THE GREAT DEPRESSION
REVISITED

ROCHESTER STUDIES IN ECONOMICS
AND POLICY ISSUES, VOLUME 2

Published in cooperation with

The Center for Research in Government
    Policy & Business
Graduate School of Management
University of Rochester
Rochester, New York

THE GREAT DEPRESSION REVISITED

EDITED BY
KARL BRUNNER

Kluwer·Nijhoff Publishing
Boston/The Hague/London

DISTRIBUTORS FOR NORTH AMERICA:

Kluwer Boston, Inc.
190 Old Derby Street
Hingham, Massachusetts 02043

DISTRIBUTORS OUTSIDE NORTH AMERICA:

Kluwer Academic Publishers Group
Distribution Centre
P.O. Box 322
3300 AH Dordrecht, The Netherlands

Library of Congress Cataloging in Publication Data

Main entry under title:
The Great Depression revisited.

(Rochester studies in economics and policy issues; v. 2)
1. Depressions—1929—United States—Congresses.
2. Depressions—1929—Sweden—Congresses.
I. Brunner, Karl, 1916–
HB3717   1929.G69 338.5'42   80–19940

ISBN 0-89838-051-0

CONTENTS

INTRODUCTION

The fateful days of the great stock market crash entered modern history almost 50 years ago to this day. The cyclic turning point of the U.S. economy occurred, however, around June 1929, and economic activity receded substantially over the subsequent months. The onset of an economic downswing thus became clearly visible before the famous crash. But the October event stays in the public's mind as the symbol of the Great Depression. For nearly four years, until the spring of 1933, the U.S. economy plunged into a deep recession. Activity declined, prices fell, and there emerged a massive unemployment problem. The economy ultimately overcame this shock in 1933. Prices rose rapidly in spite of substantial margins of unusual resources. Activity expanded, but occasionally at a somewhat hesitant rate. The expansion, however, was interrupted by another recession of major proportions during 1937–38.

The tragic sequence of events shaped public consciousness and influenced new approaches and views in economic policymaking. The activist approach to "stabilization policy" and a wide range of regulatory policies were essentially justified in terms of this experience. These policies were crucially influenced by our understanding and interpretation of the Great Depression. The view of a radically unstable economic process perennially on the edge of serious collapse gained wide popularity and became a central element of the Keynesian tradi-

1

tion. It encouraged, with supplementary interpretations, an interventionist and expanding role of the government in our economic affairs.

Milton Friedman and Anna Schwartz initiated in their remarkable volume *A Monetary History of the U.S. 1867–1960* a thorough reexamination of the events. Their investigation of the actual policies pursued and of the conceptions and interpretations governing institutional and financial policies effectively challenged many prevalent views. This work influenced our profession in many ways. Further detailed research about the causes of the Great Depression and resulting policy patterns appeared, however, only with some delay in the 1970s. The books published by Peter Temin and Charles Kindleberger attempted to rebut some central propositions of the Friedman-Schwartz explanation pertaining to the initiating causes, the accompanying conditions, and the role of policy.

The cognitive interest expressed by systematic endeavors to understand the business cycles and the pragmatic interest in the nature and role of policy institutions determined the various attempts to comprehend the economic evolution of the 1930s. The Center for Research in Government Policy and Business at the University of Rochester sponsored a conference in March 1978 in order to encourage further exploration of major outstanding issues.

The commissioned papers by Anna J. Schwartz and by Robert J. Gordon and James A. Wilcox present analyses of the causes and conditions of the Great Depression. Their contribution is usefully supplemented by detailed comments developed by Peter Temin, Peter H. Lindert, James R. Lothian, and Allan H. Meltzer. These papers examine the role of monetary and nonmonetary causes and conditions initiating the Great Depression and influencing its course.

The second set of papers, prepared by Charles C. Cox and George D. Green, addresses, on the other hand, the pattern of policies favored by the political process under the influence of the traumatic experiences suffered in the 1930s. These two authors investigate the nature of policies directed toward the nonfinancial and financial sectors, respectively, under the influence of pervasive misinterpretations of the events. Thoughtful contributions on the second set of papers were prepared by William Poole, Thomas Mayer, George J. Benston, and James L. Pierce.

The effects of the National Industrial Recovery Act are assessed in the paper by Michael M. Weinstein and the comments by Phillip Cagan. Lars Jonung offers an analysis of the radically different experience of Sweden during this period. An epilogue chapter added by the editor explores the state of cognitive efforts directed at business cycles and, more specifically, the Great Depression. The epilogue does not offer a balanced view of the contributions made at the conference. Rather, it submits to the reader a critical assessment of the discussion according to the author's best judgment.

A reader should find that even with a substantial array of unresolved issues, some central trend seems to emerge in some respects. Meltzer's attempt to circumscribe a range of consensus with Gordon appears particularly fruitful in this context. But the reader may best judge for himself. He will also find ample aspects deserving further inquiry and critical examination.

1 UNDERSTANDING 1929–1933

Anna J. Schwartz

Nearly half a century after August 1929 the debate has resumed about what produced the unusual length and extreme severity of the ensuing 43-month contraction. No new facts about that business contraction have become available that have led to revision of earlier judgments. Rather, new hands have imposed new, or reimposed old, patterns on the known facts. So we must ask whether the new hands do explain the known facts better than did earlier investigators or whether their explanations must be rejected because they do not fit the full set of known facts.

In the '30s, '40s, and '50s, the prevailing explanation of 1929–33 was essentially modeled on Keynesian income-expenditure lines. A collapse in investment as a result of earlier overinvestment, the stock market crash, and the

For the Granger causality tests and the preparation of tables 1 and 2, I am indebted to Thomas J. Sargent. Milton Friedman, who read the first draft of this paper, suggested that I include the Granger test results and the chart of the inverse of the price level. I have also restructured the paper on his advice. My indebtedness to him in a more general sense should be obvious. I have also benefited from comments by Arthur E. Gandolfi and James R. Lothian. R. A. Gordon gave me detailed comments, which I acknowledge, as I also do the views expressed by the discussant, Peter H. Lindert. I am grateful to Linda Dunn for preparing the charts and tables other than 1 and 2.

5

subsequent revision of expectations induced through the multiplier process a steep decline in output and employment. The collapse in investment was consistent with a procyclical movement in interest rates and velocity. The revision of expectations in turn set off a demand for liquidity that could not be met. The attempt to meet it, however, forced widespread liquidation of bank loans with a resultant decline in the value of private claims and debts, leading to the failure of nonfinancial corporations, to bank insolvency, and to runs on banks. Try as the Federal Reserve System might, its easy money policies—as evidenced by the decline in short-term interest rates until the summer of 1931—did not stabilize the economy.

In the Keynesian story, the quantity of money as such played no important part in the explanation of 1929–33. The story was faithful to the prevailing belief that the importance of money can be measured by the behavior of interest rates, and since econometric tests that included an interest rate revealed no significant effect of the variable, that seemed to dispose of the need to consider the behavior of money.

Fifteen years ago when Milton Friedman and I reviewed the facts about 1929–33, we did, of course, have at hand a new monthly series on the quantity of money outstanding. Earlier estimates by Currie (1935) and Warburton (1945), however, had measured the extent of the decline in the quantity of money over the contraction, so we did not discover the fact of sharp decline. What we did illuminate was the process by which the decline in the quantity of money was produced. This shed a new light on the course of the contraction. There were distinct stages of the contraction—it was not all of one piece.[1] The stages we noted included: (1) The period prior to the first banking panic—that is, August 1929 to October 1930. This period encompassed the stock market crash in October 1929, to which the Federal Reserve responded by a short-lived increase in the quantity of money. Subsequently, an earlier decline in the quantity of money was resumed, but there was no attempt by banks to liquidate loans or by depositors to shift from deposits to currency. During this interval, the contraction would have been defined as severe relative to earlier ones. (2) The first banking panic, covering the final quarter of 1930, when the real economy markedly worsened. (3) The first quarter of 1931, when signs of revival were nipped upon the onset of a second banking crisis in March 1931. (4) The last half of 1931, when the response of the Federal Reserve to Britain's departure from gold was accompanied by another outbreak of banking panic and a substantial deepening of the real decline that persisted through the first quarter of 1932. (5) The second quarter of 1932, when the Federal Reserve undertook open-market purchases, following which there was a widespread revival in the real economy in the summer and fall. (6) The final six months of the contraction, when problems with the banks spread, the real economy turned downward again, and the contraction ended with a collapse of financial markets.

Thus, after the 1929 peak in business, five negative shocks in turn destabilized the economy: the stock market crash and four episodes of banking panic—in the final quarter of 1930, from March to June 1931; from August to the end of the year (the response to the currency crisis abroad); and a final outbreak of panic in the last quarter of 1932, culminating in the Bank Holiday of March 1933. There was at least one positive shock—the open-market purchases of March–July 1932—and possibly a second, if we count the short-lived open-market purchase following the stock market crash. In our analysis, we distinguished the contraction in general from the banking and liquidity crises that punctuated its course. Our main theme was that the effect of whatever economic forces produced the contraction was magnified by the unprecedented decline in the quantity of money resulting from the banking crises. Our ancillary judgment was that the Federal Reserve System could have prevented the monetary consequences of the banking crises but failed to do so.

Two published studies by Kindleberger (1973) and Temin (1976) have recently challenged the interpretation of 1929–33 in *A Monetary History,* and an unpublished study by Abramovitz incidentally also offers a dissenting opinion.

Kindleberger's focus is on the world economic system in the interwar period. He attributes an important role, in propagating the world depression, to rising stocks and falling prices of world primary products after 1925 and to maladjustments inherited from World War I.[2] He believes that the contraction in the United States was initiated by a decline in housing—that it started as a mild contraction and was transformed into a depression by the stock market crash. In his view, during the initial phase of the depression, money was abundant and cheap, but the spread between interest rates on high-grade and low-grade assets proves that an increase in the quantity of money by itself would not have been helpful, that "one also had to improve credit-worthiness by improving the outlook" (p. 138). He traces the intensification of the depression to repercussions of the initial world contraction on the economies of the countries producing primary products, not to developments in the United States, and emphasizes the halt in international lending to peripheral countries. Given their limited gold and foreign exchange reserves, they were forced to sell their primary products for whatever they would bring. Tariff increases and quota restrictions by the industrial countries exacerbated the problems of the primary-producing countries and reduced world trade. On his reading, falling security prices and commodity prices, for which Kindleberger assigns no special responsibility to the United States, made banking systems everywhere vulnerable and led to the financial crisis of 1931. He argues that the open-market purchases by the Federal Reserve in 1932 did little to relieve the squeeze on

the economy outside financial markets and that only two means were available
to achieve world recovery: (1) simultaneous programs of government spending
in all countries and (2) simultaneous devaluations to create gold profits that
would be available for spending. Conspicuous by its absence is any discussion
of monetary expansion and the liberation of monetary policy made possible by
floating exchange rates in the 1930s, a regime Kindleberger deplores.

Peter Temin's story about the contraction concentrates on the United States
during the period beginning with the stock market crash through the end of
1930. It seems that it was not a disturbance in investment behavior but an
unexplained decline in consumption and a decline in exports as a result of
world agricultural depression that produced a decline in U.S. income. This set
off a decline in the demand for money to which the supply of money passively
adjusted. Action by the Federal Reserve to meet the demand for increased currency holdings, as depositors attempted to convert deposits into currency in the
several rounds of bank runs that characterized the contraction, or to provide
increased reserves to banks would not, in his view, have prevented a decline in
the quantity of money. Had there been no endogenous bank failures that served
to reduce the quantity of money, the deposit-reserve ratio would have declined
in response to the fall in short-term interest rates, and the decline in the quantity of money would simply have occurred through a different route. Temin does
not deny that action by the Federal Reserve to restrict monetary growth may
have played a role in initiating the economic downturn in 1929. What he disputes is whether the Federal Reserve engaged in such restrictive monetary action subsequently, until the Federal Reserve's sharp rises in discount rates in
response to gold outflows in September 1931 when Britain abandoned gold. I
defer until a later point the specific points on which he challenges *A Monetary
History*.

Abramovitz's perspective is much broader than cyclical developments in
1929–33. In his unpublished study, he attempts to introduce the behavior of
money into his analysis of U.S. long swings, which hitherto had concentrated
on their real aspects. The usual model of long swings views waves in real
income as an interaction between real expenditures on the one hand and
growth of stocks of labor and capital on the other, each explained by real
variables. In his current work, Abramovitz finds that nominal income growth
parallels real income growth and proceeds to partition the swings in nominal
income growth into its monetary elements—money-stock growth and velocity
change—and, in turn, money-stock growth into its components. He proposes a
model in which nominal income growth and its handmaiden, money-stock
growth, are governed by the growth rate of the sum of current merchandise
exports and net capital imports. U.S. factors affecting immigration, internal
migration, railroad profits, the demand for urban buildings, territorial settle-

ment, and other real matters, on this view, were important through their effects on the growth of merchandise exports and net capital imports. He then applies this hypothesis to the long swing centering on 1929–33 and suggests that the great declines in merchandise exports both after World War I and after 1929 limited the scope for Federal Reserve action. He regards the great declines of nominal income as inevitable, short of implausibly drastic accelerations in the creation of Federal Reserve credit or in the high-powered money multiplier sufficiently large to offset the declines in the sum of merchandise exports and capital movements.[3]

Underlying these three reevaluations of old facts is the view that income changes dominated money changes during the interwar period. A test of that view is now possible and is presented in the first section. I consider the appropriate measure of monetary stringency in the second section. The reciprocal of the price level in the interwar period counters what Temin regards as the decisive evidence on the price of money as measured by short-term interest rates.[4] I then comment in the third section on the decline-in-spending explanations, including Temin's version, and in the fourth section on the explanations stressing international factors, referring not only to Kindleberger and Abramovitz but also to recent work on the Great Depression by Haberler, Meltzer, and Brunner and Meltzer, among others. I conclude in the fifth section with some summary observations about cyclical experience with particular reference to 1929–33. In an appendix, I take up explicit criticisms of the explanation offered in *A Monetary History*.

MONEY AND INCOME: A TEST OF CAUSALITY

The three reevaluations of the interwar years implicitly or explicitly regard the direction of change between income and money as running from income to money. Temin says his purpose is to discriminate between the "spending hypothesis" and the "money hypothesis," with which he identifies *A Monetary History*, as an explanation of 1929–33. As he states the money hypothesis, for Friedman and Schwartz:

> Either changes in the stock of money caused income to change, or vice versa. The resolution was equally simple. The stock of money was determined by a variety of forces independent of the level of income . . . and the direction of causation therefore must be from money to income, not the other way. [P. 14]

Temin cites as the source of this passage our article on "Money and Business Cycles." Let me therefore quote from it:

The key question at issue is not whether the direction of influence is wholly from money to business or wholly from business to money; it is whether the influence running from money to business is significant, in the sense that it can account for a substantial fraction of the fluctuations in economic activity. If the answer is affirmative, then one can speak of a monetary theory of business cycles or—more precisely—of the need to assign money an important role in a full theory of business cycles. The reflex influence of business on money, the existence of which is not in doubt in light of the factual evidence summarized above, would then become part of the partly self-generating mechanism whereby monetary disturbances are transmitted. . . . As noted above, Cagan shows that the public's decisions about the proportion in which it divides its money balances between currency and deposits is an important link in the feedback mechanism whereby changes in business affect the stock of money. [1963*b*, pp. 49–50]

Whatever our view was, it clearly cannot be described as one-way causation. Since we wrote, there have been important advances in the statistical analysis of the interdependence between two series. One test of the existence and direction of causality between two series in the sense of Granger (1969) is reported here.[5] According to Granger, "We say that Y_t is *causing* X_t if we are better able to predict X_t using all available [past] information than if the information apart from [past] Y_t had been used" (p. 428). The statistical test of this formulation, using the method of least squares, is to estimate the linear regression of X_t on lagged X's and lagged Y's as

$$X_t = \sum_{j=1}^{m} \hat{\alpha}_j X_{t-j} + \sum_{j=1}^{n} \hat{\beta}_j Y_{t-j},$$

where the $\hat{\alpha}_j$'s and $\hat{\beta}_j$'s are least-squares estimates. On the null hypothesis that Y does *not* cause X, the parent parameters j, $j = 1, \ldots, n$, equal zero. The null hypothesis, with current income on the left-hand side (X_t) and money on the right-hand side (Y), is that income is not *caused* by money, in which case the Y variable (money) will have zero coefficients. Alternatively, with current money on the left-hand side (X_t), the null hypothesis is that money is not caused by income, in which case the Y variable (income) will have zero coefficients.

For money, the variable I used was monthly M_2. The choice of an income variable for the interwar years is limited. The monthly personal-income series first becomes available beginning 1929. A proxy for income—bank debits to deposit accounts at 140 centers excluding New York City—is available for the period beginning 1919.[6] The equations fitted, including a constant, a residual term, a trend term, and alternatives with and without seasonal dummies, were the following:

$$\hat{\text{MONSUP}}_t \;=\; \sum_{j=1}^{m} \hat{a}_j \; \text{MONSUP}_{t\text{-}j} \;+\; \sum_{j=1}^{n} \hat{b} \; \text{PERINC}_{t\text{-}j} \,,$$

$$\hat{\text{MONSUP}}_t \;=\; \sum_{j=1}^{m} \hat{a}_j \; \text{MONSUP}_{t\text{-}j} \;+\; \sum_{j=1}^{n} \hat{c} \; \text{BKDED}_{t\text{-}j} \,,$$

$$\hat{\text{PERINC}}_t \;=\; \sum_{j=1}^{m} \hat{a}_j \; \text{PERINC}_{t\text{-}j} \;+\; \sum_{j=1}^{n} \hat{K} \; \text{MONSUP}_{t\text{-}j} \,,$$

$$\hat{\text{BKDED}}_t \;=\; \sum_{j=1}^{m} \hat{a}_j \; \text{BKDED}_{t\text{-}j} \;+\; \sum_{j=1}^{n} \hat{m} \; \text{MONSUP}_{t\text{-}j} \,.$$

Table 1, covering the shorter period beginning 1929, with personal income as the income variable, and table 2, covering the longer period beginning 1919, with bank debits to deposit accounts as the income variable, report the probability of obtaining a value of F greater than that actually obtained if the null hypothesis is valid [Prob $(F > f)$]. If this probability is low, it indicates that the null hypothesis is implausible and can be rejected. Over the shorter period, one cannot reject exogeneity in either direction, though the probability of exceeding the observed f is, with one exception [(13), (14)], uniformly lower for those equations testing the influence of money on income than for those testing the reverse relation.

For the longer period, the situation is very different: not one of six regressions yields any evidence that income had a significant influence on money— the lowest of the probabilities associated with the observed f is 0.24, which means that in at least one time in four, chance alone would yield as strong an influence of income on money as that observed. In sharp contrast, every one of the six regressions testing the influence of money on income yields a far stronger relation than could be expected by chance if money really had no influence on income. The least-favorable regression yields a probability of 0.003 for the computed f, which means that a relation this strong would occur by chance less than 3 times in 1,000.

So far as these results go, then, for the interwar years as a whole, they clearly support unidirectional causality running from money to income. The reverse hypothesis that Temin, Kindleberger, and Abramovitz appear to embrace receives no support at all. For the shorter period, the results are not inconsistent with the passage I quoted above from "Money and Business Cycles"—mutual interdependence of money and income, with money the senior partner; but neither do they give it much support. Perhaps the only conclusion they support is that eight years[7] is too short a period to give very much evi-

Table 1.   Granger Causality Test Results, 1929–39

Reg. No.	X_t	Y_t	Prob $(F > f)$		F- Statistic	NOBS	Lags (min)
(1)	MONSUP	PERINCN	0.8851	~	$F(24,47)$	108	(24,24)
(2)	PERINC	MONSUP	0.3767		$F(24,47)$	108	(24,24)
(3)	MONSUP	PERINCN	0.8027	~	$F(18,65)$	114	(18,18)
(4)	PERINC	MONSUP	0.3971		$F(18,65)$	114	(18,18)
(5)	*MONSUP	PERINCS	0.6334	~	$F(24,58)$	108	(24,24)
(6)	*PERINCS	MONSUP	0.3488		$F(24,58)$	108	(24,24)
(7)	*MONSUP	PERINCS	0.7685	~	$F(18,76)$	114	(18,18)
(8)	*PERINCS	MONSUP	0.5034		$F(18,76)$	114	(18,18)
(9)	MONSUP2	PERINCN	0.9850	~	$F(24,47)$	108	(24,24)
(10)	PERINCN	MONSUP2	0.2501		$F(24,47)$	108	(24,24)
(11)	MONSUP2	PERINCN	0.7807	~	$F(18,65)$	114	(18.18)
(12)	PERINCN	MONSUP2	0.0771		$F(18,65)$	114	(18,18)
(13)	*MONSUP2	PERINCS	0.6130	~	$F(24,58)$	108	(24,24)
(14)	*PERINCS	MONSUP2	0.6508		$F(24,58)$	108	(24,24)
(15)	*MONSUP2	PERINCS	0.8030	~	$F(18,76)$	114	(18,18)
(16)	*PERINCS	MONSUP2	0.2760		$F(18,76)$	114	(18,18)

Sources: MONSUP $=M_2$, from Friedman and Schwartz, 1970, table 1, col. 9. MONSUP2 $=M_2$, as above, adjusted for exclusion of deposits in unlicensed banks, March 1933–May 1935, by applying the ratio of licensed and unlicensed bank to licensed bank deposits (Friedman and Schwartz 1963a, table 15, cols. 4, 2). PERINC = Personal income, OBE from Moore 1961, 2: 139.

Note: All regressions include a constant and linear trend, and regressions (5)–(8) and (13)–(16) (shown with asterisk), seasonal dummies also. Regressions are of the form

$$X_t = \sum_{i=1}^{m} \alpha_i X_{t-i} + \sum_{i=1}^{n} \beta_i Y_{t-1} + \text{residual}.$$

Table reports marginal significance level of F-statistic pertinent for testing null hypothesis $\beta_1 = \beta_2 = \cdots = \beta_n = 0$, which is the null hypothesis "Y fails to Granger-cause X." Where f is the calculated value of the pertinent F-statistic, the marginal significance level is defined as prob $[F > f]$ under the null hypothesis.

dence on direction of causation, given the large random element in the month-to-month movements of both money and personal income.[8]

MEASURING MONETARY STRINGENCY

Temin has revived the Keynesian view that the importance of money can be measured by the behavior of interest rates. In Keynesian analyses, the measure of monetary stringency is a rise in interest rates. The interest rate is regarded

Table 2. Granger Causality Test Results, 1919–39

Reg. No.	X_t	Y_t	$(F > f)$		F-Statistic	NOBS	Lags (min)
(1)	MONSUP	BKDED	0.2685	~	$F(36,131)$	216	(36,36)
(2)	BKDED	MONSUP	0.0007		$F(36,131)$	216	(36,36)
(3)	MONSUP	BKDED	0.4401	~	$F(24,167)$	228	(24,24)
(4)	BKDED	MONSUP	0.0008	~	$F(24,167)$	228	(24,24)
(5)	*MONSUP	BKDEDS	0.2410	~	$F(18,185)$	234	(18,18)
(6)	*BKDEDS	MONSUP	0.00003	~	$F(18,185)$	234	(18,18)
(7)	MONSUP2	BKDED	0.7318	~	$F(36,131)$	216	(36,36)
(8)	BKDED	MONSUP2	0.0031	~	$F(36,131)$	216	(36,36)
(9)	MONSUP2	BKDED	0.9634	~	$F(24,167)$	228	(24,24)
(10)	BKDED	MONSUP2	0.0011	~	$F(24,167)$	228	(24,24)
(11)	*MONSUP2	BKDEDS	0.7854	~	$F(18,185)$	234	(18,18)
(12)	*BKDEDS	MONSUP2	0.0002	~	$F(18,185)$	234	(18,18)

Source: BKDED = Bank debits to deposit accounts, except interbank accounts, 140 centers (excluding New York City), from U.S. Board of Governors of the Federal Reserve System 1943, pp. 236–37.
Note: See note to table 1. Here, regressions (5)–(6) and (11)–(12) (shown with asterisks) include seasonal dummies.

as "the price of money." In quantity theory analyses, the price of money is $1/P$, the inverse of the price level. In the former case, stringency is reflected in credit markets. In the latter case, money is an asset, actual and desired holdings of which are adjusted through prices, so that stringency is reflected in a rise in the reciprocal of prices.

Figure 1 plots the reciprocal of the U.S. wholesale price index, monthly, 1919–39. It is of some interest that every monetary event of significance during these two decades is mirrored in the movements of the price of money. Moreover, the reaction of prices to each monetary event is either observed in the coincident month or within five months of the event. The monetary events in the three deep contraction phases of the interwar period—1920–21, 1929–33, and 1937–38—are marked by vertical lines on the chart and identified by number above the chart. Table 3 shows the lag in months in the price response to the monetary events listed.[9]

Figure 1 refutes the allegation that Temin makes that there is no evidence of monetary stringency in 1930 and 1931 before Britain abandoned gold. I might also have entered dates of monetary events between 1921 and 1929 but refrained from doing so, because during this period the Reserve System attempted to anticipate business movements, so the monetary events and the

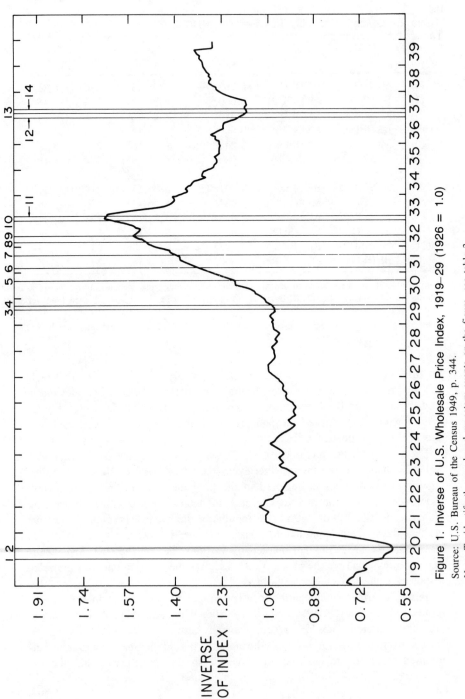

Figure 1. Inverse of U.S. Wholesale Price Index, 1919–29 (1926 = 1.0)

Source: U.S. Bureau of the Census 1949, p. 344.

Note: To identify the numbered monetary events on the figure, see table 3.

Table 3. Monetary Events Reflected in Inverse of U.S. Wholesale Price Index in Three Interwar Deep Cyclical Contractions

Cyclical Contraction			Date of Monetary Event	Lag (in months) of Initial Response of $1/P$
1920–21	1.	1/20	Rise in discount rate	+5
	2(a).	6/20	Final rise in discount rate	
	(b).	6/20	Peak in M_2	+1
1929–33	3.	8/29	Rise in discount rate	+1
	4.	10/29	Stock market crash	0
	5.	10/30	Onset of first banking crisis	0
	6.	3/31	Onset of second banking crisis	+1
	7.	9/31	Britain leaves gold	0
	8.	3/32	Onset of open-market purchases	+4
	9.	6/32	Last of large monthly declines in M_2	+1
	10.	1/33	Final banking crisis	+1
	11.	3/33	Bank Holiday	0
1937–38	12.	1/37	Announcement of final rise in reserve requirements	+4
	13.	3/37	Peak in M_2	+2
	14.	5/37	Effective date of final rise in reserve requirements	0[a]

[a]+5 for date of onset of rapid rise in 1/P.

reaction of the price of money could be regarded as the common result of movements in autonomous spending or whatever third other force produces the cycle. For the three deep contractions of the interwar years, however, the Federal Reserve took policy steps that cannot be regarded as necessary consequences of contemporary changes in business activity. The restrictive actions were followed, with brief lags, by sharp declines in the quantity of money and sharp rises in the inverse of the price level. The one important expansive action—the 1932 open-market purchases—was followed three months later by an end to large monthly declines in the quantity of money, and four months later by the largest decline in the inverse of the price level during the whole 1929–33 period.

As it happens, we had never before made this particular use of the inverse of the price level, yet we had earlier dated the numbered monetary events, so this comparison is fresh and unbiased evidence. Frankly, we were surprised at how uniform the connection was.

DECLINE IN SPENDING

I now turn to the detailed profile of the 1929–33 contraction provided by different investigators. Temin himself (1976) has reviewed critically earlier versions of what he terms the "spending hypothesis," the class of explanations that account for the severity of the Great Contraction by the collapse of one or another category of expenditure. Temin finds that the data do not support a fall in autonomous investment—the leading candidate in the Keynesian approach.

Temin reviews[10] the versions of the spending hypothesis associated with the names of Alvin Hansen, R. A. Gordon, Joseph Schumpeter, Thomas Wilson, and Keynes himself and econometric models of the interwar period constructed by Ben Bolch and John Pilgrim, Lawrence Klein, Jan Tinbergen, and John B. Kirkwood. He concludes that all of these versions are unacceptable because they rest on untested assumptions. He also reviews the long-swing or Kuznets cycle hypothesis. He asserts that it assumes that only a large shock—presumably, World War I—could have produced a large cycle in income. He then dismisses it because it cannot explain why the World War I shock did not generate a downturn until a decade later. He leaves open the possibility, but is half-hearted in offering it, that the stock market crash and the fall in construction might have been the channels through which a mild downturn was converted into a severe one.

In part, then, Temin provides a critique of both Kindleberger's and Abramovitz's approaches to 1929–33. His own version of the spending hypothesis, however, turns out to be equally vulnerable. According to him, two unexplained developments in 1930 changed the nature of the downturn. The minor one was a decline of approximately $1 billion in constant prices in American exports as a result of "the deepening world agricultural depression" and "European troubles independent of the United States. Events outside the United States therefore exerted a deflationary impact within this country" (p.68).

The major unexplained development, according to Temin, was an autonomous fall in consumption in 1930 (see table 4). He specifically rejects an explanation of the fall in consumption as reflecting the effect on wealth of the stock market crash, on the ground that the wealth effect was too small. In this sense he regards the fall as autonomous and unexplained.

Temin's conclusion that there was such a fall in consumption is based on regressions of total and nondurable nominal consumption spending on nominal current disposable income and nominal wealth for the period 1919–41. Actual

Table 4. Changes in Macroeconomic Variables in Three Periods

	1920	1921	Change (in percent or percentage points)	1929	1930	Change (in percent or percentage points)	1937	1938	Change (in percent or percentage points)
GNP, current prices (billion $)	91.5	69.6	− 23.9	103.1	90.4	− 12.3	90.4	84.7	− 6.3
constant (1958) prices	140.0	127.8	− 8.7	203.6	183.5	− 9.9	203.2	192.9	− 5.1
Personal consumption expenditures				139.6	130.4	− 6.6	143.1	140.2	− 2.0
Gross private domestic investment				36.9	28.0	− 24.1	24.5	19.4	− 20.8
Net exports of goods and services				1.5	1.4	− 6.7	− .7	1.9	+371.4
Government purchases of goods and services				22.0	24.3	+ 9.5	30.8	33.9	+ 10.1
Implicit price index (1958=100)	65.4	54.5	− 16.7	50.6	49.3	− 2.6	44.5	43.9	− 1.3
Unemployment rate	5.2	11.7	+ 6.5	3.2	8.7	+ 5.5	14.3	19.0	+ 4.7
							(9.2)	(12.5)	(+ 3.3)

	1919	1921	Change (in percent or percentage points)	1928	1930	Change (in percent or percentage points)	1936	1938	Change (in percent or percentage points)
GNP, current prices (billion $)	84.0	69.6	− 17.1	97.0	90.4	− 6.8	82.5	84.7	+ 2.7
constant (1958) prices	146.4	127.8	− 12.7	190.9	183.5	− 3.9	193.0	192.9	− 0.1
Implicit price index (1958=100)	57.4	54.5	− 5.1	50.8	49.3	− 3.0	42.7	43.9	+ 2.8
Unemployment rate	1.4	11.7	+10.3	4.2	8.7	+ 4.5	16.9	19.0	+ 2.1
							(10.1)	(12.5)	(+ 2.4)

Sources: U.S. Bureau of the Census 1975, series F-1, F-3, F-5, F-48, F-53, F-63, F-66, D-86. Figures in parentheses are Darby's (1976) estimates of unemployment rate.

consumption expenditures were above the level predicted by these regressions for 1921 and 1938 but below the predicted level for 1930. Hence Temin concludes that 1930 was unusual since consumption expenditures declined by more than would have been predicted from the associated decline in income and from the behavior of consumption expenditures in the other interwar major contraction years.[11]

Temin also compares yearly first differences in residuals from his regressions for 1921, 1930, and 1938 on the ground that a movement from a high positive to a low positive residual indicates a deflationary effect on the autonomous component of consumption. The year-to-year changes in residuals based on the regression were $6.1 billion in 1921, −$1.43 billion in 1930, and $1.81 billion in 1938. He then averages the changes in residuals for 1921 and 1938, subtracts the change in residuals in 1930, and concludes:

> On the assumption that the [average] overprediction of decline in consumption shown for 1921 and 1938 is the norm for this function in depression years, the predicted decline in consumption was $5 billion too low in 1930. [P. 72]

This is his current price estimate of the autonomous fall in consumption between 1929 and 1930, two-thirds of the total fall. In constant prices, the estimate is $3 billion of the actual fall in real consumption expenditures of $4.3 billion. Thus, according to Temin, before the onset of the October 1930 runs on banks, the economy was set on a course of deep contraction by the combined autonomous fall of $1 billion in exports and $3 billion in consumption expenditures.

Questions immediately arise with regard to these estimates. With respect to exports, the obvious question is whether the decline in U.S. exports was attributable to events abroad independent of the U.S. cyclical contraction. I shall deal with this question when I turn to explanations stressing international factors.

Temin's estimate of the autonomous decline in consumption expenditures raises questions of an entirely different order. In the first place, the consumption functions he fits are so crude by standards of the present state of the art that it is hard to take them seriously. Second, his assertion that the positive residuals he observes for 1921 and 1938 from this questionable regression are the norm for interwar contractions is strictly an obiter dictum. He gives no basis for regarding 1921 and 1938 as in some unspecified sense "normal" contraction years. But unless this is granted, he has no basis for regarding his small negative residual for 1930 as abnormal.

Thomas Mayer (1978a) in a recent paper has reestimated Temin's equations for the interwar years and has found larger negative residuals in other years of the period. Why did the negative residual in 1930 cause a deep contraction but the larger negative residual in 1925, for example, not cause one? This is ad hoc economics without qualification.

Gandolfi and Lothian (1977), in a review of Temin's book, fit a more sophisticated consumption function for the longer period 1899–1941. They regressed the log of real per capita total consumption on the log of real per capita permanent income and the log of transitory income, defined as the difference between the logs of measured and permanent income. The inclusion of the transitory income variable is designed to reduce the effect of purchase of durable goods, as opposed to their flow of services, as a component of total consumption expenditures. Since purchases of durable goods are more cyclical than their service flows, they are more dependent on transitory than on permanent income. For the sake of comparison with Temin's results, Gandolfi and Lothian also examined year-to-year changes in residuals as well as their levels. They found 1930 far from unique. Of the five severe contractions other than 1930 (1894, 1896, 1908, 1921, and 1938), only 1921 had a very large positive residual. Overprediction of the fall in consumption expenditures, then, is hardly a normal feature of deep contractions. The negative value for 1930 is not abnormal by comparison with all years, not simply deep contraction years. Of 41 changes in residuals, 14 are positive, 27 negative, of which 15 are larger than 1930. Of all 41 changes, 25 are larger in absolute value, 15 smaller. Why is it that these 15 did not produce a violent reaction in economic activity, while the 1930 shift did?

Temin combines his hypothesis that there was an autonomous decline in (nominal and real) spending relative to output with the hypothesis that the demand for (nominal) money was falling more rapidly than the quantity of money during 1930 and the first three quarters of 1931. The decline in the quantity of money itself he regards as a movement along a stable supply-of-money function in response to a downward shift in the demand function. For logical rigor, this statement needs to be supplemented by a more precise specification of the arguments of the demand and supply functions—changes in which would equate quantity demanded with quantity supplied.

For the demand for nominal money, Temin would presumably include as arguments the price level (or, the inverse of the price level), real income, and interest rates. Assume, now, with Temin that for fixed values of the arguments, the nominal quantity of money demanded fell relative to the quantity supplied. To eliminate the putative excess supply of money (that is, make money holders willing to hold it), prices would have to rise—but they fell, which exacerbated the excess supply; real income likewise would have to rise, but it fell, again exacerbating the excess supply. The one remaining possibility is that interest rates would have had to fall, which they did. As a formal matter of monetary theory, then, Temin treats the whole process as an autonomous *decline* in liquidity preference reinforced by declines in prices and in real income produced by other (spending) equations in the system, and wholly countered by lower interest rates—in other words, a large-scale shift of flow demand from goods to securities, and of stock demand from money to securities. But then, why no stock market boom? As Allan Meltzer (1976) points out, perhaps the temporary rally in the market in the spring of 1930 is consistent with Temin's construction; so also, of course, is the decline in interest rates in 1930, but hardly anything else is. Indeed, put this way, the notion of a sharp *decline* in liquidity preference is hard to square with a severe contraction accompanied by increasing industrial bankruptcies and unprecedented failures of banks.

With respect to the supply function, under the gold standard in effect in 1930 and 1931, both declining prices and declining real income would be expected to produce a gold inflow (which they did) and thereby increase the nominal quantity of money. Here too, therefore, Temin must treat the decline in interest rates as a sufficiently powerful force reducing the nominal quantity of money to have overcome the opposite influences of the other two variables. And apparently he does, since he argues that in the absence of bank failures the same decline in the quantity of money would have occurred through a decline in deposit-reserve ratios.

Temin presents no independent evidence of such great sensitivity of either demand for or supply of money to interest rates as would be required for his explanation. The general conclusion of most studies is that quantity of money supplied is largely insensitive to the interest rate (see Cagan 1965; Fand 1967; Rasche 1972) and that the quantity of money demanded is only moderately sensitive to the interest rate, displaying an elasticity a good deal less than unity with respect to long-term rates.

The various versions of the spending hypothesis—one of which attributes the Great Contraction to an autonomous decline in investment, another to an autonomous decline in housing, a third to an autonomous decline in consumption and exports—cast doubt on the value for cyclical analysis of the Keynesian distinction among investment, consumption, and net exports. The authors of the various versions write as if the cycle is necessarily propagated by the component of GNP that first reaches a peak or that is most volatile. Is this more than the most vulgar post hoc–propter hoc reasoning? If not, where is the evidence? The particular category of expenditure that first reaches a peak may not be the trigger of the downturn but the first to respond to a common influence on all expenditures, and similarly the variability of housing or investment or of exports is not an indicator of causal dominance, as Temin, for example, assumes in analyzing the German national product in constant prices, 1924–29 (p. 156).

One other general comment needs to be made about Keynesian models. It is difficult to understand how the experience of 1929–33 could have spawned the notion of the need for the replacement of the classical assumption of a price-adjustment by a quantity-adjustment system of movement toward equilibrium. One key aspect of the contraction was that the decline in nominal income was divided almost equally between a fall in quantities and in prices. Real income fell by more then one-third, implicit prices by more than one-quarter. Why quantities changed as they did in response to price changes should be the goal of analysis. A model in real terms to explain a contraction in which price declines were so prominent is bound to serve imperfectly the cause of historical understanding.[12]

Finally, no decline-in-spending model has ever been able to explain the detailed development of the contraction.

INTERNATIONAL EXPLANATIONS

The main problem with Kindleberger's account of the world in depression is his assumption that, because the contraction was worldwide in scope once it got under way, it therefore did not originate in the United States. The U.S. share in world trade, world capital and financial markets, and the world's stock of gold has been sufficiently large since World War I to give the United States the capacity to initiate worldwide movements and not merely to react to them. Of course, once having initiated a worldwide disturbance, it would in turn be subject to reflex influences.

From 1923 on, the Federal Reserve sterilized much of the gold inflow into the United States, preventing the kind of expansionary effect on the stock of money and thence on prices that would have occurred under the prewar gold standard. Instead, the system sought, and to a large measure achieved, stable economic growth with falling wholesale prices. This achievement was largely at the expense of economic stability in Great Britain and the peripheral countries tied to sterling. Britain's return to gold in 1925 at a parity that overvalued sterling would have caused less difficulty for Britain if prices in the United States had risen instead of falling thereafter.

Similarly, any problems of agricultural depression in the peripheral countries before 1929 were not independent of U.S. policy. For the contraction itself, the record is equally clear. The stock market boom, which is said to have drained funds from the rest of the world, and the stock market crash occurred in the United States. The downward movement in the U.S. money stock, including the sequence of bank failures, was not the consequence of influences from abroad. The gold inflow into the United States (during the first

two years of the contraction) to which reference will be made below is further
evidence that other countries were being forced to adapt to the U.S. monetary
policies rather than the reverse. The decline in U.S. lending abroad and the
protectionist Smoot-Hawley Tariff Act were clearly U.S. actions that destabilized the world financial system[13].

The United States was no pitiful, helpless giant on whom the rest of the
world inflicted the Great Contraction. It is true that when the pound and other
currencies were cut loose from gold in 1931, the U.S. trade balance was ad-
versely affected and speculative pressure on the dollar developed. These devaluations, however, were themselves the reflex consequences of the U.S.
contraction, and even so, their subsequent effects were not crippling, given the
size of the U.S. economy.

This point is also relevant to both Temin's assumption that the decline in
U.S. exports was independent of U.S. actions and to Abramovitz's analysis.
Temin never alludes to the monetary standard of fixed exchange rates that enforced a worldwide decline in income and prices after 1929.[14] The central role
of the United States in the worldwide scope of the contraction is attested to by
the balance of payments.[15] If the decline in income in the rest of the world was
being transmitted to the United States, we should have observed a balance-of-
payments deficit in the United States, leading to a gold outflow. However, the
U.S. gold stock rose by nearly $200 million from the annual average of 1929
to that of 1930. From August 1929 to August 1931, the gold stock rose by
over $600 million. The gold inflow strongly suggests that any decline in U.S.
exports to the rest of the world was attributable to the effects on the rest of the
world of contraction here.

Likewise, Abramovitz, by assuming that there were forces making for a
major decline in the dollar value of U.S. exports independently of U.S.
monetary actions, is able to conclude that there was a significant constraint
on the power of the Federal Reserve to sustain the growth of the money
stock. In fact, however, there were no such forces. The gold inflows contradict the assumption that the initiating force was a serious decline in the dollar value of our export market independent of what was happening in the
United States. The other exogenous factor for Abramovitz's analysis—net
capital imports—is also an item that was crucially determined by events
within the United States. In the 1930s the decline in U.S. capital exports
may have been exogenous in the sense that the state of the capital market
abroad and the prospective yields on investment in various foreign countries
discouraged capital exports. But equally the volume of saving available for
capital export relative to the volume of investment demand at home were
important endogenous elements. Internal developments in the United States
enormously affected U.S. capital exports.

Is the monetary approach to the balance of payments helpful in understanding 1929–33? The theory asserts that the active element in the balance-of-payments adjustment process is the equalization of the quantity of money demanded with the quantity of money supplied. Flows of specie are interpreted as responses to changes in demand for or domestic supply of money in various countries. A reduction in the public's demand for goods and securities leads to reduced imports and expanded exports on the goods side and to higher interest rates and capital imports on the securities side. The current account or the capital account or both move into surplus. Although the law of one price has frequently been associated with the monetary approach, some adherents allow for significant slippage between the rate of change of domestic prices and of world prices. Similarly, some adherents also accommodate interest rate differentials between domestic and foreign assets in their versions of the monetary approach.

Are the gold flows and price movements, 1929–33, consistent with the monetary approach to the balance of payments? As already noted, from August 1929 to August 1931, there was a gold inflow of $600 million. An increase in the demand for money in the United States relative to other countries, or a decrease in the supply of money in the United States relative to other countries, or any combination would be required by the monetary approach to account for the inflow. Such a change in the relative demand or supply of money would be manifested in a decline in U.S. wholesale prices relative to those in the rest of the world—either along with the inflow or as an intermediate step in producing the inflow. If changes in wholesale prices shown in table 5 for various countries are reliable, the 1929–31 decline in U.S. prices was steeper than in France and Germany, but not in the other countries. From the time Britain cut the pound loose from gold in September 1931 until July 1932, the United States had a gold outflow of $1 billion, absorbed principally by France, Belgium, Switzerland, and the Netherlands. The outflow would be interpreted as a relative increase in the demand for or decrease in the supply of money in those countries. The data on wholesale prices in the United States and France confirm an only slightly steeper rate of price decline in France than in the United States during this interval. The return flow of gold to the United States until the climactic weeks before the Bank Holiday in March 1933 restored the U.S. gold stock so that it was only $80 million lower than at the cyclical peak in business in 1929. Again, a relative increase in the demand for money in the United States and a steeper rate of price decline in the United States than abroad would be consistent with the inflow. This seems to be the case from September 1932 to February 1933.

It does not seem to me that the discussion of the international setting of 1929–33 as set forth in A Monetary History requires modification. Countries

Table 5.   Percentage Changes in Wholesale Prices at Annual Rates for
Various Countries, 1929–33

		Annual Rates of Change						
From	To	U.S.	France	Japan	Cana-da	U.K.	Ger-many	Italy
Aug. 1929	Mar. 1933	−13.1	−11.9	− 5.8	−11.8	− 9.2	−11.6	−12.3
Aug. 1929	Sept. 1930	−12.2	− 6.7	−22.3	−16.0	−14.9	−10.8	−14.1
Sept. 1930	Sept. 1931	−17.0	−16.2	−13.6	−16.9	−15.2	−12.3	−16.2
Sept. 1931	June 1932	−13.0	−14.3	− 3.0	− 6.5	− 1.5	−16.2	− 9.5
June 1932	Sept. 1932	+ 6.5	−11.5	+53.7	− 3.1	+16.0	− 4.6	+ 4.0
Sept. 1932	Feb. 1933	−17.6	− 5.3	+16.8	− 8.5	− 7.6	−10.0	−11.5

Sources: U.S.: U.S. Bureau of the Census, 1949, p. 344. France: Librarie de Recueil Sirey 1937,
table 11. Japan, Canada, U.K., Germany, Italy: League of Nations 1929–33, table 10. The U.K.
index was constructed by the Board of Trade; the Italian index is labeled "Bachi."

within the British orbit along with Britain were depressed during the '20s
while the rest of the world prospered, partly thanks to U.S. capital exports.
When the U.S. capital flow declined in 1928 and virtually ceased in the succeeding years, the economic position of the formerly recipient countries deteri-
orated. The gold exchange standard made the international financial system
vulnerable. Given the attachment to fixed exchange rates, there was no way
for other countries to insulate themselves from the effects of U.S. contraction.
Deflation in the United States forced an adjustment on the rest of the world
reflected partly in the gold inflows to the United States, partly in internal deflation necessary to avoid or reduce further gold flows. We exported deflation
and depression to the rest of the world. Even though deflation abroad then
reacted unfavorably on the United States, much leeway still remained for U.S.
policy.

UNDERSTANDING 1929–33

For Temin, 1929–33 was characterized by the absence of two equilibrating
factors: a decline in real wages and a strong real-balance effect. Real wages in
manufacturing, as the quotient of nominal wages divided by wholesale prices,
were higher on both hourly and weekly bases in 1930, 1931, and 1932, and
also on an hourly basis in 1933. Real wages in manufacturing, as the quotient
of nominal wages divided by consumer prices, were higher on an hourly basis
in every year except 1932 but lower in every year on a weekly basis. From
the hourly wholesale price deflated series, Temin concludes that the marginal

physical productivity of labor rose as employment fell, which is consistent with the classical theory of factor substitution: lowering the wage rate further might have avoided unemployment. The weekly consumer price deflated series shows, however, that this was a vain hope, since lower wages decreased the level of demand. He adds that if the real hourly wage series deflated by consumer prices is more accurate than the wholesale price deflated series, then no part of the classical theory is accurate.

I do not believe, however, that we can gain an understanding of 1929-33 by assigning a central role to real wages. Further, by dismissing the evidence of the hourly wholesale price deflated series, Temin fails to see a link between it and the aborted recoveries that Mitchell and Burns (1936) noted in 1930, 1931, and 1932.

The second equilibrating factor that Temin alleges was absent in 1929-33 was a strong real-balance effect. He defines that effect, however, as relating to the stock of money or the stock of money plus other financial assets. Yet the proper measure of the real-balance effect is the effect of the change in the net indebtedness of the government sector—that is, the sum of noninterest- and interest-bearing government liabilities. The nominal value of currency plus government debt increased 27 percent from 1929 to 1933; the real value increased 62 percent. This may be described as a strong increase in real balances, whatever the strength of the effect on spending for consumption.

In Temin's account, an unexplained change in spending set the economy on its downward slide. No monetary change could stop the downward slide. An increase in the supply of money would not help, since the public had an excess supply of money. Things could get worse, as they did, when in September 1931 the Federal Reserve for the first time since 1929 in his view exerted a deflationary effect on the economy. Temin's analytical structure is a throwback to the Keynesian position of the quarter century after 1933. It has no theoretical explanation of the price level. It makes no distinction between nominal and real magnitudes. It presumes that no evidence exists on the relation of monetary change to income change. It ignores recent theoretical developments.

The period 1929-33 began as a cyclical contraction much like others, this time in response to the immoderate concern of the Federal Reserve Board about speculation in the stock market. Application of the theory of stock values as affected by expectations of the growth of earnings now suggests, as Irving Fisher believed, that marked overvaluation of stocks was not general (Sirkin 1975). Had high employment and economic growth continued, prices in the stock market could have been maintained. In the event, restriction of the growth of money from 1928 on produced a peak in business and some months later the stock market crash. A temporary increase in the money stock in October 1929 eased the effect of the shock of the crash. This may account for the increase in output recorded in early 1930 as a lagged effect of monetary growth.

The economy was thus subjected to two sharp shocks: the initial restrictive money growth and then the collapse of stock prices. Still, what followed suggests an adjustment that moved the economy toward equilibrium, but not for long. It is not hard to explain why an unanticipated decline in aggregate demand will lead employers to hire fewer workers at each real wage rate as perceived by them and will lead workers to refuse offers of work at lower nominal wages on the basis of unchanged anticipations. Along rational-expectations lines, however, employers and workers will in time revise their anticipations in accordance with the change in opportunities. If the Federal Reserve had maintained the initial moderate rate of decline in the money stock, presumably the economy after a time would have adjusted to this condition. But this is not what happened. The screw was tightened again and again, until 1932, and unanticipated change in each case required a new period of adjustment. To add to the problem, leading government officials and industrialists exhorted employers to maintain wage rates and share employment, which must have contributed to shorter average work weeks and higher layoffs.

Still, one must acknowledge the resilience of the economy after the first shocks in 1929 and the first banking crisis at the end of 1930. In early 1931, some industries with relatively smaller price declines revived. Again, the adjustment was aborted by a second round of banking failures, subsequently compounded by the Federal Reserve's reaction to gold losses, in the autumn of 1931. The favorable shock in April 1932, when the Federal Reserve System finally began an open-market purchase program in response to congressional pressure, produced a positive reaction in the economy. Prices began to move upward and output increased. The adjustment was short-lived. The purchase program ended in early August, and the political campaign spawned rumors about the condition of banks the Reconstruction Finance Corporation (RFC) had aided. The consequence was a series of runs that ended with the shutdown of all banks as the new administration took office. The economy was at its lowest ebb. Yet vigorous growth was not precluded during the expansion phase that followed.

A far more satisfactory explanation of 1929–33 than Temin's is, therefore, that a series of negative shocks, monetary in origin, reduced real output and the demand for labor and shifted the demand for securities to short-term instruments and high-grade, long-term securities. Destroy a banking system, and the real economy will grind to a halt. There are no unexplained changes in spending that serve as deus ex machina. The presence of equilibrating forces is attested to by the interludes during the course of the contraction when real output increased. The behavior of the economy was determined by public policies. Different policies would have resulted in different behavior.

APPENDIX: DISSENTS FROM THE VIEWS IN
A MONETARY HISTORY

Temin rejects the account in *A Monetary History* of the way an initial mild decline in the money stock from 1929 to 1930, accompanying a decline in Federal Reserve credit outstanding, was converted into a sharp decline by a wave of bank failures beginning in late 1930. I shall discuss in turn five items in Temin's catalog of dissent: (1) the money-stock identity, (2) the behavior of high-powered money, (3) the behavior of interest rates, (4) the price of deflation and the behavior of real money balances, (5) the role of bank failures; and I will comment finally (6) on his and others' approaches to monetary policy during the contraction.

The Money-Stock Identity

In *A Monetary History,* we used an identity that relates money broadly defined to three proximate determinants: high-powered money, the deposit-reserve ratio, and the deposit-currency ratio. The three proximate determinants reflect, respectively, the behavior of the monetary authorities (in the United States, the Treasury and the Federal Reserve System), the commercial banks, and the public. The monetary authorities provide high-powered money—the sum of reserves and currency—that the banks and public divide between themselves in light of the factors influencing the two sets of ratios. The deposit-reserve ratio is affected by legal reserve requirements, banks' expectations of currency movements into and out of their vaults, and interest rates. The deposit-currency ratio is affected by interest rates, income, and the public's preference for holding coin and currency. The ratios clearly reflect demand factors that interact with the supply of high-powered money. The argument of *A Monetary History,* as already noted, is that the Federal Reserve System through its control of the issue of high-powered money can offset any undesired change by the other actors in some short run, and hence the system plays a dominant role in the control of the quantity of money.

Temin believes he has isolated a fatal error in *A Monetary History,* because the identity suggests to him that the stock of money is determined by supply factors alone, instead of being joined with a demand equation to determine equilibrium supply in the market for money. Temin writes:

> Consider the stock of bonds. The size of the stock is the product of past decisions about corporate and government finance. It is fixed at any moment of time by these previous supply decisions. If the demand for bonds shifts, it will not change the number of bonds in existence immediately; it will change their price. In the short run, therefore, the quantity of bonds is determined by the supply,

and the price is determined by the demand. In the longer run, the price will be a function of both the supply and demand working through a recursive relationship. Friedman and Schwartz employed the short-run part of this argument; they appear to have rejected the long-run part. [P. 18]

According to Temin, we treat changes in the demand for money as affecting only the price of money, meaning the interest rate, and not quantity, the equilibrium stock of money. This is standard Keynesian doctrine, in which the price of money is defined as the interest rate rather than the reciprocal of the price level.

The problem with Temin's analysis, as with much Keynesian analysis, is the assumption that the price level is predetermined and the resulting failure to treat the price level as a variable that helps to equate nominal demand for money with the nominal supply of money or, alternatively, to enable any level of real balances demanded to be attained for any level of nominal balances. Temin's failure to recognize the importance of the distinction between nominal and real magnitudes leads him to stress instead the distinction between long run and short run, but this distinction is not highly relevant to the determination of the stock of money. Undoubtedly, different forces exert different influences on the behavioral patterns underlying the proximate determinants in the short and long run. But in both runs, it is the behavioral patterns underlying the proximate determinants that determine the size of the nominal quantity of money outstanding. The demand forces emanating from the public that affect the nominal quantity of money are those that have to do with the forms among which they choose to distribute their nominal (or real) assets—the fraction they choose to hold in real assets, securities of various kinds, bank deposits of various kinds, and high-powered money. These demand forces interact with the supply conditions of high-powered money, and of various forms of deposits or securities, to determine the nominal quantity of money. The demand for real money balances interacts with the nominal quantity of money to determine the price level. Of course, this is an oversimplified statement. A more sophisticated statement would assert that all of these variables are determined simultaneously and that some of the variables that enter into the demand for real money balances may also enter into the functions that determine the distribution of the total balance sheet among various forms of assets. But the important point is fully brought out by the simplified picture: to leave price expectations out of the picture in the short run from 1929 on is to leave out a major part of the picture—both for monetary analysis and for income analysis. As the public adjusts discrepancies between its actual real money balances and desired real money balances, nominal income is altered and the breakdown into prices and output is determined.

Temin alleges that the supply of money in our specification is "determined by forces independent of income and interest rates" (p. 19). Yet we specifically note that the deposit ratios are functions of the interest rate, among other variables (contrary to Temin's discussion, which suggests that we do not include it) and that the deposit-currency ratio is a function also of income. He is right that we regard banking panics as "far and away the most important single determinant"(p. 20) of the ratios, not only in the early 1930s, but also during other panic episodes. How do we know this? By studying the pattern of behavior in these ratios during panic episodes. The early 1930s do not stand alone. We have evidence on the behavior of the ratios in all the post–Civil War panics in the United States. They tell a uniform story of a shift from deposits to currency by the public once the economy is engulfed in panic and of a belated attempt by banks to increase reserves relative to their deposits once the panic subsided.

We have evidence also from Canadian experience in 1929–33. The percentage fall in Canadian nominal income over these years was about the same as in U.S. nominal income, yet the percentage fall in the Canadian stock of money was considerably smaller. The reason is that Canada was spared the ordeal of bank failures. There was no shift from deposits to currency in Canada comparable to that in the United States, and so there was no effect from this proximate determinant in producing a decline in the stock of money. There was no decline in the "quality" of deposits comparable to that in the United States because of a loss of confidence in banks, and hence there was less of a decline in the demand for real money balances in Canada. That is why a smaller decline in the quantity of money was consistent with almost the same decline in income and prices. The sharp decline in Canadian income and prices occurred because Canada kept its exchange rate with the United States fixed until September 1931 and then maintained its exchange rate at a new level involving a smaller depreciation than that undergone by the pound sterling. For Canada, it is entirely appropriate to regard the quantity of money as adapting in large measure to movement in income and prices, rather than as an exogenous force. It was the tail. The United States was the dog.

The Behavior of High-Powered Money

The decline in the quantity of money from August 1929 to October 1930, before the first banking panic, did not result from any weakness of the private economy. The decline was entirely the result of a decline in Federal Reserve credit outstanding. There were no problems with the banking structure, no attempted liquidation of loans by banks, no attempt by depositors to shift from deposits to currency that contributed to reducing the quantity of money. In fact, the banks were reducing reserves relative to deposits, and the public was increasing its deposits relative to currency—enough to offset half the decline in Federal Reserve credit.

Temin counters that a decrease in bank discounts at the Fed, in response to the decline in market interest rates, and not any failure of the Fed, was responsible for the decline in Federal Reserve credit outstanding. Bank borrowings declined from a peak of $1,096 million in July 1929 to $189 million by September 1930. Total bank reserves fell about $40 million. Temin does not allude to the punitive attitude of the system toward member bank borrowing, hence bypasses the reason there was little incentive for them to increase rediscounting, absent any panic, when the Reserve Banks lowered discount rates—"dramatically," according to him (p. 21)—and he takes the absolute amount of discounting to be "low."[16]

In fact, the discount rate was not reduced uniformly at all Reserve Banks. By mid-1930, New York had reduced its rate in six steps from 6 to 2.5 percent, while at other Reserve Banks the rate had gone from 5 to 4 and 3.5 percent. By the end of 1930, the New York rate stood at 2 percent, the rates at two other banks at 3 percent, and at the remaining nine at 3.5 percent. The discount rate fell less than the commercial paper rate even in New York; a lot less, in other districts. The spread between the commercial paper rate and the discount rate at New York was a shade lower in 1930 than in 1929; at other Reserve Banks, much lower. Of course, under the lash of runs by the public, the banks did increase their borrowings—from $189 million in September 1930 to $338 million in December. But this increase in Reserve Bank credit outstanding was smaller than the increase in the public's currency holdings.

Temin's general Keynesian tendency to treat interest rates as the crucial monetary variable leads him astray in evaluating both the role of the Fed and our views about its responsibility. For example, he writes that the Federal Reserve "could have offset changes in interest rates by changing the discount rate, and it could have avoided the banking panics by changing its procedures" (p. 20). That is not our view. We put major emphasis, not on discount rate changes or on "procedures," but on Federal Reserve control of high-powered money, or bank reserves, through open-market operations.

From our view, the crucial question is whether the Federal Reserve was powerless to engage in open-market purchases to restore the level of its credit outstanding, given that, until the first banking panic, the banks, for whatever reason, were not willing to come to the discount window. Temin's discussion of the system's behavior is ambiguous, to say the least:

> No one disputes that the Fed has the power to undertake open-market operations. And most people agree that these actions have effects on the economy. But very few of the monetary changes in the early 1930's were the results of conscious

> decisions to undertake open-market operations. Friedman and Schwartz argued
> that the decline in the stock of money in 1930 was the result of a fall in discounts
> at the Fed in response to a fall in market rates not fully duplicated by the dis-
> count rate, and that the fall in 1931 was due to a decline in the two deposit ratios
> produced by the banking crises. These events are not the same as open-market
> purchases. [P. 25]

These events clearly are the opposite of open-market purchases, which would
have increased Reserve credit outstanding and high-powered money. They are
precisely the kind of events that conventional central-bank wisdom would regard as requiring open-market purchases in order to offset their effects. Temin
objects that we imply that "all changes in the stock of money were the results
of actions by the Federal Reserve" (p. 25). They are the results of actions or
inactions by the Federal Reserve. In 1930 before the panic condition developed
at the end of the year, the Federal Reserve could have readily reversed the
decline in Federal Reserve credit outstanding. Temin evades the central issue
of why they did not do so.

Temin makes much of the fact that high-powered money on an annual average continued to increase except in 1930. Hence, he argues, there was no
restraint on the supply of money. High-powered money grew after the first
banking crisis, not because member bank reserves were expanding, but because the public's currency holdings began to climb in the usual shift of its
preferences toward currency as an aftermath of the banking crisis. By August
1931, the public's currency holdings had increased by $583 million over its
holdings in October 1930, but high-powered money was only $558 million
higher. High-powered money growth, barely adequate to meet the public's
growing distrust of bank deposits, had contractionary effects on the reserve
position of the banking system—hardly impressive evidence of monetary ease.

The Behavior of Interest Rates

According to Temin, the money hypothesis fails its most important test because there is no evidence in interest rates of monetary stringency at the end of
1930 as the result of bank failures. Temin has not examined the data for earlier
panics, but it is true that short-term rates in those episodes did rise during the
weeks of panic, and we do not observe a comparable rise during the weeks of
the first banking crisis in the last quarter of 1930 or of the second banking
crisis from March to June 1931.[17] The failure of short-term rates to rise, however, is not necessarily inconsistent with the presence of monetary stringency—both because monetary stringency might be reflected in prices rather than
in interest rates and because other factors were simultaneously impinging on
short-term rates. In particular, the failure of short-term rates to rise may have

reflected, first, declines in the 1920s in the supply of short-term instruments issued by both private borrowers and the government and, second, the special role of the commercial banks as demanders of these short-term instruments. There are two markets to consider, the commercial paper market and the market for short-term government securities.

The commercial paper market today is a different market from the one that existed in the 1920s through the Great Contraction.[18] In today's market, the finance companies are the dominant borrowers. In the 1920s, corporate enterprises in textiles, foodstuffs, metals, and leather were the main borrowers. There was a dramatic decline in the market from 1924 to 1933, interrupted by a brief expansion from the stock market crash to April 1930. Outstandings fell from a peak of $925 million in October 1924 to a low of $265 million in September 1929, largely because firms that had formerly borrowed in the commercial paper market found it more advantageous to float stocks and bonds. The stock market crash and the reduction in commercial paper rates relative to bank lending rates led to a rise in outstandings in April 1930 to $553 million. Thereafter, the volume declined to $358 million in December 1930 and $275 million in August 1931.

Currently, nonfinancial corporations are the main holders of commercial paper. In the 1920s through the Great Contraction, the banks were virtually the sole buyers of commercial paper, with country banks the mainstay of the market. From the member bank call date of December 31, 1930, through the September 29, 1931, call date, member bank holdings of commercial paper ranged from 102 to 141 percent of the reported total amount outstanding, the excess over the reported amount outstanding rising steadily over the interval covered. The explanation for the excess is that the banks purchased paper from dealers other than those reporting to the Federal Reserve Bank of New York and is one indication of the strength of member bank demand for commercial paper.

The chief advantage of commercial paper to member banks apart from its yield was its eligibility for rediscount at the Reserve Banks. This advantage gained in importance during a panic, so that, from the demand side, a panic, rather than putting pressure on commercial paper rates, to some extent relieved the pressure. Instead of selling commercial paper, banks increased borrowings using commercial paper as collateral to meet depositors' demand for currency. As we have seen, bills discounted rose in the last quarter of 1930 and again in June 1931, the culmination of the second banking panic. With limited supply and persistent demand, the failure of commercial paper rates to rise during the panic in no way contradicts the money hypothesis.

With respect to the government securities market, the reduction of the public debt, dating from 1919, continued through December 1930. This constituted an increase in the supply of loanable funds, thereby reducing the interest rate that would clear the market at any given price level. The increase in the public debt was small through August 1931, so the influence on the supply of loanable funds and hence on the upward pressure on interest rates from this source must likewise have been small (see table A–1).

As is true for later years also, we lack adequate data on the maturity distribution of the debt, 1929–31. Treasury bills—first issued in December 1929—and certificates of indebtedness had a maturity of less than one year when issued; Treasury notes, of three to five years; and bonds, of more than five years. When purchased or held, however, the remaining maturity might be quite different from the original maturity. So the distribution of security holdings among the indicated categories is only a rough index of their distribution by maturity.

Of the reduced total of the public debt, through December 1930, less than 10 percent of member bank holdings were in less than one-year maturities when issued; four-fifths were in long-term bonds (see table A–2). Their holdings amounted to less than one-quarter of the bills and certificates outside the Federal Reserve from the October 1929 call date through the June 1930 call date, rose to three-tenths at the September 1930 call date when the first banking panic had not yet erupted, and then to three-eighths by the call date in December after the Bank of United States had been suspended. In 1931, the composition of member bank holdings of government securities shifted toward the short-term when issued, probably reflecting a shift in the composition of outstandings, but also reinforcing the growing concentration of bank demand on these issues, already manifested in December 1930. Bank holdings of short-term governments were more than 50 percent of outstandings in September 1931, and 60 percent of outstanding medium-term governments.

Mayer (1978*b*) asks whether one would not expect "the demand for other assets to decline, and hence their yields to rise" (p. 140) when bank failures reduced the money supply. But the short-term assets for which we have yield information, primarily commercial paper and short-term governments, are not those for which demand declined. The banks dominated these markets, and with good reason. After the experience of two banking panics, the remaining banks chose to acquire assets with assured convertibility into cash sums at need and at short notice.

Short-term governments did not experience the unremitting declines in rates that characterized the commercial paper market in 1930. Continuous monthly data are available only for the yields on three- to six-month Treasury notes and certificates (see figure A–1). (There were only five issues of Treasury bills that year, so there are quotations only on new offerings.) As the chart in figure A–1 shows, small increases in yields occurred during three months in 1930—5 basis points in April, 27 in September, and 8 in December, the month the Bank of United States failed.

Table A-1.   U.S. Federal Government Interest-Bearing Debt Outstanding,
Various Months, 1929–31 (in millions of dollars)

Situation as of Last Day of:	Bonds	Treasury Notes	Certificates of Indebtedness	Treasury Bills	Total
June 1929	12,124	2,254	1,640	—	16,018
Aug. 1929	12,126	2,781	1,620	—	16,527
Oct. 1929	12,115	2,649	1,658	—	16,422
Dec. 1929	12,110	2,513	1,306	100	16,029
Mar. 1930	12,112	2,570	1,385	56	16,123
June 1930	12,112	2,390	1,264	156	15,922
Sept. 1930	12,113	2,345	1,247	120	15,825
Oct. 1930	12,113	2,345	1,247	223	15,928
Nov. 1930	12,113	2,343	1,247	230	15,933
Dec. 1930	12,113	2,342	1,192	128	15,775
Mar. 1931	12,709	1,129	2,228	214	16,280
June 1931	13,531	621	1,924	445	16,520
Aug. 1931	13,536	644	1,883	523	16,586
Sept. 1931	14,336	644	1,545	524	17,049
Dec. 1931	14,298	795	1,860	576	17,529

Source: U.S. Treasury Department 1929–31.

Given these conditions in both the commercial paper and short-term government markets until Britain cut loose from gold on September 21, 1931, why did the commercial paper rate rise from 2 percent, during the week ending October 3, to 4.13, during the week ending November 14, after which it continued an uninterrupted decline to the week ending with the Bank Holiday—its low point during the contraction of 1.38 percent? Why did the average rate on new issues of Treasury bills, which reached a low of 0.485 percent in July 1931, rise steadily thereafter to 3.253 percent in December 1931? Outstandings of commercial paper continued to decline to the end of the year, but outstanding Treasury bills rose somewhat. It is clear from the pattern of short-term rates of private instruments that the rate rise followed the increase in the discount rate at New York on October 9, from 1.5 to 2.5 percent, and on October 16, to 3.5 percent. In this instance, the Federal Reserve led the market. In the discount rate reductions from November 1929 to May 1931, it followed the market. In the short-term government market, an added factor contributing to the rise in interest rates may have been the increase in Treasury notes.

Table A–2. Chief Kinds of U. S. Government Direct Obligations Held by Member Banks, Member Bank Call Dates, 1929–31

	Member Bank Holdings (millions of dollars)				Percent of Total Member Bank Holdings in:			Holdings as Percent of Total Amounts Outside FR Banks			
	Total (1)	Bills and Certificates (2)	Notes (3)	Bonds (4)	Bills and Certificates (5)	Notes (6)	Bonds (7)	Total (8)	Bills and Certificates (9)	Notes (10)	Bonds (11)
1929											
June 29	4,155	446	704	3,005	10.8	16.9	72.3	26.3	28.8	32.6	24.8
Oct. 4	4,022	365	665	2,992	9.1	16.5	74.4	25.0	24.0	26.5	24.8
Dec. 31	3,863	249	520	3,094	6.4	13.5	80.1	24.9	21.0	22.6	25.7
1930											
Mar. 27	4,085	273	524	3,288	6.7	12.8	80.5	26.3	23.4	21.9	27.5
June 30	4,061	259	463	3,340	6.4	11.4	82.2	26.5	22.6	21.0	27.9
Sept. 24	4,095	334	418	3,343	8.2	10.2	81.6	26.9	30.7	19.4	27.9
Dec. 31	4,125	369	485	3,271	8.9	11.8	79.3	27.4	37.6	22.9	27.4
1931											
Mar. 25	5,002	899	332	3,771	18.0	6.6	75.4	31.9	42.2	30.1	30.3
June 30	5,343	901	403	4,039	16.9	7.5	75.6	33.7	44.5	67.8	30.5
Sept. 29	5,564	914	371	4,279	16.4	6.7	76.9	34.1	54.2	60.5	30.5
Dec. 31	5,319	679	441	4,199	12.8	8.3	78.9	31.8	33.7	57.9	30.1

Sources, by columns: (1): Sum of cols. (2)–(4). (2)–(4): U. S. Board of Governors of the Federal Reserve System 1943, p. 77. (8): Holdings of the Federal Reserve Banks were deducted from the total of the three kinds of debt outstanding (ibid., pp. 332, 343, 375, 509–10); col. (1) was expressed as a percentage of the difference. (9)–(11): Procedure similar to that for col. (8), except that no breakdown of Federal Reserve holdings was available except at Dec. 31; the percentage distribution of the three kinds of debt was assumed the same at other dates in each year as on the following Dec. 31.

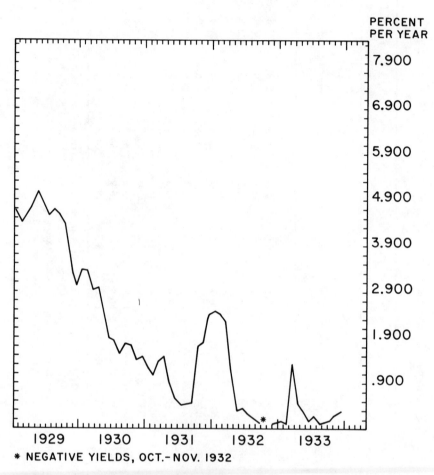

Figure A–1. Yields on Three- to Six-Month Treasury Notes and Certificates, 1929–33
Source: U.S. Board of Governors of the Federal Reserve System 1943, p. 460.

Bills discounted had been rising from July 1931, when discounts averaged $169 million, to $282 million in September. They then rose to $614 million in October, peaking at $848 million in February 1932.

In addition to the increase in their indebtedness, member banks lost $74 million in reserves between July and September 1930 and a further $426 million between September 1931 and February 1932.

Interest rate behavior is not, then, inconsistent with monetary stringency both before and after September 1931. The pattern of short-term interest rate declines before September 1931 reflected firm demand by commercial banks for commercial paper and short-term government securities and a generally declining supply of these instruments. When the Federal Reserve increased discount rates sharply in October 1931, it led market rates, pulling them up, whereas its earlier discount rate reductions followed market rate declines.

Temin, however, is right in arguing that short-term interest rates are the ones to examine because they most nearly resemble holding-period yields. For long-term rates, only yields to maturity are available, although investors make plans on the basis of holding-period yields. Temin therefore regards long-term rates as unsuitable for analysis because they are complicated for the years 1928–31 by the growing risk of default for some bonds and the rising price of risk.

In A Monetary History, we noted that while both long- and short-term interest rates had been declining before the first banking crisis, a widening spread began to emerge, synchronous with the first crisis, between yields to maturity on lower-grade corporate bonds and on government bonds as yields on corporate bonds rose sharply and yields on government bonds continued to fall. Temin says "this suggestion will not stand up" (p. 105) because bond prices began to fall well before the panic, and only the prices of lower-grade bonds fell; the prices of high-grade corporate and government bonds stayed roughly constant.

The point of Temin's insistence that the value of bank portfolios declined well before the bank panic of 1930 is that the price decline of bonds was not a result of the liquidity scramble but rather a cause. He argues that bonds were being moved from one quality class to another so that movements in the Baa rate do not show the change in the price of banks' portfolios. The price decline in any actual bond portfolio in the 1930s was the result of both the decline in the price of a given quality class and the decline in the quality ratings of the bonds in the portfolio. The yields on the fixed sample of bonds that Temin constructed for December and June dates 1928–31 rise continuously and far exceed the yields on Baa bonds.

No one disputes that bond prices were depressed in 1928 and 1929 while the boom in equities was in full swing. Temin's assertion that yields on high-grade corporate and on government bonds thereafter were constant is hard to assess. Yields on high-grade corporate bonds fell from December 1929 through October 1930, from 4.67 to 4.42. At the end of 1930, during the months of panic, they rose to 4.52. They then resumed a decline to 4.36 in July 1931. Yields to maturity on government bonds fell from 3.43 in January 1930 to 3.19 in November 1930, then rose to 3.30 in February 1931, falling thereafter until June, when the yield was 3.13. These small changes are consistent with monetary stringency before the first banking panic—given the steady decline in commodity prices, so that real rates rose appreciably; and the upward movements and subsequent declines at the end of 1930 are consistent with an intensification of monetary stringency during the panic.

In any event, the relative constancy of high-grade yields does not contradict the argument that the sale of low-grade bonds was induced by a scramble for liquidity. Temin counters that banks were net sellers of bonds in 1931 because "they perceived the risk more quickly or because they were more risk averse than individuals. The fact that they sold while individuals bought is not evidence of a liquidity scramble" (p.106 n.). This ignores the effect that dumping securities, for whatever motives, by some banks produced on the values of the investment portfolios of other banks. As for money and income, there is no reason to expect a one-way relation. The reflex influence of bond sales in setting off other bond sales is the essence of a liquidity crisis that Temin fails to recognize.

Price Deflation and the Behavior of Real Balances

Temin argues that the distinction between nominal interest rates and real interest rates can be neglected. To begin with, he doubts that anyone apart from professional economists makes such a distinction. Further, even if the distinction were made, it would not salvage the monetary explanation. If high real interest rates dominated all other explanations of 1929–33, he asks, why do we not observe a similar effect in 1920–21 with a greater deflation and the same institutional constraint that nominal interest rates cannot be negative? There were indeed high real rates in 1920–21, but their effect was not prolonged by banking panic effects on the money stock.

The final major indication for Temin that monetary causes cannot account for the severity of the economic decline is that real balances did not decline. Because prices fell so rapidly, the stock of real money balances did not fall from 1929 to 1931; hence, in his view there could not have been any deflationary effect from the decrease in the nominal stock of money. He asks:

> Why . . . should the level of real expenditures and hence of employment have been lower in, say, 1931 than in 1929 since the real stock of money was larger by all of the measures shown in Table 23? [P. 142]

For Temin, there is no contradiction between his assertion that the demand (i.e., demand function) for nominal balances declined while real balances (i.e., quantity of real balances held) were constant or increased. Real money balances are a statistical construct that he examines merely because quantity theorists consider it important. If he thought it represented the basic monetary total demanded, he would have had to explain why a decline in the demand for money did not produce a rise in prices, for a fixed nominal stock, to produce a decline in real money balances.

If one regards real money balances as the basic monetary total demanded, there is no evidence that the demand function declined. Gandolfi and Lothian (1976) have shown that the function that predicts actual real money balances for 1900–1929 predicts actual real money balances during the Great Contraction with no loss in predictive power. The demand for real money balances is conventionally defined as related positively to real income and negatively to the rate of interest. Hence the movement of real balances over the cycle depends on the relative movements of the determinants. There is no evidence of a leftward shift in the demand curve during the Great Contraction. The rise in real money balances to 1931 and similarly the decline from 1931 to 1933 were due to changes in the determinants of the demand. There were movements along the demand function, not a shift in the function, as Temin would have it.

Gandolfi and Lothian have also challenged Temin's assumption that a fall in the nominal quantity of money accompanied by a corresponding fall in prices should leave real output unchanged, since real balances remain constant. In this case, Temin fails to note a distinction between anticipated and unanticipated price change. Suppose output depends on the price of output relative to expected price of inputs. An unanticipated fall in all prices, given imperfect information on input prices, will be perceived by producers as a relative fall in output prices. Temin ignores a growing literature on the supply effect of unanticipated price changes on real output change. Hence his assertion that the behavior of real balances is inconsistent with a monetary explanation of the contraction is untenable.

The Role of Bank Failures

As indicated earlier, Temin's explanation of the role of bank failures is that they served as the channel through which the supply of money adjusted to the falling demand. He alleges that the banking panic of October 1930 was induced by the decline in agricultural income and in the prices of relatively risky long-term securities presumably held by banks and, in particular, that the failure of the Bank of United States in the course of that panic did not precipitate a liquidity crisis. In *A Monetary History* we devoted a section to the question of the origin of bank failures during the contraction. Did the failures arise primarily because of imprudent financial practices of the 1920s? Or were they the product of developments of the early 1930s?

> Whatever may have been true of the initial bank failures in the first banking crisis, any ex ante deterioration in the quality of loans and investments in the later twenties or simply the acquisition of low-quality loans and investments in that period, even if no different in quality than in earlier periods, was a minor factor in the subsequent bank failures. As we have seen, the banking system as a whole was in a position to meet the demands of depositors for currency only by a multiple contraction of deposits, hence of assets. Under such circumstances, any runs on banks for whatever reason became to some extent self-justifying, whatever the quality of assets held by banks. Banks had to dump their assets on the market which inevitably forced a decline in the market value of those assets and hence of the remaining assets they held. The impairment in the market value of assets held by banks, particularly in their bond portfolios, was the most important source of impairment of capital leading to bank suspensions, rather than the default of specific loans or of specific bond issues. [P. 355]

So even if we were to concede that all the banks that failed in the first banking panic beginning October 1930 were bad banks that deserved to fail, this series of failures would have provoked difficulties for other good banks, the market value of whose assets would have been affected by the dumping of assets by the failing banks. Such failures could well have promoted panic among all depositors. In a panic the public is mired in doubts that institutions are as sound as they are said to be.

I believe that the concession to Temin about the first banking crisis is not supported by the evidence, however. Good banks went down in that panic. His allegation that the Bank of United States failed because of fraudulent practices of its officers will not be sustained by an impartial examination of the record of the bank. The charge of fraud tells you something about the temper of the times, not the facts of the case.

Moreover, the panic of October 1930 does not stand alone in the U.S. monetary history if we look back this time, not forward to the succeeding banking crises from 1931 to 1933. Cagan (1965) noted in his study, to which Temin does not refer, that panics in U.S. monetary history appeared in the early stages of cyclical contraction and therefore themselves could not have been the major cause of the contractions. He concluded that panics made ordinary business contractions severe when they led to a substantial decline in the rate of monetary growth and not otherwise. "Substantial decline in this rate, by itself, and with no panic, could and has produced severe business contraction" (p.267).

Monetary Policy

I turn finally to the issue of monetary policy during the Great Contraction. In *A Monetary History* we argued that alternative policies were available that the Federal Reserve System could have pursued and that would have made the contraction less severe. Temin refuses to be drawn into a discussion of alternative policies. "The question posed" in his book "is not whether some alternative policy would have worked, but rather what happened to make such a corrective policy desirable" (p.7). Nevertheless, he has himself referred to alternative policies, himself conducted a counterfactual "thought experiment," as he labeled our section on alternative policies. It is counterfactual for Temin to state that, had there been no bank failures, the quantity of money would have been reduced to the same extent by a rise in the reserve-deposit ratio rather than the rise in the currency-deposit ratio that actually occurred. And this counterfactual assertion is refuted by Cagan's study. Temin assumes that the reserve-deposit ratio would have risen as a result of the decline in interest rates in the absence of bank failures. Cagan finds little interest elasticity in this ratio and concludes that the larger part of the change in the ratio was related to panics. A lagged reaction to a panic on the part of banks was to raise the ratio of their reserves to their deposit liabilities.

But to turn to the main question: We do have some evidence for 1930–31 on what alternative policies would have accomplished. We know that when the Federal Reserve System finally undertook open-market purchases of $1 billion between April and August 1932, the money stock grew at a 1.75 percent annual rate of rise from September 1932 until January 1933 compared with the preceding 14 percent annual rate of decline. We know that industrial production rose 14 percent in the second half of 1932 after sharp earlier declines and that commodity prices rose in the second and third quarters of 1932 after declining in the two preceding years. Temin counters that we merely assume that the change in the quantity of money changes the level of income and do not disprove the possibility of reverse causation. Can he really mean that the Federal Reserve undertook the open-market purchases in 1932 as a passive response to an increased demand for money that was a result of rising output and prices that lagged the change in monetary policy? There is evidence also on what alternative policies would have accomplished if we turn to the system's open-market purchases in 1924 and 1927. The omission of discussion of these policy measures in Temin's book reflects his assumption that money is passive. Supply simply adjusts to the demand. This is a real-bills vision with a vengeance.

In *A Monetary History* we found a contrast between the policy actions of the Federal Reserve in 1924 and 1927 on the one hand and 1930–33 on the other. Elmus Wicker (1966) denies such a contrast, arguing that international considerations accounted for the open-market purchases in the '20s and that international considerations were unimportant in 1930–33. In his view, the Federal Reserve never accepted domestic economic stability as a goal of monetary policy. Brunner and Meltzer (1968) also deny the contrast, arguing that in all three contractions, if market rates, particularly short-term rates, fell, policy was regarded as expansive, and if market rates rose, policy was regarded as contractionary. In the earlier contractions, gold inflows and a decline in the demand for currency and bank loans produced a decline in interest rates accompanied by an increase in high-powered money. As a result, money supply rose and the economy recovered. In 1929–30, gold inflows and declines in the demand for currency and bank loans also produced a decline in interest rates, but high-powered money and the money supply fell. Hence the economy continued to deteriorate. But, as Brunner and Meltzer document, nearly all of the members of the Open Market Committee regarded monetary policy as easy.

We regard Wicker's view as untenable. If the Federal Reserve did not accept domestic economic stability as a goal of monetary policy, why did the system allocate resources to improving the data on economic activity, why did the staff prepare detailed studies on the state of the domestic economy in preparation for open-market committee meetings, why did the system claim credit for domestic prosperity when it occurred? There is without doubt some merit to the Brunner-Meltzer analysis, yet it cannot be accepted as a complete description of the situation. After all, the governor and the chief economists on the staff of the New York Federal Reserve Bank all recognized that the decline in interest rates was not equivalent to monetary ease; they urged, and with some support from others in and outside the system, extensive open-market purchases at various times in 1930, 1931, and 1932 and were not dissuaded from doing so by the decline in interest rates. And these were the people who, so long as Benjamin Strong was alive, effectively dominated Federal Reserve policy. Hence, we continue to believe that had Strong lived or had he been succeeded by someone of similar views and equal personal force, the same monetary growth policies followed in 1924 and 1927 would have been followed in 1930, hence the decline in high-powered money either would not have occurred or would have been promptly reversed, and the economy would have been spared its prolonged ordeal.

NOTES

1. In their study of production during the business-cycle contraction of 1929–33, W. C. Mitchell and A. F. Burns (1936) noted:

> The long decline was interrupted by three partial and abortive revivals. Of these, the first, in the early months of 1930, was brief and restricted mainly to automobiles, steel, and heavy construction. The second, in the first half of 1931, had wider scope, lasted longer, and went further. It was especially pronounced in the textile, rubber tire, shoe, and leather industries. The revival in the summer and autumn of 1932 was fairly general, as is indicated by the preceding discussion of the "double bottom" in the terminal trough of this cycle. In some industries one of these abortive revivals lasted long enough and went far enough to produce an "extra" specific cycle during the depression. [P. 18]

2. Haberler (1976, pp. 22–23) notes that the Majority Report of the Gold Delegation of the Financial Committee of the League of Nations in 1932 also attributed the depression to maladjustments caused by the war, but Gustav Cassel in a Memorandum of Dissent disputed the importance of maladjustments and stressed instead monetary phenomena—the undervaluation of the French franc, the overvaluation of the pound, the cessation of U.S. capital exports, and the U.S. depression. Maladjustments were also the explanation of the Great Depression advanced in later studies issued by the Royal Institute of International Affairs (Arndt 1944) and the United Nations Economic Commission for Europe (Svenillson 1954).

3. Abramovitz, in private correspondence with me, has called to my attention qualifications to this statement in his paper. He notes that since the "small-country" model in that paper was designed to apply to long swings, it was inappropriate for use within a single business-cycle contraction and, in any event, could not apply in full force to the United States. On the basis of a subsequent paper (1977), in which he analyzed models of a "large country" and a "small country," Abramovitz believes efforts by the Federal Reserve to sustain the growth of the U.S. money supply in 1930–31, unaccompanied by similar actions by leading European countries, would not have been adequate to prevent the massive decline in income that in fact occurred.

4. See the appendix for a demonstration that Temin's interpretation of interest rate movements as showing no monetary stringency in 1930 and 1931 is contradicted by evidence on the supply of and demand for the relevant money-market instruments during that period.

5. Christopher Sims (1972) introduced a sophisticated alternative test of Granger causality between a pair of variables by running two regressions, with each as dependent variable and both leading and lagged values of the other as independent variables.

6. George Garvy (1959, pp. 71–73) has shown that bank debits to deposit accounts at these centers is a good proxy for nominal income. Peter Lindert (1981) objects to this conclusion since Garvy (p. 87) also reports a lack of perfect conformity of cyclical movements in debits with interwar NBER reference dates (debits lag the turns in January 1920 and July 1921 and skip turns in October 1926 and November 1927). Nonetheless, Moore (1961, vol. 1, chap. 5) includes debits in his list of coincident indicators for that period. Gordon and Wilcox (1981), using quarterly GNP estimates, obtained results similar to those in table 2.

7. Eight years because of the need to include lagged values.

8. One other approach to determine unidirectional relationship that some investigators have reported involves cross-correlations of the innovations in X and Y processes derived from Box-Jenkins procedures. Christopher Sims (1977a) has criticized that approach as biased "for any null hypothesis except the null hypothesis of no relation between the series." The defect in testing whether "x causes v," he points out, in a formulation

$$y = a(L)y + b(L)c(L)x + v, \tag{1}$$

"with a, b, and *c* as polynomials in positive powers of the lag operator, *L,* and *v* uncorrelated with past values of *y* or *x,"* is as follows:

> The null hypothesis "*x* does not cause *y*" is represented by $b(L) = 0$. Whether or not *a, b,* and *c* are linear in the problem's parameters, maximum likelihood will be, for stationary *x, y,* asymptotically equivalent to choosing *a, b,* and *c* to minimize the sum of squares of *v* in the sample period. With any fixed *c,* an asymptotically valid test of the null hypothesis can be obtained by estimating *a* and *b jointly* by maximum likelihood or nonlinear least squares, then applying standard test statistics. Though this is not a difficult procedure, [the criticized author] instead chooses *c* as a filter which makes *c(L)x* serially uncorrelated, and chooses *a* as a filter which makes *a(L)y* serially uncorrelated, then *holding a and c fixed,* estimates *b.* But this amounts to testing the significance of *b* by first estimating the regression (1) with *b* set to zero, then testing for the contribution of *b* to the regression by examining correlations between the *residuals* of this first-stage equation and the omitted variables of the form *c(L)x.* Anyone versed in the theory of least-squares regression will recognize this as involving a bias in favor of the null hypothesis, except in the special case when the omitted variables are uncorrelated with the included variables. [P. 24]

9. Contrary to Temin (1981), the monetary events listed in the tabulation are, in the main, not "changes in the quantity of money" or "changes in [market] interest rates." They are events, like a change in the Federal Reserve discount rate or an episode of bank runs or Britain's departure from gold or the 1932 open-market purchase program, that are newsworthy and attract attention. They have immediate announcement effects. Moreover, a quick adjustment of prices does not preclude a long distributed lag adjustment. A partial adjustment that shows up quickly is not equivalent to the full adjustment of prices.

10. In a journal article that postdates Temin's review, Barber (1978) traces the origins of the Great Depression to demographic factors that he links to a decline in the residential construction market in the United States and to "a markedly unfavourable influence on the capital spending plans of business firms throughout the developed world" (p. 453).

Annual growth in standardized nonfarm households declined from 3 percent per year to under 2 percent per year from 1924 to 1932. This is supposed to have triggered the decline in U.S. residential construction. Yet the annual growth in standardized nonfarm households from the early 1950s to 1970 was lower than growth of households in any year from 1924 to 1932. Barber attempts to rationalize this inconsistency by citing the availability of mortgage finance since World War II. In that case, the demand for housing is not dependent on demographic factors exclusively.

Similarly, a rapid decline in the rate of population growth after World War I in developed countries, which was accompanied by a lower rate of labor-force growth in the United States and Germany, need not have had the consequence he assumes on capital spending. What evidence is there that firms throughout the world were aware of this demographic trend?

Essentially, Barber fails to establish a connection between his empirical evidence on the decline in population and disequilibrium in the steady-state growth model he presents and a model that would explain recessions. Disequilibrium in a steady-state sense does not explain why the peak in capital spending occurred in 1929 rather than 1928 or 1930.

11. Temin tries to determine (1976, p. 64) from the components of real GNP whether 1930 was a more depressed year than 1921 or 1938. Table 4, based on Commerce annual estimates of GNP in current and 1958 prices, the GNP implicit price deflator, and the unemployment rate, is an alternative to Temin's table which shows percentage changes in Kendrick's annual GNP estimates in 1929 prices, the consumption and investment expenditures components of GNP, and merchandise exports deflated by wholesale prices. For the Commerce estimates, the components of GNP are available only since 1929. The first part of table 4, following Temin, relates the changes in the year following the peak in 1920, 1929, and 1937, to the magnitudes of the peak year. The bottom

half of the table relates the changes in the year following those peaks to the year preceding the peaks on the ground that the 1929 magnitudes were not typical of the interwar years. One may ask whether 1920 or 1937 was any more typical. In any event, such comparisons between consecutive or nearly consecutive annual figures are subject to substantial error because of possible differences in patterns within the base year and the comparison year. For example, a cyclical peak in December preceded by a rapid rise during the year might be accompanied by a zero year-to-year change, despite a severe recession.

For whatever such comparisons may be worth, the real income decline was somewhat greater in 1930 than in 1921, the rise in unemployment was smaller, and the price decline was much smaller. In all of these respects, 1938 was much the mildest of the three contraction years. Over a two-year span, the results show the 1930 change to be even milder relative to 1921. Of course, 1930 was a contraction year from beginning to end, whereas in 1921 a trough was reached in July, and in 1938, in June. In addition, Temin's use of gross merchandise exports as if that were an independent component of GNP is misleading. The variable normally examined in the national income accounts is net export of goods and services. The change in the variable from 1929 to 1930 is one-third the magnitude of the change Temin reports for gross merchandise exports.

What sets 1930 apart from both 1921 and 1938 is that a banking panic that changed the monetary character of the contraction occurred in the last quarter of the year. In 1921 there were many bank suspensions—triple the number in 1920, for a total of 505 banks with deposits of $172 million. In 1930, there were 1,350 bank suspensions, with deposits of $837 million. In 1938, post-FDIC, suspensions were negligible, 54 banks with $10 million in deposits. Despite the increase in bank suspensions in 1921, there were no runs on banks. That is what distinguishes 1930 from 1921—there was panic in 1930 but not in 1921. Bank suspensions in 1921 were perceived by the public as special problems of agricultural and rural areas but not as affecting confidence in banks generally.

12. On the role of real wages, see the final section of this paper.

13. The fall in prices made the Smoot-Hawley tariff level even higher than it otherwise would have been since specific duties are automatically raised with a declining price level (Haberler 1976, p. 34, n. 65). Meltzer (1976, pp. 459–60) assigns a large role to the Smoot-Hawley tariff and subsequent tariff retaliation by many countries in exacerbating the 1929–33 contraction. The effect of the tariffs was to impede the price-specie flow mechanism and the adjustment of the U.S. and the world economy. Absent the tariff, U.S. prices would have fallen relative to those abroad and led to an increase in foreign demand and net exports.

The protectionist policy that influential British economists in 1930 advised the British government to adopt played a role there parallel to that of the Smoot-Hawley tariff in the United States. In his memoir about the "golden age" of the great British economists, Colin Clark (1977) discusses a "might-have-been":

> It is now unmistakably clear that what Britain, being still a power strong enough to give a lead to the world, should have done in 1930–31, irrespective of whether or not other countries so acted, would have been to have preserved Free Trade, accompanied by an expansionist demand policy, and allowing the exchange rate to move freely in response to market pressures. It is now universally agreed that the exchange rate had been overvalued on the return to the Gold Standard in 1925, and a reduction would, in any case have been required. (Though he had protested strongly against the over-valuation in 1925, Keynes himself was not recommending devaluation in 1930–31—the only prominent men to recommend the policy were R. G. Hawtrey, the Treasury's economic adviser, and Ernest Bevin.) Once the exchange rate had been freed, a strongly expansionist policy would have been possible. The preservation of free trade would have allowed the benefits of this expansion to flow to other countries and also, a matter of equal importance, would have set the right example, and spread economic expansion more widely over the world. [P. 90]

Clark's "might-have-been" applied a fortiori to the case of the United States.

14. In *A Monetary History,* we noted that since China was on a silver standard, it was hardly affected internally, 1929–31, by the worldwide economic contraction. Choudri and Kochin (1977) provide similar evidence for Spain for those years. Spain then had flexible exchange rates and a reasonably stable monetary policy.

15. Allan Meltzer (1976) traces the start of the contraction to "economic policies in the United States and other countries operating under the rules of the interwar gold standard" (p. 457). In his view, a relative decline in prices in the United States, as in 1928–29, under the price-specie flow mechanism can induce a recession abroad. He attempts to account for subsequent U.S. price change by relating anticipated price change at the start of the year to the average rate of monetary growth in the preceding three years relative to the rate of monetary expansion in the most recent year, with acceleration from the maintained average having much the larger effect under the gold standard. He regards his predicted rates of U.S. price change for 1930–31 and 1933 as not substantially different from actual price change. For 1932, when the predicted rate was only half the actual rate of price decline, he concludes the decline cannot be explained by the price-specie flow mechanism and the expected response to monetary contraction.

16. The percentage of eligible paper offered for rediscount rejected by the Reserve Banks of New York, Dallas, Philadelphia, and St. Louis (of those reporting such figures) was higher in 1930 than in 1929, possible evidence that acceptability standards were higher despite the decline in discount rates. Of course, member banks had the option of borrowing against their 15-day promissory notes secured by government obligations. See Beckhart, Smith, and Brown (1932).

17. Minor increases in yields on short- and long-term governments and on municipals are reported for December 1930, and March-April 1931.

Brunner and Meltzer (1968) interpret the persistent decline in short-term interest rates despite currency drains and bank failures as the result of adventitious factors offsetting the effects on short-term market rates that would otherwise have been observed. They cite an inflow of gold— mostly from South America and Japan—in the last quarter of 1930 (p. 343).

18. On the change in the character of the commercial paper market since the 1920s, see Selden (1963). The commercial paper market during the 1920s is discussed in Beckhart (1932).

REFERENCES

Abramovitz, M. 1977. "Determinants of Nominal-Income and Money-Stock Growth and of the Level of the Balance of Payments: Two-Country Models under a Specie Standard." Unpublished. Stanford University.

———. N. d. "The Monetary Side of Long Swings in U.S. Economic Growth." Stanford University Center for Research in Economic Growth, Memorandum No. 146.

Arndt, H. W. 1944. *The Economic Lessons of the Nineteen-Thirties.* London: Oxford University Press.

Barber, C. L. 1978. "On the Origins of the Great Depression." *Southern Economic Journal* 44: 432–56.

Beckhart, B. H. 1932. *The New York Money Market.* Vol. 3. New York: Columbia University Press.

Beckhart, B. H.; Smith, J. G.; and Brown, W. A., Jr. 1932. *The New York Money Market.* Vol. 4. New York: Columbia University Press.

Brunner, K., and Meltzer, A. H. 1968. "What Did We Learn from the Monetary Experience of the United States in the Great Depression?" *Canadian Journal of Economics* 1: 334–48.

Cagan, P. 1965. *Determinants and Effects of Changes in the Stock of Money, 1875–1960*. New York: Columbia University Press, for the National Bureau of Economic Research.

Chandler, L. V. 1970. *America's Greatest Depression, 1929–1941*. New York: Harper & Row.

Choudri, E., and Kochin, L. 1977. "International Transmission of Business Cycle Disturbances under Fixed and Flexible Exchange Rates: Some Evidence from the Great Depression." Unpublished. Carleton University and University of Washington.

Clark, C. 1977. "The 'Golden' Age of the Great Economists: Keynes, Robbins et al. in 1930." *Encounter* 49: 80–90.

Currie, L. 1935. *The Supply and Control of Money in the United States*. Cambridge, Mass.: Harvard University Press.

Darby, M. R. 1976. "Three-and-a-Half-Million U.S. Employees Have Been Mislaid; Or, an Explanation of Unemployment, 1934–41." *Journal of Political Economy* 84: 1–16.

Fand, D. 1967. "Some Implications of Money Supply Analysis." *American Economic Review* 57: 380–400.

Friedman, M., and Schwartz, A. J. 1963a. *A Monetary History of the United States, 1867–1960*. Princeton, N.J.: Princeton University Press, for the National Bureau of Economic Research.

———. 1963b. "Money and Business Cycles." *Review of Economics and Statistics* 45: 32–78.

———. 1970. *Monetary Statistics of the United States*. New York: Columbia University Press, for the National Bureau of Economic Research.

Gandolfi, A. E. 1974. "Stability of the Demand for Money during the Great Contraction—1929–1933." *Journal of Political Economy* 82: 969–83.

Gandolfi, A. E., and Lothian, J. R. 1976. "The Demand for Money from the Great Depression to the Present." *American Economic Review* 66: 46–51.

———. 1977. "Review of 'Did Monetary Forces Cause the Great Depression?'" *Journal of Money, Credit and Banking* 9: 679–91.

Garvy, G. 1959. *Debits and Clearings Statistics and Their Use*. Rev. ed. Washington, D.C.: Board of Governors of the Federal Reserve System.

Gordon, R. J., and Wilcox, J. A. 1981. "Monetarist Interpretations of the Great Depression: An Evaluation and Critique." In this volume.

Granger, C. W. J. 1969. "Investigating Causal Relations by Econometric Models and Cross-Spectral Methods." *Econometrica* 37: 424–38.

Haberler, G. 1976. *The World Economy, Money and the Great Depression, 1919–1939*. Washington, D.C.: American Enterprise Institute for Public Policy Research.

Kindleberger, C. P. 1973. *The World in Depression, 1929–1939*. Berkeley, Calif.: University of California Press.

League of Nations. 1929–33. *Monthly Bulletin of Statistics*. Vols. 10–14. Financial and Economic Intelligence Service. Geneva.

————. 1932. *Report of the Gold Delegation of the Financial Committee*. Document C.502, M.343. Geneva.

Librarie de Recueil Sirey. 1937. *L'Evolution de l'economie Francaise, 1910–1937*. Paris.

Lindert, P. 1981. "Comments on 'Understanding 1929–1933.' " In this volume.

Mayer, T. 1978*a*. "Consumption in the Great Depression." *Journal of Political Economy* 86: 139–45.

————. 1978*b*. "Money and the Great Depression: Some Reflections on Professor Temin's Recent Book." *Explorations in Economic History* 14: 127–45.

Meltzer, A. H. 1976. "Monetary and Other Explanations of the Start of the Great Depression." *Journal of Monetary Economics* 2: 455–71.

Mitchell, W. C., and Burns, A. F. 1936. *Production during the American Business Cycle, 1927–1933*. New York: National Bureau of Economic Research, Bulletin 61.

Moore, G. H., ed. 1961. *Business Cycle Indicators*. 2 vols. Princeton, N.J.: Princeton University Press, for the National Bureau of Economic Research.

Rasche, R. H. 1972. "A Review of Empirical Studies of the Money Supply Mechanism." Federal Reserve Bank of St. Louis *Review* 54: 11–19.

Selden, R. T. 1963. *Trends and Cycles in the Commercial Paper Market*. New York: National Bureau of Economic Research, Occasional Paper 85.

Sims, C. A. 1972. "Money and Causality." *American Economic Review* 62: 540–52.

————. 1977*a*. "Comment on D. A. Pierce, 'Relationships—and the Lack Thereof—between Economic Time Series, with Special Reference to Money and Interest Rates.' " *Journal of the American Statistical Association* 72: 23–24.

————. 1977*b*. "Macroeconomics and Reality." Department of Economics, University of Minnesota, Discussion Paper 77–91.

Sirkin, G. 1975. "The Stock Market of 1929 Revisited: A Note." *Business History Review* 49: 223–31.

Svennilson, I. 1954. *Growth and Stagnation in the European Economy*. Geneva: United Nations, Economic Commission for Europe.

Temin, P. 1976. *Did Monetary Forces Cause the Great Depression?* New York: W. W. Norton.

————. 1981. "Notes on the Causes of the Great Depression." In this volume.

U.S. Board of Governors of the Federal Reserve System. 1943. *Banking and Monetary Statistics*. Washington, D.C.: National Capital Press.

U.S. Bureau of the Census. 1949. *Historical Statistics of the United States*. Washington, D.C.: Government Printing Office.

————. 1975. *Historical Statistics of the United States, Colonial Times to 1970*. Bicentennial ed., pt. 1. Washington, D.C.: Government Printing Office.

U.S. Treasury Department. 1929–31. *Statement of the Public Debt*. Monthly. Washington, D.C.: Government Printing Office.

Warburton, C. 1945. "Monetary Theory, Full Production, and the Great Depression." *Econometrica* 13: 114–28.

Wicker, E. R. 1966. *Federal Reserve Monetary Policy, 1917–1933*. New York: Random House.

2 MONETARIST INTERPRETATIONS OF THE GREAT DEPRESSION:
An Evaluation and Critique
Robert J. Gordon and James A. Wilcox

Explanations which run in terms of one single cause have been more and more discredited and should be regarded with suspicion.

—Haberler (1958, p. 5)

Between the early 1960s and mid-1970s the Great Depression received surprisingly little attention from economists. This fascinating period, the original combat zone that pitted monetarists against nonmonetarists, seemed until recently a neglected orphan, too young to be worthy of serious study by economic historians but too old to possess the easily accessible Commerce Department quarterly national-income data that today's macroeconometricians view as qualifying an era for detailed scrutiny. Only within the past few years has the

This paper is dedicated to the memory of the late R. A. Gordon. The research was supported by the National Science Foundation. The authors are grateful to James Glassman for his help. They benefited from the helpful suggestions of Clarence L. Barber, Frank Brechling, Louis Cain, Steve Easton, Robert Eisner, R. A. Gordon, James Lothian, Robert Lucas, Thomas Mayer, Donald McCloskey, Allan Meltzer, Frederic Mishkin, Joel Mokyr, George R. Neumann, and Steve Sheffrin.

orphan grown up sufficiently to attract the attention of a prominent economic historian, Peter Temin, whose attack (1976) on the Friedman-Schwartz (1963a) monetary explanation of the depression has helped to open up a new round of controversy, including the recent contributions of Meltzer (1976), Mayer (1978a, 1978b), and Schwartz (1981).

A limitation of the Temin book and the subsequent debate has been its relatively narrow focus on the first two years of the contraction (1929–31) and on the relation between money and income. As Mayer (1978b) points out, a study that emphasizes conditions in 1929 and 1930 cannot effectively criticize the main thrust of the Friedman-Schwartz analysis, which pays scarcely any attention to the first year of the contraction and concentrates on the period subsequent to the first wave of bank failures in October 1930. In a sense, monetarists and their opponents are like two knights in a jousting match who ride by each other without ever making contact. Monetarists consider virtually the only interesting question to be the source of the unique depth and severity of the depression and naturally concentrate on the 1931–33 phase when the contraction exhibited an unprecedented acceleration. The nonmonetarist opponents tend to concentrate on the initial decline in private spending, which, they claim, brought the bank failures and monetary collapse in its wake.

This paper rejects the proposition that there is only a single interesting question to ask about the decade of the 1930s. It is concerned not only with the role of money in the 1929–33 contraction but also with the relative role of monetary and nonmonetary factors in the recession of 1937–38 and subsequent recovery and, in addition, with the division of nominal-income change between prices and real output.[1] New empirical evidence bearing on each of these issues is provided.

The results suggest that both extreme monetarist and nonmonetarist interpretations of the decade of the 1930s are unsatisfactory and leave interesting features of the data unexplained. Arguing against acceptance of an extreme monetarist interpretation are (1) the inability of changes in the money supply alone to explain the severity of the initial collapse in income between 1929 and the fall of 1931, (2) the steady weakening of the correlation between changes in nominal income and money as the 1930s progressed, (3) the failure of monetary factors to explain the nature and timing of the 1938–41 recovery, and (4) the apparent absence of any tendency for the mechanism of price flexibility to provide strong self-correcting forces as required by an approach that stresses monetary rules and opposes policy activism. Arguing against acceptance of an extreme nonmonetarist interpretation are (1) the close association between the collapse in income and the lagged effect of monetary changes after the fall of 1931, (2) the milder contraction and earlier recoveries associated with the more expansive monetary policies pursued in Europe, (3) the close association between money and income in the 1937-38 recession, and (4) the failure of the price-change data to adhere to the expectational Phillips curve approach imbedded in many postwar econometric models constructed by nonmonetarists.[2]

The debate surrounding monetarist interpretations of the Great Depression does not center on the potency of monetary changes as a cause of income variation. Although some economists in the early 1960s treated the quantity theory and the Keynesian income-expenditure theory as mutually exclusive analytical frameworks, from today's vantage point the 1965 "battle of the radio stations" regarding whether only money matters or money never matters seems quaintly anachronistic.[3] Recently the monetarist controversy has been reoriented, as a result of an emerging consensus on both sides that both monetary and nonmonetary factors "matter" for the determination of income (Stein 1976). Instead, the central issues separating the monetarists and their opponents include the merits and potential benefits and costs of government policy activism, both monetary and fiscal, and the stability and inherent self-correcting properties of the private economy.

This new perspective can be summarized by constructing a "monetarist platform," which brings together in four "planks" the monetarist position on the remaining areas of disagreement:[4]

Plank 1:   Without the interference of demand shocks introduced by erratic government policy, private spending would be stable, because people base their consumption plans on a relatively stable "permanent" concept of income.

Plank 2:   Even if private planned spending is not completely stable, flexible prices create a natural tendency for it to come back on course.

Plank 3:   Even if private planned spending is not completely stable and prices are not completely flexible, an activist monetary and fiscal policy to counteract private demand swings is likely to do more harm than good.

Plank 4:   Even if prices are not completely flexible, so that the economy can wander away from equilibrium in the short run, there can be no dispute regarding the increased flexibility of prices, the longer the period of time allowed for adjustment.

From this orientation, a modern monetarist would not be required to devote excessive attention to showing that money played a major causal role in the Great Depression, because the potency of money is no longer a matter for debate.[5] He would be more interested in denying that autonomous swings in private spending, not explainable by movements in government policy or in permanent income, played a major role in the contraction of 1929–33 or in the subsequent recovery. And he would be particularly concerned with the issue of price behavior in the 1930s. Did the economy display strong self-correcting forces in the form of flexible prices that would have tended to bring the economy back to its natural unemployment rate without the need for government intervention?

This paper is divided into two main sections. The first evaluates the relative contributions to nominal-income behavior of private spending behavior and government actions. The central focus is the same question that concerns both Temin (1976) and Schwartz (1981)—whether money played no role in the first two years of the contraction (the Temin position), or whether autonomous private spending movements played no role (the Schwartz position). But the scope of our analysis is broader than an evaluation of the Temin-Schwartz debate regarding 1929–31, and our purview extends to the whole decade of the 1930s.

The final section of the paper investigates the potency of the economy's self-correcting mechanism of price flexibility—a pivotal question in the monetarist controversy but one that is given no attention at all by Temin, Schwartz, or most other recent writers. Monetarists not only tend to give greater credence to price flexibility as a source of self-correction in the private economy but also tend to adopt an analytic framework that differs from that of nonmonetarists.

Monetarists tend to view deviations of output from equilibrium ("natural output") as being a voluntary response of firms and workers to deviations of actual prices from their expected level. This "price surprises cause output changes" framework is evident both in theoretical writings and in empirical research.[6] Nonmonetarists, on the other hand, tend to discuss the same problems in terms of a disequilibrium-adjustment framework.[7] Empirical nonmonetarist explanations of wage and price change tend to place deviations between actual and expected inflation on the left-hand side of the equation and measures of commodity-market or labor-market disequilibrium on the right-hand side.[8]

The most dramatic recent contribution tending to support the monetarist belief in self-correction is Darby's (1976b) attempt to remeasure unemployment during the Great Depression and show that in the late 1930s unemployment was rapidly returning to its natural level as agents adjusted the deviation between actual and expected prices. In this paper we present new evidence on the relation between prices, expected prices, unemployment, and output, in an attempt to reassess the potency of the economy's self-correcting mechanism of price flexibility.

MONETARY AND OTHER EXPLANATIONS
OF NOMINAL-INCOME CHANGE

Distinguishing Hypotheses

Temin's entire book (1976) is devoted to an examination of two views: the "money hypothesis" and the "spending hypothesis." In order to clarify the positions held by the various protagonists and to judge their consistency with the data, we will distinguish a broader spectrum of four views, ranging from hard-line monetarism to hard-line antimonetarism.

(a) "Hard-line monetarism." The 1929–33 contraction was both initiated and aggravated by monetary factors, and nonmonetary factors played no role. The prime exponent of this view is Schwartz (1981), who has departed from her earlier advocacy in Friedman and Schwartz (1963a) of view (b), which admits the possible role of nonmonetary forces in initiating the contraction.[9]

(b) "Soft-line monetarism," the Friedman-Schwartz position. Any combination of factors, both monetary and nonmonetary, could have caused the initial stage of the contraction through the first wave of bank failures in late 1930. But from that point, bank failures played a crucial role in converting a serious recession into a deep depression. The decline in the stock of money, while itself aggravated by the severity of the contraction, did not play a purely passive role but instead worsened the decline in income. As a result, aggressive open-market purchases by the Federal Reserve could have lessened the severity and duration of the depression. This view differs from the more extreme position (a) in its explicit admission that the initial phase of the contraction could have been due to nonmonetary factors, that the money supply is at least partly endogenous, and that at least part of the 1929–33 decline in the supply of money could therefore have been caused by nonmonetary factors.[10] Following Hicks (1974), we may identify this version of soft-line monetarism as the theory of the "double slump," in which a first phase of a severe depression was followed, not by a recovery, but by a second, more severe phase caused by monetary factors.[11]

(c) "Soft-line nonmonetarism." This position emphasizes nonmonetary factors as sources of the 1929–33 contraction, while not denying the possible role of money in aggravating the slump. The behavior of housing construction and international factors are most often emphasized. Bolch and Pilgrim's (1973) study linking the housing slump to a decline in household formation is an example of this genre and is classified under category (c) because of the explicit inclusion of monetary factors in individual equations in the model. R. A. Gordon's work (1951, 1974) emphasizes overinvestment in both housing and other industries but does not deny a role for monetary factors.[12]

(d) *"Hard-line nonmonetarism."* Temin's recent work is the most notable example of this extreme view, which was predominant in the 1940s and 1950s but which has become increasingly rare since the early 1960s. Temin limits his advocacy of this extreme view to the interval between October 1929 and September 1931, but within this two-year period his sweeping claim is unguarded: "There is no evidence of *any* effective deflationary pressure from the banking system between the stock-market crash in October, 1929, and the British abandonment of the gold standard in September, 1931" (1976, p. 169, emphasis added).

Since the views labeled (b) and (c) differ only in emphasis, it is impossible to distinguish their validity with any degree of precision. Although their emphasis is very different, Friedman and Schwartz and R. A. Gordon would probably agree that both bank failures and other nonmonetary factors played at least *some* role in the 1929–33 contraction. Since interactions between money and spending may dominate the effect of either force taken by itself, any attempt to split up the contraction into the share due to money and the share due to a particular nonmonetary factor—for example, housing—is an unproductive scientific enterprise that is bound to satisfy no one. Instead, the real question is whether either extreme view (a) or (d) can be excluded.

The Temin Claim That Money Did Not Matter at All

The data show that the money-supply concept M_2 declined by 2.5 percent during the first four quarters of the contraction and by another 7.9 percent during the second four quarters.[13] For Temin to hold the extreme position (d), he must deny that this decline, whatever its source, had any effect at all on the level of nominal income. His position is surprising, since it conflicts with almost all econometric work on postwar data, ranging from the St. Louis model of Andersen and Jordan (1968), to the reduced-form money-income equations of Sims (1972, 1977), to the large-scale structural models best represented by MPS (Ando and Modigliani 1976).

Temin's case rests on two propositions. First, for the decline in real output to have been caused by monetary stringency, interest rates should have been observed to increase. In terms of the classroom *IS–LM* model, if it is claimed that *IS* movements (autonomous shifts in investment and consumption spending) were unimportant, then the decline in output could only be explained by a leftward shift in the *LM* curve, which would have caused interest rates to increase unless the *IS* curve were horizontal. But short-term interest rates on risk-free securities actually exhibited a sharp decline throughout the 1929:3–1931:3 period. Second, Temin adds, the position of the *LM* curve depends on the level of real balances and thus could not have shifted leftward in the light of the increase in real balances that actually occurred through 1931:3

Figure 1 plots the level of real balances (M_2/P) and exhibits the increase observed by Temin during the interval 1930:2–1931:2.[14] Temin's defense of view (d) collapses, however, if we can show that the 1929–31 decline in interest rates and increase in M_2/P are logically consistent with a model in which nominal spending depends positively on nominal money.

The situation described by solid lines in figure 2 describes an initial IS–LM equilibrium. The positive slope of the LM curve reflects a nonzero interest elasticity of the demand for money, and its position depends on the level of real balances (M/P). The negative slope of IS reflects a nonzero interest elasticity of investment and/or consumption spending, and its position depends on the level of "autonomous spending" ($\overline{A}$—exports, government spending, and the autonomous components of consumption and investment, which in turn depend partly on tax rates). When the LM and IS curves have the designated slopes, the aggregate demand curve DD in the bottom frame in P, Q space has a negative slope and a position that depends on autonomous spending and the *nominal* money supply. DD traces the locus of all intersections of IS and LM for given $\overline{A}$ and M. So this is a model in which a shift in nominal money shifts the DD curve and nominal income and thus is consistent with the positive effects of money on spending found in postwar econometric results.[15]

But the model in figure 2 can also easily explain the decline in short-term interest rates and increase in real balances on which Temin rests his argument. The necessary ingredient is a drop in the level of autonomous spending from $\overline{A}_0$ to $\overline{A}_1$. If we initially hold constant the level of nominal money at M_0, the IS curve shifts left from IS_0 to IS_1, and the aggregate demand curve shifts left from DD_0 to DD_1. The price level drops from P_0 to P_1, output falls from Q_0 to Q_1, and the interest rate drops from r_0 to r_1.

So the movements in the variables all go in the direction noted by Temin; nevertheless, nominal money *does matter*. Let nominal money drop from M_0 to M_1, and both output and prices will drop further to Q_2 and P_2. Because the aggregate supply curve is positively sloped, rather than vertical, the price level must fall by less than the money supply, and so M/P must fall and the interest rate must rise in situation E_2 as compared to E_1. Because the price level is altered by a change in nominal money, one cannot deduce monetary impotence from movements in real balances or interest rates.[16]

Because the argument in figure 2 relies on a shift in autonomous spending from $\overline{A}_0$ to $\overline{A}_1$, it is incompatible with the extreme hard-line monetarist view (a). In principle the economy could reach point E_2 by a different process. The argument presented in figure 2 assumes a zero expected rate of deflation. If in fact the negative 1929–31 rate of change of prices was rapidly incorporated

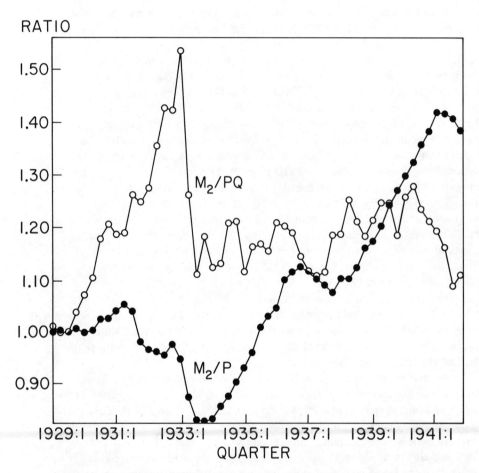

Figure 1. The Real Money Supply (M_2/P) and the Inverse of Velocity (M_2/PQ), 1929:1–1941:4 (1929:3 = 1.0)

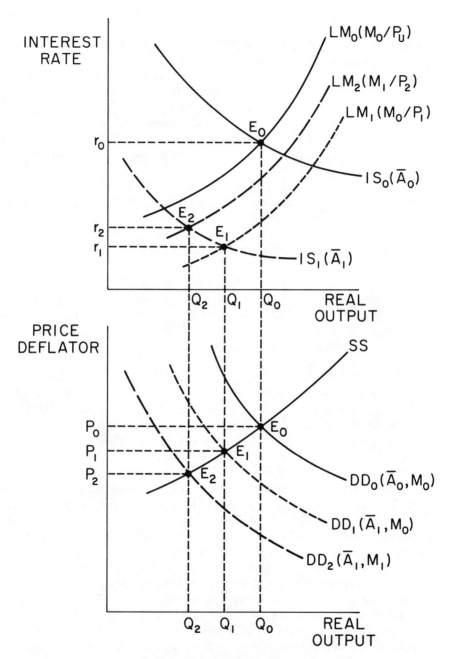

Figure 2. Effects of Nominal Money and Autonomous Spending Changes

into expectations, then the real interest rate would lie above the nominal interest rate. Because the LM curve is defined for the nominal rate (on which the demand for real balances depends) and the IS curve is defined for the real rate, it would be necessary to draw in a second IS curve in terms of the nominal interest rate. This would be displaced vertically below IS_0 by the rate of expected deflation. There is no reason why this lower curve, call it IS_i, could not yield the same intersection point E_2 in figure 2. Thus all the earlier statements about position E_2 would hold, even though autonomous spending had remained completely constant.[17]

Yet those who would rely completely on price deflation caused by a declining money supply to explain the first year of the 1929–33 contraction—leaving no room at all for autonomous spending to play a role—surely strain credulity. Consider the situation in 1930:2. M_2 had fallen only 1.8 percent from its 1929:3 peak. The GNP deflator had declined by only 2.2 percent. In the entire period between 1921:3 and 1929:3, eight full years, the GNP deflator varied over a range of only 4.4 percentage points, and the 1929:3 observation was almost exactly in the middle of the range. Why should economic agents in the spring of 1930 suddenly have started to expect a deflation substantial enough to explain the observed decline in nominal interest rates, when actual price behavior still remained within the range of an eight-year period that had been characterized by remarkable price stability?

Despite the very small declines in M_2 and P over this first three-quarter period, real output declined by 9.6 percent. Velocity declined by 9.9 percent.[18] Without a sudden and inexplicable shift from stable-price expectations to expectations of deflation, the first three quarters of the contraction must be explained by a leftward shift in the IS curve due to a decline in autonomous spending. This conclusion is consistent with the more formal simulation results presented later in figure 3 and table 3.

The expected-deflation argument becomes increasingly plausible after the summer of 1930. In 1930:3 the GNP deflator broke out of the range observed during the 1920s. By 1931:3 it had declined 13.6 percent below the 1929:3 peak and 11 percent below the lowest value observed in the 1920s. It is not implausible that expectations of deflation began in late 1930 to shift the IS curve downward, although in figure 1 it appears that the decline in velocity (increase in $1/V$) was interrupted between 1930:3 and 1931:2. Thus a scenario that appears consistent with the ratios in figure 1 would have the initial three quarters of the contraction explained by a sharp leftward shift of IS due to a decline in autonomous spending. After 1930:2 the decline in M_2 began in earnest, offsetting the downward pressure on velocity of the continuing IS shift. After 1931:2 a deflationary spiral began, in which deflationary expectations shifted down IS, while M_2 began falling more rapidly than prices, thus shifting the *LM* curve to the left as well. And, as Tobin (1975) has recently reminded us, the depressing impact on expenditures of a price deflation can include not only upward pressure on the real interest rate and resulting postponement of spending, but also redistribution toward creditors with low spending propensities from debtors with high spending propensities.[19]

The Granger Test Results and Extreme Monetarism

So far we have rejected Temin's arguments for view *(d)* by showing that the observed facts are consistent with a model in which money influences spending. This does not, however, constitute proof that such a model represents an accurate description of the 1929–33 economy. It is still conceivable that the observed facts could have been generated by an economy in which money had no effects on spending and in which the observed correlation between money and income was caused by an entirely endogenous and contemporaneous response of the money supply to bank failures due in turn to the *IS*-induced weakness of spending.[20]

At present the main argument against the extreme position (*d*) is the consensus among reduced-form and structural econometricians that "money matters" in the postwar economy. But there is no reason why the same techniques applied to postwar data cannot be used to analyze interwar data. In a frequently cited study, Sims (1972) developed a method to test the direction of causation between money and income and found that he could reject a reverse-feedback effect of income on money, while he could not reject an impact of lagged money on income.

A related method introduced by Granger (1969) involves regressing Y_t on a constant, a time trend, its own lagged values, and lagged values of X_t:

$$Y_t = \alpha_0 + \alpha_1 t + \sum_{i=1}^{K} \beta_i Y_{t-i} + \sum_{j=1}^{L} \gamma_j Y_{t-j} + u_t. \tag{1}$$

Now, Y is exogenous with respect to X if the lagged X's fail to make a significant contribution to the explanation of Y over and above the influence of the serial-correlation process in Y captured by the lagged values of Y.[21]

Table 1 displays the results of the estimation of equation (1) and contains two sections, each with four lines. Within each section the four regressions consist of one pair with nominal GNP as dependent variable and M_1 and M_2 alternatively as independent variables, and another pair with the two money

Table 1. Granger Test Results, Quarterly Data, 1920:2–1941:4 and Subperiods

			F-Ratio for Significance of Lagged X's			t-Ratio on Current X		
Dependent (Y)	Independent (X)	1920–41	1920–28	1929–41	1920–41	1920–28	1929–41
(1)	(2)	(3)	(4)	(5)	(6)	(7)	(8)
A. Levels							
Y	M_1	2.68**	1.75	1.50	4.17**	1.62*	4.60**
M_1	Y	1.10	0.85	0.38	4.17**	1.62*	4.60**
Y	M_2	3.95**	1.78	1.43	5.57**	0.78	4.95**
M_2	Y	0.38	0.76	0.43	5.57**	0.78	4.95**
B. Growth rates							
Y	M_1	2.21**	2.81**	1.15	3.97**	0.46	3.25**
M_1	Y	0.63	1.68	0.10	3.97**	0.46	3.25**
Y	M_2	2.42**	3.06**	1.69	4.85**	0.18	3.71**
M_2	Y	0.45	1.35	0.42	4.85**	0.18	3.71**

Note: * indicates significant at 10 percent level. ** indicates significant at 5 percent level.

Table 2. Granger Test Results, Monthly Data, 1929–41

	Variables		F-Ratio for Significance of Lagged X's (3)	t-Ratio on Current X (4)
	Dependent (Y) (1)	Independent (X) (2)		
A. Levels	IPC	M_2	3.26**	3.20**
	M_2	IPC	1.12	3.20**
	S	M_2	1.17	3.24**
	M_2	S	0.92	3.24**
B. Growth rates	IPC	M_2	3.26**	3.64**
	M_2	IPC	1.40	3.64**
	S	M_2	0.83	2.98**
	M_2	S	1.04	2.98**

Note: ** indicates significant at 5 percent level. All data are seasonally adjusted; S is an index of department store sales published by the Federal Reserve Board; IPC is the Federal Reserve Board's index of industrial production multiplied by the CPI.

concepts as alternative dependent variables. Section A defines each variable in its level form, while section B defines each variable as a one-quarter rate of change. Table 1 reports the results for quarterly data estimated for the period 1920:2–1941:4 and two subperiods.[22] Table 2 reports analogous results for monthly data using M_2 and two proxies for aggregate nominal activity, nominal industrial production, and an index of nominal department store sales.[23]

Turning first to table 1, the first three columns report F-tests on the significance of the lagged independent variables. Lagged nominal income has no significant feedback effect on either M_1 or M_2, though its impact on both approaches significance in growth-rate form in the 1920–28 subperiod. Thus the endogeneity of money, upon which Temin rests much of his argument, is not evident in the form of an impact of lagged income on money in quarterly data for either the 1929–41 subperiod or the complete 1920–41 period. However, a current effect of income on money, as we shall see, is an important feature of these periods.

Lagged money has an ambiguous effect on income. In the level equations (section A of table 1) there is a very significant impact for the overall period but not for either of the subperiods. In rate-of-growth form the significance levels increase substantially for 1920–28 but fall for 1920–41. There is an insignificant impact on income during the 1929–41 period for both M_1 and M_2, just as in the level form of the equations.

The three right-hand columns of table 1 report t-ratios for current values of the independent variables. By far the most important characteristic of the 1929–41 period is the simultaneity of movements in money and income. Schwartz could claim that within the current quarter, money has a very rapid and powerful positive effect on nominal GNP, while Temin could claim that within the current quarter, money is responding passively to changes in GNP caused by nonmonetary factors.

The next step, in the light of simultaneity for the 1929–41 subperiod, is to look inside the contemporaneous quarter by examining results for monthly data in table 2. Once again we find no influence of the lagged income proxies on money, while lagged M_2 does appear to have a significant influence on industrial production (although not on retail sales). Once again there is a strong contemporaneous relation within the current month that could go either way, and so still it is not possible to reject the hypothesis that there is significant feedback from income to money within the current month. In the light of the impact of lagged money on industrial production and the consequent rejection of view (d), however, nothing important depends on our inability to untangle the direction of causation within the current month. Certainly, proponents of the middle-ground views (b) and (c) can feel comfortable with an instantaneous feedback from income to money, described by Friedman and Schwartz as "the reflex influence of business on money, the existence of which is not in doubt" (1963b, p. 49).

The Dynamic Simulations and Extreme Monetarism

It is one thing for us to reject the extreme nonmonetarist claim that money did not matter at all, but it is quite another for an extreme monetarist to argue that "only money matters" and that there are "no unexplained changes in spending that serve as deus ex machina" after accounting for a series of "negative shocks, monetary in origin" (Schwartz 1981, pp. 33–34). Similarly, Darby (1976a) asserts that the first stage of the contraction was entirely monetary in origin:

> The contraction began, in fact, during the summer of 1929, as the decline in fluidity due to the initial monetary shock slowed and reversed. This early part of the contraction from 1929 to 1930 was in no way different from the sharp recession that would be expected from a 6 percent decrease in the money-supply growth rate. [P. 239]

A possible method to test the Darby-Schwartz proposition about the monetary origin of the contraction is to use the average statistical relation between lagged money and income during the 1920–28 interval, during which there were three separate recessions, to establish what might be expected to follow a deceleration in the growth rate of the money supply. Can the first year or two of the contraction be attributed in its entirety or in part to the prior monetary deceleration? In this section we report the results of a dynamic simulation in which equation (1) is estimated for the period 1920:2–1928:4 with income as dependent variable and lagged income and money as right-hand variables, and then the predicted behavior of income is calculated based on the fitted coefficients.

A number of possible variants of the dynamic simulation could be presented, corresponding to the different lines in table 1. The monetary definition could be M_1 or M_2, and the variables could be in the form of levels or rates of change. To economize on space, only one version is presented, based on the level form with the M_2 definition of money, because this simulation is most favorable to the hypothesis (a) that monetary shocks were solely responsible for the contraction. The M_2 variant in level form is more favorable both because M_2 fell relatively more than M_1 during the contraction and also because the pattern of coefficients during the sample period for the M_2 level variant yields a greater simulated contraction in income.[24]

In figure 3 and table 3 the actual values of nominal income are compared with the values of $\hat{Y}_t$ calculated as

$$\hat{Y}_t = \hat{\alpha}_0 + \hat{\alpha}_1 t + \sum_{i=1}^{4} \hat{\beta}_i \hat{Y}_{t-i} + \sum_{j=1}^{8} \hat{\gamma}_j X_{t-j}. \qquad (2)$$

The "hatted" coefficients are those estimated from equation (1) for the sample period 1920:2–1928:4. The X_{t-j} are the actual values of lagged M_2, and $\hat{Y}_{t-i}$ are the fitted values of the equation when the time period $t-i$ equals 1928:4 or earlier and are the values calculated in equation (2) after 1928:4.

The differences between actual (Y_t) and simulated $(\hat{Y}_t)$ nominal income presented in figure 3 must be interpreted carefully. $\hat{Y}_t$ measures the estimated contribution to the behavior of Y_t of the *actual* behavior of lagged M_2, given the structural relation between lagged M_2 and Y_t present in the 1920–28 data. The values of lagged M_2 fed into the dynamic simulations are the actual historical values. To the extent that money was partly endogenous, and the observed decline in M_2 during the contraction partially reflects the contemporaneous influence of nonmonetary factors on income, $\hat{Y}_t$ would tend to exaggerate the contribution of exogenous monetary factors.

On the other hand, monetarists may object to the limitation of the influence of money to a lagged effect. To the extent that the contemporaneous correlation of money and income represents the money-to-income channel of causa-

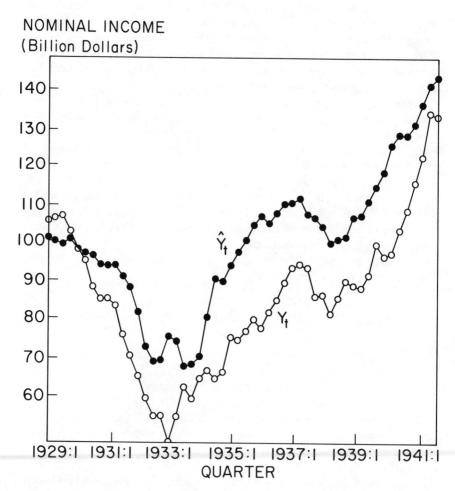

NOMINAL INCOME
(Billion Dollars)

Figure 3. Comparison of Actual and Simulated Nominal Income, 1929–41

Table 3. Summary of Simulation Results on the Role of Lagged Money, 1929–33

	Actual Y_t (1)	Simulated with Lagged Money $\hat{Y}_t$ (2)	Cumulative Change (billion $) from Line A			Marginal Change (billion $) from Line Above		
			Y_t (3)	$\hat{Y}_t$ (4)	(4)/(3) (5)	Y_t (6)	$\hat{Y}_t$ (7)	(7)/(6) (8)
A. Peak level (1929:3)	106.0	98.8	—	—	—	—	—	—
B. Half-years								
1. 1929:4–1930:1	100.0	98.8	− 6.0	0.0	0.0	− 6.0	0.0	0.0
2. 1930:2–1930:3	91.3	96.2	−14.7	− 2.6	17.7	− 8.7	− 2.6	+ 29.9
3. 1930:4–1931:1	84.9	93.5	−21.1	− 5.3	25.1	− 6.4	− 2.7	+ 42.2
4. 1931:2–1931:3	79.5	92.0	−26.5	− 6.8	25.7	− 5.4	− 1.5	+ 27.8
5. 1931:4–1932:1	67.9	84.6	−38.1	−14.2	37.3	−11.6	− 7.4	+ 63.8
6. 1932:2–1932:3	57.2	70.9	−48.8	−27.9	57.2	−10.7	−13.7	+128.0
7. 1932:4–1933:1	51.8	72.4	−54.2	−26.4	48.7	− 5.4	+ 1.5	− 27.8
8. 1933:2–1933:3	58.5	71.0	−47.5	−27.8	58.5	+ 6.7	− 1.4	− 20.9

Source: Figure 3.

tion, the exclusion of the current money supply understates the contribution of monetary change. But the addition of current money, somewhat surprisingly, actually dampens the 1929–33 decline in the simulated income series, because the coefficient on current money in the 1920–28 income regression is a small and insignificant *negative* number.

How well does the lagged-money simulation explain the Great Contraction? Figure 3 indicates that $\hat{Y}_t$ consistently lies above the actual value of nominal GNP (Y_t). Dividing up the 1929–33 contraction into two-quarter intervals to facilitate analysis, we can examine the averages presented in table 3. According to the Hicks theory of the "double slump," we should find that the simulation based on lagged money ($\hat{Y}_t$) explains only a portion of the actual slump in Y_t during the first two years of the contraction but that monetary forces then take over and account for most of the decline in Y_t. According to Friedman-Schwartz, the contraction changed its character one year earlier, at the time of the first wave of bank failures during the last quarter of 1930. According to Darby-Schwartz, the $\hat{Y}_t$ series should trace the 1929–31 decline in Y_t quite closely.

Both the contribution of money to the cumulative change in $\hat{Y}_t$ in column (5) and the contribution to the marginal change from one half-year to the next in column (9) are more consistent with the Hicks timing than with the Friedman-Schwartz timing and are not consistent at all with the Darby-Schwartz money-only explanation. Between line A and line B2, money contributes 17.7 percent of the total decline in income; on line B4 the cumulative contribution rises only to 25.7 percent. And the marginal contribution on line B4 is only 27.8 percent. In contrast, there is a dramatic change beginning on line B5, where the marginal contribution of money jumps to 63.8 percent, and to more than 100 percent on line B6. Although a subsequent zigzag causes the simulated Y_t series to miss the timing of the last stage of the contraction in late 1932 and early 1933, the cumulative contribution of $\hat{Y}_t$ to the actual decline in Y_t nevertheless remains in the vicinity of 50 percent in lines B6 through B8.

As we have seen, both Darby and Schwartz have pointed to slow monetary growth in 1928 and early 1929 as the fundamental underlying cause of the first year of the contraction. Indeed, between 1928:1 and 1929:3, M_2 grew by only 0.6 percent at an annual rate in contrast to a rate of 5.2 percent in the preceding five quarters. But even greater decelerations of monetary growth had happened before without causing a drastic drop in nominal income. For instance, while the growth of M_2 slowed from an annual rate of 8.8 percent in the seven quarters preceding 1925:4 to a 0.5 rate in the next four quarters, the subsequent decline in nominal income between peak and trough in the 1927 recession was only 2.8 percent. Thus the simulated value $\hat{Y}_t$, which combines the average relation between lagged money and income observed during the 1920s with the actual behavior of money in 1929–33, essentially says, "Though monetary growth decelerated in 1928 and 1929, such a monetary slowdown had happened before and can only account for 18 percent of the observed decline in nominal income in the first year of the contraction and 26 percent cumulatively in the first two years."

The 1937–38 Recession and Subsequent Recovery

Monetarist interpretations of the Great Depression are not limited to the 1929–33 contraction phase. In addition, monetarists have long taken the position that the proximate cause of the 1937–38 recession was the three-stage doubling of reserve requirements between August 1936 and May 1937. The same simulation technique can be used to evaluate the validity of this claim. The technique is exactly the same as in the preceding discussion, except that two different simulation results are reported. The first is based on the money-income equation fitted to the 1920–28 period that is used in the simulations in figure 3 and table 3. As is evident in table 4 and figure 4, the value of $\hat{Y}_t$ calculated from the dynamic simulation that starts in 1929:1 remains above the actual value of Y_t throughout the 1937–41 period. Nevertheless, $\hat{Y}_t$ declines between the peak quarter (1937:2) and early 1938 by almost as much as actual income. In short, the simulation based on the 1920–28 coefficients implies that the 1937–38 recession was almost entirely a monetary phenomenon.

A second simulation is based on the same specification extended to the longer 1920:2–1936:4 sample period. The results of the 1937–38 recession confirm the verdict that the simulated $\hat{\hat{Y}}_t$ series explains most of the downturn in Y_t—68 percent in this case as compared to 91 percent for the first simulation.

Although the simulated series $\hat{Y}_t$ and $\hat{\hat{Y}}_t$ indicate that most of the 1937–38 recession can be explained as a consequence of the behavior of lagged money and lagged income, the ability of the two simulated series to track actual income nevertheless deteriorates markedly after early 1938. As indicated in both table 4 and figure 4, the simulated series recover much more markedly than actual Y_t between the first half of 1938 and the first half of 1940. In the latter interval, actual nominal income had exceeded the 1937 peak by only $2.4 billion, or 2.6 percent. But the $\hat{Y}_t$ series had grown by 9.1 percent and $\hat{\hat{Y}}_t$ by 16.8 percent.

After the first half of 1940 the relationship between the actual and simulated series shifted in the direction of rapid actual growth relative to simulated growth. Only about half of the actual growth in nominal income between the first half of 1940 and the last half of 1941 can be explained by the growth of

Table 4. Summary of Simulation Results on the Role of Lagged Money, 1937–41

	Actual Y_t	Simulated with Lagged Money $\hat{Y}_t, \hat{\bar{Y}}_t$	Nominal Income (billion $)					
			Cumulative Change (billion $) from Peak			Marginal Change (billion $) from Line Above		
			Y_t	$\hat{Y}_t, \hat{\bar{Y}}_t$	(4)/(3)	Y_t	$\hat{Y}_t, \hat{\bar{Y}}_t$	(7)/(6)
	(1)	(2)	(3)	(4)	(5)	(6)	(7)	(8)
A. Simulation based on 1920–28 ($\hat{Y}$)								
1. Peak, 1937:2	93.7	110.5	—	—	—	—	—	—
2. 1938:1–1938:2	83.5	101.2	−10.2	− 9.3	91.1	−10.2	− 9.3	91.1
3. 1940:1–1940:2	96.1	120.6	+ 2.4	+10.1	420.8	+12.6	+19.4	154.0
4. 1941:3–1941:4	131.7	140.3	+38.0	+29.8	78.4	+35.6	+19.7	55.3
B. Simulation based on 1920–36 ($\hat{\bar{Y}}$)								
1. Peak, 1937:2	93.7	88.8	—	—	—	—	—	—
2. 1938:1–1938:2	83.5	81.9	−10.2	− 6.9	67.6	−10.2	− 6.9	67.6
3. 1940:1–1940:2	96.1	103.7	+ 2.4	+14.9	620.8	+12.6	+21.8	173.0
4. 1941:3–1941:4	131.7	121.4	+38.0	+32.6	85.8	+35.6	+17.7	49.7

Source: Figure 4.

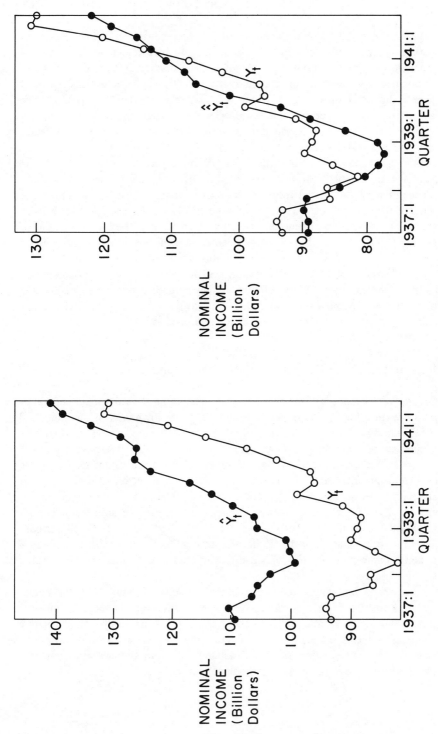

Figure 4. Comparison of Actual and Simulated Nominal Income, 1937–41

lagged money and income. These results appear consistent with a model of income determination in which shifts in private investment and government expenditures play an important role, given the behavior of money. Private investment was sluggish during the interval 1937–40, leading to a weak recovery despite the rapid growth in M_2 that was occurring.[25] Then, after mid-1940, rapid growth in government defense spending shifted the *IS* curve rapidly rightward and caused an accelerated growth in income without any acceleration in the growth rate of money.[26]

Our interpretation is that shifts in the *IS* curve must be relied upon to explain the timing of income growth in the 1938–41 period, just as *IS* shifts appear to have dominated the explanation of income change in the first two years of the Great Contraction, 1929:3–1931:3. This suggests a puzzle. 1Given the weak impetus to spending provided by the monetary acceleration of 1938–40, why should the monetary deceleration of early 1937 have been so potent? One answer is that monetary tightness *per se* was not particularly potent, and instead the 1937–38 recession was due at least partly to nonmonetary factors. One candidate that stands out is the increase between 1936 and 1937 in the full-employment federal surplus equal to fully 3 percent of GNP (equivalent to a \$60 billion fiscal swing in today's economy).[27]

Implications of the Regressions and Simulations

Several additional questions can be raised concerning the regression and simulation results. First, do the 1929–33 and 1937–38 downturns in the simulated series $\hat{Y}_t$ and $\hat{Y}_t$ reflect just the lagged effect of the decline in money, or is part of the decline contributed by the lagged-income variables? We have examined separate simulations based on regressions in which lagged values of money are excluded, in order to study the postsample predictions based solely on the autoregressive structure of the income variable. There is a minor cycle in the *growth rate* of income in such a dynamic autoregressive simulation but no actual decline in the level of income during the 1929–33 or 1937–38 periods. Thus it appears that all of the decline in the simulated series in figures 3 and 4 is being contributed by the lagged effect of money and none by the lagged-income variables.

Second, is the failure of the simulated series to capture fully the actual 1929–33 decline in income in figure 3 due in any part to the inclusion of a time trend in the original regression equation (1)? The results of alternative simulations based on regressions without time trends can be summarized by showing the contribution of the simulated series to the actual cumulative change by the two alternative methods of estimation:

		With Trend	Without Trend
Table 3, peak to	1931:2/1931:3	25.7%	31.3%
Table 3, peak to	1932:4/1933:1	48.7	57.6
Table 4, peak to	1938:1/1938:2 (Line A)	91.1	95.1
Table 4, peak to	1938:1/1938:2 (Line B)	67.6	22.5

Thus the omission of the time-trend variable does increase by a minor amount the contribution of lagged money to an explanation of the 1929–33 and 1937–38 contractions based on the 1920–28 regressions where the time trend is positive. The same omission, however, substantially reduces the contribution of lagged money to an explanation of the 1937–38 contraction based on the 1920–36 regressions where the time trend is negative.

Third, why is there such a difference in the contribution of lagged money to an explanation of the 1937–38 contraction between the two sets of simulations based on the alternative 1920–28 and 1920–36 sample periods? There are very substantial shifts in the coefficients of these reduced-form regression equations when the sample period is altered. Table 5 exhibits the shifts in coefficients on lagged and current money in alternative overlapping eight-year sample periods. There appears to be an inverse correlation between the sum of coefficients on lagged money in column (1), which is greatest in the first three lines, and the coefficient on current money in column (3), which is much larger in the last four lines than in the first three. Thus the relation between money and income appears to have shifted to a mainly contemporaneous one in the 1930s, with a substantial lagged effect of money on income evident only in the earlier periods.

The results in table 5 cast additional doubt on the hypothesis that changes in the money supply were primarily responsible for the behavior of income in the Great Depression. In all of the subperiods in table 5 the t-ratio on the sum of lagged coefficients is extremely small. Although some individual coefficients are significant, they tend to alternate in sign. The dominance of the contemporaneous correlation in the decade of the 1930s adds plausibility to the reverse-feedback hypothesis that the reflex effect of business on money was a primary determinant of shifts in the money supply. Further, it is awkward for monetarists to rely upon an entirely contemporaneous money-to-income effect to support their case, because long lags between policy changes and income changes play an important part in their argument against countercyclical activism in Plank 3 of the monetarist platform.[28]

It is important, however, to distinguish hypothesis (1), that observed movements in the money supply during the 1930s were largely passive and endogenous, from hypothesis (2), that an alternative monetary policy that substituted

Table 5.   Effect of Lagged and Current Money on Income in Alternative Eight-Year Sample Periods, Quarterly Data, 1920–40

	Lagged Money		Current Money	
Sample Periods	Sum of Coefficients (1)	t-Ratio of Sum (2)	Coefficient (3)	t-Ratio (4)
1. 1920:2–1928:4	0.936	0.15	−1.118	−0.77
2. 1922:1–1930:4	1.405	0.27	+0.289	+0.21
3. 1924:1–1932:4	1.249	0.19	+0.871	+1.16
4. 1926:1–1934:4	0.262	0.05	+2.357	+2.77
5. 1928:1–1936:4	0.628	0.12	+3.083	+3.47
6. 1930:1–1938:4	0.413	0.07	+3.938	+6.05
7. 1932:1–1940:4	0.595	0.12	+2.748	+3.11

active countercyclical open-market operations could have lessened the severity of the contraction and brought about an earlier and more robust recovery. Both hypotheses (1) and (2) could be correct, but hypothesis (2) cannot be tested on data from the period if hypothesis (1) is correct as well. Coefficients would have shifted, as the work of Robert Lucas (1976) suggests, if an activist monetary policy had been pursued. For this reason, econometric studies of U.S. money and income data are unlikely to settle the debate regarding the potential role of alternative monetary policies, however much they may indicate that the lagged changes in monetary growth that actually did occur are capable of explaining little if any of the fluctuations in income in the decade of the 1930s.

A comparison of the United States with Europe, where both money and income followed quite different paths after the devaluation of sterling in the fall of 1931, helps to overcome the inherent limitations of the U.S. data. In figure 5 the European data exhibit a dramatic divergence from the U.S. behavior of money and income after 1931.[29]

Some of this difference may represent nonmonetary factors that raised income and pulled up the money supply through a reverse-feedback mechanism—for example, the stimulus of the 1931 devaluation in several European countries and the impact on income of activist fiscal stimuli (especially in Germany beginning in 1933). But some of the explanation for the earlier European recovery may rest with activist monetary policy, as described for Sweden by Jonung (1981), lending some credence to Schwartz's (1981) statement that "different policies would have resulted in different behavior."

The comparison between European and U.S. velocity in the bottom frame of figure 5 reveals some interesting similarities and differences. The simultane-

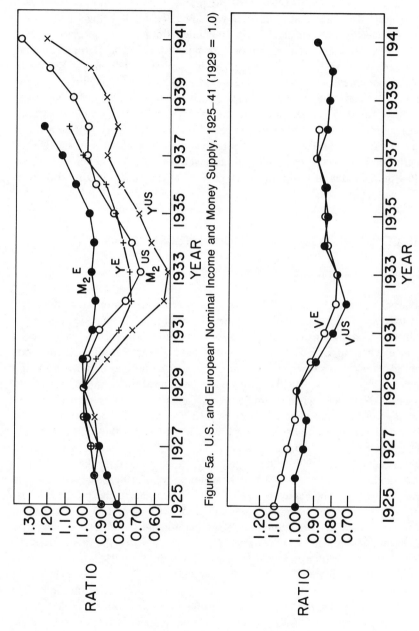

Figure 5a. U.S. and European Nominal Income and Money Supply, 1925–41 (1929 = 1.0)

Figure 5b. U.S. and European Velocity, 1925–41 (1929 = 1.0)

ous sharp decline in 1929–32 suggests the presence of a common nonmonetary shift factor. The fact that European velocity declined less than that in the United States is not consistent with the predictions of an ordinary *IS–LM* model, given the less restrictive monetary policy pursued in Europe. Finally, the decline in velocity in the United States in 1939 and 1940, and in Europe in 1938, is consistent with the hypothesis that the *LM* curve is positively sloped but does not constitute a demonstration that it is horizontal. In short, the comparison in figure 5 is consistent with the basic themes of this paper that both monetary and nonmonetary factors mattered, that nonmonetary factors were of prime importance in 1929–31, that different monetary policies in the United States after 1931 would have reduced the severity of the contraction, and finally that the stimulus of rapid monetary growth on economic activity in the late 1930s was quite weak.

THE CONTRIBUTION OF NONMONETARY FACTORS

Searching for Nonmonetary Explanations

It is easier to show that nonmonetary factors must have been at work in the first two years of the contraction than to determine what those factors were, much less to assign specific quantitative contributions to each of them. Most recent discussions of nonmonetary factors have suffered from three methodological weaknesses, which we may label "monocausal blinders," the "endogenicity fallacy," and "postwar second-guessing." An analyst wears monocausal blinders when he claims that Factor X could not have possibly been *the* cause of the contraction because it was not quantitatively important enough, or it happened at the wrong time. For instance, "the fall of construction in the late 1920s was deflationary, but too small to precipitate a major depression" (Temin 1976, p. 68). "Construction spending peaked in 1926," some might say, "so if construction spending was the cause, why did the Great Depression not begin in 1927?" This view ignores the possibility that there may have been several causes and timing patterns. Imagine that there were two causes, X_1 (construction), which continuously exerted a downward influence on nominal spending after 1926, and X_2 (say the stock market), which exerted an expansionary influence in 1928 and early 1929 and a contractionary influence after mid-1929. The fact that the economy slumped in late 1929 rather than early 1927 does not deny that cause X_1 made the post-1929 contraction more severe than otherwise. In the same way, table 3 indicates that in the early quarters of 1930, the decline in the money supply probably made the contraction more severe, even if money *alone* can account for only a fraction of the total decline in spending. As the decline in Y_t fed into investment planning, it in turn made investment decline more rapidly than otherwise.

An analyst suffers from the "endogenicity fallacy" when he dismisses X_1 as a possible cause because it is "endogenous and declined because income declined." For instance, Temin writes that "the major part of the fall in construction in the 1930's can best be seen as the result of the fall in income rather than as the result of a change in some alternative variable" (1976, p. 66). Thus, the construction hypothesis is abruptly dismissed. Similarly, money is dismissed as a cause by Temin because the bank failures that were primarily responsible for the decline in the stock of money are viewed as an endogenous response to the decline in income. But this cavalier approach neglects the possibility of interactions among a number of possible causes, an interaction of which Friedman and Schwartz were well aware when they wrote that the endogenicity of money was "part of the partly self-generating mechanism whereby monetary disturbances are transmitted" (1963b, p. 50). In the same way, the endogenicity of construction—which is influenced by income, on which the desired stock of structures depends, but which at the same time is part of GNP—is part of the "partly self-generating mechanism whereby nonmonetary disturbances are transmitted."

Finally, "postwar second-guessing" occurs when an analyst claims that X_1 could not have been a cause of the 1929–33 contraction because slumps in X_1 have been observed to occur in the postwar years without resulting in a Great Depression. This ignores possible differences in factors other than X_1 that may have served to insulate the economy from the effects of the X_1 slump. More formally, this point may be made in terms of the national-income identity:

$$S \equiv I + D + F, \tag{3}$$

where S is gross saving, I is gross investment, D is the government deficit, and F is the foreign trade surplus. Dividing both sides by "full-employment" or "natural-employment" output (Q^*), and designating the ratio of gross saving to actual output (Q) as s $(=S/Q)$, we have:

$$\frac{sQ}{Q^*} \equiv \frac{I}{Q^*} + \frac{D}{Q^*} + \frac{F}{Q^*}. \tag{4}$$

Imagine, for the sake of argument, that the gross saving ratio, s, is roughly fixed. If there is a decline in the ratio of gross domestic investment to natural output (I/Q^*), then the economy must adjust in some way, either by an offsetting shift in the natural-output government deficit (D/Q^*) or in the natural-output trade surplus (F/Q^*) on the right-hand side of the equation or by a contraction in the output ratio (Q/Q^*) on the left-hand side.

In the postwar period there have been repeated multiyear booms and slumps in the I/Q^* ratio. To some extent these have been offset by the willingness of the federal government to incur budget deficits; nevertheless, their impact has not been entirely offset, and the economy has adjusted by experiencing prolonged periods of persistent above-average or below-average unemployment.[30] The absence of a depression in the postwar period testifies to (1) potent built-in stabilizers and (2) monetary policy, which aggravated cycles in the short run by allowing procyclical slumps in money at the beginning of recessions but nevertheless managed to get money growing again after a quarter or two. It is not inconsistent to say that the actual behavior of investment in 1929-31 would have caused only a 1958- or 1975-size recession had it been accompanied by postwar-size built-in stabilizers and postwar monetary policy and at the same time to say that the behavior of investment caused a much more serious contraction in the 1930s, given the smaller built-in stabilizers and the endogenous procyclical monetary policy conducted by the Fed.[31] Put another way, one can simultaneously claim that the contraction was a nonmonetary phenomenon in origin and that it was monetary in the sense that the actual monetary policy aggravated the slump and an alternative expansionary monetary policy would have moderated it. One can agree with Schwartz that "different policies would have resulted in different behavior" and simultaneously disagree with her statement that "there are no unexplained changes in spending that serve as deus ex machina"(1981, p. 26).

In searching for the nature of the nonmonetary deus ex machina, we do not imply that money did not play an important role, particularly in the 1931–33 phase of the contraction. But we reject the contention that there is only one "main question" to be answered about the contraction—why it was so severe and "why recovery was so slow in coming" (Mayer 1978b, p. 130.) An episode as dramatic as the contraction is capable of raising more than a single issue. While monetarists may be content to limit their analysis to a demonstration that inept monetary policy explains the unique magnitude of the contraction, we find equally interesting a search for nonmonetary forces that appear to have been primarily responsible for the 28 percent decline in nominal income in the interval 1929:3–1931:3 and that in turn must have played at least some role in causing the bank failures that the Fed failed to counteract.[32]

Just as there can be more than a single "main question" of interest suggested by the 1929–33 experience, so there may have been more than a single nonmonetary explanation of the severity of the decline in income during the 1929–31 phase. Several possible explanations share the common theme that any excess of spending breeds its own self-correcting contraction. Many authors have constructed business-cycle models based on the interaction of the multiplier and the accelerator. In Goodwin's model the expansion phase is eventually terminated by supply constraints, which slow the growth of the capital stock and hence the level of net investment. The economy "is always straining to get to the full employment limit, but by the mere fact of being there for a time, it is projected downward again" (1955, p. 209).

Our explanation can be summarized within the flexible-accelerator framework as follows:

1. Net investment in both consumer and producer goods is a function of the deviation between the desired and actual stocks of those goods.
2. A decline in net investment can occur when there is a decline in the desired stock or when something has occurred in the past to raise the current stock too high relative to today's desired stock.
3. Within the framework of the identity (4) above, any such decline in net investment will cause a decline in the output ratio (Q/Q^*) unless offset by a decline in the saving ratio, the natural-employment government deficit, or the natural-employment trade surplus.
4. The major factor that reduced the desired capital stock was the effect of declining population growth on residential housing.
5. The major factors that raised the actual capital stock too high were the overbuilding of residential housing in the mid-1920s and the effect on consumer spending of the overshooting of the stock market during its 1928–29 speculative bubble.

Construction

In a recent paper Hickman (1973) has documented both the effect of the decline in population growth on the desired housing stock and also the extent of overbuilding in the mid-1920s. Hickman's model of the residential housing sector improves on previous work by treating the rate of population growth as endogenous, due to the effect of income on the rate at which individuals in various age groups choose to form households. Hickman is able to decompose the observed decline in the rate of population growth between the early 1920s and mid-1930s into two components—that due to the effect of declining income, and a remaining exogenous decline in "standardized households" due primarily to the decline of immigration.[33]

In order to isolate the effect of the exogenous component of the decline in household formation, Hickman calculated two dynamic simulations of his model, one in which standardized households are assumed to increase steadily at the 1924–25 rate of growth, and another in which income and other economic variables are identical but in which standardized households follow their actual declining growth path after 1925. The impact of the actual demographic slump gradually becomes more important as the 1930s progress, accounting for a decline in housing starts between the two simulations of 28.3 percent for the year 1933 and 39.1 percent for the year 1940.[34]

It has been suggested that the effect of declining immigration on the desired capital stock of residential housing could not be a contributing factor to a worldwide depression. Such a change in immigration patterns, the argument runs, would reduce the demand for housing in the United States but raise the demand for housing in the former source countries, for example, Italy and Poland. But this position is flawed for several reasons. First, many of the immigrants came from rural areas where their departure led to housing abandonment. A lower immigration flow would reduce the demand for housing in the United States but would to a large extent reduce the rate of abandonment in Italy and Poland rather than stimulate new construction. Second, the marginal product of U.S. immigrants instantly increased upon arrival as compared to their previous situation because of the much greater amount of physical capital available in the United States. Third, there is a long oral tradition in labor economics which claims that increases in immigration led to an expansion in the demand for all types of reproducible capital goods, not just residential housing. Immigrants initially hold a proportionately greater share of their non-human wealth in liquid capital, particularly gold and jewelry, but after some period of adjustment to their new environment, this liquid wealth is converted into physical capital.[35]

But the deflationary impact of demography was only the first of the two important causes of the housing problem. The second was the extent of overbuilding in the mid-1920s. For six years (1923–28) real residential construction achieved a level more than double the average of the entire decade before World War I. In four successive years (1924–27) the ratio of real residential construction to real GNP reached by far its highest level of the twentieth century.[36] Hickman's simulations dramatize the extent to which housing starts had risen in 1925 to a rate higher than was consistent with current income, prices, and the rate of household formation. In the most optimistic of his simulations—that which assumes that standardized household growth *continues* at its 1924–25 rate, rather than declining, and that there is no decline in income—predicted housing starts still fall by 35 percent between 1925 and 1930.

Combining the two effects, how much could housing have contributed to the decline in income in the Great Contraction? Hickman's simulation that holds income constant but allows standardized households to follow their actual growth path generates a decline in housing starts between 1925 and 1930 of 49 percent, amounting to about 4 percent of 1925 GNP. The impact of this deflationary force on the economy was delayed by the buoyant behavior of consumption and inventory accumulation in 1929, but when these components

Table 6. Ratios of Real Spending Components to Natural Real Output in
1926, 1929, and 1930

	1926	1929	1930	Change, 1926–30
Consumption expenditures	66.4	68.1	61.8	− 4.6
Nonresidential fixed investment	13.0	12.9	10.3	− 2.7
Residential fixed investment	8.6	5.1	3.0	− 5.6
Other	12.3	13.2	11.9	− 0.4
Total	100.3	99.3	87.0	−13.3

Sources: The natural output series (Q^*) is from Gordon 1978, Appendix B. The 1926 spending components are from Hickman and Coen 1976, table A.2, p. 222. The 1929 and 1930 spending data are in 1958 dollars, to retain comparability with the Hickman and Coen data, from the *Economic Report of the President* 1968.

of spending collapsed in 1930, the downward pressure on income from the housing sector interacted to aggravate the severity of the contraction. Table 6 displays the ratios to real natural output of the major components of real spending in 1926, 1929, and 1930.

Consumption Expenditures

Table 5 indicates that several components of spending declined sharply between 1929 and 1930, with the decline in consumption contributing the most to the decline in real GNP. The behavior of consumption spending partly represents an endogenous reaction to the decline in other components of spending, but in addition some portion of the consumption decline may reflect the influence of the stock market crash or may be an unexplained autonomous puzzle. Unfortunately, the recent debate between Temin (1976) and Mayer (1978a) does little to elucidate the role of the stock market in explaining consumption. By focusing on the significance in 1930 of *residuals* from consumption equations, both Temin and Mayer neglect to calculate the contribution of changes in stock market wealth to the *fitted* value of consumption. Yet the timing of the stock market boom and crash must partly explain why the level of consumption spending was so high in 1929 and so low in 1930.

Taking the position that data inadequacies preclude estimation of an interwar macroeconometric model, Mishkin (1978) has used coefficients from a postwar model to assess the impact on consumption expenditures and residential housing of changes in the household balance sheet in the 1930–41 period. Wealth effects are potent enough to explain 45 percent of the decline in these spending components in 1929–30. This is probably an overstatement of the true impact of the exogenous component of the financial developments, because the endogenous response of the financial variables to the decline in income is neglected. When the Hickman housing simulations and Mishkin calculations are combined, we emerge with an explanation of several crucial features of the depression.

First, the housing collapse helps to explain both why the contraction was so severe and why it lasted so long. As late as 1940 the ratio of housing to natural output had not regained even half of its level of the mid-1920s. Real GNP in 1940 was able to exceed its absolute 1929 level through the contribution of government pump-priming that filled in the gap left by the missing investment.[37] Given the fact that M_2 had risen 18 percent in 1940 relative to 1929 and that M_1 had risen by 49 percent, a purely monetary approach cannot provide an explanation of the duration of the depression.

Second, the relation between the stock market and consumption spending helps to explain why the initial 1927–29 collapse of construction did not initiate the depression earlier; the 1928–29 stock market bubble induced a consumption boom that postponed the impact of the housing slump. The stock market collapse precipitated a drastic decline in consumption spending that interacted with and further aggravated the continuing decline in residential construction. This interpretation makes the behavior of consumption at least partly a monetary phenomenon, to the extent that easy money helped boost stock prices and that tight money helped bring on the crash. But no one has ever claimed that the tripling of stock prices between the business-cycle peaks of 1923 and 1929 could be more than partly explained by the 27 percent increase in M_2 over the same interval; a large residual portion of the behavior of stock market prices must be classified as due to a speculative bubble that at some point had to burst. In this sense the behavior of the stock market and its impact on consumption can be termed both autonomous and essentially nonmonetary in origin, even if the precise timing of the stock market crash may depend in part on the timing of monetary policy.

International Interactions

Meltzer has argued that American adherence to the rules of the gold-exchange standard was a factor contributing to the initial decline in spending in 1929.

"A recession can be induced by the changes in [international] relative prices that occurred in 1928 and 1929. A recession induced by changes of this kind is a response to monetary policy if we include in monetary policy a commitment to operate under the rules of the gold standard" (1976, p. 458).

To the extent that the money stock is endogenous and responds negatively to relative output advances, Meltzer has identified a little-noticed monetary influence. Consider a domestic monetary expansion. As domestic output and prices advance relative to output and prices abroad, net exports decline, tempering and possibly reversing the rise in output. Under the gold-exchange-standard rules, the decline in net exports would also result in a gold outflow and subsequent fall in the money supply.

The evidence in favor of adherence to the principles of gold standard during this period is extremely weak, however. Actually, U.S. policy through most of the 1920s was to sterilize gold flows. "From 1923 on, gold movements were largely offset by movements in Federal Reserve credit so that there was essentially *no* relation between the movements in gold and in the total of high powered money; the fairly irregular dips and rises in the gold stock were transformed into a horizontal movement in total high powered money" (Friedman and Schwartz 1963*a*, p. 382).

This policy of sterilization eliminates the link between gold and the money supply central to Meltzer's hypothesis. Further refutation of Meltzer's thesis that monetary policy should have been expected to lead to a recession after the 1927–28 recovery lies in the fact that the ratio of export to import prices in the past had not always risen when U.S. output advanced relative to that of its trading partners. Though an increase in U.S. relative to world income was accompanied by an increase in U.S. relative prices in 1928–29, this was not the case in 1922–23, when the price of U.S. exports fell over 9 percent relative to the price of imports and U.S. output advanced relatively.[38]

Even with the deterioration of U.S. relative international prices at the end of the 1920s, a demonstration of the impact of these price changes on net exports is problematical. Hickman and Coen (1976) attempt to capture the effect of relative price on imports over this era but cannot uncover any significant effect when income and other factors are allowed for. More recently, Artus and Sosa attempt to estimate these price elasticities for the 1963–74 period, concluding that these elasticities "are not extremely large and are felt rather slowly" (1978, p. 46). In addition, real net exports barely changed between 1929 and 1930. Exports and imports declined together. If a relative price change were responsible for causing the United States to export less and import more, a deterioration in the trade balance should be observed. The absence of any change in the real trade balance is an indication that some other factor or combination of factors, both monetary and nonmonetary, was responsible for the simultaneous reduction in income of the United States and its trading partners, which in turn caused both exports and imports to decline together. The fact that European nominal income fell less than that in the United States, as indicated in figure 5, is consistent with the hypothesis that the depression spread from the United States to Europe but does not support any particular hypothesis about the effect of relative prices on the trade balance.[39]

The most important qualification of all to Meltzer's hypothesis is that a change in relative prices of a particular nation should have caused expenditure *switching*, not a worldwide depression. European output should have been stimulated and U.S. output depressed, with aggregate world output left unaffected.[40] The data show that income and output on both sides of the Atlantic fell together, a pattern consistent with causation from another factor.

Meltzer is on firmer ground when he blames another international factor, the Hawley-Smoot Tariff Act of June 1930, as responsible for converting "a sizeable recession into a severe depression" (p. 469). The tariff was responsible for an increase of almost 50 percent in the effective rate of duties paid on imports between 1929 and 1932. This aggravated the contraction through three main channels:

1. Directly, without any retaliation, the resulting increase in the price of U.S. imports and close domestic substitutes altered the division of the nominal-income decline between output and prices in 1930–32, so that output fell more than otherwise and prices fell less.
2. Foreign retaliation reduced the demand for U.S. exports, which aggravated the contraction through the standard Keynesian multiplier mechanism.
3. Foreign retaliation against U.S. exports of food products, which dropped 66 percent between 1929 and 1932 (Meltzer 1976, p. 460), aggravated the decline in U.S. farm prices, which was an important cause of rural bank failures and in turn of the decline in the supply of money due to currency hoarding.

Whether the impact on output and unemployment of the Hawley-Smoot tariff was more or less important than that of housing and the stock market is probably impossible to determine. The important point is that there was more than one source, not just the behavior of the money supply but also several nonmonetary factors, and that their effects interacted and amplified the severity of the contraction. The role of the tariff, while not explicitly involving the money supply, is nonetheless a factor that is consistent with Plank 3 of the monetarist platform with its emphasis on the harmful effect of government intervention, of which the tariff is a classic example.

Other international factors caused differences in the timing and magnitude of the contraction in individual countries. The end of capital outflows from the

United States to Germany in 1928 helped cause an early downturn in that country. In addition, reparations "greatly intensified the German depression" (Haberler 1976, p. 29). Then devaluations by Britain, Scandinavia, and other countries in September 1931 stimulated early recoveries there while deepening the slide in the United States and Germany. The devaluation of the dollar in 1933–34 caused a late trough in France and some other countries that had not devalued earlier.

PRICES, OUTPUT, AND AGGREGATE SUPPLY

Equilibrium and Disequilibrium Approaches

Monetarists tend to rely on equilibrium aggregate supply (EAS) theories to explain the division of nominal income between prices and quantities. These theories—embodied, for example, in the work of Friedman (1968), Lucas (1973), and Sargent (1976)—view changes in the actual relative to the "natural" rate of output as the response to deviations of actual from expected prices, which cause a divergence of economic agents' expected and actual real wages.

Nonmonetarists, on the other hand, tend to discuss the same issue of price and quantity determination in terms of a disequilibrium-adjustment framework. In response to a demand shock, prices do not typically adjust rapidly enough to clear markets, so agents find themselves constrained by a level of sales or employment different from what they would voluntarily choose to demand or supply at prevailing wages and prices (see Barro and Grossman 1976, chap. 2). Under these circumstances, the demand for labor becomes a function not only of real wage, the capital stock, and technology—as in EAS theory—but also of actual or expected output or sales. Nonmonetarists do not claim that wages and prices are completely rigid but rather assert that in the short run wage and price adjustment to a situation of excess supply or demand is partial rather than complete.

Empirical Explanations of Unemployment and the Output Ratio

Empirical tests of the EAS approach have been carried out by Lucas and Rapping (1969) and more recently by Darby (1976b). Though Lucas and Rapping examined the period from 1930 through 1965 and concluded that their model was "consistent with the U.S. experience," in the ensuing debate with Rees (1972), they admitted that their approach could not account for the failure of the unemployment rate to decline more rapidly after 1933.

In an attempt to resuscitate the EAS explanation of the 1930s, Darby has presented new unemployment data that treat government workers on CCC and WPA projects as employed rather than unemployed. Darby's corrected data are claimed to exhibit a strong movement toward the natural rate of unemployment in the post-1933 period.[41] Darby expresses the actual unemployment rate at time t, U_t, as a function of a constant, representing the natural rate of unemployment, and the unanticipated component of the price level:

$$U_t = \alpha_0 + \alpha_1 \log (P_t/P_t^*),\qquad(5)$$

where α_0 is the natural rate of unemployment, P_t is the current level of the implicit price deflator, and P_t^* is the expected level of the deflator. Darby specifies the expected component of prices, P_t^*, as being formed adaptively:

$$P_t^* = \lambda P_t + (1-\lambda) P_{t-1}^*,\qquad(6)$$

with λ being the adjustment coefficient.[42]

Table 7 replicates Darby's results using Lebergott's original unemployment rate series U^L, Darby's "corrected" version of that series, U^D, and a measure of output relative to trend output, Q/Q^*. Each equation is estimated using a maximum-likelihood technique. The regression that minimizes the sum of squared residuals over various values of the expectations parameter is listed in table 7, along with the implied mean expectations-adjustment lag, calculated as $(1-\lambda)/\lambda$.

The annual regressions in section A indicate that regardless of the output measure used, Darby's measure of unanticipated prices is correctly signed and has a significant impact on output; for each of the output variants employed, the t-ratio on "price surprises" is very large. As in Darby's original paper, the estimate of the natural rate of unemployment obtained with the U^D unemployment series is relatively high, around 8 percent. The natural-rate estimate obtained using the Lebergott data is 5.9 percent.[43] Section B contains the results obtained when the output-ratio version is reestimated using quarterly data. The quarterly and annual regressions tell the same story, with a strongly significant impact of "price surprises" on output and an infinite lag in the adjustment of expectations.[44]

Darby's adjustments to Lebergott's unemployment series sharply alter the profile of unemployment in the Great Depression, especially in the late 1930s. A comparison of lines A1 and A2 in table 7 indicates, however, that the regression evidence in favor of the EAS hypothesis is no stronger using the Darby data then when the original Lebergott data is used. In fact, the natural-rate estimate and the t-ratio on the price-surprise variable are both more favorable to the EAS theories in line A1. Thus, we cannot conclude that the

Table 7. Effect of "Price Surprises" on Output, 1930–41

Dependent Variable	Estimate of U^* (1)	Unanticipated Price Coefficient (2)	Mean Expectations Adjustment Lag (in years) (3)	SEE (4)	D-W (5)	Mean Expectations Lag Constrained Equal to 1 Year	
						SEE (6)	D-W (7)
A. Annual data							
1. U^L	0.059 (13.7)	−0.716 (−13.3)	∞	0.0123	2.22	0.0453	0.52
2. U^D	0.080 (14.2)	−0.631 (−12.3)	9.0	0.0133	1.98	0.0302	0.66
3. Q/Q^*	0.970 (46.4)	+1.208 (+9.5)	∞	0.0292	1.83	0.0790	0.56
B. Quarterly data							
1. Q/Q^*	0.990 (70.2)	+1.183 (15.2)	∞	0.0374	0.72	0.0876	0.13

Note: t-ratios in parentheses.

"corrected" data reveal that kind of consistency with the EAS framework where none previously existed.

One disconcerting element in these test results is the extremely long implied expectations formation lag. Column (3) indicates that only the Darby unemployment rate regression has a finite mean lag, and that lag is nine years.[45] The infinite adjustment lag estimated for the remaining regressions in table 7 means that expected price level remains a constant equal to the actual price level in 1924.

While it is true that prices in the 1920s exhibited little variance, so that expectations of nearly constant prices like those implied by a 9-year mean lag seem credible, from 1929 through 1940 prices fell sharply and then recovered appreciably. In every year during this 12-year stretch, agents overestimated the price change, whether the adjustment lag is 9 years or infinite. These overestimates are both large and persistent. For instance, in 1931 with the economy sliding further and further into depression, the estimated expected 1932 inflation rate implied by a 9-year lag is over 12 percent. Actually, 1932 brought 11 percent *deflation*. The question must be whether these estimates can plausibly describe the behavior of rational economic agents. We think not. And we suspect that many monetarists, particularly those who stress the excess of real over nominal interest rates in 1931–33, would agree (see Meltzer 1976).

Columns (6) and (7) of table 7 present standard errors of the estimates and Durbin-Watson statistics for the models described above under the restriction that the mean expectations adjustment lag is limited to one year.[46] The imposition of this restriction in each case substantially decreases the explanatory power of the EAS hypothesis. The standard errors more than double, and the Durbin-Watson statistics indicate strong serial correlation in the residuals, suggesting that Granger and Newbold's (1974) warning regarding the possibly spurious nature of the entire relation cannot be disregarded.

Thus Darby's new unemployment data make a minimal contribution to the case for the EAS framework. Unconstrained expectations estimates imply incredibly long, sometimes infinite, lags. Lag estimates restricted to a one-year mean revive problems of serious autocorrelation. The EAS theory cannot yet account for the behavior of prices and output in the Great Depression in a manner consistent with the rational formation of expectations.

Explaining Price Change

If the EAS explanation cannot satisfactorily account for the behavior of prices and output during the Great Depression, how adequate is the expectations-augmented Phillips curve (EPC) favored in recent postwar econometric work?

Table 8 presents the results of an attempt to determine whether the level or change in either unemployment concept in table 7 can explain the rate of change of prices in annual data.

Contrary to the usual Phillips curve relation between the level of the unemployment rate and the rate of change of prices, table 8 indicates that there is no significant effect of the level of unemployment in equations that also include the change in the unemployment rate. These equations and numerous others not reported here demonstrate conclusively that the relation between prices and unemployment (or the output ratio) in the interwar period links levels of each variable or the rates of change of each. There is no evidence of any empirical effect of the *level* of unemployment on the *rate of change* of prices, as called for by the Phillips curve hypothesis. The EAS results in table 7 are completely consistent with this finding, of course, because an infinite adjustment lag causes equation (5) to be converted into a relation between the *level* of unemployment and the *level* of a price index with 1924 as base:

$$U_t = a_0 + a_1 \ \log \ (P_t/P_{1924}). \tag{7}$$

The role of government intervention as a source of price and wage behavior in the 1930s has been stressed by several recent authors (R. J. Gordon 1976; Darby 1976b; Weinstein 1981). One method of identifying such effects is to introduce dummy variables into time-series regressions for years identified as "special" by external evidence. For instance, we know that the NRA (the National Recovery Administration) was established in June 1933 and abolished in May 1935. Any effects of the NRA on price behavior must therefore contaminate the annual-average data for each year between 1933 and 1936. To allow for the possible effect of the NRA, the equations in table 8 have been reestimated with the addition of annual dummy variables for 1933–36.

The results are interesting, particularly those presented in line 3. The coefficients on the individual dummies for the years when the NRA operated (1933 and 1934) are positive and are almost exactly counteracted by negative coefficients for the years of the dismantling of the NRA after its enabling legislation, the National Industrial Recovery Act, was declared unconstitutional (1935 and 1936).[47] It appears that the addition of these annual dummy variables fails to change the conclusion that the Darby unemployment variant (line 4 of table 7) provides a relatively poorer explanation of price change in the interwar period. The addition of the NRA dummies reduces the standard error of the estimate, as compared with line 2, but the sum of the dummy-variable coefficients in that version is an implausible, albeit insignificant, -8.4 percent.

Meltzer argues that "anticipations of inflation depend upon the prevailing monetary standard" (1977, p. 189), implying that empirical schemes that ap-

Table 8. Effect of the Lebergott and Darby Unemployment Concepts on the Rate of Change of Prices in the United States, Annual Data, 1922–41

Sum of Two Lagged Rates of Price Change (1)	Coefficients of				Dummy Variables				SEE (10)	D-W (11)
	U_t^L (2)	ΔU_t^L (3)	U_t^D (4)	ΔU_t^D (5)	1933 (6)	1934 (7)	1935 (8)	1936 (9)		
1. 0.135 (1.04)	0.042 (0.59)	−0.951 (−6.67)	—	—	—	—	—	—	0.0237	2.51
2. 0.203 (1.36)	—	—	−0.037 (−0.34)	−0.921 (−5.31)	—	—	—	—	0.0265	2.50
3. 0.432 (3.05)	0.042 (0.49)	−0.957 (−6.75)	—	—	0.029 (+1.03)	0.049 (1.76)	−0.050 (−1.89)	−0.035 (−1.40)	0.0200	2.94
4. 0.495 (2.73)	—	—	0.069 (+0.41)	−1.060 (−4.35)	−0.001 (−0.02)	0.029 (0.78)	−0.059 (−1.64)	−0.053 (−1.66)	0.0241	2.81

Note: Additional variants yield the conclusion that U_{t-1}^L, U_{t-1}^D, $(U^L-U^D)_t$, and $(U^L-U^D)_{t-1}$ have no significant effect when added to the listed equations.

proximate expectation formation with fixed coefficient functions of past inflation rates may provide poor estimates of rationally formed expectations when the operation of the monetary system undergoes a basic alteration, as when "the international gold standard ended after . . . 1931" (p. 190). In order to test whether the relationship between the changes of prices and of output is sensitive to the empirical method used to estimate expectations, we have drawn upon Meltzer's method and estimated expectations as a function of lagged money growth and lagged average money growth.[48] Regardless of whether expectations of inflation are proxied by lagged inflation rates or are independently estimated functions of lagged money growth, and regardless of whether or not separate annual dummies for 1933–36 are included, and regardless of whether the whole sample or various subsamples are examined, the same result emerges: the rate of change of prices is significantly influenced, not by the level of output, but only by its current rate of change.

The European Experience

While dummy variables provide a crude method to gauge the impact of government intervention, another approach is to compare the division of nominal income between price and output change in the United States and some other countries or group of countries where government intervention was less important. This section compares the behavior of the United States with that of an aggregate of six European countries.[49] Without further research, it is impossible to determine whether any or all of these countries were completely free of new government measures that interfered with the setting of prices; the presumption here is that the degree of New Deal intervention in the 1933–38 period represents an extreme case that might be identified by a comparison with countries with less intervention.[50]

Figure 6 displays real output and the GNP deflator for the United States and Europe during the period 1925–38. It is clear that the division of nominal income change between price and output change was quite different in Europe. Expressed on a 1929 base, the U.S. output index was lower than its price index in every year between 1930 and 1935, whereas the reverse was true in Europe for every year of the 1930–38 period. On an annual basis, only 45 percent of the decline in U.S. nominal income during the 1929–33 contraction was expressed as price change, whereas during the same interval the equivalent figure for Europe was 73 percent. Because the greater extent of price flexibility in Europe was evident well before the advent of New Deal intervention in the price system, it appears that some other factor must have been primarily responsible for sluggish price adjustment in the United States. One possibility

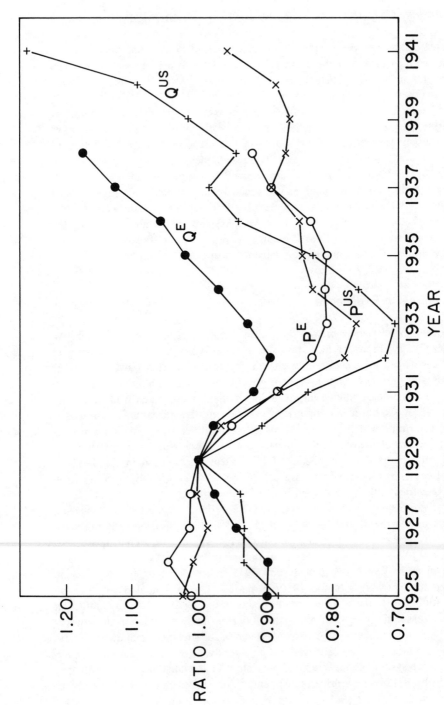

Figure 6. U.S. and European Prices and Real Output, 1925–41 (1929 = 1.0)

is the influence of the Hawley-Smoot tariff discussed above, although Melt-zer's analysis (1976) relies heavily on retaliation by foreign countries to ex-plain how the tariff contributed to the severity of the U.S. contraction.[51]

The difference between the U.S. and European aggregate-supply response is summarized in table 9, which presents the same specification as table 8 but replaces the alternative unemployment variables by the ratio of output to a trend (Q/Q^*), in order to compensate for the lack of comparable unemploy-ment data for this period. The equations for Europe duplicate the U.S. result that the rate of price change is a function of the rate of change of the Q/Q^* level, not its level. Further, in the European equations the coefficient on the rate of change of Q/Q^* is significantly higher than in the United States, indi-cating that any given change in nominal income was reflected more in the form of price change and less as quantity change in Europe than in the United States.[52]

Since an identity links the rates of change of nominal income, the price level, and real output, the equations in table 9 can be reestimated in a form that makes the rate of change of prices a function of the current rate of change of nominal income and the lagged rate of change of prices. This allows a direct comparison of the impact of the differences between the European and the U.S. aggregate-supply functions, holding constant the behavior of nominal income. In figure 7 are plotted the annual level of the U.S. implicit GNP deflator (P_t) and the fitted values of prices in two dynamic simulations. The first $(\hat{P}_t)$ is based on coefficients from a regression of U.S. price change on U.S. nominal-income change and lagged price change. The second $(\hat{\hat{P}}_t)$ is based on coefficients from a regression of European price change on European nominal-income change and lagged price change fitted to 1928–38. Each simu-lation is calculated by multiplying these two alternative sets of coefficients by the *actual* rate of change of U.S. nominal income and the *fitted* values of lagged U.S. price change.

Several interesting features of figure 7 stand out prominently. First, the im-pact of government intervention on the price level is evident in the difference between P_t and $\hat{P}_t$. The rise in actual P_t relative to the simulated series in 1934 reflects the influence of NRA, and the subsequent slowness of increase in P_t presumably reflects the demise of NRA in 1935. Even more notable is the increase in P_t relative to $\hat{P}_t$ in 1937, caused at least partly by the influence of unionization.[53] Further, the simulated $\hat{\hat{P}}_t$ series based on European coeffi-cients indicate that, given actual U.S. nominal-income behavior, the U.S. price level would have declined by 33 rather than only 24 percent during the period 1929–33 if prices had been as flexible as in Europe. The rapid increase in the U.S. price level during the period 1933–37, often cited as evidence of cost-push, instead appears to have been due to the very rapid growth of nomi-

Table 9. Effect of Output and Output Change on the Rate of Change
of Prices, United States and Europe, Annual Data

		Coefficients of				
	Sample Period	Sum of Two Lagged Rates of Price Change	Q/Q^*	Rate of Change of Q/Q^*	SEE	D-W
A. United States						
1.	1922–41	0.156	0.031	_____	0.0460	1.42
		(0.61)	(0.33)			
2.	1922–41	0.016	_____	0.423	0.0318	2.44
		(0.09)		(4.20)		
B. Europe						
1.	1928–38	0.380	0.195	_____	0.0339	1.32
		(0.56)	(0.48)			
2.	1928–38	0.467	_____	0.794	0.0188	2.10
		(1.46)		(4.08)		

Note: t-ratios in parentheses.

nal income during this interval. In fact, the simulated series $\hat{P}_t$ based on European coefficients and actual U.S. nominal-income growth registers a 1933–37 increase of 19.3 percent, greater than the 16.6 percent increase in the actual U.S. deflator during the same period. Thus, if the degree of price flexibility in the United States had been greater, U.S. prices would have rebounded even more in 1933–37 than they actually did.

CONCLUSION

Sources of Income Change

This paper has examined two different aspects of macroeconomic behavior in the United States during the 12-year period between 1929 and 1941—both the proximate determinants of the severity and duration of the slump in nominal income, and the factors influencing the division of those changes in nominal income between changes in the price level and in real output. The first topic involves the sources of shifts in aggregate demand, and the second concerns the slope and source of shifts in the aggregate-supply function. The link that unifies attention to both issues in a single paper is their relation to present-day monetarism. The preference of monetarists for monetary rules rather

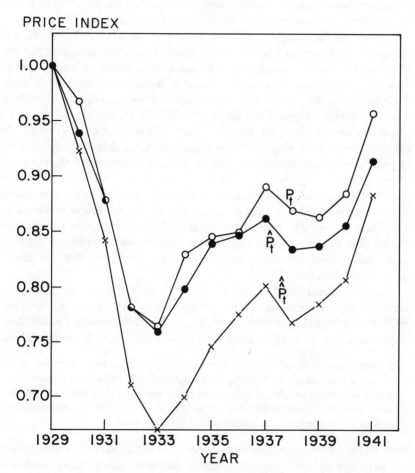

Figure 7. Comparison of Actual and Simulated Prices, 1929–41
(1929 = 1.0)

than countercyclical activism is based on their assumptions that private spending is basically stable in the absence of government interference, that government intervention does more harm than good, and that the price mechanism provides a powerful self-correcting force that insulates the economy from long-lasting swings in real output in the absence of government activism.

The first question, the sources of nominal-income movements, has been the subject of much recent controversy and debate, but we are persuaded that most of the heat has been unproductive. The common weakness of recent work has been its polemical and unscientific attempt to demonstrate that a single factor, the behavior of the money supply and monetary policy, either was solely responsible for the Great Contraction of 1929–33 (Schwartz and Darby) or played no role at all in the first two years of the contraction (Temin). The inherent weakness of single-factor explanations, or of denials of the influence of particular factors, is that they can be so easily contradicted. Schwartz and Darby must deny that *any* factor besides the 1928–29 deceleration in monetary growth was responsible for the rapid collapse of spending in the first quarters of the contraction. Temin must deny that a *single* deposit holder at a bank that failed in 1930 or 1931 was forced to cut back his spending on current goods and services by as much as a single dollar! Because such extreme positions fly in the face of common sense, we must register our surprise that they are still so firmly maintained.

This paper concludes that both nonmonetary and monetary factors played an important role in determining changes in nominal income during the period 1929–41. In holding that there must have been multiple causes rather than a single cause, we are only echoing a conclusion reached long ago by Haberler:

> Explanations which run in terms of one single cause have been more and more discredited and should be regarded with suspicion. The majority of modern writers on the subject are careful to point out that a whole set of factors, and perhaps not always the same combination of factors, contribute towards producing an alternation of prosperity and depression. [1958, pp. 5–6]

Four views ranging from extreme monetarism (*a*) to extreme nonmonetarism (*d*) were initially distinguished. Evidence has been presented that leads us to reject both views (*a*) and (*d*), leaving the intermediate soft-line monetarist and nonmonetarist views (*b*) and (*c*) as plausible explanations that differ only in emphasis.

View (*b*) essentially states that, while nonmonetary factors may partially have initiated the 1929–33 contraction, it was the failure of the Federal Reserve to offset the deflationary impact of bank failures that converted a serious recession into a severe depression. View (*c*) emphasizes the nature of the nonmonetary factors that played an important role in 1929–33 without denying that a countercyclical stimulus applied by the Federal Reserve could have lessened the severity and duration of the contraction. The difference between views (*b*) and (*c*) is inconsequential, representing mainly the greater interest of nonmonetarists in the 1929-31 phase of the contraction and of monetarists in the 1931–33 phase, and the two views are in fact almost perfectly complementary, each filling in the gaps left in the other's analysis.[54]

Weaknesses in a Purely Monetary Explanation

The present paper contains new evidence against a monocausal monetary explanation of the first two years of the contraction. Simulations based on the average relation between lagged values of the money supply and current values of nominal income in the 1920–28 interval suggest that the deceleration in monetary growth beginning in early 1929 cannot explain why the initial contraction of income was so severe. The initial slowdown of monetary growth in 1928–29 was no greater than in previous minor recessions in the 1920s, leaving unanswered the question why nominal income should have dropped by almost 30 percent during the first two years of the contraction.

The statistical relationship between lagged money and income is sufficiently weak, even in the 1920s, to raise serious questions about the ability of changes in the money supply and monetary policy to explain changes in nominal income during the interwar period. While an F-ratio on the joint contribution of the lagged money variables is significant in the 1920–28 period when the variables are expressed as growth rates, the F-ratio is insignificant for the level form of the variables. The t-ratios on the sum of the lagged money coefficients are insignificant in every period and for every variant of the equations. And questions may be raised as to whether a significant lead of money before income would have any meaning even if it could be found; some nonmonetarists might claim that money-supply swings reflect changes in the need of businessmen to finance inventory changes and that swings in these working-capital needs could precede business-cycle turning points.

As the sample period of the income-on-lagged-money regressions is extended into the 1930s, the coefficients on lagged monetary change become even weaker. After 1929 the relationship between money and income appears to be entirely contemporaneous, adding plausibility to the reverse-feedback hypothesis that the reflex influence of business on money was a primary determinant of money-supply swings during the period 1929–41. In the light of postwar time-series evidence indicating that swings in monetary growth induced by policy shifts require several quarters to influence income growth, it appears dubious that the purely contemporaneous relation of the 1930s could mainly reflect a money-to-income chain of causation.

Not only is a statistical relation between lagged money and income nonexistent after 1929, but in addition a purely monetary explanation cannot account for the duration of the slump of nominal income in the 1930s. The money supply grew very rapidly between 1938 and 1940 and in 1940 exceeded its 1929 average by almost 20 percent, yet income grew at a sluggish pace during the same period and in 1940 was still below its 1929 level.

A purely monetary explanation leaves unanswered why nominal income fell so rapidly during the 1929–31 period, why income grew so slowly during the 1938–40 period and so rapidly between 1940 and 1941, and why the relation between money and income in the 1930s should have been contemporaneous without the long lags that monetarists have emphasized in their critiques of policy activism. Yet nonmonetary explanations are available for each of these features of the period.

The first nonmonetary source of the 1929–31 contraction in income was the decline in residential housing construction, due both to a decline in population growth following the 1921 and 1924 legislation limiting immigration and to overbuilding during the mid-1920s. The decline in housing began in 1927 and became very steep in 1928 and 1929, and yet its impact on the aggregate economy was delayed by a temporary boom in consumption (and to some extent in nonresidential investment) stimulated by the speculative stock market bubble. The collapse in stock values brought about a rapid decline in consumption spending that added to and interacted with the impact of the housing slump. After the summer of 1930 the Hawley-Smoot tariff added to the contractionary pressure.

The timing of income change in the late 1930s also requires a mainly nonmonetary explanation. While money-supply growth was rapid and relatively steady between early 1938 and late 1941, nominal income grew slowly through mid-1940 and rapidly thereafter. Nonmonetarists point to the sluggishness of investment demand in 1938–40, and the enormous increase in defense spending in 1940–41, as an obvious explanation of this timing pattern. And, in the light of the weak relation between money and income in 1938–41, they would suggest that at least part of the simultaneous 1937–38 decline in money and income reflects, not the influence of an exogenous monetary policy shift, but rather the reverse-feedback effect of income on money following a very marked contractionary swing toward a full-employment fiscal surplus during the period 1936–37.

Weaknesses in a Purely Nonmonetary Explanation

There is no contradiction between the statements that (1) in the absence of a strong countercyclical monetary policy, the money-income relation in the

1930s was dominated by a contemporaneous feedback effect of income on money, and (2) an alternative activist monetary policy would have yielded a different set of data exhibiting a significant impact of lagged money on income. Nonmonetarists may rightly claim that, *given* the absence of monetary activism, nonmonetary factors were mainly responsible for the collapse in both money and income in 1929–33, but they thereby provide no proof that such activism could not have been effective.

Since the U.S. data are incapable of revealing the effects of behavior that did not occur, monetarists make a valuable contribution by pointing to the differences between European and U.S. behavior. The similarity in the behavior of velocity in Europe and the United States during the decade of the 1930s supports the monetarist conjecture that, had the United States followed Europe in preventing a collapse of the money supply, U.S. nominal income would have exhibited the milder contraction and earlier recovery actually observed in Europe.

Monetarists might also claim that the weakness of the effects of money-supply growth in 1938–40 could have been a consequence of earlier monetary inaction. As Hawtrey (1933) pointed out, once a depression has occurred and business expectations have become dominated by pessimism, a monetary expansion may not have the same stimulating effect that would have occurred earlier, and a combined monetary and fiscal expansion may instead be necessary to bring about a full recovery. It was such an expansion in 1940–41, of course, that finally brought the depression to an end in the United States.

Finally, the primary role of nonmonetary forces in explaining the initial phase of the 1929–33 contraction, and the inability of the small deceleration in monetary growth to explain why the contraction was so severe, may be admitted without precluding a role for money in determining the timing of the 1929 turning point. Without easy money in 1927–28 and tight money in early 1929, the stock market and consumption boom and collapse might have been dampened, and the course of nominal income might have more directly followed the path of the ongoing slump in housing investment.

The Aggregate-Supply Response

Neither the equilibrium aggregate supply (EAS) approach nor the expectational Phillips curve (EPC) appear at all adequate as explanations of the division of U.S. nominal-income changes between price and output changes in the 1930s. Deviations of unemployment or output from their natural levels, according to EAS, occur only when economic agents are surprised by the emergence of a price level different from that which they previously expected. While the EAS approach provides a plausible explanation of 1929–33, it cannot explain why output remained so low and unemployment so high from 1933 to 1940. Price movements were sufficiently modest after 1934 to make surprises small by any reasonable version of how agents formed expectations; the computer is forced to conclude that an EAS econometric specification can explain unemployment and output in the late 1930s only if it is implausibly assumed that agents each year expected the price level to return to its 1924 value in the face of continuing evidence that no such return was occurring!

The EPC approach fails completely as well, because there is no evidence at all of a relation between price *change* and the *level* of unemployment or output during the 1930s, either for the United States or for an aggregate of six European countries. The statistical relation appears to have been between price change and output change, or between the level of prices and the level of output. These results lead to an interesting set of research questions to be explored in subsequent work. The finding that price change responds to output change but not the level of output is consistent with Meltzer's (1977) development of a price-specie-flow model of an economy operating under the gold standard. Changes in demand cause simultaneous changes in both output and prices, but the emergence of unemployment and an output gap is anticipated and has no independent effect on the rate of price change, as required in the EPC approach. Why the EPC appears to describe the postwar years but not the interwar years is attributed by Meltzer to the shift from the gold to the dollar standard, although R. J. Gordon's recent work (1977) on the postwar years suggests that even recently the dominant explanation of the rate of price change is the rate of change of the output gap rather than its level.[55]

Because the high *level* of unemployment had no independent effect on prices in the 1930s, the monetarist belief in the recuperative self-correcting powers of the private economy receives no support from the data. Some monetarist writings have stressed the role of government intervention as a source of cost-push pressure in the 1930s, but our results lead us to discount any crucial role for government in explaining the puzzles of U.S. aggregate supply behavior during that decade. With the exception of a temporary upward blip in prices in 1934, which vanished in 1935, and of a high rate of price increase in 1937, the year of greatest unionization, we find that a simple relation between price change, output change, and lagged price change fits the interwar data for both the United States and Europe quite well. Because Europe has much less price-raising intervention than the United States but exhibits the same type of supply response, doubt is cast on intervention as the main cause of U.S. behavior. The main difference between the United States and Europe—the steeper slope of the European supply function—was evident in 1929–33, well before the advent of the New Deal. The sources of sluggishness in U.S. price behavior prior to 1933 must stand high on an agenda of future research topics, with an initial avenue of investigation being an attempt to quantify the role of the Hawley-Smoot tariff of 1930.

A Final Scorecard

In concluding that nonmonetary factors are essential in a complete explanation of the magnitude and timing of income movements in the 1930s, we deny the validity of Plank 1 of the monetarist platform with its emphasis on the inherent stability of private spending. But in agreeing with the basic Friedman-Schwartz proposition that a different policy response would have reduced the severity and duration of the Great Contraction, and in pointing to the harmful role of the Hawley-Smoot tariff, we lend our support to the message of Plank 3 that past government policy actions (and in 1929–33 the *absence* of appropriate policy actions) have done more harm than good. Finally, while denying any potency to the self-correcting mechanisms of price flexibility during the 1930s, as stressed in Planks 2 and 4, we must add that the underlying sources of aggregate supply behavior in the United States during the interwar period, and the reasons for changes in this behavior between the nineteenth century and the 1930s, and between the 1930s and the present day, must stand high on any agenda of unsolved research puzzles in macroeconomics.

APPENDIX: DATA SOURCES, 1919–41

IPC: Index of nominal value of industrial production. Calculated as the index of industrial production (Federal Reserve *Bulletin,* various issues) times the CPI (BLS).

M: Money.
United States: Friedman and Schwartz 1963a, Appendix A.
Europe (France, Germany, Italy, the Netherlands, Sweden, United Kingdom): Mitchell 1975, pp. 676–83.

P: Implicit price deflator.
United States: Annual—1919–21: Kuznets 1941; 1922–28: Hickman and Coen 1976; 1929–41: U.S. Department of Commerce 1976. Quarterly—generated using the Chow-Lin (1971) technique that distributes annual series into quarterly series using related, quarterly series; the related series used were the CPI and the WPI.
Europe (except France): Mitchell 1975, pp. 785–90. Calculated as the quotient of current-dollar divided by constant-dollar gross national product.

France: The German implicit price deflator was regressed on the German WPI, both in logs. The resulting coefficients were then multiplied by the French WPI to obtain an estimate of the French implicit price deflator. French and German WPI data series are from Mitchell 1975.

Q: Real output.

United States: Annual—1919–21: Kuznets 1941; 1922–28: Hickman and Coen 1976; 1929–41: U.S. Department of Commerce 1976. Quarterly—three related series (industrial production, real department store sales, and a linear trend) were employed to generate quarterly real output using the Chow-Lin (1971) technique. See *P.*

Europe: Mitchell 1975, pp. 785–90. The aggregate for Europe is the sum of real GNP for the six European countries, converted into dollars using 1929 exchange rates.

Q*: Natural rate of output. 1913–29: calculated as the exponential trend between the real GNP levels of 1913 and 1929; 1930–41: calculated as the extrapolation of the 1913–29 annual trend rate of growth of 2.54 percent using the actual rate of output in 1929 as the natural rate of output in 1929.

S: Index of department store sales. Federal Reserve *Bulletin,* various issues.

U^D: Unemployment rate. Darby 1976*b.*

U^L: Unemployment rate. Lebergott 1964.

Y: Nominal GNP.

United States: P multiplied by *Q.*

Europe: Mitchell 1975, pp. 785–90. The aggregate for Europe is the sum of nominal GNP for the six European countries converted into dollars using 1929 exchange rates.

NOTES

1. Outside of the context of the Temin debate, several monetarist authors have provided important recent interpretations of the price-output division of nominal income. See especially Meltzer (1977) and Darby (1976*b*).

2. The primary emphasis in this paper on monetarist interpretations reflects the topic selected by the organizers of the conference on the Great Depression and does not imply any belief on our part that nonmonetarist interpretations should be immune from detailed scrutiny.

3. The phrase "battle of the radio stations" comes from the initials (AM-FM) of the main protagonists in a 100-page debate published in 1965 in the *American Economic Review.* See Ando and Modigliani (1965) and Friedman and Meiselman (1965).

4. The development of the monetarist platform benefited from the suggestions of Milton Friedman, Allan Meltzer, Franco Modigliani, and Arthur Okun. It is supported by a more extensive discussion in R. J. Gordon (1978, pp. 335–43).

5. This explains the apparent oddity that the word *money* does not appear in the platform. Were it not for the popularity of the word *monetarist* among both economists and journalists, the platform might be better described by the term *antiactivist*.

6. A clear example is Friedman's (1968) statement that "the simultaneous fall *ex post* in real wages to employers and rise *ex ante* in real wages to employees is what enabled employment to increase." Empirical studies by Lucas and Rapping (1969), Darby (1976*b*), and Barro (1977) place unemployment or real output on the left-hand side of the equation and deviations of nominal variables from their expected values on the right-hand side. Schwartz writes in the same vein, "Why quantities changed as they did *in response to* price changes should be the goal of analysis" (1981, p. 21, emphasis added).

7. In response to a demand shock, prices do not typically adjust rapidly enough to clear markets, and so agents find themselves constrained by a level of sales or employment different from what they would voluntarily choose to supply at going prices and wages (Barro and Grossman 1976, chap. 2). Prices and wages are not completely sticky; instead, their adjustment to excess demand or supply in any given time period is partial rather than instantaneous and complete.

8. R. J. Gordon (1977) presents both wage and price equations with the coefficient of expectations constrained to be 1.0, thus placing the difference between actual and expected values on the left-hand side.

9. "A far more satisfactory explanation of 1929–33 than Temin's is, therefore, that a series of negative shocks, monetary in origin, reduced real output. . . . There are no unexplained changes in spending that serve as deus ex machina. . . . The behavior of the economy was determined by public policies. Different policies would have resulted in different behavior" (Schwartz 1981, p. 26).

10. The clearest admission of the possible role of nonmonetary forces comes in Friedman and Schwartz (1963*a*): "True, as events unfolded, the decline in the stock of money and the near-collapse of the banking system can be regarded as a consequence of nonmonetary forces in the United States, and monetary and nonmonetary forces in the rest of the world. . . . Prevention or moderation of the decline in the stock of money, let alone the substitution of monetary expansion, would have reduced the contraction's severity and almost as certainly its duration. The contraction might still have been relatively severe" (pp. 300–01). On the endogenicity of the money supply, see Friedman and Schwartz (1963*b*): "The reflex influence of business on money, the existence of which is not in doubt in light of the factual evidence summarized above, would then become part of the partly self-generating mechanism whereby monetary disturbances are transmitted" (pp. 49–50).

11. "The first thing to be said about [the Great Depression] is that it was a *double* slump. It began with the Wall Street crash in 1929, a repetition, at least at first sight, of that of 1907, leading to a depression just as that had done. But the recovery from the depression, which on previous experience might have been expected to follow within a year or two, did not take place. Instead there was a double slump, superimposed upon the first. Now there is no doubt at all that this second slump was monetary in character" (p. 210). Hicks dates the second stage from the fall of 1931, thus differing from the Friedman-Schwartz emphasis on the role of bank failures in the fall of 1930.

12. In 1974 R. A. Gordon was close enough to the Friedman-Schwartz position to agree that "vigorous action by the Fed could have substantially reduced the severity of the depression" (p. 72).

13. The peak of the cycle was 1929:3. Sources of data are identified in the Appendix at the end of the paper.

14. P is the quarterly GNP deflator. See Appendix.

15. Econometric studies of consumption functions generally support a real-balance effect that makes IS depend on M/P, but this added factor does not alter our conclusions; it simply makes the DD curve flatter without changing the variables that cause it to shift its position.

16. We believe that Temin was unwise to use $IS–LM$ curves in a problem involving variable prices without also examining the $SS–DD$ diagram shown in the bottom frame of figure 2. For a full development of this diagrammatic apparatus, and a discussion of the variables that make SS shift its position, see R. J. Gordon (1978, pp. 143–98).

17. This represents a graphic translation of an argument made by Schwartz (1981). The distinction between nominal and real interest rates is incorporated into $IS–LM$ analysis in R. J. Gordon (1978, pp. 289–91).

18. The inverse of velocity, M_2/PQ, is displayed in figure 1.

19. This aspect of the Great Depression is emphasized by Fisher (1933).

20. Two channels by which the decline in nominal GNP could have caused the bank failures are (1) by reducing the nominal sales of individuals and firms to which banks had lent money, turning initially sound loans into loans that could not be repaid, and (2) by reducing the prices of bonds, as securities markets reflected the increased "price of risk," thus contributing to the insolvency of banks holding risky bonds (Temin 1976, pp. 103–21).

21. Schwartz (1981) has independently used the Granger method to evaluate the Temin interpretation of the 1929–33 contraction. While our results are consistent with hers in rejecting Temin's extreme position (d), we go beyond her results by running simulations that tend to reject her own extreme position (a).

22. In table 1, $K = 4$ and $L = 8$ when money is the independent variable, and $L = 4$ when income is the independent variable. This difference in the value of L occurs because quarterly income data are not available before 1919, and we were urged by a discussant to start our sample period in 1920:2 in order to capture the relation between money and income in the 1920–21 recession.

23. In table 2, $K = L = 8$. Inclusion of extra lagged values beyond eight yielded insignificant coefficients and did not alter the results displayed in table 2.

24. Between 1929:3 and 1933:2, M_1 fell by 31.8 percent and M_2 fell by 35.1 percent. The sums of coefficients on lagged money in the 1920–28 sample period are as follows in each version:

	Level	Rate of Change
M_1	0.970	0.213
M_2	0.936	0.520

25. Nonresidential fixed investment in 1940 was exactly the same as in 1937 in real terms and grew only 3 percent in nominal terms, whereas nominal M_2 grew 18.5 percent between 1937:2 and 1940:2.

26. Between 1940 and 1941 nominal defense spending grew by an amount equal to 11.5 percent of 1940 nominal GNP. The annual growth rate of M_2 in the six quarters after 1940:2 (12.2 percent) was little different from that in the six quarters before 1940:2 (11.0 percent).

27. For sources and data, see Gordon (1978, p. 496).

28. In the case of the regressions in which the variables are in the form of growth rates, the sums of coefficients on lagged money are almost always negative and are never significantly different from zero. Also, the F-ratio on the significance of lagged-M_2 growth rates declines appreciably as the sample moves through the 1930s.

29. The European data refer to the total of France, Germany, Italy, the Netherlands, Sweden, and the United Kingdom aggregated with weights according to 1929 GNP in dollars. Sources are described in the Appendix.

30. As examples, the ratio of real fixed gross investment to Q^* was 0.144 in 1955–57, 0.130 in 1958–61, 0.150 in 1965–69, and 0.124 in 1975–77.

31. Hickman and Coen (1976, p. 194) estimate a multiplier for changes in real autonomous spending (for five years after the change) of 5.09 under the conditions of 1926–40 and only 2.10 under the conditions of 1951–65. R. J. Gordon (1978, p. 494) calculates that the automatic fiscal stabilizers absorbed only 5.5 percent of the decline in GNP in 1932, but 36.9 percent in 1975.

32. Meltzer himself shows that industrial production had already fallen by 25 percent at the time of the first bank failures in October 1930 (1976, p. 464).

33. "Standardized households" are calculated by applying fixed 1940 household-headship rates to each age group. Since headship rates among children are negligible, the endogenous decline in the birth rate caused by the drop in income during the depression could not have altered the number of standardized households in the 1929–41 period.

34. See Hickman's presentation (1973, table 3, p. 307) of results for each year both for simulation II (standardized households grow at 1924–25 rate) and simulation III (standardized households follow actual path). Temin's summary of this same paper states that "holding income constant in this model eliminates most of the fall in construction in the 1930's by eliminating the observed fall in the rate of family formation in that decade" (1976, pp. 46–47). But Hickman's simulation III, which holds income constant while allowing standardized households to follow their actual path, does *not* eliminate the observed fall in the rate of household formation (in simulation III the rate of household formation falls from 579 million in 1925 to a trough of 377 million in 1937, for a decline of 34.9 percent). Nor is most of the decline in construction eliminated, since housing starts fall in simulation III from 977 million in 1925 to 372 million in 1940, for a decline of *61.9 percent*.

35. The oral tradition was passed on to us by George R. Neumann, to whom we are indebted.

36. The ratio was 8.6 percent in 1924–27 (Hickman and Coen, 1976, table A.2, p. 222). None of the postwar *individual* peak years of residential construction spending (1950, 1955, 1959, 1964, and 1972) came close to the ratio of *any* of the four successive peak years of the 1920s (the ratios for these postwar years are 6.2, 5.4, 5.3, 5.0, 5.3).

37. The expanding role of government is evident in the following comparison of ratios to actual real GNP in 1929 and 1940:

	1929	1940	Change
Consumption expenditures	68.5	67.1	−1.4
Gross private domestic investment	17.8	13.0	−4.8
Net exports	0.7	0.9	+0.2
Government purchases	13.0	19.1	+6.1

38. Between 1922 and 1923 U.S. real output grew 13.1 percent, compared to 3.5 percent in the United Kingdom, 8.2 in France, and 6.3 in Canada. At the same time, the relative price of exports fell by 9.2 percent. The Emergency Tariff Act of 1921 and the Fordney tariff of 1922, in the absence of perfectly elastic supply schedules, prevented relative export prices from falling further.

39. If income elasticities for U.S. exports and imports were equal, the smaller decline in European income should have led to a smaller decline in U.S exports, abstracting from relative price effects. The zero change in the trade balance argues that relative price effects cut the trade balance. But this result depends on equal income elasticities and would be invalidated by an income elasticity higher for U.S. exports than for imports.

40. In this era the economy of western Europe plus Canada was about equal in size to that of the United States. The GNP in dollars of the subset of six countries plotted in figure 5 was 75 percent of U.S. GNP in 1929 (see Appendix).

41. For a critique of Darby's redefinition of unemployment, see R. J. Gordon (1976, pp. 195–96) and Kesselman and Savin (1978).

42. Actual and expected prices were assumed equal in 1924.

43. This may still be an overestimate, since, even in the presence of far more lucrative welfare and unemployment benefits in the 1970s, current estimates of the natural rate hover around 6 percent (R. J. Gordon 1977).

44. At the suggestion of Robert Lucas, we conducted separate experiments in which lagged dependent variables were added to each of the regressions reported in table 7. In each case the lagged variables were insignificant.

45. This exceeds Darby's estimate of 5.7 years, presumably because of our use of a slightly different price series prior to 1929. The methods and other data series used here are identical to Darby's.

46. This lag restriction is arbitrary but is much closer to postwar estimates than a nine-year or infinite lag.

47. The sum of the individual-years coefficients is -0.7 percent, implying that whatever impetus the NRA gave to price and wage increases was completely reversed after the NRA was abolished. Since the NRA was both established and declared unconstitutional in midyear, the significance of the NRA's initial (1933)- and terminal (1935)-year coefficients are probably understated. An F-ratio on the joint significance of the 1933–36 coefficients, which is probably similarly understated, passes a significance test at the 10 percent level.

48. Over the 1922–41 period, agents choosing between predictions of inflation based on lagged inflation rates or on measures of lagged money growth would have been better off choosing the former. The R^2's and standard errors of the two versions are 0.22 and 0.0455, and 0.24 and 0.0448, respectively, in equations explaining the annual rate of change of the GNP deflator.

49. The six European nations are the same as those identified in n. 29 and for which money and nominal-income data are plotted in figure 5.

50. The most important cases of intervention in Europe were the German price and wage controls and the French Blum experiment. Bry (1960) suggests that German price controls caused the official cost-of-living index to be understated from 1937 on. Kalecki (1938) concludes that the Blum experiment raised wages and wholesale prices by 60 percent in France in 1937, without having any appreciable effect on real output. The upward push on prices in France in 1937 thus, to some extent, offsets the German controls, which became tighter in 1936–38.

51. If retaliation had been complete and instantaneous, then the tariff could make no contribution to the explanation of the greater degree of price flexibility in Europe.

52. The fraction of nominal income going into price change in the short run (given lagged prices) is equal to $\alpha/1 + \alpha$, where α is the coefficient on the rate of change of Q/Q^* in table 9. This fraction is 30 percent for the United States on line A2 and 44 percent for Europe in line B2.

53. The ratio of union members to civilian employment more than doubled between 1936 and 1938 and showed little change before 1937 or between 1938 and 1942.

54. Mayer (1978b) and others comment on the notable lack of attention to the nature of the 1929–30 phase of the contraction by Friedman and Schwartz.

55. Our research here supports Meltzer's in linking the rate of change of prices and the rate of change of output but conflicts with his in finding no conclusive evidence that price expectations were based on the recent behavior of monetary growth. Instead, we find that price change is better predicted by past price change than by past monetary change and that the money-to-prices link was particularly weak in 1937–40 (in 1940 the GNP deflator was below

its 1937 value, despite the 20 percent growth in M_2 and 30 percent growth in M_1 that occurred during the interval). In part, our differences with Meltzer may reflect the fact that Meltzer actually fits no equations that include only the interwar period. In his regressions for 1901–40, any looseness of the money-to-prices relation in 1937–40 must be dominated by the high variance of both money and prices during the World War I period, 1916–1920.

REFERENCES

Andersen, L. C., and Jordan, J. L. 1968. "Monetary and Fiscal Actions: A Test of Their Relative Importance in Economic Stabilization." Federal Reserve Bank of St. Louis *Review* 50: 11–24.

Ando, A., and Modigliani, F. 1965. "The Relative Stability of Monetary Velocity and the Investment Multiplier." *American Economic Review* 55: 693–728.

———. 1976. "Impacts of Fiscal Actions on Aggregate Income and the Monetarist Controversy: Theory and Evidence." In *Monetarism,* ed. J. L. Stein. Amsterdam: North-Holland.

Artus, J. R., and Sosa, S. C. 1978. "Relative Price Effects on Export Performance: The Case of Nonelectrical Machinery." *IMF Staff Papers* 25: 25–47.

Barro, R. J. 1977. "Unanticipated Money Growth and Unemployment in the United States." *American Economic Review* 67: 101–15.

Barro, R. J., and Grossman, H. I. 1976. *Money, Employment, and Inflation.* Cambridge: Cambridge University Press.

Bolch, B. W., and Pilgrim, J. D. 1973. "A Reappraisal of Some Factors Associated with Fluctuations in the United States in the Interwar Period." *Southern Economic Journal* 39: 327–44.

Bry, G. 1960. *Wages in Germany, 1871–1945.* Princeton, N.J.: Princeton University Press.

Chow, G. C., and Lin, A. 1971. "Best, Linear, Unbiased Interpolation, Distribution, and Extrapolation of Time Series by Related Series." *Review of Economics and Statistics* 53: 372–75.

Darby, M. R. 1976a. *Macroeconomics.* New York: McGraw-Hill.

———. 1976b. "Three-and-a-Half-Million U.S. Employees Have Been Mislaid; Or, An Explanation of Unemployment, 1934–41." *Journal of Political Economy* 84: 1–16.

Fisher, I. 1933. "The Debt-Deflation Theory of Great Depressions." *Econometrica* 1: 337–57.

Friedman, M. 1968. "The Role of Monetary Policy." *American Economic Review* 58: 1–17.

Friedman, M., and Meiselman, D. 1965. "Reply to Ando and Modigliani and to Deprano and Mayer." *American Economic Review* 55: 753–85.

Friedman, M., and Schwartz, A. 1963a. *A Monetary History of the United States.* Princeton, N.J.: Princeton University Press, for the National Bureau of Economic Research.

_____. 1963*b*. "Money and Business Cycles." *Review of Economics and Statistics* 45: 32–78.

Goodwin, R. M. 1955. "A Model of Cyclical Growth." In *The Business Cycles in the Post War World,* ed. E. Lundberg. London: Macmillan.

Gordon, R. A. 1951. "Cyclical Experience in the Interwar Period: The Investment Boom of the Twenties." In Universities-National Bureau Committee for Economic Research, *Conference on Business Cycles.* New York: National Bureau of Economic Research.

_____. 1974. *Economic Instability and Growth: The American Record.* New York: Harper & Row.

Gordon, R. J. 1976. "Recent Developments in the Theory of Inflation and Unemployment." *Journal of Monetary Economics* 2: 185–219.

_____. 1977. "Can the Inflation of the 1970's Be Explained?" *Brookings Papers on Economic Activity* 8: 253–79.

_____. 1978. *Macroeconomics.* Boston: Little, Brown.

Granger, C. W. J. 1969. "Investigating Casual Relations by Econometric Models and Cross-Spectral Methods." *Econometrica* 37: 424–38.

Granger, C. W. J., and Newbold, P. 1974. "Spurious Regressions in Econometrics." *Journal of Econometrics* 2: 111–20.

Haberler, G. 1958. *Prosperity and Depression.* Cambridge, Mass.: Harvard University Press.

_____. 1976. *The World Economy, Money, and the Great Depression, 1919–39.* Washington, D.C.: American Enterprise Institute.

Hawtrey, R. G. 1933. *Trade Depression and the Way Out.* London: Longmans.

Hickman, B. G. 1973. "What Became of the Building Cycle." In *Nations and Households in Economic Growth: Essays in Honor of Moses Abramovitz,* ed. P. David and M. Reder. New York: Academic Press.

Hickman, B. G., and Coen, R. M. 1976. *An Annual Growth Model of the U. S. Economy.* New York: American Elsevier.

Hicks, J. R. 1974. "Real and Monetary Factors in Economic Fluctuations." *Scottish Journal of Political Economy,* November: 205–14.

Jonung, L. 1981. "The Depression in Sweden and the United States: A Comparison of Causes and Policies." In this volume.

Kalecki, M. 1938. "The Lesson of the Blum Experiment." *Economic Journal* 48: 26–41.

Kesselman, J. R., and Savin, N. E. 1978. "Three-and-a-Half Million Workers Never Were Lost." *Economic Inquiry* 16: 205–25.

Kuznets, S. 1941. *National Income and Its Composition.* New York: National Bureau of Economic Research.

Lebergott, S. 1964. *Manpower in Economic Growth.* New York: McGraw-Hill.

Lucas, R. E., Jr. 1973. "Some International Evidence on Output-Inflation Trade-Offs." *American Economic Review* 63: 326–34.

_____. 1976. "Econometric Policy Evaluation: A Critique." In *The Phillips Curve and Labor Markets,* ed. K. Brunner and A. Meltzer. *Journal of Monetary Economics* 2 (supp.): 19–46.

Lucas, R. E., Jr., and Rapping, L. A. 1969. "Real Wages, Employment, and Inflation." *Journal of Political Economy* 77: 721–54.

Maddison, A. 1964. *Economic Growth in the West*. New York: Twentieth-Century
Fund.

Mayer, T. 1978*a*. "Consumption in the Great Depression." *Journal of Political Economy* 86: 139–46.

———. 1978*b*. "Money and the Great Depression: A Critique of Professor Temin's
Thesis." *Explorations in Economic History* 15: 127–45.

Meltzer, A. H. 1976. "Monetary and Other Explanations of the Start of the Great
Depression." *Journal of Monetary Economics* 2: 455–72.

———. 1977. "Anticipated Inflation and Unanticipated Price Change." *Journal of
Money, Credit and Banking* 9: 182–205.

Mishkin, F. S. 1978. "The Household Balance-Sheet and the Great Depression." *Journal of Economic History* 38: 918–37.

Mitchell, B. R. 1975. *European Historical Statistics, 1750–1970*. New York: Columbia
University Press.

Rees, A. 1972. "Real Wages and Inflation: Rejoinder." *Journal of Political Economy*
80: 192.

Sargent, T. J. 1976. "A Classical Macroeconometric Model for the United States."
Journal of Political Economy 84: 207–38.

Schwartz, A. J. 1981. "Understanding 1929–1933." In this volume.

Sims, C. A. 1972. "Money, Income, and Causality." *American Economic Review* 62:
540–52.

———. 1977. "Macroeconomics and Reality." Department of Economics, University
of Minnesota, Discussion Paper No. 77–91.

Stein, J. L. 1976. *Monetarism*. Amsterdam: North-Holland.

Temin, P. 1976. *Did Monetary Forces Cause the Great Depression?* New York:
W. W. Norton.

Tobin, J. 1975. "Keynesian Models of Recession and Depression." *American Economic Review* 65: 195–202.

U. S. Department of Commerce. 1976. *The National Income and Product Accounts*.
Washington, D.C.: Government Printing Office.

Weinstein, M. 1981. "Some Macroeconomic Impacts of the National Industrial Recovery Act, 1933–1935." In this volume.

3 NOTES ON THE CAUSES OF THE GREAT DEPRESSION

Peter Temin

However consistent may be the relation between monetary change and economic change, and however strong the evidence for the autonomy of the monetary changes, we shall not be persuaded that the monetary changes are the source of the economic changes unless we can specify in some detail the mechanism that connects the one with the other.

— Friedman and Schwartz (1963*b*, p. 59)

There are two issues at hand in the discussion of the causes of the Great Depression, one substantive and one methodological. The substantive issue is simple: Friedman and Schwartz asserted (1963*a*) that the banking panic of 1930 was a major—probably the major—factor in turning an ordinary depression into the Great Depression. I contested that view and asserted (1976) that the banking panic of 1930 was not a major deflationary shock to the economy.

This issue can be placed in its historical perspective. Everyone agrees that the economy began to decline in 1929, and everyone agrees that the Fed's response to the British sterling crisis in the fall of 1931 furthered the decline. The open issue concerns the two years between the fall of 1929 and the fall of 1931. Friedman and Schwartz argued that an additional, major deflationary shock occurred midway through that two-year period: the banking panic at the

108

end of 1930 decreased the money supply in a deflationary way. I argued that the initial shocks to the economy in 1929 were severe enough to explain the observed decline in 1930–31 and that the banking panic of 1930 did not deepen the depression in the critical two-year period.

The methodological issue follows naturally from this definition of the substantive one: how to choose between the two stories. In order to discriminate between the two accounts, and in sympathy with Friedman and Schwartz's view expressed in the epigraph, I examined the *mechanisms* by which the banking panic of 1930 might have acted. In addition to specifying mechanisms, I tried to see if they were operating in the early 1930s. The data for this exercise are embarrassingly simple. It is enough to note that real income, commodity prices, short-term interest rates, and the nominal money stock all fell between the fall of 1929 and the fall of 1931 while the real money stock rose.

Because there exists some confusion about this test, I will restate it here. It is hoped that this restatement will be clearer. I will use the familiar *IS–LM* model with an aggregate supply curve as my basic model. This is a static model, with all the defects of static models. I use it because it illuminates more clearly than dynamic models the short-run adjustment mechanism of the economy to various shocks and because it is, as well, more generally known than the dynamic models. I will discuss dynamic considerations at the relevant places in the argument.

The discussion has four parts. First, the two stories are told in the context of this simple formal model. Second, two tests of the alternative stories are carried out, one involving real balances and one involving different mechanisms by which monetary changes are communicated to the rest of the economy. Third, some implications of the models that figure in the discussion of the depression will be described. And finally, the argument here will be related to the conference papers by Schwartz and by Gordon and Wilcox.[1]

THE ALTERNATIVE MODELS

Figure 1 shows the curves for what I called the spending hypothesis in the two-year period from late 1929 to late 1931. In response to a downward shift of the *IS* curve, the economy has gone from A to C in the upper panel and from D to E in the lower.[2] Real income, prices, and interest rates are all lower after the shift than before. The transition path can be specified under the assumption that the money market returns to equilibrium rapidly enough after shocks to stay in or near equilibrium. The economy could not move from A to C immediately, despite the shift in the *IS* curve, so it moved down along the *LM* curve until it reached C. Income, prices, and interest rates declined contin-

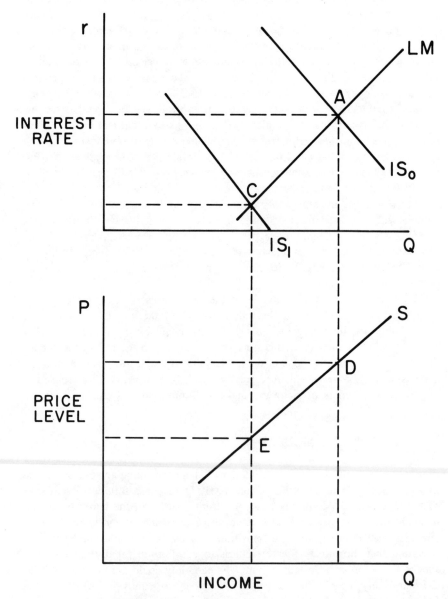

Figure 1. Spending Hypothesis Model

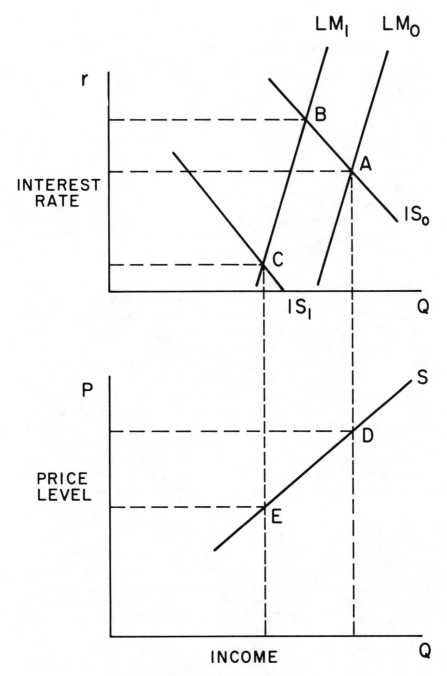

Figure 2. Money Hypothesis Model

uously in the course of this transition. The money market remained in equilibrium, and any excess supply of goods (as the *IS* curve shifted faster than the economy) was offset by an excess demand for (certain types of short-term) bonds.

Figure 2 shows the curves for what I called the money hypothesis in the same period. It is almost the same as figure 1. Points A, C, D, and E, as well as the *S*, IS_0, and IS_1 curves are the same. Only the *LM* curves are new. The *LM* curve is steeper in this figure, in keeping with the monetarist position that monetary shocks are more potent than fiscal, and it has shifted in the transition from A to C.

The money hypothesis goes like this: The *LM* curve shifted to the left, from LM_0 to LM_1 as a result of the banking panic. The economy moved from A to B by a path above IS_0, the distance between the economy's path and IS_0 being a function of the relative speed of adjustment of the money and goods markets. As the economy moved from A to B, it was also moving down along the supply curve, and the fall in prices created expectations of further deflation. As a result of these expectations, the real rate of interest rose relative to the nominal rate, causing the *IS* curve—which depends on the real rate—to fall as a function of the nominal interest rate. This is shown in figure 2 as a movement from IS_0 to IS_1, resulting in a further movement from B to C. As real income continued to fall, the economy continued to move down the supply curve in the bottom panel, ending up at E.

As the similarity between figures 1 and 2 suggests, the two stories are very close. They both involve movements along the aggregate supply curve and shifts of the *IS* curve. There are two important differences. First, the *LM* curve shifts only in the money hypothesis (figure 2). Second, while the *IS* curve shifts in both stories, in the money hypothesis it shifts only because of deflationary expectations initiated by the shift in the *LM* curve. Are these differences enough to allow the two stories to be tested against each other?

TESTS OF THE MODELS

Each difference suggests a test. First, the *LM* curve is drawn for a given supply of real balances. It shifts inward when the stock of real balances falls. But the stock of real balances rose during the critical two-year period under discussion from late 1929 to late 1930.[3] This suggests strongly that the *LM* curve did not shift inward.

The power of this test is diminished by the movement of prices during this period. Real balances rose because prices fell faster than the nominal money supply. While the static model shows an unchanged *LM* curve, keeping real balances constant by having both nominal money and prices fall can be deflationary through their effect on expectations. As noted above, deflationary expectations shift the *IS* curve (relative to nominal interest rates).

More importantly, a rise in real balances resulting from a fall in prices can be made consistent with both stories. In the spending hypothesis, real balances should have risen as the economy moved down the aggregate supply curve, so there is no inconsistency. The monetarist story relies on an initial fall in real balances (to shift the *LM* curve inward), but this could have been offset by an induced fall in prices if the aggregate supply curve were steep enough. If the deflation produced by the monetary stringency were fast enough, the result might be to increase real balances as income fell. The two stories consequently could end up at the same place; the only difference is at the beginning.

To use the path of real balances to test these two stories, therefore, attention has to be paid to the beginning of the process. Both stories are consistent with an eventual rise in real balances; only the money hypothesis implies an initial fall. It asserts that the banking panic in late 1930 was an important deflationary shock. The fall in real balances should have followed that panic. Yet real balances rose from the fourth quarter of 1930 (when the banking panic occurred) to the first quarter of 1931.[4] There is no evidence of a fall in real balances as a result of the banking panic of 1930. This test consequently rejects the monetary hypothesis.

It should not be surprising that the test involves only events immediately after the banking panic. Both stories were constructed to explain the same events, and they both consequently describe the same overall movements of the relevant variables. To find different implications of the two stories, we need to examine smaller movements in the variables that were not included among the "facts" to be explained.

In keeping with this view, the second test also involves the events surrounding the banking panic of 1930. The issue in this test is the *IS* curve. Unlike the first test, we are not asking whether a curve shifted; both stories assert that the *IS* curve did. Instead, the issue is *why* the *IS* curve shifted inward. And this issue can be clarified by returning to figures 1 and 2.

Both stories describe a movement from A to C and from D to E during 1930 and 1931. The money hypothesis argues that the *LM* curve shifted inward halfway through that period and was the cause of the decline in real income and prices thereafter. If we take points A and D to represent the economy on the eve of the banking panic in late 1930, we can describe the transition path from there to C and E in the two stories. The different transition paths can then be compared with the data to see which is a better summary of the facts.

The most important part of the transition for the present argument involves interest rates. The spending hypothesis argues that the nominal interest rate declined steadily. The money hypothesis argues that the nominal interest rate rose as the economy went from point A to point B in figure 2 before declining as the economy continued on to point C. In fact, the money hypothesis implies that the interest rate rose above point B, since the *IS* curve is almost completely inelastic in the very short run. The full impact of the shift in the *LM* curve was taken up by the interest rate in the first instance and only gradually shifted to income, according to the theory of how monetary shocks are transmitted to the rest of the economy.

There are many interest rates, and they moved in many contrary directions during the 1930–31 period. It seems clear, however, that short-term interest rates on safe securities are the appropriate rates, and they did not rise just following the banking panic of 1930.[5] So this test, too, rejects the money hypothesis.

While the interest rate is a primary means of communication between the monetary and real parts of the economy, it is not the only one. Other mechanisms by which monetary shocks are transmitted to the economy in general need to be considered as well. Two alternative channels can be found in the literature: the real-balance effect, and changes in expectations. For the purposes of discussion, the latter needs to be subdivided into perfect foresight and slowly adaptive expectations. These three possible channels, then, can be discussed in turn.

A decrease in real balances may affect spending behavior directly—without going through the financial markets—if the spending plans of individuals are affected by their holdings of real balances. In terms of figure 2, this argument says that the inward shift of the *LM* curve would be mirrored by a *simultaneous* inward shift of the *IS* curve. Equilibrium would be displaced directly from A to C. If the money market equilibrates much faster than the goods market, the economy might still pass through or close to point B on its way to C, since the equilibrium curves during the transition period would be IS_1 and LM_1. But if the goods market equilibrates relatively quickly, the rise in the interest rate might be avoided altogether.

However important this transmission mechanism may be in general, it is not relevant to the present discussion. As noted above, real balances did not fall immediately after the banking panic of 1930. This mechanism consequently could not have been activated.

Changes in the supply of money may also change expectations, and these changing expectations provide another channel by which monetary changes can affect the rest of the economy. Rapid changes in expectations may be grouped under the term perfect foresight and discussed first. If the people making spending decisions perceive and understand immediately the implications of monetary changes and incorporate them into their decisions, then there is no need for the communication from monetary to real markets to go through the markets for financial assets.

This observation does not advance the discussion very far, because the existence of perfect foresight—rapidly adjusting expectations—is inconsistent with figures 1 and 2 as drawn. The upward slope of the aggregate supply curve derives from the existence of sticky expectations. If people can foresee accurately the effects of monetary changes, then the long run collapses into the short run, and the aggregate supply curve is vertical. The depression could not have taken place in such a world, and we do not need to discuss it further.

Slowly adjusting expectations pose a different problem. If expectations change slowly, then the immediate adjustment to monetary contraction takes place with essentially fixed expectations. In other words, the arguments given above about the behavior of interest rates immediately after the monetary shock are still appropriate. The banking panic of 1930 may have changed expectations as 1931 unfolded, but there was no immediate deflationary pressure on the economy—as shown by the preceding arguments about interest rates.

In addition, if expectations were changing in the second half of 1930, this change must have come about as a result of earlier events. Since expectations changed slowly, the events that caused expectations to change in late 1930 must have come before that period. In short, if a change in expectations caused the *IS* curve to shift downward in late 1930, it was the result of events before and separate from the banking panic of 1930.

This discussion of expectations can be summarized briefly. Perfect foresight is irrelevant in an explanation of the depression because it is inconsistent with the occurrence of the depression. Sticky expectations do not affect the preceding arguments about interest rates for two reasons. First, the effects of the banking panic of 1930 on expectations would have been delayed by their stickiness, and they would have followed—as opposed to circumvented—the transmission mechanisms described above. Second, any change in expectations around the time of the banking panic of 1930 must have been the result of events prior to the banking panic, making them independent of the panic. The test incorporating adaptive expectations into the model again rejects the money hypothesis.

The history of this critical two-year period, therefore, may be given as follows. It was preceded and followed by deflationary shocks to the economy in which monetary conditions played a prominent part, as shown by the behavior of interest rates in mid-1929 and late 1931. But the neo-Keynesian story summarized by figure 1 describes the events between those shocks better than the monetarist story described in figure 2. The economy slid into its greatest depression without an additional effective monetary deflationary shock for two years after the stock market crash.

IMPLICATIONS

Three implications can be drawn from this story. I will discuss these briefly: the policy implications, the reasons for the shift in the *IS* curve shown in figure 1, and a counterfactual assertion about the banking panic.

The policy implications of the two stories are not very different. They both start from points C and E, differing only in the presumed slope of the *LM* curve. Whatever the slope of this curve, deflationary monetary policy would still be effective. Expansionary policy poses a more difficult problem. Given the low level of interest rates as the economy approached C, monetary expansion could easily have led to a disequilibrium situation with effectively zero nominal interest rates. The effectiveness of this policy would then have depended on the relative speeds with which the money and goods markets reached equilibrium. If the money market equilibrated faster than the goods market, expansionary monetary policy would have been effective. If not, as asserted in some versions of the real-balances communication mechanism, it would simply have created excess money balances.

Even among those investigators who agree that the downward shift of the *IS* curve was a critical part of the story in 1930–31, there is still disagreement over the reasons why it shifted. Several reasons have been offered. Consumption was unusually low in 1930, even after correcting for the fall in income. This can be related in large part to the fall in the stock market, both because of the effect of the stock market crash on wealth and its effect on the liquidity of consumers. The latter effect—in which the leverage of consumers is more important than their net asset position—appears to have been the most important (Mishkin 1978). In addition, expectations became more and more pessimistic starting in late 1930, whether originating from monetary or other causes. And problems in the housing and foreign exchange markets may have added to the decline (Gordon and Wilcox 1981). More work is needed to disentangle these varied influences.

Finally, there remains the question of what would have happened in the absence of the banking panic of 1930. Two possibilities can be envisaged. The stock of money decreased during 1930 in response to a decline in the quantity of money demanded, that is, to a movement along the demand curve for money. This process might have continued through 1931 as income fell and consumers moved further down along the demand curve for money. In this case, banks would have accumulated excess reserves as the economy declined. Alternatively, banks would have been able to extend loans at reasonable rates and the *LM* curve would have shifted outward. The effects of this would have been the same as those indicated under the description of expansionary monetary policy above. In the absence of banking panics, the money supply might have been larger by late 1931 and deflationary expectations might have been less pessimistic. The economy could have found itself with higher real income and higher prices on eve of Britain's abandonment of the gold standard in September 1931. The effect of these changes on the Fed's reaction to this event is hard to visualize. While the depression might have been moderated, it would not have been over in 1931.

A COMPARISON OF VIEWS

This discussion has shown that there is no substantive disagreement between Gordon and Wilcox (1981) and myself, despite the tone of their paper. As they asserted, addition of an aggregate supply curve to the standard *IS–LM* diagram clarifies the analysis. But, in contradiction to their assertions, it does not impugn the story I told.

In fact, Gordon and Wilcox reached almost precisely the conclusions that I did by entirely independent means. Lest this similarity of conclusions be obscured by the tone of their paper, let me quote a few sentences from it. They say, "Without a sudden and inexplicable shift from stable price expectations to expectations of deflation, the first three quarters of the contraction must be explained by a leftward shift in the *IS* curve due to a decline in autonomous spending" (p. 58). In other words, the spending hypothesis as shown in figure 1 is a better representation of the early stages of the depression than is the money hypothesis as shown in figure 2. They go on to say, "After 1931:2 a deflationary spiral began, in which deflationary expectations shifted down *IS*, while M_2 began falling more rapidly than prices, thus shifting the *LM* curve to the left as well" (pp. 58–59). In other words, the character of the depression began to change at the time of the European currency crisis in the summer of 1931. This is the story I told in my book.[6]

Gordon and Wilcox provide evidence for their story in the form of simulations from a simple model. Their conclusion is that the decline in the supply of money accounted for only one-fourth of the decline in income through the third quarter of 1931. Starting in the fourth quarter of 1931, monetary changes became much more important (p. 65, table 3), as everyone agrees. This evidence has a variety of problems and does not describe the mechanism by which monetary forces are supposed to act, so it is not to be regarded as conclusive. But it does show clearly the substantive agreement between Gordon and Wilcox and me. A decline in autonomous spending was the primary deflationary force before Britain left gold. That is the issue, not whether I fit into one or another of Gordon and Wilcox's ideological categories.

In fact, Gordon and Wilcox's attempt to type my views in terms of their categories is hopelessly confused. As noted above, and as Gordon and Wilcox themselves note in their paper (pp. 59, 71–72), questions of history and of policy are related but not identical. And the question at issue here is not whether expansionary monetary policies could have had an effect—proponents of both stories can agree that they could have, as noted above—but whether deflationary monetary events had an important contractionary impact before the European currency crisis in 1931. Gordon and Wilcox, however, ride roughshod over this distinction at various points in their argument, conveying the appearance of substantial disagreement between us.

For example, they say, "Temin's defense of view (d) collapses, however, if we can show that the decline in interest rates and increase in M_2/P during 1929–31 are logically consistent with a model in which nominal spending depends positively on nominal money" (p. 55). It is a misunderstanding of history to think that a historical statement can be refuted by showing that an alternate story is "logically consistent." The task of history is to explain the events that actually happened, to the extent that we can see clearly with hindsight, not to specify the range of what might conceivably have happened. In addition, Gordon and Wilcox have identified me with their hard-line position (d) by correctly quoting, but incorrectly emphasizing, an important concluding sentence from my book. A more accurate reading would be: "There is *no evidence* of any effective deflationary pressure from the banking system between the stock market crash in October, 1929 and the British abandonment of the gold standard in September, 1931" (Temin 1976, p. 169, emphasis added). That conclusion is reaffirmed both here and in Gordon and Wilcox's paper.

Schwartz's paper (1981) ranges over many issues of the interwar period. But the theory underlying most of the arguments and comments in it is articulated in the brief second section. Indeed, Schwartz claims that the "figure [in the second section] refutes the allegation that Temin makes that there is no evidence of monetary stringency in 1930 and 1931 before Britain abandoned gold" (p. 13). And much of the argument in the other sections of the paper is based on the second section as well.

Schwartz asserts in her second section that "the price of money is $1/P$, the inverse of the price level." While I asserted that monetary stringency would show up in credit markets, she asserts that monetary "stringency is reflected in a rise in the reciprocal of prices." As evidence, she presents a figure showing that "the reaction of prices to each monetary event [1919–39] is either observed in the coincident month or within five months of the event." And then she progresses to the statement quoted above to the effect that this figure refutes my conclusion that the banking panic of 1930 was not a major cause of the ensuing economic decline.[7]

Now this assertion of Schwartz's is very odd. Almost all macroeconomic theories that I know of assert that money and inflation are very closely related *in the long run*. But none that I know of claims that this relationship extends down the very short run. Yet fully one-third of the price reactions that Schwartz lists to her "monetary events" take place within a month of the event, and another one-third take place with a lag of only one month. Schwartz is trying to document a claim that does not arise from any well-known macroeconomic theory.[8]

It is universally agreed that changes in the quantity of money affect the real economy with a lag of half a year or more and that interest rates follow a well-defined path in the interim. One does not need to look to orthodox Keynesian sources to find this agreement. It is present in Friedman and Schwartz's work, in Cagan's, and elsewhere. It is worth quoting Friedman and Schwartz's own rationale for this position to show how well accepted it is:

> It seems plausible that both nonbank and bank holders of redundant balances will turn first to securities comparable to those they have sold, say, fixed interest coupon, low-risk obligations. But as they seek to purchase these they will tend to bid up the prices of those issues. . . .
>
> As the prices of financial assets are bid up, they become expensive relative to nonfinancial assets, so there is an incentive for individuals and enterprises to seek to bring their actual portfolios into accord with desired portfolios by acquiring nonfinancial assets. . . . The monetary stimulus is, in this way, spread from the financial markets to the markets for goods and services. [Friedman and Schwartz 1963b, pp. 60–61; see also Cagan 1972, pp. 1–5]

This view is repeated routinely in a recent monetarist macroeconomic text:

> A decrease in the rate of growth of the money supply at first causes the nominal and real interest rates to rise because of the liquidity effect. At approximately 6 months, the income effect becomes dominant and the interest rates begin to fall. [Darby 1976, p. 169]

There is a set of assumptions under which Schwartz's contention that changes in the rate of growth of money ("monetary events") are reflected immediately in prices. This happens when the economic actors have perfect foresight, that is, if expectations adjust *instantly* to the actual rate of inflation or deflation. But under these circumstances, there are no real effects of these monetary changes. Prices adjust immediately to any monetary changes, and no resources are reallocated. Schwartz, therefore, is on the horns of a dilemma. Either her contention is true only in the long run and not in the short run, in which case monetary changes are reflected in interest rates, or else her contention is true in the short run, but monetary changes have no real effects. In the first case, my test is an appropriate one. In the second case, monetary stringency could not have caused the depression.[9]

To summarize the argument so far, the view that interest rate changes are an integral part of the mechanism by which monetary changes are transmitted to the real economy is neither outmoded nor particular to a small group of current economists. This is not the same as saying that interest rates are a measure of monetary stringency. That view—which has many problems—is not germane to the discussion here. We need only that interest rates are a channel by which monetary stringency is communicated to the economy at large. Similarly, the question of whether excess money balances are spent initially only on financial assets—and whether deficient money balances are made up initially only from these assets as well—is not at issue here. For this historical discussion, we need only agree that deficient money balances are made up by sales of a variety of assets, among which financial assets are included.

So much for theory. Let me now demonstrate how Schwartz's adherence to an untenable theoretical position has led her astray on a variety of specific issues.

First, Schwartz attempted on the basis of an examination of price movements to refute my assertion that monetary stringency was absent through 1930 and most of 1931. It is hard to see how price movements can give any useful information on this issue. Given an upward sloping aggregate supply curve, a reduction of aggregate demand from any source would cause prices to fall. Looking at prices, therefore, cannot discriminate between different hypotheses about the cause of this fall in aggregate demand.

If the fall in the stock of money affected prices directly without going through the asset markets, then real output should have been unaffected. And if the fall in the stock of money caused real output to fall, then it must have affected interest rates along the way. On the assumption that we are trying to explain a fall in real output, interest rates rather than prices are the appropriate place to look. And as I said in my book, interest rate movements are inconsistent with Friedman and Schwartz's story.[10]

Second, Schwartz maintains that I was mistaken to assert that Friedman and Schwartz ignored the identification problem and assumed that the stock of money was determined by the supply alone. In her view, the money market is equilibrated by changes in the price level—that is, in commodity prices. The supply of money determines the nominal money stock, and the demand for real balances determines the price level. In her words, I "stress . . . the distinction between long run and short run, but this distinction is not highly relevant to the determination of the stock of money" (p. 28).

As the preceding review of the theory shows, however, the distinction between the long and short run is all important. Schwartz has described the process by which the money market finds its way to long-run equilibrium; she has ignored the short run entirely. And as noted above, the assumptions needed to collapse the long run into the short run imply that monetary changes have no real impact. Under more realistic assumptions, the money market equilibrates in the short run by means of interest rate changes.

I stated in my book (1976, p. 18) that Friedman and Schwartz had neglected the long run in their account of the money market. I now see that I was mistaken. They neglected the short run, instead. But in the explanation of a depression, the short run is what matters. Without a well-specified theory of the short run, no complete story of the depression can be constructed and no hypothesis about its cause can be tested.

Finally, Schwartz argues that the characteristics of the various markets for short-term financial securities in 1930 prevented the prices of these assets from responding to monetary stringency in the normal way. Before looking at the specific arguments, a problem with this train of thought needs to be noted. As noted above, interest rate movements are an essential part of the link between the monetary and the real parts of the economy. An argument that suggests a perverse movement of interest rates suggests also that this essential part of the transmission mechanism was not operative. In other words, if "other factors were simultaneously impinging on short-term rates," monetary changes might have been prevented from having their usual real consequences.

This general problem can be seen in Schwartz's discussion of the commercial paper market. She starts by noting that commercial paper was eligible for rediscount at the Fed. She then asserts that banks used commercial paper to acquire currency during the banking panic of 1930 by increasing the volume of them discounted at the Fed. "Instead of selling commercial paper" in response to deficient money balances, she says, "banks increased borrowings using commercial paper as collateral to meet depositors' demand for currency." This increased the demand for commercial paper, preventing the price from falling or the yields from rising in response to the banking panic. Schwartz concludes: "With limited supply and persistent demand, the failure of commercial paper rates to rise during the panic in no way contradicts the money hypothesis" (p. 32).

On the contrary, the failure of interest rates to rise in response to the banking panic of 1930 shows that the banking panics did not have the macroeconomic effects Friedman and Schwartz claimed for them. Any deficiencies in money balances were not communicated to the investing and consuming public and therefore could not affect spending plans. I suggested that the failure of short-term interest rates to rise reflected an absence of deficient money balances. Schwartz argues instead that this failure reflected the institutional nature of the commercial paper market. In either case, the failure of short-term interest rates to rise meant that spenders did not find themselves paying higher rates to borrow and spend.

Schwartz's argument actually goes further than mine. She suggests that the banking panic increased the demand for commercial paper. This must have tended to increase its price and reduce the cost of borrowing to its issuers. The banking panic therefore resulted in a perverse signal to corporate borrowers: borrowing became easier. Schwartz lists the textile, foodstuffs, metals, and leather industries as the main borrowers in this market. The market incentives for them to spend were increased by the banking panic, according to Schwartz's argument (pp. 31–32).

Commercial paper was not the main short-term financial instrument of the time; it was not even a very large one (Temin 1976, p. 122). What was happening in the other markets for short-term assets? Interest rates did not rise in those markets either, so there are two choices. Either institutional arrangements similar to the one in the commercial paper market resulted in perverse signals being given as a result of the banking panic, or else the demand for short-term funds was falling more rapidly than the supply. In either case, the reduction in the stock of money resulting from the banking panic of 1930 did not have the effect attributed to it by Friedman and Schwartz.

I think I have said enough to make the point. Schwartz and I are relying on very different macroeconomic theories, so the same facts communicate different messages to us. I have argued here that the theory I am using is the one common to our profession—it is the one used by Gordon and Wilcox—and that the one Schwartz is using lacks internal consistency. Consequently, I submit that my interpretation of the facts is to be preferred to hers.

This conclusion and the form of argument used to reach it bring us back to the methodological problem mentioned at the start of this discussion. Schwartz and I do not seem to have any common ground on which to discuss our historical stories. How can we talk about the historical facts when we perceive them so differently? How can we test hypotheses unless we agree on the mechanisms by which monetary forces affect aggregate demand? Phrased more generally, on the assumption that Schwartz and I are not terribly unusual supporters of our respective macroeconomic viewpoints, can the issue of the causes of the Great Depression be debated fruitfully at all?

NOTES

1. It was to be expected that a paper on the nonmonetary causes of the Great Depression by Anna Schwartz might be hostile, but it is hard to see why a paper on the monetarist interpretations

of the Great Depression should also be hostile to my writings, particularly since (as I will show later) the authors appear to agree with my conclusions. In the absence of an explanation, I will set the tone of these papers aside and respond to their economic content.

2. This exposition is patterned after Gordon and Wilcox's. The addition of aggregate supply and demand curves extends the reach of the formal model, but it does not refute the implications of my earlier discussion based on the *IS–LM* curves alone, as the present discussion shows.

3. See Gordon and Wilcox (1981, p. 56) for quarterly estimates of M_2/P.

4. Ibid.

5. Schwartz (1981, p. 37) agrees with the use of short-term interest rates for this test, while disagreeing with the result.

6. It is also the story alluded to briefly by Hicks (1974) in a single paragraph in a lecture, although Hicks is vague on the events before 1931. Gordon and Wilcox consistently refer to this story as the Hicks story, rather than the Temin story, when indicating their agreement with it.

7. The precise definition of the price response is not given, so it is hard to evaluate the accompanying graph (pp. 12–16).

8. It is worth noting in passing that three of Schwartz's "monetary events" involve changes in interest rates, while a fourth consists of movements of stock prices. As I will state in some detail shortly, everyone agrees that spending and therefore prices (particularly wholesale prices as used in Schwartz's graph) should respond to changes in interest rates. But almost everyone would agree that changes in interest rates are not the same as changes in the quantity of money. Schwartz blurs this distinction in her chart, creating doubt about what constitutes a "monetary event" and what her theory is.

9. There is one other set of assumptions that would lead to a change in the rate of money growth to be reflected in commodity prices without affecting the price of financial assets, although it is hardly important enough to list. If money and financial assets are not even partial substitutes—that is, if the demands for money and for financial assets are completely independent of one another—then none of the deficient money balances attendant upon a slowdown of monetary growth will be made up by sales of financial assets. People will sell goods, prices will fall, and market interest rates will be unaffected. But this view clearly is not to be taken seriously. It flies in the face of all the empirical information about the demand for money and other financial assets, and it undermines the foundations of the modern theory of finance.

10. I have made the assumption that we are all trying to explain the same events, but one paragraph in Schwartz's paper has made me question even that. She states, "It is difficult to understand how the experience of 1929–33 could have spawned the notion of the need for the replacement of the classical assumption of a price adjustment by a quantity-adjustment system of movement toward equilibrium." Schwartz's confusion is itself difficult to understand; surely the depression was traumatic enough to shake the very foundations of any theory that denied it could have happened. But to the extent that Schwartz is relying on a consistent macroeconomic theory, she uses the classical model of complete and instantaneous price adjustment, which implicitly denies the possibility of depressions. Has this theoretical position led her to deny the existence of the very events we are trying to explain?

REFERENCES

Cagan, P. 1972. *The Channels of Monetary Effects on Interest Rates*. New York: Columbia University Press, for the National Bureau of Economic Research.

Darby, M. R. 1976. *Macroeconomics*. New York: McGraw-Hill.

Friedman, M., and Schwartz, A. J. 1963a. *A Monetary History of the United States, 1867–1960*. Princeton, N.J.: Princeton University Press, for the National Bureau of Economic Research.

————. 1963b. "Money and Business Cycles." *Review of Economics and Statistics* 45: 32–78.

Gordon, R. J., and Wilcox, J. A. 1981. "Monetarist Interpretations of the Great Depression: An Evaluation and Critique." In this volume.

Hicks, J. 1974. "Real and Monetary Factors in Economic Fluctuations." *Scottish Journal of Political Economy* 21: 205–14.

Mishkin, F. S. 1978. "The Household Balance Sheet and the Great Depression." *Journal of Economic History* 38.

Schwartz, A. J. 1981. "Understanding 1929–1933." In this volume.

Temin, P. 1976. *Did Monetary Forces Cause the Great Depression?* New York: W. W. Norton.

4 COMMENTS ON "UNDERSTANDING 1929-1933"

Peter H. Lindert

The subject matter of "Understanding 1929-1933" is compelling, and its authorship is promising. Explaining the onset, the severity, and the duration of the Great Depression is almost as central a task to macroeconomics as is the study of viral epidemics to medicine. It is promising to find these issues addressed again by Dr. Schwartz, who has helped to combine imagination with the finest NBER standards of documentation in past landmarks on the growth and fluctuations of the British economy and the monetary history of the United States.

Yet I found as much disappointment as reward in the present paper. I shall take up five main aspects of the paper, starting with what I liked least and building from there.

THE TONE

The title promises an exploration of issues, but it is followed by a rambling series of swipes at critics. Half the paper's energy is spent sneering at Peter

Temin's recent book (1976), perhaps in pursuit of partisan cheers. Consider this passage:

> Temin's analytical structure is a throwback to the Keynesian position of the quarter century after 1933. It has no theoretical explanation of the price level. It makes no distinction between nominal and real magnitudes. It presumes that no evidence exists on the relation of monetary change to income change. It ignores recent theoretical developments. [P. 25]

This prose is not justified by either the tone or the substance of Temin's book, though Temin did at times misrepresent the earlier position of Friedman and Schwartz. Some might argue that it advances the debate. Perhaps the sight of bludgeons and blood draws a wider audience to watch and fund scholarly debates. But such prose inevitably ties up our resources in repeating what we really said 15 years ago and finding yet another minor miscue in what our opponents said. Enough.

MONEY, INCOME, AND GRANGER CAUSALITY

Dr. Schwartz breaks new ground by offering an interwar test of causal priority between money and nominal income in order to buttress a monetarist interpretation of the Great Slump of 1929–33. Yet her present Granger causality tests add little, in my view, for two reasons.

The less serious difficulty with these tests is that they came out strongly her way only when she used bank debits to deposit accounts outside New York City as a proxy for monthly nominal income. She defended the crucial proxy in a strange way. I had expected a demonstration of how well monthly outside debits predicted monthly personal income after 1929, when the personal income series starts.[1] Instead, she cites a 1959 study by George Garvy as proof that monthly outside debits neatly match monthly national income and product.

Garvy applied two kinds of tests. First, a comparison of rates of change between periods of one year or longer did show an excellent correlation between changes in outside debits and changes in GNP (1959, p. 76). But to debate the causes of the 1929–33 slump, Dr. Schwartz needs monthly data. Garvy's second test did compare turning points in outside debits with NBER reference cycles. He concluded:

> For the period between the world wars, Table 9 shows clearly that any reliance placed on outside debits as a single-variable indicator of business would not yield a satisfactory monthly chronology of cyclical movements of aggregate business. [P. 87]

The fit was especially bad for the 1920s. There is the danger, then, that Dr. Schwartz's 1919–39 Granger tests, far from cutting the Gordian knot of money-income causality, only mirror ordinary banking mechanics. They may only show that soon after the money stock is raised by new bank lending, borrowers write checks on their new accounts.

Proxies aside, a more serious doubt is whether the Granger testing mode can resolve the questions that divide scholars of the depression era. While debating other things, most of us would agree that the money stock and income are both endogenous variables, each partly affected by the other in a structural relationship involving other variables as well. Provoked by Temin's (1976, pp. 14, 27) apparent misrepresentation of the Friedman-Schwartz position on this point, Schwartz rightly repeats that this is their view (though the language of her conclusions on causality reverts to the word *unidirectional*). If I have read Temin correctly, he agrees and wishes to explore which *exogenous* variables— Fed policy, or immigration laws, or foreign events, or Wall Street disorders— set both money and income spiraling downward. I agree, too. But if the frontiers of our consensus lie well beyond the money-income nexus, little is gained by a causality test restricted to money and income. We must all await the arrival of a better methodology for choosing among complicated hypotheses about economic structure.

WHAT IS THE PRICE OF MONEY?

Schwartz, like Temin before her, tries to get further clues about the forces cutting the nominal money stock by using a simple price-quantity test. If the price and quantity of money moved in the same direction, it is a fair guess that shifts in the demand curve were larger than supply shifts, though both may have occurred. If they moved in opposite directions, then it is a fair guess that shifts in supply were greater, though again both curves may have shifted.

Temin's variant defines the prices of money as equivalent to the inverse of the unit price of liquid bonds and bills, or one plus the short-term interest rate. On this measure the relative price of money, we well as the nominal money stock, fell between July of 1929 and the first banking crisis of October 1930. This suggests to Temin that the dominant shift involved a drop in the quantity of money demanded at any given interest rate.

Schwartz rightly regards Temin's interest-rate measure as too narrow to be "the price of money." The interest rates on high quality bills and bonds are affected by movements between these instruments and other assets and commodities besides money. There seems to have been a shift from other nonmoney assets into liquid bills and bonds in the 12 months after the Wall

Street crash. Both Schwartz's appendix and Temin's chapter 4 support this conclusion, though they have preferred different labels for the same behavior. The point remains that short term interest rates do not reflect monetary stringency so well in 1930 as in the standard *IS–LM* model.

Schwartz embarks on her own quest for the price of money by inverting the wholesale price index. Comparing its movement to the nominal money stock gives a clear answer: price of money up, quantity down; ergo, supply restriction dominated, and the Fed is to blame.

Two worries remain about her use of the amended price and nominal quantity of money. The first relates to the narrower task she has set herself, namely, the measurement of the price of money. If money is an alternative to more than bonds, it is also an alternative to more than currently produced goods. Just as Friedman's restatement of the quantity theory has made the demand for cash depend on all sorts of prices and returns, so the best "price of money" measure should also reflect all alternatives to money. The usual rules of the price-index game suggest a transactions-weighted average of the nominal price relatives for *all* nonmoney assets, goods, and services as the inverse of the price of money.

If someone were to go to the trouble of calculating such a transactions-weighted index, it would slightly modify the Schwartz view of monetary stringency in the crucial early-slump period, July 1929–October 1930. The prices of most interest-bearing assets rose slightly. On the other hand, the prices of common stocks and farm land fell much faster than the usual commodity price indices (yes, Virginia, there was a Wall Street crash even in real terms, and the shareholders who committed suicide suffered from more than just money illusion). The net result would come out slightly in Schwartz's favor, with the overall price of money still rising while the nominal money stock fell.[2]

A second worry about the simple price-quantity tests is more serious. When the two sides of a market respond to different price and quantity variables, it is arbitrary and dangerous to select one set of definitions of price and quantity and to try to identify shifts in behavior from changes in this price and this quantity.[3] One way to see this arbitrariness is to ask: Should we be discussing the real or the nominal price and quantity of money? Presumably we should focus on either real magnitudes or nominal magnitudes for both price and quantity in order to sustain the analogy to a simple demand-supply diagram. Yet most of us, including Friedman and Schwartz, focus on the nominal money stock in judging the Fed but on the real money stock in discussing the demand for money. For all the interest in the demand for money, nobody has empirically measured the real price of money that accompanies the real money stock. If this were measured, the results would be murky. In the Great Slump the "real" price of money (using the GNP goods and services as the numeraire) fell slightly (i.e., nonmoney assets on the whole fell less in nominal price than did nominal commodity prices) while the real money stock remained essentially unchanged.

There is thus a basic ambiguity in the simple price-quantity testing mode used by both Temin and Schwartz. In 1929–30 or 1929–33, the supply curve for nominal money shifted to the left, à la Schwartz, but the supply curve for real money, the curve supposedly seen by the demanders of real cash, did not. Here again, as with Granger causality, a laudable search for a simple decisive test has not panned out. This is a shame, partly because the arguments on both sides are plausible. I share Temin's view that a *proximate* cause of the onset of the Great Depression in 1929–30 was a large shift from demanding goods and services (and equities) toward demanding liquid (especially nonmoney) assets, but his frequent discussion of a demand-side shift in the money market confuses things.[4] For her part, Schwartz tries to gather support for the plausible Friedman-Schwartz policy counterfactual that more nominal reserves could have made the difference in 1930 and 1931 with a side trip into the murky area of measuring a single price for money, but she ends up adding to the confusion.

THE BILLION-DOLLAR PRESCRIPTION

These worries about some current tests should not obscure a basic contribution of the *Monetary History* that transcends any of the tests offered by Temin or Schwartz. I refer to the Friedman-Schwartz indictment of Fed policy in 1930 and 1931, after the slump had progressed. They have carefully spelled out three billion-dollar missed opportunities. First in January–October 1930, then in January–August 1931, and finally in September 1931–January 1932, the Federal Reserve could have arrested or even eliminated the decline in the money supply and, less directly, GNP by pumping an extra billion dollars of reserves into the banking system. The argument is well structured: the counterfactual is made very explicit; the policy prescription is appropriate to the banking sector, whose breakdown profoundly shocked the public; and Friedman and Schwartz follow up with sound arguments about the free-gold excuse and other explanations of why the Fed decided against more monetary expansion (1963, pp. 391–419).

To this argument well put, I would add only two additional reasons for accepting it. One is that one must adopt an extreme position indeed to deny that some strong dosage of extra reserves from the Fed could not have checked much or all of the slump. One would have to argue first that extra reserves could not have kept banks from closing—or that bank failures did not feed loss of confidence, decline in aggregate demand, and flight from the dollar. This is untenable, whatever one's view of the prior events triggering the bank failures. If it is conceded that extra reserves would have propped up the money stock, a gainsayer would then have to argue that the extra money stock would have no effect whatsoever on aggregate demand. The extensive empirical literature on the money-income relationship precludes this extreme view.[5] And once one concedes that extra reserves and money have some significant effect on aggregate, the debate is largely over: for any given desired effect on GNP, there must be *some* dosage of extra reserves, if not one billion dollars exactly, that would have done the job.

A second support for the Friedman-Schwartz monetary prescription should be accepted by anybody believing that *fiscal* policy matters. Both Keynesians and conservatives would agree that a sudden tax hike like the Revenue Act of 1932 should have reduced GNP—the Keynesians because the tax hike should have cut aggregate demand, and the conservatives because higher tax rates should have stifled initiative and cut aggregate supply. What has not been appreciated is that the dreaded tax increases of 1932 were largely a response to the bank failures and thus to the prior failure of monetary policy.

Neither President Hoover nor the Democratic majority in Congress found it easy to advocate higher tax rates when business was depressed. Both had to be forced into supporting tax increases by the severity of the banking crisis. Hoover said as much in his State of the Union address on December 8, 1931:

> Whatever the causes may be, the vast liquidation and readjustments which have taken place have left us with a large degree of credit paralysis, which together with the situation in our railroads and the conditions abroad, are now the outstanding obstacles to recovery. . . . Many of our bankers, in order to prepare themselves to meet possible withdrawals, have felt compelled to call in loans, to refuse new credits, and to realize upon securities, which in turn has demoralized the markets. . . .
>
> Our first step toward recovery is to reestablish confidence and thus restore the flow of credit which is the very basis of our economic life.
>
> The first requirement of confidence and of economic recovery is financial stability of the United States Government.
>
> Even with increased taxation, the government will reach the utmost safe limit of its borrowing capacity by the expenditures for which we are already obligated and the recommendations here proposed. . . . [Cited in Stein 1969, pp. 33–34]

The initial reaction of most Congressmen was to back the tax hikes in principle but to try to avoid voting for any of several increases that would be most unpopular with their constituents. The resulting stall in Congress was broken by "Cactus Jack" Garner, Speaker of the House, in the spring of 1932. Giving up the speaker's gavel and descending into the well of the House, he made an eloquent plea for fiscal responsibility:

> I think more of my country than I do of any theory of taxation that I may have, and the country is in a condition where the worst taxes you could possibly levy would be better than no taxes at all. . . . It is your duty, your paramount duty, to restore some taxes to this bill in order that the country's financial integrity may be maintained. . . . I believe that if this Congress today should decline to levy a tax bill there would not be a bank in the United States in existence in sixty days that could meet its depositors. [Cited in Paul 1954, p. 155]

Garner successfully forced the entire House to stand and be counted as in favor of balancing the budget with higher taxes. That day a third of the ultimate tax increases were restored to the Revenue Act of 1932. Such was the power of bank failures and related signs of monetary breakdown over fiscal policy at the time. This must be reckoned as part of the contractionary impact of the Fed's failure to expand bank reserves in 1930 and 1931.

THE SEARCH FOR ORIGINAL SIN, 1928–29

Schwartz has made a bold new departure on an issue that Temin has so insistently emphasized: What explains the *onset* of the Great Depression? Why was policy after Wall Street faced with such a tough test, a test it failed? Her present paper makes it clear that she considers tight money between April 1928 and late 1929 to have been the main culprit. The *Monetary History* had not stated things so forcefully. It had followed what looked like the start of a monetarist *coda*—

> the contraction is in fact a tragic testimonial to the importance of monetary forces

—with a striking disclaimer:

> True, as events unfolded, the decline in the stock of money and the near-collapse of the banking system can be regarded as a consequence of nonmonetary forces in the United States, and monetary and nonmonetary forces in the rest of the world. [1963, pp. 300, 301]

This passage had always struck me as evidence that Friedman and Schwartz felt more agnostic and less enthused about explanations of the onset of the depression than they were about indicting the Fed for not arresting it. The Schwartz paper now reveals her firmer belief that the failure of the Fed to allow the money stock to grow after April 1928 really accounts for much of the severity of the test put to the Fed in 1930 and 1931.

This provocative hypothesis is most welcome, and I cannot regard it as easily refuted. It does put a disturbing story before us, though. In 1928–29 the Fed did commit the sin of tightening the money supply more than was usual in booms, but it did so only moderately and gradually. The money stock did not actually decline but grew slightly from the December 1926 trough. Schwartz could argue that this was sin enough. Yet at the same time she has argued that the private economy was able to adjust well enough to the absolute contraction of the money supply in the wake of the crash in 1929–30:

> Along rational-expectations lines, however, employers and workers will in time revise their anticipations in accordance with the change in opportunities. If the Federal Reserve had maintained the initial moderate rate of decline in the money stock, presumably the economy after a time would have adjusted to this condition. But this is not what happened. The screw was tightened again and again. . . . [1981, p. 26]

She further cites with approval Gerald Sirkin's recent article (1975) arguing that the Wall Street bulls were not crazy and that the bears in the crash were only adjusting rationally to a change in information. It is hard to see how the private economy adjusts with such explosive (rational) response to the lesser provocation of tight money in 1928–29 yet is capable of rolling readjustment to the stiffer blows of 1929–30.

I see some conflict between the monetarist view that the slight extra tightness of monetary policy in 1928–29 triggered so severe a slump and the conservative view that the private economy adjusts smoothly to changing conditions. Given the facts of 1929–33, it is hard to have it both ways.

NOTES

1. In postconference correspondence, Dr. Schwartz informed me that there is a very high correlation between monthly personal income and monthly outside bank debits for 1929–39, without lags and with or without removal of long trends. This would seem to make the proxy a good one for 1929–39. There remain the bothersome points (1) that personal income, to which bank debits are now tied for 1929–39, did not reveal clear unidirectional influences from money to income for this period and (2) that the clearer-looking unidirectionality of 1919–39 needs cautious interpretation in view of the questions about cyclical correspondence between outside debits and personal income mentioned in the text here.

2. The same result would obtain even if one departed from Schwartz's focus on the nominal instantaneous purchase price of money and substituted the nominal price of the holding of money over time. To calculate the overall price of the use of money over time, one should mark up real asset prices by their rate of inflation over the relevant time period—the expected rate of inflation if one wants the expected price of money, and the actual rate if one wants the actual price. Since these asset prices were dropping faster in the slump than in mid-1929, the actual nominal price of the use of money had a steeper trend if this adjustment is made. It is not clear whether changing to

this use-of-money measure would alter the text's conclusion that the *real* price of money did not rise.

3. A similar ambiguity plagues the analysis of labor markets, where employers watch the pre-tax wage deflated by the price of their own products and prospective employees watch the after-tax wage deflated by consumer prices. When the earnings tax rate shifts, or the ratio of industry prices to the cost of living shifts, whether supply shifted or demand shifted again depends on which price one puts on the axis.

4. Temin's discussion of the market for money may have invited the view that he was trying to document an initial behavorial shift in the money-demand function, a Walrasian shift away from money toward bonds. As I read his book, however, his "spending hypothesis" pivots on an initial shift away from goods and services, principally toward liquid bonds, which sets in motion a (non-Walrasian) downward spiral in income and in the quantities of goods and money demanded, without his having posited any shift in the money-demand function.

5. The present argument is not undermined by the fact that the United States was an open economy in the 1930s. By checking bank failures, extra reserves would have had some tendency to keep down capital outflows, thus offsetting some of the usual response to lower interest rates. It also seems unlikely that international capital flows were so interest-elastic (even apart from bank-failure effects) that any attempt to expand the money supply would have been frustrated with fixed exchange rates. Finally, the United States had sufficient free gold reserves to ride out a considerable gold outflow, buying enough time so that the public could later accept a switch to gold embargoes and floating exchange rates as a reasonable response to international crisis in a U.S. economy where banks were not failing.

REFERENCES

Friedman, M., and Schwartz, A. J. 1963. *A Monetary History of the United States, 1867-1960*. Princeton, N.J.: Princeton University Press, for the National Bureau of Economic Research.

Garvy, G. 1959. *Debits and Clearings Statistics and Their Use*. Rev. ed. Washington, D.C.: Federal Reserve Board of Governors.

Paul, R. E. 1954. *A History of Taxation in the United States*. Boston: Little, Brown.

Schwartz, A. J. 1981. "Understanding 1929-1933." In this volume.

Sirkin, G. 1975. "The Stock Market of 1929 Revisited: A Note." *Business History Review* 49: 223-31.

Stein, H. 1969. *The Fiscal Revolution in America*. Chicago: University of Chicago Press.

Temin, P. 1976. *Did Monetary Forces Cause the Great Depression?* New York: W. W. Norton.

5 COMMENTS ON "MONETARIST INTERPRETATIONS OF THE GREAT DEPRESSION"
James R. Lothian

As an agenda for research, Gordon and Wilcox's is a good one. Many of the topics they cover fall into areas in which I believe further work on the depression is particularly needed. Reading through the initial draft and listening to their conference presentation, I found myself in substantial agreement with many of their observations. There is, however, something disturbing about the paper—both in substance and in tone.

They begin with an excursion into the history of economic thought, discussing various views of what caused the depression before focusing on one—the recent contribution of Peter Temin—and analyzing it in more depth. They then turn to several empirical issues: the relationship of nominal income to money, the behavior of prices and real output and the role of nonmonetary factors in the depression. The first two they investigate econometrically with data for both the United States and six European countries in aggregate; the last they deal with more discursively.

I would like to thank Ramachandra Bhagavatula, Phillip Cagan, Michael R. Darby, Arthur E. Gandolfi, Robert J. Gordon, and Anna J. Schwartz for their helpful discussions in the course of preparing this paper. Donna Bettini, Richard Burrell, Edward Colby, Charles Wainhouse, and Carol Williams also provided comments and assistance at various stages, for which I am grateful.

The problem is that, after all of this material, I was not sure exactly what to conclude. Gordon and Wilcox provide a final summing up, but the words they use to describe their results are not the words I would have used. For one thing, I find the underlying perspective of their paper—their attempt to give it doctrinal roots—both misleading and distracting. More important, in many instances I would interpret many of their actual empirical findings quite differently from the way they do. In others, in which I agree with their interpretations, I would have emphasized the results to a much greater extent than others that they regard as significant.

VIEWS OF THE DEPRESSION

To set the stage for their subsequent examination of the data, Gordon and Wilcox (1981) review various explanations of what caused the depression. Like Gaul, these are divided into parts; Gordon and Wilcox list four: hard-line monetarist, soft-line monetarist, soft-line nonmonetarist, and hard-line nonmonetarist. They place Anna Schwartz's paper in this volume in the first set, Milton Friedman and Anna Schwartz (1963a) in the second, Ben Bolch and John Pilgrim in the third, and Peter Temin in the fourth.

At first glance, Gordon and Wilcox's broader taxonomy appears as if it will free their analysis from the constricting effects of Temin's framework of "spending hypothesis" versus straw-man "money hypothesis."[1] In actuality, it suffers from many of the same problems. "The real question," they say, at the end of their doctrinal discussions, "is whether either extreme view [Schwartz's or Temin's] . . . can be excluded" (p. 54). But that is just replaying Temin's game, with slightly different sides. Schwartz alone now fills in for Friedman and her together, and Temin proxies for the rest of those espousing the spending hypothesis. Not only is this misleading in and of itself—Schwartz's position in the current paper hardly differs from, and certainly does not conflict with, that of the *Monetary History*; it is also symptomatic of the broader and no more accurate revisionist interpretation of economic thought that permeates their whole discussion.[2]

To illustrate what I mean, let us consider Gordon and Wilcox's reasons for focusing on the so-called extreme views. Their justification is that, since the soft-line monetarist and soft-line nonmonetarist views "differ only in emphasis, it is impossible to distinguish their validity with any degree of precision" (p. 54). What's wrong here is that degree of emphasis does matter. There's a fundamental difference between a view that money was the prime mover in the depression, that in the absence of its unprecedented decline the depression would have been severe but not great, and a view that, to use Gordon and Wilcox's terminology, "does not deny a role for monetary factors" (p. 53).

In the first instance, money is the critical—but not the only—factor in explaining the differences among depressions. In the second, it plays at most a minor part. And that's a good deal closer to Temin than to Friedman and Schwartz. About the only thing Friedman and Schwartz's position has in common with the soft-line nonmonetarist view that Gordon and Wilcox describe is explicit acknowledgment of the world's complexity, which is a rather weak bond.

GORDON AND WILCOX ON TEMIN

As evidence that changes in the supply of money were an unimportant factor in the early part of the cyclical decline, Temin had cited the failure of interest rates to rise or of real balances to fall in 1930, neither of which he could reconcile with a decline in the supply of money in the context of a simple *IS–LM* model. Gordon and Wilcox raise two objections to this analysis.

Consider a fall in autonomous expenditures, they say. Interest rates will fall; nominal aggregate demand, and along with it, prices and output, will fall. With a given nominal stock of money, real balances will rise. In such an environment, money still could have an influence on economic conditions without interest rates rising or real balances falling relative to their initial levels. The effect of a decrease in the nominal stock of money on both variables could have been more than counterbalanced by the prior effects of the decrease in autonomous expenditures.

Their second objection is that Temin's analysis takes no account of price expectations. Nominal interest rates would fall with expectations of deflation. A reduction in the nominal stock of money (or its rate of growth) then would cause real interest rates to rise temporarily. But given the expected negative rate of change of prices, nominal rates could still end up being below their initial levels.

Having levied this second objection, however, they dismiss its empirical importance. As evidence against it, they cite the low actual rate of price deflation—by their calculations, a 1.8 percent fall in the GNP deflator between 1929:3 and 1930:2—and the relative stability of prices from 1921:3 on. That leaves their first scenario, 1a decline in money preceded by an actual decline in autonomous expenditures, as the only way for money to have played an active role in 1930.

These two scenarios do not, however, exhaust the possibilities. As Arthur Gandolfi and I have pointed out (1977), interest rates tend to fall at some point during recessions for reasons other than expectations of deflation alone. There is also an income effect of a reduction in monetary growth, something the conventional *IS–LM* apparatus is not really equipped to handle.

After the waning of the initial upward effect on interest rates of a decrease in monetary growth, rates begin to fall in response to the fall in real income and in credit demand. Then, temporarily, they drop below their initial levels. In this scenario, a further monetary decline would cause interest rates to rise somewhat, but not necessarily to their initial levels or above. The point is, then, that in the realm of logical possibility, autonomous expenditures or money, or both, could have been important in 1929. To argue that money was important a year later—the period of dispute for Temin—does not preclude its having been a causative factor earlier.

On the question of price expectations, I am considerably less willing than Gordon and Wilcox to say anything very categorical. I do not think we really know enough about how expectations are formed to rule out a negative price-expectations effect. After all, prices were declining, only slightly when measured by the deflator, but by a good deal more—9.2 percent from 1929 to 1930—when measured by the WPI.

Furthermore, why should people's horizons only extend back to 1921:2? Why not 1920 or even 1902? Both would surely give us much bigger numbers for the range of rates of change of prices, and the periods seem no less arbitrary. Or, why wouldn't some Americans have looked abroad? Britain experienced substantial deflation in the 1920s. There must have been some tendency here to extrapolate on the basis of that experience or on the basis of movements in underlying U.S. variables.

MONEY AND INCOME

In their analysis of the actual effects of money in the depression, Gordon and Wilcox run a series of quarterly regressions for various periods in the interval 1920:2–1941:4 in which a proxy for nominal income alternates with M_1 or M_2 as the dependent variable and in which contemporaneous and lagged values of both income and the relevant monetary measure are the independent variables. They run these regressions in both level and rate-of-change form and use them to perform tests of causation of the Granger-Sims variety. The results that emerge from this part of the analysis are similar to those reported by Schwartz:

no evidence of reverse causation from income to money, other than contemporaneous correlation, and ample evidence of direct causation from money to income.

To investigate the contemporaneous correlation further, they conduct a similar exercise for the period 1929–41, with monthly industrial production and an index of department store sales used as income variables and M_2 as the monetary variable. The results are qualitatively the same as for the quarterly data. Their overall conclusions are that the data clearly do not support Temin's hypothesis but that "proponents of the middle-ground views . . . can feel comfortable with an instantaneous feedback from income to money" (p. 62).

Their next step is to use the quarterly nominal-income-to-nominal-M_2 regression, estimated in level form for various subperiods in the interwar years, in a series of postsample dynamic simulations. Their conclusion is that something is awry: the 1920–28 regressions fail to account adequately for the fall in nominal income from 1929 to 1931; the lag period appears to shorten as the 1930s proceed; and the 1920–36 regression underestimates the rise in nominal income after 1938.

I find the results of the Granger-Sims tests surprising. In a period as turbulent as the depression, I would have expected to see more reverse causation than shows up in their tests—or, put better, reverse causation showing up over a longer time period. That it does not may in part, however, be a reflection of the data they use. They are all that are available, but given their quality—the interpolated nature of the income series, in particular—fine distinctions of the type Gordon and Wilcox want to make may be impossible.

The same problem—trying to get too much out of too little—plagues their simulations. They use a quarterly nominal-income series that contains the same flaws as the real series to estimate a very simple relationship over a short sample period encompassing only one major and two minor cyclical contractions and then go on to make strong inferences from the simulation errors from that equation during the most severe depression in over a century. I just do not know what to make of the results of that kind of exercise. More evidence would be needed to make them at all convincing.

One procedure would be to reestimate their equation over a more reasonable sample period, one containing more information about the cyclical relationship between money and income. I have done this using annual data for the period 1893–1928. The estimates of equations in both logarithmic level and first-difference forms are contained in the top half of table 1. In the bottom half, I have reproduced an abbreviated version of the table Gordon and Wilcox use in analyzing the forecast errors from their equation, along with a similar table derived from my level equation.

Table 1.   Money and Nominal Income in the Great Depression: A Comparison with Gordon and Wilcox's Simulation Results

Nominal Income Regressions (1893–1928)

Type of Equation (Lothian)	Intercept	M_t	M_{t-1}	M_{t-2}	M_{t-3}	Time	R^2/SEE	D-W
			Coefficients of[a]					
log	+0.952	+1.161	+0.217	−0.263	+0.101	−0.026	0.993	0.96
	(5.979)	(5.165)	(0.733)	(0.906)	(0.500)	(2.066)	0.61	
Δlog	−0.017	+1.178	+0.205	−0.238	−0.053		0.620	2.60
	(0.766)	(6.537)	(1.125)	(1.312)	(0.296)		0.059	

Simulation Results

Equation[b]	Date	Y_t (1)	$\hat{Y}_t$ (2)	ΔY_t (3)	$\Delta\hat{Y}_t$ (4)	$\Sigma\Delta Y_t$ (5)	$\Sigma\Delta\hat{Y}_t$ (6)	(6)/(5) (7)
				Variables[c]				
G-W	1929:3	106.0	98.8	—	—	—	—	—
	1930:2–1930:3	91.3	96.2	−14.7	− 2.6	−14.7	− 2.6	0.18
	1931:2–1931:3	79.5	92.0	−11.8	− 4.2	−26.5	− 6.8	0.26
	1932:2–1932:3	57.2	70.9	−22.3	−21.1	−48.8	−27.9	0.57
	1933:2–1933:3	58.5	71.0	+ 1.3	+ 0.1	−47.5	−27.8	0.59
log (Lothian)	1929	105.8	96.0	+ 6.4	− 1.8	—	—	—
	1930	92.5	90.9	−13.2	− 5.2	−13.2	− 5.2	0.39
	1931	77.9	81.2	−14.7	− 9.7	−27.9	−14.9	0.53
	1932	59.5	64.6	−18.3	−16.7	−46.2	−31.6	0.68
	1933	57.2	54.2	− 2.3	−10.4	−48.5	−42.0	0.87

Sources: Nominal income, U.S. Department of Commerce 1973, 1976; money (M_2), Friedman and Schwartz 1970.

[a] The absolute values of the t-statistics are in parentheses beneath the coefficients.
[b] Gordon and Wilcox's (G-W) results are contained in table 3 of their paper. My results given below theirs are derived from the equation in log form reported above.
[c] Actual nominal income in period t is Y_t; simulated is $\hat{Y}_t$. The marginal changes in both are denoted by a Δ, and the accumulation of these changes (starting point 1929) by a Σ.

Both equations seem fairly reasonable. The first-difference form in which autocorrelation and multicollinearity are less severe is probably the better of the two. The coefficient of current year's money indicates that most of the effect of a change in monetary growth is felt within one year. The lagged money terms have the correct signs and pattern to produce overshooting, and the sum of the coefficients of all of the money terms is close to unity. These lagged terms, however, are statistically insignificant at the conventional levels.

What is most noticeable about both equations, however, is their clearly superior tracking ability (in the early years of the depression) vis-à-vis the Gordon-Wilcox equation. Judged on the basis of either actual versus estimated level of nominal income (first and second columns) or actual versus estimated cumulative changes in nominal income from 1929 on (fifth and sixth columns), the level equation is much closer to target in 1930 and 1931 than is Gordon and Wilcox's. Accumulated from 1928 on, the year in which my equation predicts the start of the cyclical decline, the simulated and actual changes from the level equation are virtually identical in 1930. The first-differenced equation, though missing the decline in nominal income in 1930, shows some cyclical forces at work. Like the level equation, it produced a slight decline in 1929; and in 1930, estimated nominal-income growth remains well below its average of 5.4 percent per year over the sample period. By 1931, the equation is getting back closer to track with 54 percent of the cumulative change in nominal income accounted for.

Neither equation, therefore, supports Gordon and Wilcox's contention that the depression pre-1931 was primarily a nonmonetary phenomenon. On the contrary, taken at face value, the equations indicate that money can account for at least a slowdown in the growth and perhaps a sizable portion of the decline in the level of nominal income up until 1930 and virtually all of the decline in the level after that.[3]

NONMONETARY EXPLANATIONS AND THE DIVISION OF NOMINAL INCOME

Two other areas that Gordon and Wilcox cover at some length I will consider only briefly: the first, nonmonetary explanations, because it only warrants a short comment; the second, their investigation of price equations, because I have no independent evidence to offer one way or the other.

The section on nonmonetary explanations does not really tell us anything new. Housing and consumption are pointed to as the culprits in the early years of the depression. There was overbuilding in the late 1920s, they say. Its initial effects were masked by the effects of the stock market boom. Then when the market fell to pieces, consumption also fell. That, combined with housing, led to the start of the depression. As evidence, they point to the falling shares in GNP of both consumption and residential housing and cite studies of housing by Hickman and of consumption by Mishkin.

We obviously cannot rule either out. In a severe recession like the 1930s, real factors must have played some, and perhaps a sizable, independent part, at least once things got rolling. But Gordon and Wilcox just provide us with candidates and ones that have been around for awhile, at that.

In any episode, be it inflation or deflation, some components of an economic aggregate will always be more volatile than the aggregate itself. Looking at one episode alone, singling out the components that diverge the most from the average, and attaching causal significance to their movements is a haphazard business. When there are reasons why those particular components will behave that way, it becomes even more suspect. And this is the case for both consumption and housing, since both are influenced to some extent by fluctuations in transitory income and are, therefore, endogenous.[4] In fact, as Gandolfi and I (1977) have shown, once we include transitory income in an aggregate-consumption equation, we can account for the apparent shift in the consumption function that both Temin and Gordon and Wilcox claim took place.

I think Gordon and Wilcox are essentially correct in pointing out the deficiency of our explanation for how nominal-income changes were divided between price and quantity changes in the depression. And, if we can trust the comparisons of European and American experience, about which I have some doubts—both because of inaccuracies in the European data and because of potential problems of aggregation—their finding of greater price responsiveness abroad is an important one. I do, however, have several sets of questions about this part of the analysis.

The first concerns their attempt to replicate Michael Darby's (1972) results. They neglect to mention that they estimate a quite different functional form from Darby's. His equation includes both nominal wages and prices; their equation only includes the latter. Furthermore, they couch their discussion purely in terms of point estimates of the coefficient of adjustment.

Given the few data points—12 years' worth—underlying these equations, a more useful procedure would have been to compare the confidence interval around that estimate with Darby's. His is hardly precise—the range is from 0.075 to 0.35, which translates into a range for the estimated mean lag of 1.9 to 12.3 years. I would suspect that theirs is similarly broad. In the same vein, it would be a useful exercise to reestimate the equations, constrain the adjustment coefficient to various values within this range, and then test for serial correlation. I suspect that it would have brought them closer to Darby's conclusion that his results "are best interpreted as negating the view that anticipations-search models have no role in explaining unemployment during 1934–41" (1976, p. 12).

What may be a more serious problem with Gordon and Wilcox's interpretations of their results is their confusion of two separate effects—autocorrelation of cyclical changes and the effect of price shocks on output.[5] To illustrate, suppose we consider the Lucas (1973) aggregate-supply equation in which the current period's cyclical component of output, $y_{c,t}$, bears the following relationship to price $(P_t - P_t^*)$ shocks and to the previous period's cyclical component of output, $y_{c,t-1}$:

$$y_{c,t} = \alpha + \beta y_{c,t-1} + \lambda (P_t - P_t^*).$$

The coefficient β on the lagged income term provides a measure of the stability of the economy in the absence of shocks. If it were zero, the economy would return to trend growth immediately; if it were unity, there would be no such tendency. The coefficient λ measures the sensitivity to shocks rather than the tendency of the economy to self-correct. A slow return to equilibrium may, therefore, reflect something about the magnitude of either coefficient or about how price expectations are formed. Gordon and Wilcox do not disentangle the three.

One possible reason for a relatively sluggish response of real output to the acceleration of money after 1933 (which I assume to be at least in part unanticipated) is that λ had fallen. In Lucas's model, it depends upon the relative variances of relative prices and the general price level. Their finding that the cyclical component of output responds slowly to price shocks—alternatively stated, that in their framework the price-shock term is best defined statistically with an extremely long horizon for the formation of price expectations—may be a reflection of the phenomenon treated by Lucas. Given the variations in policy from 1929 to 1933, it may not be surprising, therefore, that unemployment and the cyclical component of output showed a sluggish response to more expansive aggregate-demand policies. This explanation, moreover, would explain why in Europe, where the depression was, in general, less severe, there appeared to be a greater degree of response.

INTERNATIONAL COMPARISONS

The most interesting parts of the Gordon and Wilcox paper are the international comparisons. These sections of the paper, however, are the least developed, which is unfortunate, since comparisons of this sort are potentially a very valuable source of information. They add degrees of freedom in a way that more intensive investigation of relatively short time series for a single country cannot, since the diversity of experiences among countries presents an opportunity for counterfactual investigations of alternative macroeconomic policies. This, in turn, provides a means of disentangling complex questions about causality in a simultaneous world.

One particularly striking comparison, which warrants some mention, is between the British and the American experience in the first two interwar depressions—1920–21 and the Great Depression. In table 2, I present data for both countries for both episodes and for periods of several years before and after each. If we focus on 1920–21 initially, what stand out are the similarities in the behavior of the stock of money in the United States and the United Kingdom up until 1920 and the dissimilarities in the years immediately thereafter. In the United States, as in the United Kingdom, money growth averaged over 12 percent per year from 1914 until 1920. It then turned negative in 1921 but picked up in the next two years, thus making up the initial absolute decrease. In the United Kingdom, the 1920–21 monetary shock was only slightly less severe, but a subsequent turnabout never materialized. The money stock actually declined between 1921 and 1923, after growing by only 0.8 percent in 1921.

The real sides of the two economies reacted as one might expect, real GNP and industrial production initially falling in each by substantial amounts. In the United States—the country with the postcontraction expansion in money—both real aggregates picked up much more rapidly and hence made up their initial declines much sooner than in the United Kingdom. By 1923, each had risen enough to far exceed their 1920 levels. In the United Kingdom, however, neither had reached its 1920 level by then, and not until 1925 did both even approach a level consistent with a fairly modest long-term growth trend of 2 percent per annum from 1920 on.

A reversal of roles took place in the next major contraction, in 1929–32. Initially, monetary growth in both countries turned down in a similar fashion: in the United Kingdom, from 1.4 percent in 1927–29, peaking at 2.2 percent in 1928, to 0.9 percent in 1930; in the United States, from 1.9 percent in 1927–29 to 1 percent in 1929–30.[6] As the contraction continued, the two countries diverged more and more. In the United Kingdom, the money stock grew slowly on average from 1929 to 1932 and up until 1931 actually declined. Real GNP fell by 1.9 percent per year and industrial production by 3.8 percent per year. In the United States, the money supply declined by a substantial amount during the full course of the contraction—an average fall of 8.7 percent per year from 1929 to 1932—followed by a further decrease of 2 percent per year from 1932 to 1934. Both GNP and industrial production fell precipitously— GNP by 11.5 percent per year from 1929 to 1932 and industrial production by 20.9 percent per year. Moreover, GNP continued to fall through 1933 and, unlike the United Kingdom, neither aggregate reached its 1929 level until almost the end of the decade.

What these comparisons indicate, then, is that it is at the very least plausible to regard both cycles in each country as having monetary roots being deter-

Table 2. Comparison of the United States and the United Kingdom in Two Interwar Cycles

		Average Annual Percentage Changes		
	Country	Precontraction 1914–20 1927–29	Contraction 1920–21 1929–32	Postcontraction 1921–23 1932–34
Money supply				
1914–23	U.K.	+12.9	+ 0.8	− 3.9
	U.S.	+12.5	− 6.3	+ 5.7
1927–34	U.K.	+ 1.4	+ 0.6	+ 2.7
	U.S.	+ 1.9	− 8.7	− 2.0
Nominal GNP				
1914–23	U.K.	+14.4	−21.7	− 8.9
	U.S.	+14.4	−27.4	+10.0
1927–34	U.K.	+ 1.4	− 4.6	+ 3.2
	U.S.	+ 4.1	−19.2	+ 5.7
Real GNP				
1914–23	U.K.	− 2.7	− 4.9	+ 3.9
	U.S.	+ 1.8	− 9.1	+13.0
1927–34	U.K.	+ 2.0	− 1.9	+ 4.3
	U.S.	+ 3.5	−11.5	+ 3.3
Industrial production				
1914–23	U.K.	+ 1.1	−20.9	+10.1
	U.S.	+ 4.6	−21.4	+18.3
1927–34	U.K.	+ 1.1	− 3.8	+ 8.0
	U.S.	+ 6.8	−20.9	+12.8
GNP deflator				
1914–23	U.K.	+17.1	−16.8	−12.8
	U.S.	+12.6	−18.3	− 3.0
1927–34	U.K.	− 0.6	− 6.5	− 1.3
	U.S.	+ 0.6	− 7.7	+ 2.4
Velocity				
1914–23	U.K.	+ 1.5	−22.5	− 5.0
	U.S.	+ 1.9	−21.1	+ 4.3
1927–34	U.K.	+ 0.0	− 5.4	+ 0.5
	U.S.	+ 2.2	−10.5	+ 7.7

Sources: U.K. real GNP, nominal GNP, GNP deflator, and industrial production from Feinstein, tables 2, 7, 51; U.K. money (M_2) from Sheppard 1971. U.S. real GNP, nominal GNP, and industrial production from U.S. Department of Commerce 1973; money (M_2) from Friedman and Schwartz 1970.

mined to some, and perhaps a large, extent by unanticipated changes in the supply of money.[7] More important, they suggest that, regardless of the initial causes of the business declines, monetary factors contributed to both their severity and their duration. The initial declines in 1920–21 in both countries, and the contraction of 1929–32 in the United States, all were of greater magnitude than the contraction of 1929–32 in the United Kingdom; all were accompanied by larger declines in money growth. Moreover, the contractions of 1920–21 in the United Kingdom and 1929–32 in the United States, both of which were more protracted than their counterparts in the other country, were both accompanied by more protracted declines in the supply of money that in each instance took the form of a series of successive sudden shocks.

A final implication is for the conduct of monetary policy. A standard argument about the Great Depression is that the U.S. monetary authorities were powerless in the face of the substantial declines in income and interest rates that took place. Money was purely passive. If this were the case, however, there would be no reason to expect any differences between the United States and the United Kingdom in either 1920–21 or 1929–32. Such differences clearly exist, however. History has thus provided us with almost a controlled experiment. Unless it can be shown that there was a factor other than monetary growth that varied in the same way between the two countries, the passivity of money in these major contractions has to be considered a highly dubious hypothesis.

CONCLUSION

The initial salvo from Gordon and Wilcox is aimed at Peter Temin. Temin, they contend, is too rigid in denying almost any role to money in the depression. Their own conclusion is that money was not purely passive as Temin alleges, that the Federal Reserve's failure to offset the decline in the nominal stock of money produced by the fall in the deposit-currency ratio was the reason the depression became so severe. Once we get beyond that difference, however, their position and Temin's are virtually identical. In their eyes, nonmonetary forces—Temin's consumption plus one more, housing—explain virtually everything before 1931.

I find their evidence unconvincing. Nonmonetary factors probably were important, but their framework, like Temin's, precludes any firm conclusions. Given the limited number of relevant episodes both he and they examine, an eclectic point of view is virtually guaranteed. Only by considering other episodes in which severe contractions actually took place, or logically could have been expected to take place but did not, are we apt to gain very much useful knowledge of the depression.[8]

NOTES

1. For a critique of the Temin framework, see Gandolfi and Lothian (1977).
2. Even the quotation from Schwartz that they cite as evidence of a hard-line position, "A far *more* satisfactory explanation of 1929–33 than Temin's is, therefore, that a series of shocks, monetary in origin, reduced real ouput" (emphasis added), is hardly a statement that only money matters.
3. These results also need to be interpreted with caution. They are less plagued by data constraints than are Gordon and Wilcox's, but they still are based on a relatively simple form of the equation. Other results consistent with these are presented by Gandolfi (1974) and by Gandolfi and Lothian (1976, 1977).
4. See Darby (1972).
5. Discussions with Arthur Gandolfi led to the development of this point.
6. If we use quarterly or monthly data, the monetary decreases appear more severe. In the United States, M_2 fell at an annual rate of -1.1 percent from April 1928 to October 1920 after having risen by close to 6 percent the year before. In the United Kingdom, M_2 had been growing at an annual rate of 3.2 percent from early 1928 to early 1929. Between then and early 1930, it dropped slightly over 2 percent. The source of the U.S. money data is Friedman and Schwartz (1970); the U.K. series is my own as described in Lothian (1976).
7. Additional work does, however, need to be done on the question of causation in the United Kingdom. In 1920–21, monetary factors definitely seem to have been active forces. The policy of the British government was to return to gold at the prewar price. To do so, high-powered money was reduced drastically, starting in 1920, with the initial impact on its rate of growth having come the year before. In 1929–32, the situation is less clear, particularly at the beginning of the contraction. After 1929, reductions in high-powered money, due to gold outflows, appear to have been the important factor. Only in 1932 after Britain went off the gold standard was there sufficient expansion in the domestic component of high-powered money to produce an increase in M_2. And only then did the contraction come to an end.
8. Evidence of this sort is presented by Jonung (1981) and by Choudri and Kochin (1977) for several foreign countries and by Cagan (1965) for the United States.

REFERENCES

Barro, R. J. 1977. "Unanticipated Money Growth and Unemployment in the United States." *American Economic Review* 67: 101–15.

Bolch, B. W., and Pilgrim, J. D. 1973. "A Reappraisal of Some Factors Associated with Fluctuations in the United States in the Interwar Period." *Southern Economic Journal* 39: 327–44.

Cagan, P. 1965. *Determinants and Effects of Changes in the Stock of Money, 1875–1960*. New York: Columbia University Press, for the National Bureau of Economic Research.

Choudri, E., and Kochin, L. 1977. "International Transmission of Business Cycle Disturbances under Fixed and Flexible Exchange Rates: Some Evidence from the Great Depression." Unpublished. Carleton University and University of Washington.

Darby, M. R. 1972. "The Allocation of Transitory Income among Consumers' Assets." *American Economic Review* 62: 928–41.

――――. 1976. "Three-and-a-Half-Million U.S. Employees Have Been Mislaid; Or, an Explanation of Unemployment, 1934–41." *Journal of Political Economy* 84: 1–16.

Feinstein, C. H. 1972. *National Income Expenditures and Output of the United Kingdom, 1855–1965*. Cambridge: Cambridge University Press.

Friedman, M., and Schwartz, A. 1963a. *A Monetary History of the United States*. Princeton, N.J.: Princeton University Press, for the National Bureau of Economic Research.

――――. 1963b. "Money and Business Cycles." *Review of Economics and Statistics* 45: 32–78.

――――. 1970. *Monetary Statistics of the United States*. New York: Columbia University Press, for the National Bureau of Economic Research.

Gandolfi, A. E. 1974. "Stability of the Demand for Money during the Great Contraction—1929–1933." *Journal of Political Economy* 82: 969–83.

Gandolfi, A. E., and Lothian, J. R. 1976. "The Demand for Money during the Great Depression to the Present." *American Economic Review* 66: 46–51.

――――. 1977. " 'Did Monetary Forces Cause the Great Depression?' A Review Essay." *Journal of Money, Credit and Banking* 9: 679–91.

Gordon, R. J., and Wilcox, J. A. 1981. "Monetarist Interpretations of the Great Depression: An Evaluation and Critique." In this volume.

Jonung, L. 1981. "The Depression in Sweden and the United States: A Comparison of Causes and Policies." In this volume.

Lothian, J. R. 1976. "Interwar Britain: A Comparison with American Experience." Unpublished. Citibank, N. A., New York.

Lucas, R. E., Jr. 1973. "Some International Evidence on Output-Inflation Trade-Offs." *American Economic Review* 63: 326–34.

Schwartz, A. J. 1981. "Understanding 1929–1933." In this volume.

Sheppard, D. K. 1971. *The Growth and Role of U.K. Financial Institutions, 1880–1962*. London: Methuen.

Temin, P. 1976. *Did Monetary Forces Cause the Great Depression?* New York: W. W. Norton.

U.S. Department of Commerce. 1973. *Long Term Economic Growth, 1860–1970*. Washington, D.C.: Government Printing Office.

――――. 1976. *The National Income and Product Accounts*. Washington, D.C.: Government Printing Office.

6 COMMENTS ON "MONETARIST INTERPRETATIONS OF THE GREAT DEPRESSION"

Allan H. Meltzer

Are the courses of fluctuations in economic activity and prices entirely monetary or entirely nonmonetary? One has reason to expect that the answer to that question has been so well understood for so long that it does not require a paper, much less a book or a conference to report the answer. The earliest attempts at systematic thinking about fluctuations recognized wars, crop failures, plagues, weather, and money—real and monetary shocks—as causes of fluctuations. Evidence supported this explanation. Although there was no single accepted formal theory of business-cycle dynamics, few economists have argued that all fluctuations have a unique cause (Haberler 1958).

Keynesian economists, until recently, assigned no important role to money as a force in the initiation and propagation of business cycles and often assigned no role at all. Books by Hansen (1951) and Duesenberry (1958), written in the Keynesian heyday, are examples. Recently, Peter Temin revived this position; in Temin (1976), he argued that there is no evidence that U.S. monetary policy was an independent cause of the start of the 1930s' depression.

This comment was started while I was a visiting fellow at the Hoover Institution and completed while I was a visitor at the Getulio Vargas Foundation in Rio de Janeiro.

Temin's claim that the decline in output and prices from 1929 to 1933 resulted solely from a decline in spending, accompanied by an induced increase in the demand for money, has neither a valid theoretical nor a correct empirical basis. Gordon and Wilcox (1981) agree with me (1976), and with all the reviews of Temin's book that I have seen, in finding Temin's argument incorrect or incomplete and by concluding that Temin's evidence is not persuasive. Further, Gordon and Wilcox show that the conclusion Temin drew from the data is false in two senses. First, they build a persuasive case that monetary factors contributed to the decline in output and prices but cannot account for the entire decline. Second, they use data from European countries to suggest that monetary expansion—a higher growth rate of money—would have reduced the severity of the decline.[1] On both points, they reinforce the conclusions reached by Friedman and Schwartz (1963).

Gordon and Wilcox go beyond the issues raised by Temin. They describe the four main conclusions of their paper as

1.   "Both monetary and nonmonetary factors mattered."
2.   "Nonmonetary factors were of prime importance in 1929–31."
3.   "Different monetary policies in the United States after 1931 would have reduced the severity of the contraction."
4.   "And finally . . . the stimulus of rapid monetary growth on economic activity in the late 1930s was quite weak."

I agree with points (1) and (4); "mattered" in point (1) refers to the effects on prices and output. I agree with point (3) but would delete "after 1931." There is no reason to exclude from criticism the monetary policies of 1929 and 1930, since the monetary base fell in both years. A more expansive monetary policy in the fall of 1929, after the recession was recognized, and in 1930 would have limited the decline.

On point (2) we are farther apart. I have argued elsewhere (Meltzer 1976) for the importance of tariffs, but I do not believe that the primacy of nonmonetary factors is established, and I am not persuaded by the case that Gordon and Wilcox make for population growth, residential construction, and the stock market as independent causal factors. Gordon and Wilcox's neglect of anticipations at critical points of their discussion is one reason we disagree. Below, I discuss anticipations and some other issues on which we differ.

There are, however, some major points on which we agree. Since we started from different positions, it may be useful to explore some of the reasons why differences remain and some issues on which we have reached agreement. I discuss, first, some of the areas of agreement and some differences in emphasis. Then I consider some of the remaining differences. A final section attempts to put the differences into perspective.

AREAS OF AGREEMENT

Gordon and Wilcox list four propositions that they believe comprise the "monetarist platform."[2] They accept, for the period of the 1930s, only one of these propositions—"that past government policy actions (and in 1929–33 the *absence* of appropriate policy actions) have done more harm than good" (1981, p. 99). They argue that the causes of the depression are neither entirely monetary nor entirely nonmonetary. I agree with their conclusion about the effects of government policy in the 1930s and with their rejection of arguments that assign no independent role to changes in money or that interpret all changes in money as a response to current or past changes in the arguments of the demand function for money.

Gordon and Wilcox also reject "hard-line monetarism," which they identify with the proposition that "the 1929–33 contraction was both initiated and aggravated by monetary factors, and nonmonetary factors played no role" (p. 53). This statement is open to more than one interpretation.[3] I accept, as one correct interpretation, that the magnitude and timing of *all* changes in output and prices cannot be explained as a response to prior changes in the quantity of money. There are, during the downswing and recovery, at least two major elements in addition to the usual white noise. First, there are nonmonetary policies, including tariff policy of 1930, the pro-monopoly and pro-cartel legislation like NIRA in the early New Deal, and later the Wagner Act. Second, there are the anticipations induced by policies and other events.

Tariff policy is a nonmonetary policy, but its effects in the early '30s depended on prevailing monetary policy. The effects of higher tariffs on output and prices, described by Gordon and Wilcox (p. 82), would have been different if the gold standard had been abandoned early rather than late. Brunner (1976) shows that the unambiguous effect of higher tariffs with fixed exchange rates is to increase the domestic money supply and lower foreign money supplies. With floating exchange rates, the deflationary effects of the Hawley-Smoot tariff on the rest of the world would have been smaller and shorter-lived, and the feedback effects on the United States through the trade balance and the money stock would have been smaller also.[4]

Gordon and Wilcox raise questions about the speed of the recovery and the effects of money and nonmonetary changes on prices and output during the recovery from 1933 to 1941 and during the intervening recession, 1937–38. I agree that the sequence of recovery, recession, and recovery in 1933–41 is a valid source of evidence on the relevance of alternative explanations, but I disagree with their analysis of the recovery, particularly their neglect of the effects on anticipations of policies and of the existence of worldwide recession.[5]

There is no disagreement, however, on a main point. The depression was deeper and the recovery slower than can be explained by models relating income to current and past values of money. Gordon and Wilcox devote considerable effort to demonstrating this point. Their simulation using the relation of current income to lagged money and income computed from the 1920s shows that "the 1937–38 recession was almost entirely a monetary phenomenon"; it also shows that nominal income rose much less than the simulation predicts (p. 67).

The results of the simulation, however, show little more than their figure 5 comparing U.S. and European velocity, where velocity is defined as the ratio of nominal income to money plus time deposits (M_2). During the 1920s, average M_2 velocity in the United States declined slightly. Velocity declined at a much greater rate per annum from 1929 to 1932, remained relatively constant from 1934 to 1937, then declined again in the next two years. Consequently, the simulations, using the coefficient of lagged money computed from data for the '20s, substantially underestimate the decline in the early '30s when money and velocity fell together and overestimate the recovery in the late '30s when velocity fell and the money stock rose.[6]

Gordon and Wilcox do not go behind the simulations to ask whether differences in the demand for money (velocity) reflect consistent, linear or nonlinear, responses to unchanged arguments of the demand function, changes in anticipations, or, at the opposite extreme, instability of the function. Nevertheless, they draw a much stronger conclusion than seems warranted by the simulations. They write, "Our interpretation is that shifts in the IS curve must be relied upon to explain the timing of income growth in the 1938–41 period" (p. 70). The implication is that most of the shift in IS is independent of past government policies—monetary and nonmonetary. The 1941 positive shift in IS is an exception and is attributed to defense spending. But the slow recovery in 1938–40 is attributed mainly to sluggish investment that led to a "weak recovery despite the rapid growth in M_2," (p. 70). This appears to be one main piece of evidence for "denying any potency to the self-correcting mechanism of price flexibility during the 1930s" (p. 99).

Gordon and Wilcox never ask whether the slow recovery of real income from the 1938 recession was, in part, a consequence of New Deal policies. The taxation of undistributed profits, higher income taxes, the Wagner Act, the regulation of wages and hours of work, growing regulation of business, rhetoric about "economic royalists," and the rising real value of the government debt held by banks and the public are among the government actions reducing incentives to invest or contributing to uncertainty about the future. Jacob Viner warned Roosevelt at the time that his criticisms of businessmen and his policies toward business reduced the effect of his spending policies on investment. According to Viner, Roosevelt became angry and barred him from subsequent meetings.[7]

An additional point on which we agree is the conclusion that, contrary to the Phillips curve, "the rate of change of prices is significantly influenced, not by the level of output, but only by its current rate of change" (p. 89).[8] Gordon and Wilcox replicate this finding using European and U.S. data and thereby provide new evidence that the classical mechanism, relating prices to output and rates of price change to rates of output change, provides a better explanation of the data than does the inflation-augmented Phillips curve.

A principal difference between the two explanations is in the interpretation of the output gap. In Keynesian analysis, and in the inflation-augmented Phillips curve, the gap (or unemployment) is a measure of disequilibrium in the output and labor markets. With a large gap, and a low expected rate of inflation, the rate of price change should be negative according to the arguments of Keynesian writers (see Modigliani and Papademos 1975). In the Keynesian interpretation, the failure of prices to fall in the '30s is a main piece of evidence showing that the self-correcting properties in the private sector were weak or absent.

Gordon and Wilcox conclude that the rise in prices from 1933 to 1937 "appears to have been due to the very rapid growth of nominal income during this interval" (pp. 91–92). They agree that prices fell in the contraction of 1929–33. For the first eight years of the depression, prices responded to market conditions. The alleged failure of the price system could only have occurred after 1937.

To sum up, we agree on three main points and a number of minor points. The main points of agreement, with some remaining qualifications, are:

1. The decline from 1929 to 1933 is not solely a response to prior or contemporaneous reductions in money. Higher tariffs under Hawley-Smoot, and retaliation abroad, contributed to the decline. I would add that the interaction of the gold-standard rules and the tariff changes also contributed to the decline. Gordon and Wilcox suggest that construction activity and the decline in stock prices exerted independent effects. I discuss both topics below.

2. The response of nominal output to money was lower in the '30s than in the '20s but was not absent. A more expansive monetary policy from 1929 to 1933 would have reduced the decline. A less restrictive monetary policy than the doubling of reserve requirements would, as a minimum, have reduced the severity of the 1937–38 recession and probably would have avoided the decline entirely.

3. The distribution of nominal income between prices and output shows that rates of price change are related to rates of change of output and not to the level of output, the full-employment gap, or the level of unemployment. These findings are contrary to the standard Phillips curve and are an important source of evidence against policy conclusions, based on the Phillips curve, suggesting that increased stimulus raises output without raising prices. Gordon and Wilcox add that equilibrium aggregate-supply theories fail, also, to explain the distribution of nominal income between prices and real income. I am content with the more modest conclusion that current versions of the equilibrium theory do not explain the movements of output and prices from 1938 to 1940 or 1941. In the following section, I suggest an explanation.

DIFFERENCES AND DISAGREEMENTS

Every reader of the Gordon and Wilcox paper must be as struck as I was by the absence, in a paper as long as theirs, of any careful discussion of interest rates, asset prices, or anticipations. These topics are mentioned rarely or not at all. To their credit, the liquidity trap is not introduced as a deus ex machina to explain interest rates and anticipations. Here, too, they depart from the usual Keynesian interpretation. But their failure to model anticipations, except as a simple adaptive rule, is as disappointing as their failure to distinguish, except in a passing way, between anticipated and unanticipated changes in government policy. Several of our differences and disagreements stem from this common source.

In this section, I concentrate on four issues that have attracted considerable attention in the past. One is the contrast between the weak response to government policy in 1938 and 1939 and the larger response to defense and war spending after 1940. A second is the importance assigned to autonomous changes in housing and stock prices in the 1929–33 decline. A third is the role of the gold standard. Fourth is reverse causation.

The Weak Recovery

If Gordon and Wilcox had devoted more attention to anticipations, they would have been less likely to deny "*any* potency to the self-correcting mechanism of price flexibility during the 1930s" (p. 99, emphasis added). Their conclusion, a main point on which we disagree, seems much too strong. There was a strong expansion from 1933 to 1937, with rising or steady velocity. After

1937, the demand for money increased more than nominal income; velocity fell. The contrast between the two periods of expansion provides evidence about the differences in anticipations during the two periods and helps to explain why the recovery was weak from 1938 to 1940.

Interest rates on long- and short-term securities fell in both periods, 1933–37 and 1937–40. Common-stock prices rose in the earlier expansion and fell in the later expansion. Table 1 shows these data. Rates of changes of the deflator are shown to permit comparison of ex post real and nominal returns.

For the years 1930–32, returns to common stocks and commodities are strongly negative; returns to money and short-term securities are high and positive. Falling prices increased net wealth, but higher interest rates and lower expected income reduced the market value of wealth. In 1933, the situation changed. Stock prices rose in 1933 and continued to rise by more than the rate of inflation until 1936. Dividends and realized capital gains were distinctly positive in the years 1933–36. The return to holding money became negative in 1934, and the nominal return on short-term securities was rarely much more, and at times less, than the rate of price change. It does not strain credulity to believe that rising stock prices reflected anticipations of rising real returns to capital and higher real income.

Contrast the situation after 1937. There are, again, positive returns to short-term securities and negative returns to common stocks. If falling stock prices in this period indicate prevailing anticipations of future returns to capital, we can conclude that anticipations become bearish. Stock prices decline in recession, when real income and real returns fall. But, real income rose 8 or 9

Table 1.   Interest Rates and Stock Prices, 1930–40 (in percent)

	Long-Term Rate	Short-Term Rate	Rate of Change, Standard & Poor's Average	Rate of Price Change
1930	4.0	3.6	−21.3	− 2.6
1931	3.9	2.6	−43.2	− 9.6
1932	4.3	2.7	−67.8	−10.8
1933	4.3	1.7	+25.7	− 2.3
1934	3.7	1.0	+ 9.4	+ 7.1
1935	3.0	0.8	+ 7.4	+ 0.9
1936	2.6	0.8	+37.8	+ 0.2
1937	2.7	0.9	− 0.4	+ 0.4
1938	2.6	0.8	−29.4	− 0.1
1939	2.4	0.6	+ 4.8	− 0.2
1940	2.2	0.6	− 9.0	+ 0.2

percent in 1939 and 1940, lending support to the interpretation that the decline in stock prices reflected increased pessimism about future returns to real capital and not an anticipated decline in real income or a new recession.

What accounts for the change in anticipations? I believe that two interrelated factors must be considered. First, the Roosevelt administration, reelected in 1936, promised a series of additional laws regulating wages and hours, retirements, and labor relations and raising taxes on corporate profits. The anticipated effects were higher labor costs and lower after-tax returns to capital. Second, confidence in the ability of government to restore prosperity and avoid recession was weakened by the 1937–38 recession. Whether the recession was entirely the result of Federal Reserve policy or partly the result of a shift in budget policy, government produced the recession. Leading economists, including a president of the American Economic Association, did not conclude that government policies had failed to restore prosperity but, instead, talked of stagnation and urged increased government spending.

There was a stream of potential and actual programs, including an attempt to "pack" the Supreme Court so as to have programs declared constitutional. These activities affected anticipations and increased uncertainty about the future. If the change in opinion had occurred suddenly, there would have been a one-time adjustment of expected returns. Asset prices would have fallen until capital values reflected the new anticipations. The stream of projects, proposals, and policies was spread over time, however. Stock prices fell sharply in 1938, recovered slightly, then fell again as the markets adjusted to the flow of new information or rumors about the administration's policies.

Once defense spending started, prices rose and nominal income increased more rapidly. Repeated experience with wartime spending strengthens the belief that wars are financed by inflation. At the time, the change in anticipations was reinforced by the shift in the administration's policy from concern with redistribution and regulation to a growing interest in expanding output. The rational response for households was to shift from money and securities to goods. Velocity rose, as Gordon and Wilcox show; so with little change in the growth rate of M_2, private spending and nominal income accelerated. In the event, the anticipations of wartime inflation proved to be correct.

The 1938–40 recovery is one piece of evidence leading Gordon and Wilcox to reject the monetarists' claim that the private sector is stable. In doing so, they again neglect studies of the demand for money. Many of these studies show that the demand for money responded, without extraordinary error, to falling nominal returns and rising income in the late '30s—that is, responded to the variables incorporating anticipations of changes in aggregates. They also neglect the evidence in their figures 5 and 6. The former shows that growth rates of money and nominal income differed for the United States and for the aggregate of six European countries, but the two indexes of velocities, computed as the ratio of nominal income to money, base 100 in 1929, were almost identical during the recovery phase 1933–37 and then appear to separate. Their figure 6 shows that by 1937 real income in Europe had passed the 1929 peak. Real income in the United States almost certainly would have passed the 1929 peak in 1937 had there not been a policy-induced recession.

Taken together, figures 5 and 6 suggest that something changed in the United States in 1937. It is plausible, but not established, that the failure of New Deal policies to maintain real expansion and the threat of increased government regulation, more redistribution, and higher tax rates changed anticipations. Once emphasis shifted from redistribution and regulation to expansion, and the threat of war awakened anticipations of inflation, the demands for money and securities fell as the demands for goods and services rose. Recovery resumed.

Housing

A second type of evidence that Gordon and Wilcox use to make the case for private-sector instability is the behavior of housing. They argue (pp. 77–79) that the desired capital stock declined after 1929 because of declining population growth. The actual capital stock was "too high" because of "overbuilding" of residential housing in the 1920s and the "overshooting" of the stock market in 1928–29. Both the "overbuilt" actual stock and the reduced desired stock contributed to an excess supply of housing. Consequently, Gordon and Wilcox argue, residential construction declined. They summarize some previous studies and present some evidence in table 6 showing that the percentage of full-employment output going to residential fixed investment declined 40 percent from 1926 to 1929 and an additional 40 percent in the following year.

Their argument about population and overbuilding suffers from two main defects. First, data on U.S. population growth show a peak in the rate of growth about 1923 and a trough in 1931. During most of the depression years, the population growth rate rose. The rate of growth of nonfarm households also declined from the early '20s to 1931, then rose about as rapidly as at any time in the previous six decades.[9] If falling population growth caused an excess supply of housing in the '20s or early '30s, rising population growth should have caused rising demand in the '30s. Second, Gordon and Wilcox do not make a persuasive case that the decline in housing after 1929 was an autonomous or independent cause of the depression. More than five years of declining population growth reduced the growth rate of nonfarm households from above 3 percent to below 1 percent by 1929. It is difficult to accept without evidence that this decline was not recognized as it occurred and that adjustment was not made in the 1920s. The fall in income after 1929, of course, changed the desired rate of purchase of durables. With real returns to short-term government securities between 6 percent and 13 percent in 1930–32, the gain from postponing purchases, and lending or purchasing securities instead of borrowing to purchase durables, was high by any historical standard. It does not require an interest elasticity as large as has been found in some recent studies to explain the decline in housing starts after 1929 as mainly a response to demand (see Arcelus and Meltzer 1973).

Stock Prices

The increase in production early in 1929 was large by past or present standards. Despite the deep recession that started in August, according to National Bureau chronology, the year 1929 as a whole shows a 6 percent growth in real output. A 6 percent rate of expansion is higher than in most peacetime years that do not culminate in a recession, so it is noteworthy that the 6 percent average increase occurred in the year that the depression started. A better indication of the surge in output early in the year is the 17 percent increase shown by industrial production in the year ending July 1929.

Industrial production fell more than 2.5 percent before the stock market collapsed in late October and fell an additional 10 percent by the end of January. Since stock prices fell after output declined sharply, and the recession was expected to continue, the decline in stock prices should not be treated as an autonomous event or an independent cause of the depression.

Many studies of the depression and the decline in stock prices ask why output and stock prices fell as much as they did in 1930. None ask why output rose as much as it did in the year ending July 1929. The causes of the very large 1929 expansion are no less difficult to discern than the causes of the 1930 collapse. An explanation of both events is more likely to be productive than explanations that start from the 1929 peak and ask why the first year of the recession is so much larger than can be explained as a response to prior changes in money.

The Gold Standard

Gordon and Wilcox deny that the gold standard and its interaction with the Hawley-Smoot tariff contributed to the decline, although they accept the tariff as a policy change that deepened the recession.[10] They do not discuss the *nominal* values of exports and imports or capital movements, the factors that affect the foreign component of the monetary base. Further, they comment that the price-specie-flow mechanism induces expenditure switching, and possibly a recession in a single country, but not a worldwide depression. I believe that in the absence of Hawley-Smoot, subsequent tariff retaliation, and the policy errors of the Federal Reserve, there would not have been a worldwide depression and almost certainly not a depression of the same magnitude and duration as the depression that occurred.[11] Without a fixed exchange rate system, the depressing effects of the tariff would have been smaller, and more of the effects would have been concentrated in the United States. The United States would not have drained as much gold from the rest of the world, so the depression elsewhere would have been less severe and the effect of that tariff would have been reflected mainly in a higher U.S. price level.

Reverse Causation

A main conclusion of the authors' lengthy discussion of the influence of money on output is that contemporaneous correlation between money and income in the decade of the '30s adds plausibility to the reverse-feedback hypothesis. This hypothesis makes changes in money the result of changes in income acting on the supply of money and implies that money is a relatively passive factor in fluctuations. Much of the evidence leading Gordon and Wilcox to accept the reverse-causation hypothesis is contained in their table 5. The table shows that during the '30s the influence of current money on current nominal income rose and the influence of lagged money fell.

I do not believe that the data in table 5 sustain the interpretation placed on them. These data appear to have been obtained from a regression equation in which nominal income depends on current and lagged money, current income, and a time trend.

$$Y_t = \alpha_0 + \alpha_1 M_t + \sum_{j=1}^{8} \alpha_{2j} M_{t-j} + \sum_{i=1}^{4} \alpha_{3i} Y_{t-i} + \alpha_{4t} + u_t.$$

The interpretation of the equation is left open, but whatever its interpretation, it is not clear why the statistical significance of α_1 tells us as much about the reflex effect of business on the supply of money as the authors claim.

One interpretation of the equation is obtained from the quantity theory using $\overline{Y}$ and $\overline{M}\,\overline{V}$ to denote average or expected nominal income and nominal expenditure; and $Y_t - \overline{Y}$ and $M_t V_t - \overline{M}\,\overline{V}$, the deviations of current from expected income and spending.

$$Y_t - \overline{Y} = M_t V_t - \overline{M}\,\overline{V}.$$

If the time trend had been omitted, the regression estimates obtained by Gordon and Wilcox would have a clearer interpretation. The coefficients α_1 and α_{2j} would measure the velocity of current and lagged money—the effects of money on spending holding $\overline{Y}$ constant—and the $\Sigma\ \alpha_{3i}$ would measure the effect of $\overline{Y}$ on Y. The coefficient of current M would be approximately equal to current velocity. In their table 5, α_1 is a bit high in the samples that include the middle '30s.[12]

I do not recommend Gordon and Wilcox's equation as a method of testing the quantity theory, but I am able to interpret the coefficients of the test using the quantity theory. I do not know how to interpret α_1 and α_{2j} as part of a supply theory of money or how to get implications about reverse causation. Do Gordon and Wilcox maintain that the current money stock depended mainly on current income? Did a dollar of current income have a more significant effect on the money stock in the 1930s than in the 1920s?

The relative rates of change of the money stock ($\hat{M}_1$) and the monetary base ($\hat{B}$) are shown in table 2.[13] The cumulative rates of changes, $\Sigma\hat{B}$ and $\Sigma\hat{M}_1$, are approximately equal up to 1938. Thereafter, the growth rate of money is substantially less than the growth rate of the base, but the positive correlation remains. To sustain the reverse-causation hypothesis, given this correlation, Gordon and Wilcox must argue that the growth of the monetary base also is a result of the growth of income.

One channel by which income can influence the base, member-bank borrowing, was removed during the mid-1930s; banks rarely borrowed from the Federal Reserve. The balance of payments is a second possible channel.

Table 2. Relative Rates of Change of M_1 and B, 1934–40

	$\hat{B}$	$\Sigma\hat{B}$	M_1	$\Sigma\hat{M}_1$
1934	+0.18		+0.09	
1935	+0.14	0.32	+0.17	0.26
1936	+0.09	0.41	+0.13	0.39
1937	−0.11	0.30	+0.04	0.43
1938	+0.15	0.45	−0.01	0.42
1939	+0.20	0.65	+0.11	0.53
1940	+0.25	0.90	+0.15	0.68

Note: The monetary base is defined as currency and bank reserves adjusted for reserves impounded by increases in the reserve requirement ratios in 1936 and 1937. M_1 is currency and demand deposits.

Gordon and Wilcox's table 1 shows why it is difficult to believe that income determined the base through the balance of payments. There is no evidence of any relation between lagged nominal income and money. The entire effect of income on the balance of payments and of the balance of payments on the stock of money would have to be synchronous. Gordon and Wilcox deny for earlier and later periods any substantial effect of prices on the trade account.[14] Given their denial, real income and price effects on the capital account would have to be large and rapid.

The remaining channel is open-market policy. Did the Federal Reserve respond to the level of income by increasing base money when nominal income rose and reducing base money when nominal income fell? My reading of the minutes suggests that when income rises, the Federal Reserve increases the base if interest rates rise and reduces money if interest rates fall. Pegged interest rates permit output to affect money; if loan demand responds to income, and the money stock rises with loan demand, there is an effect of income on money. But this would not explain an effect on the base. As table 2 shows, the growth of money was lower than the growth of the base. Moreover, in the middle '30s, the Federal Reserve conducted open-market operations rarely and in small amounts (Friedman and Schwartz 1963).

Reverse causation is not impossible, but it is implausible that the relation of base money or money to income is mainly the result of reverse causation in the '30s. The dominant effects on the base, after 1934, are the doubling of reserve requirement ratios and the flow of foreign exchange and gold—induced, to a considerable extent, by the rise in the price of gold and later by the capital flight from Europe as fears of war and confiscation rose.[15]

SOME FINAL COMMENTS

The Keynesian-monetarist dispute has moved a considerable distance from its origin. Gordon and Wilcox's paper takes another step in the direction of resolving conflicts by looking at evidence. Since their paper is long and substantive, there are many points of agreement, and disagreement, on which I did not comment. I have, however, tried to stress both major points of agreement and issues on which additional evidence is required to reduce the remaining differences.

Two issues very much a part of the discussion have been neglected: the impotence of monetary policy and the effectiveness of fiscal policy. Professional opinion on both issues has changed considerably.

In the heyday of Keynesian orthodoxy, it was not unusual to find statements about the instability of the demand for money and the impotence of monetary policy. The demand for money, or velocity, it was said, shifted erratically; so that even if money could be controlled, monetary policy could not be relied upon to influence income. Statements of this kind are still made but have little empirical foundation even for the '30s. Gordon and Wilcox present evidence (table 6) that monetary velocity in Europe and in the United States not only did not move erratically, but the two velocities changed together until 1937. Whatever affected one appears to have affected the other with about the same timing and in the same direction.

The effects of fiscal and other nonmonetary policies of the New Deal are all but completely ignored by Gordon and Wilcox. Gordon and Wilcox show (n. 37) that real government purchases increased in relative size by nearly 50 percent during the decade, rising from 13 percent to 19 percent of real GNP. Yet, aside from a single comment suggesting that the increase in the Federal budget surplus in 1937 contributed to the recession, fiscal policy has no role in the analysis.

The Keynesian-monetarist dispute has not lacked controversy about the potency of fiscal policy financed by debt issues. The '30s is the decade in which economists are alleged to have discovered the potency of debt finance, but recent studies find weak effects or no effects at all (Stein 1976). Neglect of fiscal policy by the authors may be entirely a consequence of their attempt to limit the scope of their effort to extract evidence on the role of money. A careful study of the response to fiscal policy in an economy with idle resources remains to be done.

The authors' major conclusion denies that the price system would have restored equilibrium at full employment. I believe this conclusion stands on a weak foundation. The authors' discussion of anticipations never goes beyond a simple adaptive scheme. Generally, anticipations are ignored. The failure of Keynesian policies and New Deal legislation to restore prosperity is taken as evidence of the failure of the price system. Neither the disincentive effects of many of the New Deal policies nor their stimulative effects are considered.

An alternative explanation of the very gradual recovery is that, after the policy-induced recession of 1937–38, people no longer anticipated that the New Deal policies would promptly produce rising real, after-tax returns to private investment. A series of announced policy changes and proposed changes lowered anticipated future returns and delayed the recovery. In the absence of these policies and the policy-induced recession, the recovery would have continued as it did in Europe.

The alternative hypothesis has at least as much surface validity as the hypothesis that the price system failed. A test of the aggregative effects of New Deal policies would help to resolve this issue and is, clearly, long overdue.

NOTES

1. Lars Jonung's discussion (1981) of Swedish experience provides additional evidence.

2. Mayer (1978) lists twelve. There is considerable overlap between the two lists, but neither is complete. Both fail to mention the international monetary system, particularly the role of fluctuating versus fixed exchange rates. Gordon and Wilcox use descriptive words and phrases—"stable," "natural tendency"—that are open to many interpretations. My discussion of Mayer (in Mayer 1978, pp. 145–75) assigns much more importance to differences in the interpretation of unemployment than do Mayer or Gordon and Wilcox. For these reasons, I do not accept either list as complete.

3. I believe "hard-line monetarism" is an empty box that owes its existence mainly to a desire for symmetry. Gordon and Wilcox cite several times a summary statement by Schwartz (1981) but neglect her statement (n. 13) accepting the Hawley-Smoot tariff and tariff retaliation as factors contributing to the decline.

4. My agreement with Gordon and Wilcox is less than complete. Their discussion of the effects of tariff changes makes no mention of effects on capital movements and money stocks in the United States and abroad. I return to this point below in the discussion of disagreements.

5. Their complaint that monetarists express interest only in the depth and severity of the decline (p. 50) and neglect the recovery and recession is without foundation. Friedman and Schwartz (1963) and Friedman and Meiselman (1963) are but two of the studies of the recession and recovery that can be cited.

6. I do not agree, however, with the conclusions based on table 5, particularly the finding that "the contemporaneous correlation in the decade of the 1930s adds plausibility to the reverse-feedback hypothesis that the reflex effect of business on money was a primary determinant of shifts in the money supply" (p. 71). The amount of "reverse causation" is not independent of policy. If the Federal Reserve pegs the interest rate, increases in the public's supply of earning assets to banks increase bank credit and money.

7. The story was told to me by Viner. Viner was a consultant to the Treasury in the mid-1930s, and Secretary Morgenthau's published diaries record a brief version of the story. Gordon and Wilcox consider the effect on prices of NRA price fixing and attribute some of the unexplained rise in prices in 1937 to the growth of labor union membership fostered by the National Labor Relations Act (Wagner Act). But they do not mention that a change in the monopsony power of unions that raises the price level can lower aggregate real output.

8. To correct a misinterpretation on p. 98, let me add that I do not claim (1977) that the expectations-augmented Phillips curve works under the dollar standard. On the contrary, I conclude that the output gap had no significant effect on the rate of price change under the dollar standard of the postwar years.

9. Clarence Barber (1978) also argues that declining population growth reduced housing demand. I have used charts 2 and 4 of his paper for data on growth rates of population and nonfarm households.

10. Although Gordon and Wilcox are scornful of writers with "monocausal blinders" (p. 74), when dismissing the gold standard they ignore this stricture and neglect the interaction discussed earlier between tariffs and money-stock changes under the gold standard.

11. Figure 6 in Gordon and Wilcox shows a decline in real output and a rise in the price level for their European composite in 1929. The Maddison indexes used in my study (Meltzer 1976) do not include the Netherlands and Sweden; however, they do not show a decline in any of the larger countries and show a sizable increase in real output for France. Wholesale prices fell in Europe, but Gordon and Wilcox show an increase. Under the price-specie-flow theory, a fall in income abroad lowers U.S. exports and the U.S. money stock.

12. The sum of the coefficients of lagged Y is never significantly different from zero or one. Information supplied by Gordon and Wilcox, however, shows that the coefficient of Y_{t-1} is significant in all samples and is usually the only coefficient of the lagged Y's that passes the standard test of statistical significance. The coefficient of Y_{t-1} is generally in the neighborhood of one, as implied by the quantity theory; for the seven regressions in table 5, the average is 0.94.

13. I have used M_1 rather than M_2 because it was available at the time of writing. It is unlikely that the observed pattern is affected by the change in a way that would change the conclusion.

14. Gordon and Wilcox do not mention that the t-statistics for lagged money on income and lagged growth rates of money on growth rates of income are always higher, usually substantially higher, than the comparable statistics for reverse causation in their table 1. As Zellner (1979) and Schwert (1979) show, Granger tests are tests of temporal precedence and not tests of causation as the term is generally used in science.

15. The reverse-causation hypothesis of Gordon and Wilcox is, of course, entirely different from the Temin (1976) argument that the effect of falling income on money from 1929 to 1933 produced an *excess supply* of money.

REFERENCES

Arcelus, F., and Meltzer, A. 1973. "The Markets for Housing and Housing Services." *Journal of Money, Credit and Banking* 5: 78–98.

Barber, C. 1978. "On the Origins of the Great Depression." *Southern Economic Journal* 44: 432–56.

Brunner, K. 1976. "A Fisherian Framework for the Analysis of International Monetary Problems." In *Inflation in the World Economy,* ed. M. Parkin and G. Zis. Manchester: University of Manchester Press.

Duesenberry, J. 1958. *Business Cycles and Economic Growth.* New York: McGraw-Hill.

Friedman, M., and Meiselman, D. 1963. "The Relative Stability of Monetary Velocity and the Investment Multiplier in the United States, 1897–1958." In *Stabilization Policies,* Commission on Money and Credit. Englewood Cliffs, N.J.: Prentice-Hall, for the Commission on Money and Credit.

Friedman, M., and Schwartz, A. J. 1963. *A Monetary History of the United States, 1867–1960.* Princeton, N.J.: Princeton University Press, for the National Bureau of Economic Research.

Gordon, R. J., and Wilcox, J. A. 1981. "Monetarist Interpretations of the Great Depression: An Evaluation and Critique." In this volume.

Haberler, G. 1958. *Prosperity and Depression.* Cambridge, Mass.: Harvard University Press.

Hansen, A. H. 1951. *Business Cycles and National Income.* New York: W. W. Norton.

Jonung, L. 1981. "The Depression in Sweden and the United States: A Comparison of Causes and Policies." In this volume.

Mayer, T., ed. 1978. *The Structure of Monetarism.* New York: W. W. Norton.

Meltzer, A. H. 1976. "Monetary and Other Explanations of the Start of the Great Depression." *Journal of Monetary Economics* 2: 455–71.

————. 1977. "Anticipated Inflation and Unanticipated Price Change." *Journal of Money, Credit and Banking* 9: 182–205.

Modigliani, F., and Papademos, L. 1975. "Targets for Monetary Policy in the Coming Year." *Brookings Papers on Economic Activity,* no. 1: 141–63.

Schwert, W. 1979. "Tests of Causality: The Message in the Innovations." *Journal of Monetary Economics* 10 (supp.).

Stein, J. 1976. "A Keynesian Can Be a Monetarist." In *Monetarism,* ed. J. L. Stein. Amsterdam: North-Holland.

Temin, P. 1976. *Did Monetary Forces Cause the Great Depression?* New York: W. W. Norton.

Zellner, A. 1979. "Causality and Econometrics." *Journal of Monetary Economics* 10 (supp.).

7 MONETARIST INTERPRETATIONS OF THE GREAT DEPRESSION: *A Rejoinder*

Robert J. Gordon and James A. Wilcox

The primary contributions of our paper are to broaden the discussion of the depression beyond the behavior of U.S. money and income in the 1929–31 period—the issue with which Temin and his critics are mainly concerned—and to argue (with Haberler 1958) that "explanations which run in terms of one single cause . . . should be regarded with suspicion" (p. 5). Unlike the recent papers that limit their attention to the role of money and other factors as determinants of aggregate demand shifts, considerable attention in our paper is devoted to the nature of aggregate supply behavior. Finally, unlike others who concentrate exclusively on the relation of money, income, and prices in the United States alone, we base some of our conclusions on a comparison of the United States with an aggregate of six European countries.

We find that both extreme monetarist and nonmonetarist interpretations of the decade of the 1930s are unsatisfactory and leave interesting features of the data unexplained. The extreme monetarist interpretation suffers from its inabil-

This research has been supported by the National Science Foundation. Conversations with Allan Meltzer were helpful in the development of this rejoinder.

165

ity to explain the severity of the initial collapse in income in 1929–31, the steady weakening in the correlation between money and income as the 1930s progressed, the failure of monetary factors to explain the nature and timing of the 1938–41 recovery, and the weakness of the self-correcting mechanism of price flexibility. But extreme nonmonetarist explanations suffer as well by failing to place a sufficient emphasis on the causal role of money in the collapse of U.S. nominal income after the fall of 1931, on the effect of more-expansionary monetary policies in Europe as a central explanation of the relatively milder contraction that occurred there, on the close association between money and income in the 1937–38 recession, and on the inability of the Phillips curve approach to explain price behavior during the decade of the 1930s.

Given the wide range of topics covered in our paper, we naturally did not expect the comments of our discussants to be in agreement on every point. Thus we are gratified at the wide range of central issues on which Meltzer appears to be in substantial agreement. Most of Meltzer's area of disagreement involves interesting problems of interpretation on questions that have no final and definitive answers. Lothian's comments appear at first glance to contain substantive evidence that contradicts some of our main conclusions, but upon further examination his evidence appears to be fully consistent with ours. Finally, Temin's comments contain a brief section that harshly condemns our interpretation of his own position but fails to alter our view that Temin's position is both extreme and unsupported by the evidence he examines.

METHODOLOGY AND EXTREME POSITIONS

Although Meltzer's point of departure is his basic agreement with our rejection of extreme, single-cause interpretations of the depression, both Temin and Lothian are unhappy with our four-way categorization of views, albeit for opposite reasons. Temin resists being typecast as an antimonetarist extremist, whereas Lothian is uncomfortable with our middle-ground refusal to accept simple, single-cause explanations and instead wants to be told "exactly what to conclude."

Temin's objection begins with our interpretation of a quote from his book that we cited to support our categorization of his position as "extreme nonmonetarist." We emphasized Temin's denial of *"any* effective deflationary pressure from the banking system" between October 1929 and September 1931.[1] Temin prefers to add emphasis to his own words as follows: "There is *no evidence* of any effective deflationary pressure" (p. 118). Whatever the emphasis, Temin's absolute denial of "any" contractionary effect remains and seems to us prima facie evidence of any extremist approach to economic analysis.

But let us accept Temin's emphasis on the words *no evidence*. What evidence is needed to convince oneself that the bank failures must have had *some* contractionary influence? Nowhere does Temin deny any element in the following list:

1. Some banks failed in late 1930.
2. Deposits vanish when a bank fails.
3. Some individuals are forced to reduce spending when their bank deposits disappear.[2]
4. Aggregate nominal expenditure declines when some individuals are forced to reduce their spending.

At least one step in this chain of reasoning *must* be denied for Temin to claim that there was no deflationary pressure exerted by bank failures, and yet Temin provides no such denial. This is one basic element in our criticism of Temin's position.

The second basic element in our criticism is the failure of Temin's own evidence to support his extreme claim. Here Temin asserts that our analysis is "hopelessly confused" and that we "ride roughshod" over the distinction between counterfactual and descriptive history. Temin apparently believes that his own "historical statement" that explains "the events that actually happened" is immune from the test of logical consistency that we applied. Yet Temin's historical analysis of the evidence remains unconvincing in its denial of *any* role for bank failures, because every fact cited by him is logically consistent with a model in which the destruction of money reduces aggregate expenditure.

We believe that the difference between our analysis and Temin's can be clarified in terms of his *IS–LM* model by writing down two quite different statements:

1. In the absence of any leftward shift in the *IS* curve, the observed behavior of nominal risk-free interest rates and the real money supply is inconsistent with the hypothesis of a contractionary effect of the reduction in the money supply.
2. Given the acceptance of a leftward shift in the *IS* curve (that could have stemmed from either real spending shifts or deflationary expectations), the observed behavior of nominal risk-free interest rates and the real money supply are completely consistent with the hypothesis that any

decline in the money supply has a net contractionary impact on nominal
spending.

Temin's evidence, both in his book and in his comment here, consists of an
examination of the behavior of nominal risk-free interest rates and of the real
money supply. Our position is that this evidence is compatible with *either*
statement 1 or 2 and thus, for anyone (including Meltzer's present comment
and the Friedman-Schwartz book) willing to accept the relevance of nonmonetary shocks, provides no evidence at all that the bank failures had no contractionary effect. Temin's claim that we reached "almost precisely the
conclusions that I did by entirely independent means" refers to our acceptance
of the leftward shift of *IS* involved in statement 2, to our denial of the absence
of a leftward shift required for the acceptance of statement 1, and to our
Granger simulations that attribute three-quarters of the decline in nominal income in 1929–31 to nonmonetary factors.

But our agreement that nonmonetary factors played a major role in 1929–31
merely supports statement 2 above and does not imply any endorsement of
Temin's extreme claims of a zero effect of bank failures or of his own method
of analysis. The facts that we examined support a role for contradictory monetary policy, because: (*a*) monetary growth did decelerate in 1929; (*b*) there was
an impact of lagged money on income in the 1920–28 period; and (*c*) there
was therefore a contractionary influence of the effect of lagged money sufficient to explain one-quarter of the drop of nominal income in 1929–31. To the
extent that 25 percent is closer to 0 percent than to 100 percent, we are closer
to Temin than to Schwartz or Lothian. But 25 percent is *not the same as 0
percent,* and thus we must disassociate ourselves from the extreme denial of
any contractionary effect of the 1930 bank failures that Temin so relentlessly
pursues and erroneously attributes to us when he states that the conclusion of
"no evidence of any [contractionary] pressure is . . . reaffirmed both here and
in Gordon and Wilcox's paper."

The problem with many of Lothian's comments is that they evince a preference for definitive monocausal statements and an unwillingness to accept our
basic conclusion that *both* monetary and nonmonetary factors were important.
Our paper left Lothian "not sure *exactly* what to conclude." Our framework
"precludes any *firm* conclusions." Further, in his unwillingness to accept our
middle ground between monetary and nonmonetary extremes, Lothian quite
inaccurately claims that in our eyes "nonmonetary forces . . . explain *virtually
everything* before 1931."[3]

Most of Lothian's reluctance to accept our conclusion involves matters of
degree rather than kind, that is, the *choice of words* used in describing the
balance between monetary and nonmonetary factors. Our position is best char-

acterized as stating that there were several important episodes during the 1929–41 interval. The lagged behavior of the money supply explains some portion of variations in income during all phases of this 12-year period, probably a minority of the variance during the intervals 1929–31 and 1938–41, and probably a majority during the 1931–38 period. Nonmonetary factors explained a majority (*but not all*) of the variance of nominal income during the 1929–31 and 1938–40 periods. Lothian's evaluation makes no distinction between intervals and insists that "the degree of emphasis does matter" in distinguishing whether money was a "prime move" in the depression or explains "at most a minor part." Because he makes no distinction between intervals and refuses to accept the intermediate view that both monetary and nonmonetary factors were important, in varying degrees at different times, he simply misses the main thrust of our conclusion that both monetary and nonmonetary factors were "prime movers."

MONEY AND INCOME

In our discussion of Temin's evidence on the behavior of interest rates and the real money supply, we argued that a leftward shift in the *IS* curve was required to explain the evidence. The importance of nonmonetary shifts in spending as a cause of the leftward *IS* shift can be denied only if one were willing to claim that the *IS* shift was caused by the emergence of deflationary expectations. At least during the first three quarters of the contraction, neither the CPI nor interpolated GNP deflator dropped outside of the range observed in the 1923–29 period, a fact that made us dubious of the potential importance of deflationary expectations between late 1929 and mid-1930, however important they might have been later. Even if agents looked back to 1920 or 1902, or to the interwar experience in Britain, as Lothian suggests they should have done, there was no evidence available as of mid-1930 that would have led them to view the first three quarters as a prelude to an unprecedented deflation, rather than a short one-year recession of the duration of, say, the 1907–08 or 1920–21 episodes.

The evidence on money and income to which Lothian devotes most of his attention, however, does not involve price expectations but rather the relation between nominal income, current money, and lagged money on an *annual basis* over the longer period 1893–1928.[4] Unfortunately, all of Lothian's results listed in his table 1 are completely useless because of his mistake of including *current* money in an annual equation that attempts to explain movements in *current* nominal income. If there is *any* feedback from income to money, whether within the contemporaneous month or contemporaneous quarter or year, the coefficients on current money in his income equation are biased upward, perhaps by a large amount, and the Lothian simulation results are biased toward the conclusion that money fully explains the drop in income during the 1929–33 period. Put another way, without any evidence that there was no feedback from income to money within the current year (and he provides no such evidence), Lothian's results in table 1 can be interpreted as saying no more than that "income fell because money fell because income fell."[5]

Our quarterly regressions of income on money and money on income also lead Meltzer to raise a question of interpretation. In his comments on the regressions with money as a dependent variable in our table 5, he objects to our conclusion that "the dominance of the contemporaneous correlation in the decade of the 1930s adds plausibility to the reverse feedback hypothesis that the reflex effect of business on money was a primary determinant of shifts in the money supply." Instead, Meltzer argues, "Reverse causation is not impossible, but it is implausible that the relation of base money or money to income is mainly the result of reverse causation in the '30s"(p. 160).

Here the first problem is semantic. When we say that a factor, say reverse causation, was "a primary determinant," we do not mean that there were no other primary determinants. For instance, we explicitly recognize the primary role of gold inflows in expanding both base money and the money supply during the 1938–40 period. The contemporaneous correlation between money and income, even in monthly data, makes it impossible to *rule out* a role for reverse feedback. To go further and argue that reverse feedback *must have occurred,* one leaves the realm of hard evidence and must rely instead on conjecture. One conjecture is that a causal link from money to income should have taken longer than one quarter or one month to occur, based on econometric evidence from postwar quarterly models, leaving reverse feedback as a plausible explanation of the strong contemporaneous feedback observed in the 1930s.

Meltzer raises legitimate questions about the channel by which reverse feedback might have occurred. One channel he fails to discuss is the 1931–33 increase in the cash-holding ratio, and then the subsequent reduction in the ratio as the economy recovered between 1933 and 1935. If declining income and prices help to induce bank failures, and bank failures help induce changes in the currency ratio, then there is a "reverse causation" link from income to money that is independent of open-market operations or gold flows and that will cause an upward simultaneous-equations bias in any attempt (like Lothian's table 1) to include current money in an equation explaining the behavior of income.

NONMONETARY FACTORS OPERATING
DURING 1929–31 AND 1938–40

Meltzer's main disagreement is with our claim that the majority of the decline in nominal spending in 1929–31 and of the recovery in 1938–41 was due to nonmonetary factors. Regarding 1938–41, we emphasize the sluggish behavior of investment during the 1938–40 period and the contrasting buoyancy of the fiscal expansion after mid-1940 as nonmonetary factors explaining why nominal income grew at such different rates during the 1938–41 period when the growth of M_2 was rapid and relatively constant. Meltzer does not really disagree with our analysis but rather goes beyond it by linking the sluggish recovery of investment between 1938 and 1940 to pessimistic anticipations induced by antibusiness New Deal measures. It is possible to admit that Meltzer's factors are plausible as a partial explanation and consistent with monetarist emphasis on the actual harm done by government policy. But Meltzer does not actually provide any evidence that would sort out the role of governmental antibusiness measures. Pessimistic anticipations and the 1938–40 slump in stock prices, in particular, may well have been a *symptom* of the sluggish recovery of spending rather than its *cause*. Sluggish income growth and "bearish anticipations" tend to go together and presumably interact. To use a modern analogy, would Meltzer accept the hypothesis that sluggish U.S. income growth during the 1973–76 period was a result of antibusiness measures introduced by Presidents Nixon and Ford, on the basis of the pathetic performance of the Standard and Poor's average during those years?

Meltzer raises two objections to our discussion of the behavior of housing and stock prices in the late 1920s. First, the decline in household formation began in the mid-1920s; thus it is difficult to accept that the adjustment to this factor did not take place in the 1920s. We agree and in our paper pointed to the rapid decline in housing investment that occurred in 1928 and 1929. Our argument is not that the adjustment had not already begun but that the decline in household formation required a continuous downward movement in the ratio of housing investment to GNP during the 1926–31 period that aggravated the decline in income that occurred during the 1929–31 period.

Further, Meltzer argues that the decline in stock prices in late 1929 was not an autonomous event, because industrial production had already fallen by 2.5 percent before the stock market collapsed in late October. He objects to statements made about the decline in economic variables from the 1929 peak and claims that the 1929 expansion and 1930 collapse need to be explained together. Here Meltzer's position is close to ours, when we argue that the 1929 boom in consumption and the stock market was superimposed on an economy weakened by the collapse in housing investment. To the extent that the stock market boom of 1928–29 was a bubble that had to end, because stock values could not be sustained for long at triple their 1923 values, both we and Meltzer agree that the 1929–30 boom and collapse were part of the same essentially nonmonetary phenomenon. As the discussion of our paper points out, however, monetary growth was rapid in 1928 and then came to a halt in early 1929, thus aggravating the boom and collapse in both output and the stock market and requiring the conclusion that the timing of the 1929–30 episode was partially monetary in origin.

PRICES AND OUTPUT

Lothian's first criticism of our aggregate supply analysis starts from the following equation relating the cyclical component of output to price shocks $(P_t - P_t^*)$:

$$y_{ct} = \alpha + \beta\, y_{ct-1} + \lambda\, (P_t - P_t^*).$$

Our statistical analysis demonstrates that deviations of real output from trend during the 1930s cannot be explained as responding only to price "surprises" unless the expected price level totally failed to adjust downward to the deflation that had actually occurred. Otherwise, with the price level almost constant after 1934, where were the "surprises" needed in the Lucas theory to explain the low level of output and high level of unemployment? Lothian introduces his equation in order to point to a high level of β, the serial correlation of the output deviations, as another possible explanation of the long duration of the depression. But here Lothian misses the point of recent critiques of the Lucas approach. A drop in nominal income, as occurred in the 1930s, must be divided by definition between a drop in real output and a drop in the price level. If the drop in real output persists, as when β is high, then this means by definition that downward price adjustment is sluggish in the face of low output. But if price adjustment is sluggish, we are in the disequilibrium world of Barro and Grossman, and the Lucas model of price surprises simply does not apply, because individual economic agents are forced off their notional supply curves. Thus Lothian's own reinterpretation of our results reinforces our critique of the Lucas equilibrium aggregate-supply approach to the analysis of economic fluctuations.

Finally, Lothian's comparisons of the United States and the United Kingdom, while they put the evidence together in an interesting way, do not contribute any new insights that would cause us to change the main conclusions of our paper. First, Lothian's middle column labeled "Contraction" lists figures for nominal income, money, and velocity, showing that in each episode the decline in nominal income was associated with a larger decline in velocity than in money, supporting our emphasis on the relevance of nonmonetary factors. Second, the decline in nominal income mainly took the form of declining prices in 1920–21 in both countries and in 1927–34 in the United Kingdom, whereas the decline in real output was greater than that in prices in 1927–34 for the United States. This merely points to the same puzzle with which we ended our paper: the mystery is not why prices rose so much after 1933, a phenomenon that the United States and Europe shared in common despite the greater amount of U.S. government price-raising legislation, but rather why the price level was relatively less flexible downward in the United States than in Europe during the 1929–33 period.

NOTES

1. Incidentally, we must object to Meltzer's inaccurate characterization of Temin's view: "Temin (1976) . . . argued that there is no evidence that U.S. monetary policy was an independent cause of the start of the 1930s' depression" (p. 148). On the contrary, Temin is quite consistent, both in his book and in his comment here, in accepting a primal causal role for monetary policy beginning in September 1931.
2. The effect of liquidity constraints on individual consumption decisions is analyzed in Barro and Grossman (1976, chap. 2).
3. In each of these three quotes, the emphasis is added.
4. Lothian implies that our quarterly data are "plagued" by the use of interpolated income data incapable of making "fine distinctions." Yet the crucial issue is to disentangle the one-directional causation from money to income from the simultaneous two-directional causation revealed in annual data. It was precisely to avoid claims that our interpolation procedures introduced measurement error that we also ran the identical tests on published monthly money and industrial production data (our table 2) and obtained results similar to those in the quarterly data used for the simulations.
5. Lothian's remark (p. 141) that transitory income can explain the behavior of consumption and housing is, of course, plagued by the same simultaneity problem, since consumption and housing expenditures *are part of* transitory income!

REFERENCES

Barro, R. J., and Grossman, H. I. 1976. *Money, Employment, and Inflation.* Cambridge: Cambridge University Press.
Haberler, G. 1958. *Prosperity and Depression.* Cambridge, Mass: Harvard University Press.

8 MONOPOLY EXPLANATIONS OF THE GREAT DEPRESSION AND PUBLIC POLICIES TOWARD BUSINESS

Charles C. Cox

During the 1930s, a number of economists, politicians, and business reformers claimed that industrial concentration, a decline in competition, and failure of the price system explained the length and severity of the depression. The core of these explanations was the administered-price doctrine—the notion that prices in concentrated industries are rigid when demand decreases; but they linked the depression to monopoly in other ways, too. These interpretations of the Great Depression produced a wide range of proposals about regulating economic activity, and they led to a vast study of concentration of economic power by the Temporary National Economic Committee. Overall, the idea was to promote economic recovery by correcting market failures that resulted from declining competition. Among economists who held other explanations of the depression, few questioned whether some kind of reform was desirable; it was widely believed that markets were riddled with imperfections and monopoly conditions that could be improved by appropriate regulatory policies.

Today, monopoly explanations of the Great Depression are dead issues, but some propositions about pricing, concentration, and competition that were advanced as part of those explanations have become received doctrine. Interest in monopoly explanations disappeared when the depression ended. Economists embraced Keynesian models that focused on shifts in autonomous spending to explain unemployment equilibrium and secular stagnation. Reformers turned to topics that were more current and could attract the public's interest. More recently, several economists reexamined explanations of the Great Depression, and most of these studies concluded that monetary policy was the principal cause of the 1929–39 depression.[1] Some of the studies considered the influence of nonmonetary factors such as tariffs and autonomous spending; none gave any attention to monopoly as an explanation. While economists have abandoned monopoly explanations of the depression, ideas from those explanations about business behavior and industrial organization have persisted as policy issues. For years now, policymakers have attributed inflation to administered prices. Industrial concentration has been the subject of numerous studies, and recently there have been proposals for legislation to deconcentrate and reorganize industry.

Much of the regulation that started during the depression years has survived, the range of regulated activities has increased, and public regulation has become a controversial and growing field of study. New Deal policies cartelized industries, promoted labor unions, subsidized agriculture, established regulatory commissions, increased antitrust activity, and otherwise expanded the scope of public regulation. All of these policies were supposed to remedy market failures, and most were supposed to promote economic recovery. Since then, the amount of regulation has grown as new regulatory agencies have been set up for new problems and new regulatory items have been added to the domain of old agencies. This pattern of regulatory growth has led some economists and historians to regard the Great Depression as a turning point for the U.S. economy, whereby a general policy toward business of laissez faire ended, and a general policy of widespread government regulation began (e.g., Buchanan 1975, p. 14; Mund 1965, pp. 17–21; Hawley 1966). But there was a substantial amount of regulation prior to the depression, and no one, so far as I know, has shown specifically how the pattern of regulatory policies has been influenced by ideas from the depression.

This essay examines effects of monopoly explanations of the Great Depression on the regulation of economic activity. In particular, I consider issues that were raised by those explanations and have had long-run influences on the direction of policy toward competition, monopoly, and pricing. First, I sketch the major monopoly explanations, describe the policy issues that they raised, and trace the subsequent development of those ideas. Then, I investigate the characteristics of regulation before, during, and after the depression to see how, in fact, regulatory policies have changed. Next, I consider the development of antitrust enforcement in the light of the depression arguments. Finally, I relate the administered-price doctrine to price-control policies.

MONOPOLY EXPLANATIONS AND POLICY ISSUES

The basis for monopoly explanations of the Great Depression is the idea that increasing industrial concentration during the first part of the twentieth century had substantially destroyed the competitive nature of the price system by the 1930s. This image of the organization of industry was portrayed in influential studies such as Berle and Means (1932) and Burns (1936). Chamberlain's theory of monopolistic competition and Robinson's work on imperfect competition reinforced the idea by emphasizing the ubiquity of monopoly power. Even though there was little evidence of an increase in monopoly, the belief was widely held.[2] Then the notion of administered prices linked the depression to concentration and declining competition.

Administered Prices

The administered-price doctrine was set out in the early '30s by Gardiner Means (1935). It maintains that the economy has two different kinds of markets: traditional markets in which flexible prices equate supply and demand, and administered markets in which supply and demand are equated at an inflexible price that is administered by the seller. In traditional markets, adjustments to changes in demand occur primarily through changes in price. In administered markets, adjustments to changes in demand occur primarily through changes in production. Consequently, rigid administered prices caused large decreases in output and employment during the depression, but industries with flexible prices had small decreases in output. The difference was critical because administered prices had come to dominate the economy. On the basis of price changes over the period 1926–33, Means classified more than half of the commodities in the BLS wholesale price index as having administered prices. "Indeed, the whole Depression might be described as a general dropping of prices at the flexible end of the price scale and a dropping of production at the rigid end with intermediate effects between" (Means 1935, p. 8).

According to Means, administered prices are found in concentrated industries because, where there are few sellers, firms can choose between changing price or output when demand decreases, and profits are usually maximized by reducing output and holding price at its original level. Means never explained why a rigid price policy maximizes profits in a concentrated industry, although he conjectured that demand was very inelastic and a rigid price policy was less risky than a flexible price policy. Later, economists tried to rationalize rigid prices by assuming a kink in the demand curve facing an oligopolist, but empirical work showed there is virtually no correspondence between the price patterns implied by the kinky-demand-curve theory and the price patterns observed in oligopolistic industries.[3] Even without a theoretical basis, the administered-price doctrine incited much controversy and a number of empirical studies.

Two different views of industrial concentration produced two schools of thought about policy toward administered prices. One school attributed concentration to technology and advocated economic planning; the other attributed concentration to monopoly and advocated antitrust policy. Means viewed increasing concentration and administered markets as the result of organizational efficiency and technological development. He explicitly said that administered prices resulted from large firms and high concentration but should not be attributed to monopoly or collusion; therefore, he thought that policy to deconcentrate industries, restore competition, and eliminate administered prices would be very costly:

> Few realize the extent to which it would be necessary to pulverize industry. Each of the big automobile companies would probably have to be made into a hundred or more independent concerns; the big chemical companies would have to be broken into very much smaller units; and even after the break-up of the unregulated part of industry, the inflexible prices in the railroad and utility fields would impede economic adjustment unless they also were broken up and made competitive. In order to make a laissez-faire policy truly effective, productive efficiency would have to be greatly impaired and a lower standard of living accepted than is made possible by modern industrial organization and modern technology. [Means 1935, pp. 12–13]

Instead of antitrust, he suggested that administered prices be accepted and government regulation be used to counter the destabilizing influences of administered markets. "Our economy has developed to the point where we simply cannot rely on the actions of individuals or enterprises acting independently to produce overall co-ordination and an effectively functioning economy" (p. 35). The solution that he proposed was a scheme of coordinated controls of price and output devised on the basis of best use of resources and involving consumer, labor, and business interests, but this plan was never spelled out in detail.

Other economists (Douglas 1937; Galbraith 1936; Kreps 1939; Wallace 1936) equated inflexible prices with monopoly power. Essentially they took Means's notion of administered prices—his best-known statement of the administered-price doctrine is a paper of his that was presented in Congress by someone else as evidence of monopoly's role in the depression—and interpreted the source of concentration differently. In the monopoly argument, the primary source of concentration is firms' efforts to monopolize industries; except for natural monopolies, technology is taken as a minor determinant of concentration. The monopoly explanation was expressed by the Federal Trade Commission:

> The Commission believes that whatever may have been the immediate causes of the present depression, the effects have been aggravated by the lethargy of the capitalistic system, a lethargy due to a steady growth of monopolistic practices in American industry and trade. The failure of controlled prices to follow the falling market in 1930 was apparently a factor in prolonging and deepening the collapse of production and employment.
>
> Artificially high prices appear to have been a factor in the unwholesome lack of buying power that has so long interfered with recovery. In 1936 and 1937, it seems that artificial and excessive increases in prices were in part responsible for limiting the growth of prosperity and turning the curve of production downward. [U.S. Congress 1939, p. 1654]

Henry Simons (1934, p. 14) also thought that inflexible prices were a major factor in the depression and resulted from monopoly power, but he attributed monopoly to government regulation and labor organization as well as industrial concentration.

The proposals by men who held the monopoly view of administered prices dwelled on antitrust regulation. A general theme was that vigorous antitrust enforcement had never been tried. Some (e.g., Simons 1934; Wallace 1936) argued that a policy of deconcentration to reduce firms to the minimum efficient size was appropriate. Others (e.g., Edwards 1940; Mason 1939) doubted that antitrust regulation to break up firms was practical; they proposed that the focus of antitrust should be to prevent the growth of monopoly power and that normal economic growth would eventually reduce the problem of existing monopoly.

> Industries which were strategically important twenty years ago have been superseded by the development of substitutes. Regional markets have been expanded by the improvement of transportation. By further developments of this kind it is probable that many of our highly concentrated industries will be exposed to new competition. If we can take steps to limit the future growth of large enterprises, to preserve competition in the new industries, and to prevent expansion of the power of our present large enterprises, we may be able to reduce the problem of price leadership and group monopoly to manageable proportions. Such a policy involves peculiar care to protect the opportunities for new enterprises to enter the

market as well as care to keep them from being swallowed up by the old concerns. [Edwards 1940, p. 177]

Along these lines, stronger antimerger policy, elimination of barriers to entry, and regulation of business practices like basing-point pricing and abuses of patents that work to restrain trade were advocated. The idea was to stop monopoly in its incipiency.

Temporary National Economic Committee

In 1938 the president delivered an antimonopoly message to Congress in which he endorsed the basic monopoly explanation of the depression:

> One of the primary causes of our present difficulties lies in the disappearance of price competition in many industrial fields, particularly in basic manufacture where concentrated economic power is most evident and where rigid prices and fluctuating payrolls are general. [U.S. Congress 1938]

His policy toward this problem was to request a thorough study of concentration, competition, and monopoly in the U.S. economy in order to revise and guide the enforcement of the antitrust laws.

Congress responded by creating the Temporary National Economic Committee (TNEC) to investigate concentration, monopoly, and effects on trade and employment of the price system and price policies of industry. The TNEC produced 43 different monographs and held hearings on some 31 topics. The subjects covered a wide range: price behavior and business policy, competition and monopoly in American industry, the structure of industry, unfair competitive practices, patents, technology, antitrust, monopolistic practices, and numerous studies of individual industries. All of the topics raised by the monopoly explanation of the depression were covered, but the studies that I have read are mostly descriptive and unfocused, so that they provided few insights about concentration and monopoly and few guides for policy.

Consider the studies on price flexibility, concentration, and economies of scale. The study on price flexibility started from the premise that businesses have a high degree of discretion in setting price; it never examined the relation between concentration and rigid prices. It concluded:

> There is little doubt that the behavior of prices intimately affects the rate of business activity. Nevertheless, it seems equally evident that no simple, single approach to prices as such will solve the problem of increasing and maintaining industrial activity. The problem is far too complex. [Nelson and Keim 1940, p. 53]

The only useful information on price behavior appeared in part of the concentration study that examined the relation between concentration and rigid prices:

> Concentration in the control of production of the products does not appear to be associated with any particular and unique price or quantity behavior in either the cyclical downswing from 1929 to 1933 or in the upswing from 1933 to 1937. Products with high concentration ratios and products with low concentration ratios experienced strikingly similar changes in price and quantity. [Thorp and Crowder 1941, p. 411]

The analysis of trend in concentration was poorly done. On the basis of average concentration across a sample of industries, the concentration study reported increasing industrial concentration over the period 1914–37. Yet the data for individual industries show different patterns, and there was no clear trend in concentration (Thorp and Crowder 1941, pp. 54–81).

The major issue for policy confronting those who held monopoly explanations of the depression was whether economies of scale are the cause of industrial concentration. The study that addressed this question compared average accounting costs for firms in several industries and found that the largest firms in an industry seldom had the lowest costs. This approach would not persuade any economist about the importance of scale economies, nor did it persuade the authors of the study. "The Commission in submitting the results of these tests to the Temporary National Economic Committee offers no definite opinion as to whether they conclusively disprove the claim frequently made that large size in American business is more efficient than medium or small size" (U.S. Federal Trade Commission 1941, p.11). So much for the TNEC's studies; aside from the concentration data, they contributed little to the knowledge of industrial organization.

By the time the TNEC finished its task, it had lost sight of concentration, administered prices, and most of the other issues that it started to investigate. Many of the TNEC policy recommendations were unrelated to industrial organization (U.S. Congress 1941, pp. 20–43). Some were Keynesian recommendations: stimulate private investment spending to avoid stagnation; provide programs to transfer income to people with low incomes. Some—geographically decentralize industry to avoid depressing aspects of the factory system— were simply peculiar. Of the antitrust recommendations, several were trivial: increase the budgets for antitrust enforcement; increase the penalties for antitrust violations; require trade associations to register and report to a federal agency. There were only four substantive antitrust recommendations: (1) revise Section 7 of the Clayton Act to prohibit mergers by acquiring firms' assets; (2) revise the patent laws to require compulsory patent licensing at a fair price and without restrictions; (3) pass legislation prohibiting basing-point pricing; (4)

repeal the Miller-Tydings Act that allows firms in interstate commerce to have state resale price-maintenance contracts.

Clearly, the TNEC did not answer many of the questions about concentration and the price system that were raised by monopoly explanations of the depression, nor did the TNEC set any new directions for antitrust policy. The antimerger law was eventually enacted and has influenced antitrust policy, but the idea of tighter merger regulations did not originate with the TNEC. Some of the other policy suggestions have been implemented by the courts. Overall, though, it is fair to say that the TNEC had only a minor impact on analysis· and policy. As a 1942 review of the TNEC studies put it, "The reader will find it easy to leave the T.N.E.C. publications with much the same ideas with which he approached them" (Stigler 1942, p. 13).

Subsequent Developments

When the depression no longer interested them, economists dropped the argument that it was explainable by monopoly. But they continued to study concentration and administered prices, because those topics continued to be problems for policy.

First, the basic premise of the monopoly explanations—the belief that monopoly was widespread in the '30s and had increased significantly since 1900—which had been widely accepted as fact during the depression years, was shown to be wrong. Careful empirical studies by Nutter (1951) and Stigler (1949) showed that there is no factual basis for the belief: monopoly accounted for about 25 percent of national income in 1939 and had not increased since 1900. Later studies confirmed and updated these findings. An approximately constant amount of monopoly is now the received opinion, but the amount that does exist is commonly considered to be too much.

We have seen that during the '30s high industrial concentration came to be interpreted as monopoly power. The belief was that monopoly is positively related to market concentration. This belief was confirmed when Bain (1951) published a study showing higher profits for more highly concentrated industries. Numerous studies followed showing a weak positive relation between profits and concentration. Over the past ten years, these studies have been seriously challenged: the concentration-profits relation does not persist over time; adjusting accounting data to more closely approximate the notion of economic costs reduces the already weak relationship; the correlation may well be spurious. In another attack, those who hold that concentration reflects monopoly have been challenged to provide this belief with a theoretical basis that is consistent with the concentration-profits facts. Although there is no conclusive case that the concentration-profits relation is due to monopoly, it is my opinion that the dominant view among economists and policymakers is that industrial concentration measures monopoly power.

Numerous, probably hundreds, of empirical studies have attempted to determine the extent to which economies of scale cause industrial concentration. This is the crucial question for policy toward concentration, but it has not yet been answered. Three analytical approaches have been developed—statistical cost comparisons, engineering estimates, and survivor tests; but each has been severely criticized, and economists are undecided about which approach is best. Besides all of the methodological problems, there are enough different results that one can, by appropriate selection of evidence, support any view—large-scale economies or diseconomies or constant costs. My reading of the evidence, with a preference for the survivor technique, leads me to think that cost curves are generally L-shaped. All three types of studies tend to find substantial diseconomies for small-size firms, and the survivor and statistical cost techniques tend to find a wide range of constant costs from medium to large firm sizes. The bend in the L, however, is not at a constant absolute or relative size across industries. This is important for concentration policy because it implies that a meaningful rule of minimum efficient size cannot be specified.

After the depression, the subject of administered prices was virtually ignored until Means (1957) reformulated his doctrine to explain inflation in the 1950s. In the revised version, administered prices are not just rigid; there is, instead, a ratchet effect by which administered prices sometimes go up but do not go down. Administered-price firms have a range of discretion in which they can set price, and profits will be unchanged. But Means did not explain why the firms had started to raise prices persistently at that time. Other economists (Galbraith 1957; Ackley 1959; Blair 1959) took up the argument and advanced a variety of non–profit-maximizing theories to explain the inflationary behavior of administered prices.

One reason that many economists have readily accepted administered-price arguments is that the only theories of noncollusive oligopoly assume firms' behavior, and that behavior is usually not profit-maximizing. So, there was no well-accepted theory of oligopoly with which to analyze Means's assertions about rigid prices during the depression, nor was there any theory of oligopoly by which to judge the notion of administered inflation during the 1950s. Assertions about lagging oligopoly prices, mark-up pricing, and target-return pricing used to explain administered inflation were about as unreasonable as other theories of oligopoly.

Another reason why economists were attracted to the idea of administered-price inflations is that the Keynesian models that were in vogue had no way to explain the price level. Inflation—especially inflation at less than "full employment''—had to be attributed to some force exogenous to the model, and administered prices served as that exogenous force. Some of us now realize that arguments about administered inflation use a framework suited to analyzing relative prices in order to explain increases in the economy's price level. No advocate of administered inflation that I know of has ever demonstrated how, in a Walrasian general-equilibrium system, price increases in some markets (relative increases) raise the price level.

When the doctrine of administered prices was first set out, the only challenge to it was from two articles (Humphrey 1937; Mason 1938) that pointed out that rigid prices were not a new phenomenon and wondered why rigid prices had not caused the price system to fail earlier. Now there are empirical studies that challenge the existence of administered prices. Stigler (1962) and Stigler and Kindahl (1970) showed that administered prices are mainly a statistical illusion due to the BLS (Bureau of Labor Statistics) method of collecting prices from different numbers of sellers and due to the fact that BLS prices are list rather than transaction prices. Also, it was shown that transaction prices in ''administered markets'' are neither rigid nor unresponsive to the business cycle. As for administered inflation, Lustgarten (1975) and Weston and Lustgarten (1974) have shown that prices in more-concentrated industries increased less rapidly than prices in less-concentrated industries over the period 1954–73.

Despite the new evidence that undermines the administered-price doctrine, economists generally still believe that prices in highly concentrated industries are administered in some perverse way. So great has been the influence of Gardiner Means's ideas over the past 45 years, that the administered-price doctrine will be unlearned very slowly.

A recent development that is relevant for the analysis and policy considered here is the rational–self-interest theory of regulation advanced by Stigler (1971). This approach rejects the traditional theory that government regulation is created to improve resource allocation in cases of market failure such as natural monopoly, externalities, and public goods. Research showing that regulation seldom improved resource allocation and often was perverse led to the new view. The self-interest theory looks at regulation as a means of effecting wealth transfers, and it says that regulation—especially industry-specific regulation—is generally acquired by and administered to benefit the regulated industry. The benefits take forms such as barriers to entry, elimination of price competition, and sometimes direct money subsidies. General-purpose regulation like antitrust that covers many industries is less likely to serve special interests. Yet, the self-interest theory challenges the conventional system of beliefs about monopoly because it implies that government is a primary source of monopoly and, coupled with the view that concentration-profit relations do not show monopoly power, that public policy toward concentration and business practices has been misdirected.

Overall, the developments in thinking about concentration, monopoly, and the price system that have taken place since the depression years show that until very recently the prevailing doctrine was about the same as was set out in monopoly explanations of the depression. Early research showed that monopoly was neither growing nor as prevalent as economists had thought, but the correlation between concentration and profits, which was found at about the same time, seemed to confirm the belief that concentration measures monopoly power. Serious attacks on the conventional beliefs have been very recent and have not yet had much impact. For some three decades, then, policy has been shaped by views that came from monopoly explanations of the Great Depression. Concentration, various consequences of it like administered prices, and other market failures have been treated as problems for which markets should be regulated so as to modify business practices and, directly or indirectly, restructure industries. To examine the consequences of these beliefs about industrial organization, I turn now to regulatory policy.

PATTERNS OF ECONOMIC REGULATION

The trend in regulation over the past century can be described in different ways. The scope of regulation has expanded substantially over the years as additional industries, occupations, and other areas of economic activity have become subjects of public policy. The trend in the amount of effective regulation is more difficult to summarize. Almost everyone says that regulation is more influential now than it was in the past. This view surely seems correct, but no one has yet measured the overall magnitude of regulation at even one point in time. Trends in the direction of federal economic regulation are investigated here. First, the major regulatory laws are examined for patterns in the kinds of regulations and regulated activities. Second, expenditures of regulatory agencies are used to compare the growth of different kinds of regulation.

Regulatory Statutes

Table 1 shows major laws regulating business that were enacted by Congress over the period 1887–1976. The list contains 76 regulatory statutes, but even so, not all major federal regulations are included; for example, the list takes no account of tariffs or taxes. Furthermore, it is important to realize that only

Table 1. Federal Regulatory Statutes, 1887–1976

Year	Law	Function
1887	Interstate Commerce Act	Establishes ICC to regulate price and entry in rail and related water transportation
1890	Sherman Act	Prohibits joint action to restrain trade, monopoly, and monopolizing
1906	Hepburn Act	Extends ICC regulation to pipeline rates
1906	Food and Drugs Act	Establishes FDA to regulate adulteration and misbranding of foods and drugs
1910	Mann-Elkins Act	Extends ICC regulation to telephone, telegraph, cable
1914	Clayton Act	Prohibits anticompetitive mergers, price discrimination, and business practices
1914	Federal Trade Commission	Establishes FTC to enforce Clayton Act and police unfair trade practices
1916	Shipping Act	Establishes Federal Maritime Commission to regulate water transportation
1918	Export Trade Act	Authorizes "Webb-Pomerene" exporters' cartels
1920	Transportation Act	Extends ICC authority to set minimum prices
1920	Water Power Act	Establishes FPC to regulate power projects
1921	Packers and Stockyards Act	Establishes Packer and Stockyards Administration to regulate practices in livestock markets
1922	Grain Futures Act	Establishes regulation for future trading in grain
1922	Capper-Volstead Act	Exempts cartels of agricultural producers from antitrust
1927	Federal Radio Act	Establishes Federal Radio Commission to control use of radio frequencies
1931	Davis-Bacon Act	Requires federal construction projects to pay prevailing wages
1932	Norris-LaGuardia Act	Establishes legality of unionization and collective bargaining
1933	National Industrial Recovery Act (declared unconstitutional, 1935)	Establishes NIRA to cartelize industry and regulate wages and hours of labor
1933	Agricultural Adjustment Act (declared unconsitutional, 1936)	Establishes production controls and price supports for farm products
1933	Securities Act	Regulates public offering of new securities
1934	Securities Exchange Act	Establishes SEC to administer Securities Act and to regulate trading on securities exchanges
1934	Communications Act	Establishes FCC to administer communications regulation
1934	Fishery Cooperative Marketing Act	Exempts cartels of fishermen from antitrust

Table 1 (Continued)

Year	Law	Function
1935	Public Utility Act	Extends FPC control to all interstate electricity and required deconcentration of utilities
1935	Motor Carriers Act	Extends ICC regulation to trucking
1935	Banking Act	Establishes FDIC to insure and regulate banks
1935	National Labor Relations Act	Establishes NLRB to regulate unfair labor practices and requires collective bargaining
1936	Robinson-Patman Act	Amends Clayton Act to prohibit price differences
1936	Merchant Marine Act	Authorizes Federal Maritime Commission to subsidize shipbuilding and ship operation
1936	Commodity Exchange Act	Establishes Commodity Exchange Authority to regulate futures trading in agricultural commodities
1937	Miller-Tydings Act	Authorizes state resale price-maintenance contracts in interstate commerce
1937	Bituminous Coal Act	Establishes the Bituminous Coal Commission to set minimum prices for coal
1938	Civil Aeronautics Act	Establishes CAB to regulate entry and price and to subsidize interstate air carriers
1938	Natural Gas Act	Extends FPC regulation to transmission and resale price of natural gas
1938	Fair Labor Standards Act	Regulates minimum wages and maximum hours for labor
1938	Wheeler-Lea Act	Amends FTC Act to prohibit deceptive acts and practices
1938	Food, Drugs, Cosmetics Act	Extends regulatory authority of FDA
1938	Agricultural Adjustment Act	Reformulates regulation of farm prices and production to avoid Supreme Court objections
1940	Transportation Act	Extends ICC regulation to inland water carriers
1942	Small Business Mobilization Act	Authorizes War Production Board to grant exemptions from antitrust
1945	McCarran Act	Exempts state-regulated insurance firms from antitrust
1946	Atomic Energy Act	Establishes AEC to regulate nuclear power production
1947	Taft-Hartley Act	Prohibits unfair union practices
1948	Sugar Act	Establishes quotas on imports and production of sugar
1948	Reed-Bulwinkle Act	Exempts cartel prices approved by ICC from antitrust
1950	Cellar-Kefauver Act	Amends Clayton Act to prohibit anticompetitive mergers by acquiring assets

Table 1 (Continued)

Year	Law	Function
1950	Defense Production Act	Authorizes the president to exempt industries from antitrust for defense purposes
1953	Small Business Act	Establishes SBA to administer subsidized loans to small business
1954	Atomic Energy Act	Extends AEC regulation of nuclear power
1958	Transportation Act	Authorizes ICC to disregard effect of a regulated rate on other modes of transportation
1959	Landrum-Griffin Act	Prohibits unfair union practices
1962	Food and Drug Amendments	Extends FDA control of testing and marketing drugs
1962	Air Pollution Control Act	Establishes air pollution standards
1964	Civil Rights Act	Establishes Equal Employment Opportunity Commission to regulate job discrimination
1965	Water Quality Act	Requires state standards on pollution
1966	Fair Packaging and Labeling Act	Sets required information on product labels
1966	Child Protection Act	Prohibits sale of hazardous toys
1966	Bank Merger Act	Requires banks to notify regulators of intention to merge
1966	Traffic Safety Act	Establishes National Highway Safety Administration to set standards for autos
1967	Agricultural Fair Practices Act	Prohibits unfair practices by farm-products handlers
1967	Flammable Fabrics Act	Extends control of fabrics standards
1968	Truth-in-Lending Act	Specifies information on terms of credit transactions
1969	National Environment Policy Act	Requires environmental impact statement for projects
1970	Amendment to Banking Act	Regulates credit cards
1970	Economic Stabilization Act	Authorizes general price controls
1970	Securities Investors Protection Act	Establishes insurance for brokers accounts
1970	Occupational Safety and Health Act	Establishes OSHA to set and enforce safety standards for employment
1970	National Air Quality Act	Establishes EPA to administer pollution standards
1972	Consumer Products Safety Act	Establishes Consumer Products Safety Commission to set standards and to prohibit hazardous products
1972	Noise Pollution and Control Act	Sets limits on noise of products

Table 1   (Continued)

Year	Law	Function
1974	Federal Energy Admin- istration Act	Establishes FEA authority to require conservation of energy
1974	Employee Retirement Income Security Act	Establishes terms of firm pension plans
1974	Commodity Futures Trading Act	Establishes CFTC and extends the regulation of futures trading
1975	Consumer Goods Pricing Act	Repeals Miller-Tydings Act
1975	Magnuson-Moss Act	Sets terms and wording for product warranties
1976	Antitrust Improvements Act	Amends antitrust laws to require firms to notify FTC of intent to merge

Sources: Commerce Clearing House 1977; Wilcox 1960; Wilcox and Shepherd 1975; Weidenbaum 1977.

federal regulation is considered here; there are also innumerable state and local regulations. The series displays three different patterns in the direction of regulation: (1) industry-oriented regulation developed from the 1880s to the 1950s; (2) during the 1950s, Congress increased the scope of regulation very little; (3) starting in the early 1960s, a different kind of regulation proliferated, involving many different industries and often directed toward consumer protection, safety, and the environment.

The regulatory legislation until 1950 was mostly industry-specific in that it established or extended industry controls or exempted some industry from antitrust. Of the 45 laws listed, 35 were for this purpose. Five of the laws were concerned with organized labor, so 90 percent of the regulation was directed toward special interests. Notice that all of the traditional regulatory agencies, such as the ICC, the FDA, the FPC, and the FCC, were established prior to 1940—not one new industrial regulatory agency has been established since 1950. Of the five laws concerned with regulation of many industries, four— the Sherman Act, the Clayton Act, the Federal Trade Commission Act, and the Robinson-Patman Act—were antitrust laws; and one, the Securities Act, regulated new issues of stock.

How does the New Deal regulation (1933–40) relate to the earlier pattern? Most of the laws extended regulation that had been established prior to the depression. For example, the transportation, power, communications, and banking regulation extended the reach of old regulatory frameworks. Similarly, exemptions from antitrust had been extended to industries before the depression, too. Securities markets and new issues of stock were a new area for regulation, but the circumstances were much like those surrounding the earlier establishment of the FDA: ostensibly, both the SEC and FDA were formed in response to scandals, and both are supposed to protect consumers by prohibiting the sale of "defective" merchandise.

The National Industrial Recovery Act, which established the NRA to cartelize industry and labor, was a new direction for regulatory policy, but the NRA was short-lived. Competition persisted in many industries, and after two years, the Supreme Court ruled the NRA unconstitutional. Yet, some laws from the New Deal period did set long-lasting new directions for public regulation. Never before had federal regulation promoted the interests of labor unions or set agricultural prices and production or prescribed statutory deconcentration of public utilities. The direction of antitrust regulation was modified by the Robinson-Patman Act, which classified many price differences and low prices as anticompetitive. Aside from these innovations in the regulation of labor, agriculture, utilities, and antitrust, however, the New Deal regulation followed the same pattern as the 1887–1930 period.

The pattern of regulation shifted in the 1950s when Congress enacted only a few regulatory laws, and those laws only modified existing regulation. Unlike the previous period, there were no laws extending regulation into new areas of activity. The most important regulatory law during this decade was the Celler-Kefauver Act, which tightened the antimerger provisions of the Clayton Act and thereby substantially changed antitrust policy toward mergers. As far as extending the scope of regulation is concerned, judicial and administrative decisions became as important as congressional action. For example, a 1954 Supreme Court decision extended FPC (Federal Power Commission) control to the well-head price of natural gas without any change in a statute.

The direction of regulatory legislation shifted again in the early 1960s. This time the trend is dominated by consumer protection, safety, environmental regulation, and the like. Table 1 shows that 18 of the 25 laws enacted since 1962 are for this kind of regulation. Most of the recently established regulation focuses on controlling something specific—like pollution, product safety, job discrimination, or occupational safety—wherever it arises across industries. In this respect the new regulation is like antitrust, which attempted to control monopoly wherever it arises. It is unlike the industry-oriented regulation that is concerned with prices, profits, entry, and other aspects of a specific industry and that dominated the early trend of regulation.

No new industry-oriented regulatory agency was established in the 1960–76 period. A 1974 law established the Commodity Futures Trading Commission; but in effect, that law just renamed and granted independent status to the Commodity Exchange Authority, which had regulated futures trading since 1936.

Antitrust was changed by two laws from this later period: one repealed the Miller-Tydings Act that exempted resale price-maintenance contracts from antitrust; one required firms to notify the FTC of intent to merge so that antitrust authorities can block mergers before they occur. State resale price-maintenance had become generally ineffective by 1975, so repeal of the antitrust exemption has had little impact. The premerger notification law is too new to evaluate its influence on antitrust policy. It is interesting, though, that these two antitrust measures were recommended by the TNEC in 1941, and 35 years later they were enacted into law.

Regulatory Expenditures

Table 2 lists some of the main federal regulatory agencies and presents estimates of the long-run growth of their expenditures. The kinds of regulation that expanded most rapidly should correspond to the highest rates of growth in expenditures. The data show that the most rapid growth was in the Federal Power Commission (FPC) and the Antitrust Division. The slowest growth was in the Interstate Commerce Commission (ICC). Surprisingly, though, there are similar rates of growth for most agencies. The agencies established during the depression years—the CAB, the NLRB, the SEC, and the Wage and Hour Division—have about the same rates of growth as agencies established prior to the depression.

The growth rates for the shorter period 1950–67 reveal that the outliers for the longer-period growth are due mainly to changes in expenditures during the Great Depression and World War II. That is, the FPC and Antitrust had especially rapid growth in the '30s and '40s, and the ICC had especially slow growth because these agencies are not outliers in the 1950–67 period. For the 1950–67 period, the Food and Drug Administration (FDA) is far and away the fastest-growing agency, which is consistent with the shift in direction of regulation that took place during this period. Again, there is little difference between the growth of agencies established during the depression and the growth of agencies established before.

The pattern of expenditures for the Antitrust Division suggests that monopoly explanations of the depression were influential in rapidly expanding antitrust regulation during the 1930s and '40s. The Federal Trade Commission, however, fails to exhibit the same pattern of expenditures. The pattern of expenditures for the Interstate Commerce Commission is puzzling. On the one hand, regulation of telephone and telegraph was transferred from the ICC to the FCC in 1934, which probably reduced ICC expenditures for a time. On the other

Table 2. Growth of Expenditures of Federal Regulatory Agencies

Agency	1969 Expenditures (millions)	Initial Date of Expenditure Data	Initial Date–1969 Annual Rates of Growth[a]	1950–67 Annual Rates of Growth[a]
Antitrust Division	8.3	1925	10.0	5.3
CAB	11.3	1941	9.4	8.2
FCC	20.7	1929	9.4	6.9
ICC	27.2	1925	2.8	6.4
FTC	16.8	1925	6.3	9.0
FDA	68.9	1926	8.9	15.9
FPC	15.7	1925	12.4	8.5
NLRB	34.8	1937	9.2	8.6
SEC	18.6	1936	4.6	7.7
Commodity Exchange Authority	1.9	1925	6.0	4.6
Wage and Hour Division	25.8	1940	6.7	7.9
Tariff Commission	3.8	1925	3.8	7.0
Packer and Stockyards Administration	2.8	1925	4.6	9.9

Source: Stigler 1972.

[a] Calculated from the equation: ln (expenditure) = $a + bt$; annual rate = $100b$.

hand, the ICC began to regulate motor carriers in 1935 and inland water carriers in 1940, which should have increased expenditures.

Influence of Monopoly Explanations

The patterns of economic regulation described here show changes in antitrust policy that can be attributed to monopoly explanations of the depression. Antitrust expenditures grew rapidly when monopoly was a popular issue; an antitrust law was passed to prohibit price differences that could injure small retail merchants; and eventually antitrust laws were passed to block mergers and thereby limit industrial concentration. Also, I believe that the 1970 law authorizing price controls evolved from ideas about administered prices.

During the depression, it was argued that the NRA and the AAA were programs to counter administered prices by raising flexible farm prices, raising production in industries with rigid prices, and raising both prices and production in intermediate industries (Tugwell 1935, pp. 78–96). This argument may have persuaded some policymakers in 1933. I doubt, however, that the survival of agricultural subsidy programs and labor laws that evolved from the NRA should be attributed to administered-price arguments. Surely the political benefits from catering to agricultural and organized-labor interests explain the persistence of these policies better than notions about administered prices and monopoly.

As for the other regulatory policies, I find no indication that monopoly explanations had any long-run impact. Most of the regulation established during the depression was similar to that established before the depression. And regulatory expenditures show that both newer and older controls grew at the same pace. The regulation established in the 1960s and '70s is generally oriented toward consumer and employee protection, so it seems unrelated to monopoly arguments of the depression years.

Are these reasonable interpretations of the patterns of economic regulation? The problem with answering this question is that there is no well-developed theory of why a society adopts its regulatory policies. The most promising attempt so far is the rational–self-interest theory of regulation. Peltzman (1976) has shown that this approach yields implications about the areas in which new regulation will appear that seem to correspond with the sequence of regulations in table 1. It also implies that regulation will be more heavily weighted toward producer protection during depressions and toward consumer protection in expansions, which seems to explain regulation like the NRA. Another implication of the theory is that economic arguments about market failure have little influence on regulatory policy directed toward a specific industry or occupation, because that regulation is often dominated by the regulated interest group. Consequently, there is some basis for the conclusions about monopoly explanations. Antitrust and price control are not directed toward specific industries, so it is more likely that arguments about monopoly, concentration, and price policy will influence this kind of regulation. It is less likely that those arguments will influence the regulation of transportation, communication, utilities, and the like.

ANTITRUST POLICY

This section examines statistics on antitrust regulation to see how monopoly explanations of the Great Depression influenced antitrust policy. Specifically, we shall look at the number of cases filed, the success of enforcement agencies, the pattern of violations alleged, and the use of various remedies. The source of these data is a study of antitrust enforcement by Posner (1970).

Number of Cases Filed

The monopoly explanations of the depression, the focus on antitrust policy, and the fact that monopoly and antitrust had become public issues by the mid-1930s should show up in increased antitrust enforcement. This expected change in antitrust policy is clearly shown by the statistics in table 3.

The number of antitrust cases filed by the Justice Department jumps to a higher level at the end of the 1930s; prior to 1935, the Justice Department filed an average of 8 cases per year; after 1935, the average increases to 35 cases per year. Antitrust cases filed by the FTC exhibit the same jump; prior to 1935 the FTC filed an average of 24 cases per year; after 1935 the average increases to 51 cases per year. For both agencies the change is once-and-for-all, at the time when monopoly explanations of the depression became popular issues; and it cannot be attributed to a trend in enforcement. The stationary higher level of cases also shows, however, that there has not been any tendency for antitrust regulation to keep pace with the growth over time in business activity.[4]

A large share of FTC antitrust cases since 1936 are Robinson-Patman cases. Some of these involve true price discrimination—systematic selling at different prices when marginal cost is equal; and some involve only price differences—selling at different prices when marginal costs are different. True price discrimination is widely considered to be a restraint of trade and a matter for antitrust, but the regulation of price differences has often been anticompetitive

Table 3. Department of Justice and FTC Antitrust Cases

Period in Which Case Was Instituted	Department of Justice	Percentage Won	FTC	FTC Restraint of Trade [a]	Percentage in Which Order Issued [a]	Percentage Judicial Review in Which FTC Won
1890–94	9	38				
1895–99	7	57				
1900–04	6	83				
1905–09	39	55				
1910–14	91	67				
1915–19	43	72	206	206	27	25
1920–24	66	64	177	177	23	60
1925–29	59	93	60	60	39	40
1930–34	30	79	37	37	50	100
1935–39	57	79	215	140	73	95
1940–44	223	78	209	103	76	90
1945–49	157	82	141	47	66	63
1950–54	159	86	123	57	78	67
1955–59	195	91	319	92	70	76
1960–64	215	85	614	69	78	89
1965–69	195	96	178	76		
Total	1551		2279	1064		

Source: Posner 1970.

Note: Totals corrected for error in original table.

[a] Excludes Robinson-Patman cases that do not allege predatory pricing.

and served to control prices for special interests. Excluding questionable Robinson-Patman cases gives a truer picture of FTC policy toward restraint of trade, and it makes the FTC cases more comparable with the Justice Department cases.[5] In table 3, therefore, the FTC restraint-of-trade category excludes all Robinson-Patman cases except those that allege predatory pricing.

The FTC restraint-of-trade cases have a different pattern from that of its overall antitrust regulation. There is no persistent increase in the number of restraint-of-trade cases filed by the FTC: the average per year falls from 24 before 1935 to 16 after 1935. It is fair to say that the FTC stance toward restraint of trade remained constant, and the increase in FTC antitrust activity was due to regulation of price differences. Nevertheless, it remains true that there was a substantial and persistent increase in antitrust regulation following the monopoly explanations of the depression.

Success in Antitrust Cases

Table 3 also presents statistics on the outcome of antitrust cases. The question here is whether there is a difference in the success of antitrust enforcement that can be attributed to the thinking on monopoly that developed during the depression. Prior to 1935, the Justice Department won 70 percent of its cases; after 1935, it won 85 percent. Prior to 1935, the FTC issued a cease-and-desist order in 28 percent of the restraint-of-trade cases; after 1935, an order was issued in 74 percent of the cases. The FTC also became more successful in its restraint-of-trade cases that were reviewed by a court: the FTC won 44 percent prior to 1935 and 83 percent after 1935. The percentages given for each of the five-year periods in table 3 show that the overall percentages are approximately typical for each of the shorter periods. So, like the number of cases filed, there was a shift in the level of success for the antitrust agencies.

It could be that cases were more carefully prepared after 1935, but with the abrupt increase in number of cases, this seems unlikely to explain much of the increased success. I attribute the shift in success to a shift in judicial attitude toward vigorous enforcement of antitrust laws.

Antitrust Remedies

The choice of remedies sought in antitrust cases gives an indication of the direction of policy. If the Justice Department wants to restructure an industry or to compel or prohibit a firm's following specific practices—for example, require a firm to license patents on nondiscriminatory terms—then it must seek

Table 4. Criminal and Civil Cases Brought by the Department of Justice

Period in Which Case Was Instituted	Total Number of Cases	Criminal	Civil	Percentage Criminal	Percentage Civil
1890–94	9	4	5	44	56
1895–99	7	1	6	14	86
1900–04	6	1	5	17	83
1905–09	39	26	13	67	33
1910–14	91	37	54	41	59
1915–19	43	25	18	58	42
1920–24	66	25	41	38	62
1925–29	59	16	43	27	73
1930–34	30	11	19	37	63
1935–39	57	27	30	47	53
1940–44	223	163	60	73	27
1945–49	157	58	99	37	63
1950–54	159	73	86	46	54
1955–59	195	97	98	50	50
1960–64	215	78	137	36	64
1965–69	195	52	143	27	73
Total	1551	694	857		

Source: Posner 1970.

a civil remedy. On the other hand, where the illegality of an act is well established—for example, price fixing—a criminal remedy suffices to penalize a violator. Table 4 shows how the Justice Department's cases have been divided between civil and criminal. There is little difference in the choice of remedies before and after 1935. In the early period, 58 percent of the cases filed were civil cases, and in the later period, 54 percent were civil cases. The series of percentages for five-year periods also shows that the division of cases exhibits neither a trend over the years nor a shift at the time of the depression. One implication of this finding is that the emphasis on concentration and unfair competition in monopoly explanations did not move the antitrust authorities to rely more on remedial as opposed to punitive antitrust enforcement.

Antitrust Violations

The violations alleged in cases filed show what aspects of monopoly were emphasized in enforcement policy. Recall that one line of thought about monopoly and the depression advocated a direct attack on monopoly through measures like deconcentration; an alternative line of thought advocated policy to counter incipient monopoly by attacking business practices—especially a number of so-called abusive trade practices—which are supposed to establish or extend monopoly power. Table 5 summarizes the patterns of alleged violations and certain remedies in Department of Justice cases. Generally, the data show that antitrust policy has shifted toward preventing the growth of monopoly, that there has been virtually no change in policy toward deconcentration, and that the main focus of antitrust has always been price fixing.

The categories of violations are distinguished in table 5. Horizontal conspiracy includes all cases alleging agreements between competitors to eliminate competition. Usually, this is price fixing. Horizontal conspiracy is the most frequently alleged violation: 68 percent of the cases prior to 1935 and 62 percent of the cases after 1935 allege conspiracy. And the period-by-period statistics show that antitrust has consistently emphasized conspiracy. Monopolizing includes all cases alleging that firms enlarged monopoly power. This includes mergers that create monopoly and abusive trade practices. There has been an increase in the frequency of monopolizing allegations, especially in the 1940–54 period: prior to 1935, monopolizing was alleged in 19 percent of the cases, and after 1935 it was alleged in 25 percent of the cases. Acquisitions short of monopoly include all cases alleging that a merger will restrain trade even though it does not establish a monopoly. These allegations increased from 4 percent of the cases before 1935 to 15 percent after 1935, but the increase in this category really occurred after 1955. The Celler-Kefauver Antimerger Act of 1950 made it worthwhile for the antitrust authorities to attack mergers that do not clearly create or extend a monopoly.

The pattern of monopolizing and acquisition allegations taken together reflects the policy of attempting to prevent the growth of monopoly power. The combined percentage of cases with these allegations prior to 1935 is 23 percent; after 1935, the combined percentage increases to 40 percent. Hence, there has been a marked shift toward containing market power since that policy was proposed in the 1930s. On the other hand, deconcentration has never been very important in antitrust policy. The column of dissolution or divestiture remedies in monopolizing cases shows that antitrust has seldom broken up large firms: dissolution or divestiture occurred 13 times prior to 1935 and 19 times after. So the frequency of breaking up large firms has remained at about the same low level over the period studied, but it has decreased relative to the number of cases alleging monopolization. Deconcentration is not a dead issue—in 1968 and 1972 there were serious proposals for new legislation to deconcentrate industry, and some economists have recently argued that decon-

Table 5. Horizontal Conspiracy, Monopolizing, and Acquisitions Short of Monopoly in Department of Justice Cases

Period in Which Case Was Instituted	Number of Cases	Horizontal Conspiracy	Monopolizing		Acquisitions Short of Monopoly
			Number of Allegations	Dissolution or Divestiture	
1890–94	9	3	3		
1895–99	7	7			
1900–04	6	5	1		1
1905–09	39	28	9	3	2
1910–14	91	62	25	5	3
1915–19	43	29	3		1
1920–24	66	50	7		1
1925–29	59	36	8	2	5
1930–34	30	19	9	1	1
1935–39	57	34	14	2	3
1940–44	223	179	65	4	2
1945–49	157	114	60	1	5
1950–54	159	122	62	7	3
1955–59	195	122	45	5	26
1960–64	215	104	40	2	61
1965–69	195	75	19		80
Total	1,551	989	370	32	194

centration could be accomplished with the Sherman Act; but it has not influenced actual antitrust policy.[6]

The role of abusive trade practices in antitrust policy is another indication of the influence of views from the depression years. Abusive trade practices denote business practices by which a single firm is supposed to extend or establish monopoly power. Some examples of abuses are tie-in sales, vertical integration, predatory pricing, and exclusive dealing. As we have seen, some economists advocated attacking abuses as an indirect, long-run method to deconcentrate industry and reduce monopoly power. Table 6 shows the relative importance of abusive-trade-practices cases. Notice that abuses have been alleged since antitrust began, but the share of abuse cases rose at the time of the depression and has persisted at a level of approximately 30 percent. Before and after 1935, the shares of cases alleging abusive trade practices are 18 and 34 percent respectively. This fact confirms the conclusion that antitrust shifted toward a policy of policing business practices in order to contain monopoly.[7]

Robinson-Patman Act

The Robinson-Patman Act of 1936 amended the antitrust laws to make price differences an abusive trade practice. Even if different prices charged by a seller result from cost differences, they can be attacked as anticompetitive if they favor certain buyers. The act was passed in response to complaints from independent food brokers, retail grocers, and druggists who were unable to compete with chain stores. They claimed that the chain stores would monopolize the distribution sector and asked for legislation to preserve competition. The Robinson-Patman Act is anticompetitive and conflicts with the spirit of the antitrust laws, but even so, it has had a strong and persistent influence on antitrust policy.

The statistics in table 3 show that more than half of the FTC cases deal with Robinson-Patman price differences. A study by Posner (1976) shows that after 1969 FTC policy has been to neglect Robinson-Patman violations. Private antitrust enforcement, however, which has grown rapidly in recent years, now makes extensive use of precedents from FTC proceedings and judicial reviews of Robinson-Patman cases in order to enforce the law privately.

To summarize, antitrust policy exhibits three changes that seem to follow from the thought about monopoly and competition that developed during the depression years. (1) There was a substantial increase in antitrust activity that started in the late '30s and continued over time. (2) The antitrust authorities became more successful in winning cases. (3) Antitrust became more concerned with regulating business practices that are thought to establish or main-

Table 6. Significance of Abusive Trade Practices in Department of Justice Antitrust Cases

Period in Which Case Was Instituted	Number of Cases Involving Horizontal Combinations or Conspiracies	Cases Involving Abuse	Percentage of Abuse Cases
1890–94	5	2	29
1895–99	7	0	0
1900–04	6	0	0
1905–09	32	4	11
1910–14	78	23	23
1915–19	32	6	16
1920–24	55	5	8
1925–29	46	11	19
1930–34	23	11	32
1935–39	41	19	32
1940–44	192	75	28
1945–49	127	79	38
1950–54	137	58	30
1955–59	157	65	29
1960–64	172	66	28
1965–69	146	50	26

Source: Posner 1970.
Note: Cases in which both an abuse and a combination are alleged are counted twice in the table.

tain monopoly by coercing, destroying, or excluding competitors from a market.

PRICE CONTROL POLICIES

In 1957 the Senate Subcommittee on Antitrust and Monopoly started hearings to determine the relation between administered prices and inflation and to prescribe public policy to deal with the problem. According to Estes Kefauver, chairman of the committee, administered prices had become more common since the 1930s because agriculture had declined relative to manufacturing and because industry had become much more concentrated. As Kefauver saw it, there were two possible approaches for policy: antitrust could destroy the power of firms to administer prices, or there could be some kind of policy to directly control prices. The work of this committee was instrumental in estab-

lishing the notion of administered inflation—known variously as seller's inflation or cost-push inflation—as a phenomenon due to price increases in
concentrated industries and for which monetary and fiscal policy are ineffective. In turn, administered-inflation arguments led to price-control programs
that are supposed to operate on industry prices—relative prices—in order to
reduce inflation.

The Hearings

The Administered Prices Hearings spanned some four years. Means, Galbraith,
and other economists first testified that inflation in the 1955–57 period was
produced by administered prices (U.S. Congress 1957). The main evidence
was that prices that changed frequently in the period 1926–33—Means's flexible prices—did not on average rise from 1955 to 1957; but prices that were
rigid during the early period—Means's administered prices—rose about 7 percent from 1955 to 1957. The explanation for increases in administered prices
was that they are arbitrary: there is a wide range of discretion within which
firms can set prices without influencing profits, so relative price increases and
somehow an increase in the price level can occur without changes in demand
or costs. Then the committee moved on to investigate individual industries
such as steel, automobiles, and drugs where prices were said to be administered. The issues of increasing industrial concentration and prevalent administered prices, which opened the hearings, were never investigated for the
economy as a whole. Administered prices were never logically linked to inflation. And Stigler (1962) has pointed out additional deficiencies in the committee's work.
    Despite its lack of a sound theoretical or empirical basis, the administered-
inflation doctrine began to convince policymakers that there was a new kind of
inflation that required new kinds of policies. Some economists still argued that
antitrust could solve administered-price problems, but the idea of direct price
regulation was more influential. At one point, Senator Kefauver asked President Eisenhower to intervene in a steel price increase by setting up a program
of price guidelines (U.S. Congress 1959, pt. 9, pp. 4844–47). The Kefauver
Committee also considered a bill to require firms in concentrated industries to
notify the FTC prior to any price increase so that a public hearing could be
held to decide whether the price increase was justified (U.S. Congress 1959,
pt. 11). The president rejected Kefauver's request, and the price notification
bill was not passed. Nevertheless, the Council of Economic Advisors started to
deplore administered inflation, and eventually, when the Kennedy administra-

tion took over in 1961, anti-inflation policy turned to price guidelines and presidential intervention.

Policy Consequences

A program of price and wage guideposts to deal with administered inflation was set out in the 1962 *Annual Report* of the Council of Economic Advisors. The report stated, "There are important segments of the economy where firms are large or employees well-organized or both. In these sectors, private parties may exercise considerable discretion over the terms of wage bargains and price decisions" (U.S. Council of Economic Advisors 1962, p. 185). The guidepost program proposed to solve the problem by tying price and wage changes to productivity changes. The rate of increase in wages was supposed to equal the trend rate of overall productivity increase. Price was supposed to decrease, remain stable, or increase as the industry's rate of productivity increase exceeded, equaled, or fell short of the overall rate. The guideposts were presented as voluntary price controls with moral suasion as the only enforcement mechanism, but the president intervened forcefully when U.S. Steel announced a price increase above the guidelines: the price increase was publicly denounced as unjustified and irresponsible, and threats of antitrust action and tax penalties were made (Barber 1975, p. 172).

This set the tone of anti-inflation policy for the next six years. The CEA set annual guidepost numbers and scrutinized the price policies in various industries. Confrontations between the government and industries such as steel, automobiles, aluminum, copper, and oil have been described elsewhere; government contracts, stockpiles, export controls, and import controls were also used to threaten firms that violated the guideposts (Cochrane 1975).

Guideposts ended in 1969 when the Nixon administration took office, rejected price-control policies, and vowed to stop inflation with monetary and fiscal policy. But two years later, the president intervened in steel prices and construction wages, threatening to revoke beneficial government regulation unless price increases were reasonable (De Marchi 1975, pp. 329-34). By August 1971 the administration decided that direct controls were worthwhile and imposed mandatory price and wage controls, which Congress had authorized in the Economic Stabilization Act of 1970. These controls, the details of which have been spelled out by Kosters (1975) and others, evolved until April 1974, when they were allowed to expire.

Today, there are neither informal guidelines nor formal price controls, but price-control programs continue to be considered as anti-inflation policy alternatives. Price controls for a particular industry like petroleum are not controversial, and it is considered normal for the president to criticize price increases in industries like steel or automobiles. The administered-inflation arguments that were advanced 20 years ago are now taken for granted—neither policy-makers nor the public nor a number of economists question the belief that concentrated industries and organized labor share with the government the responsibility for inflation. No one has ever shown that price controls reduced inflation (Brunner and Meltzer 1976); but this is not surprising, because no one has ever shown how price controls could reduce inflation. Put another way, no one has ever shown that restricting price increases in concentrated industries will reduce the growth of money or increase the growth of demand for money or increase the growth of real aggregate income.

CONCLUDING REMARKS

Monopoly explanations of the Great Depression established a system of belief about monopoly and market failure that has influenced both antitrust and anti-inflation policy over the decades since the depression. First, competition started to be judged by the assumptions of the theory of competitive markets. This led to the belief that industrial concentration measures monopoly power and that business practices that injure competitors, and may thereby increase concentration, are monopolizing tactics. Second, the illusion of rigid prices in concentrated industries was interpreted as showing that oligopoly prices are administered by sellers rather than set by forces of supply and demand. At first, this seemed to explain the length and severity of the depression, and it eventually led to the belief that price increases in concentrated industries produce inflation.

Since industrial concentration came to be regarded as an economic problem, a recurring policy theme has been to deconcentrate industries in order to restore competition and eliminate administered prices. But this proposal has not had much impact on actual policies toward business. Instead, antitrust policy has attempted to deconcentrate industry indirectly by preventing business practices that could increase concentration. The problem is that these business practices are unlikely to be monopolizing tactics, and the link between concentration and monopoly is quite weak. Consequently, a substantial amount of antitrust activity has been misdirected if the goal is to reduce monopoly. Anti-inflation policy has attempted direct control of prices in concentrated industries in order to let monetary policy promote full employment, economic growth, or some other goal. The problem is that price controls divert attention away from policies that can stop inflation; and to the extent that price controls are effective, the allocation of resources and distribution of output is distorted.

Monopoly explanations may have influenced public regulation of business in areas other than antitrust and anti-inflation policy. I have focused on those two areas because the effects can be documented. If one argues that monopoly explanations of the Great Depression convinced people that markets do not work well, almost any regulation could be related to those explanations, but it would add nothing to our understanding of how policy develops.

NOTES

1. Friedman and Schwartz's (1963) account of monetary events during the depression years revived the monetary explanation of the Great Depression. Darby (1976) and Haberler (1976) have also given monetary explanations. Temin (1976) rejected the monetary explanation. But both Meltzer (1976) and Gandolfi and Lothian (1977) have maintained that Temin is wrong and that the evidence supports the monetary explanation.
2. For example, on the basis of statistics showing that nearly half of corporate assets were controlled by 200 corporations, Berle and Means (1932) argued in their influential book that industries had become highly concentrated.
3. Stigler (1947) summarizes and criticizes the kinky-demand-curve theories.
4. For example, output in the manufacturing sector grew about 390 percent in real terms over the period 1940–69, but the number of antitrust cases remained approximately constant.
5. The Justice Department has seldom been involved in a Robinson-Patman case.
6. In recent years, though, the Justice Department started actions designed to break up IBM and AT&T. At the same time the FTC has sought to break up the eight largest oil companies.
7. Antitrust concern with abusive trade practices has been controversial because several economists have argued that most of the business practices that have been labeled abusive are not methods of extending or preserving monopoly power. Either the practices are competitive tactics, or they serve as methods of increasing the profits from existing monopoly power. To the extent that antitrust attacks competitive practices, it is inefficient. To the extent that antitrust attacks symptoms of monopoly, it does nothing to eliminate monopoly and to increase efficiency.

REFERENCES

Ackley, G. 1959. "Administered Prices and the Inflationary Process." *American Economic Review* 49: 419–30.

Bain, J. S. 1951. "Relation of Profit-Rate to Industry Concentration: American Manufacturing, 1936–1940." *Quarterly Journal of Economics* 65: 293–324.

Barber, W. J. 1975. "The Kennedy Years: Purposeful Pedagogy." In Goodwin (1975).

Berle, A., and Means, G. C. 1932. *The Modern Corporation and Private Property*. New York: Macmillan.

Blair, J. M. 1959. "Administered Prices: A Phenomenon in Search of a Theory." *American Economic Review* 49: 431–50.

Brunner, K., and Meltzer, A., eds. 1976. *The Economics of Price and Wage Controls*. Carnegie-Rochester Conference Series on Public Policy. Vol. 2. Amsterdam: North-Holland.

Buchanan, J. 1975. *The Limits of Liberty*. Chicago: University of Chicago Press.

Burns, A. R. 1936. *The Decline of Competition*. New York: McGraw-Hill.

Cochrane, J. L. 1975. "The Johnson Administration: Moral Suasion Goes to War." In Goodwin (1975).

Commerce Clearing House. 1977. *Trade Regulation Reporter*. Chicago: Commerce Clearing House.

Darby, M. R. 1976. "Three-and-a-Half Million U.S. Employees Have Been Mislaid: Or, an Explanation of Unemployment, 1934–1941." *Journal of Political Economy* 84: 1–16.

De Marchi, N. 1975. "The First Nixon Administration: Prelude to Controls." In Goodwin (1975).

Douglas, P. H. 1937. "What Shall We Do about Monopoly Prices?" *Journal of the Society for the Advancement of Management* 2.

Edwards, C. D. 1940. "Can the Antitrust Laws Preserve Competition?" *American Economic Review* 30 (supp.): 164–79.

Friedman, M., and Schwartz, A. J. 1963. *A Monetary History of the United States, 1867–1960*. Princeton, N.J.: Princeton University Press, for the National Bureau of Economic Research.

Galbraith, J. K. 1936. "Monopoly Power and Price Rigidities." *Quarterly Journal of Economics* 50: 456–75.

———. 1957. In U.S. Congress (1957, pp. 32–71).

Gandolfi, A. E., and Lothian, J. R. 1977. " 'Did Monetary Forces Cause the Great Depression?' A Review Essay." *Journal of Money, Credit and Banking* 9: 679–91.

Goodwin, C. D., ed. 1975. *Exhortation and Controls*. Washington, D.C.: Brookings Institution.

Haberler, G. 1976. *The World Economy, Money, and the Great Depression, 1919–1939*. Washington, D.C.: American Enterprise Institute.

Hawley, E. W. 1966. *The New Deal and the Problem of Monopoly*. Princeton, N.J.: Princeton University Press.

Humphrey, D. D. 1937. "The Nature and Meaning of Rigid Prices, 1890–1933." *Journal of Political Economy* 45: 651–61.

Kosters, M. H. 1975. *Controls and Inflation*. Washington, D.C.: American Enterprise Institute.

Kreps, T. J. 1939. "Some Price Problems." In *Economic Problems in a Changing World*, ed. W. Thorp. New York: Farrar and Rhinehart.

Lustgarten, S. 1975. *Industrial Concentration and Inflation*. Washington, D.C.: American Enterprise Institute.

Mason, E. S. 1938. "Price Inflexibility." *Review of Economic Statistics* 20: 53–64.

———. 1939. "Methods of Developing a Proper Control of Big Business." *Proceedings of the Academy of Political Science* 18: 40–49.

Means, G. C. 1935. *Industrial Prices and Their Relative Inflexibility*. U.S. Congress, Senate. 74th Cong., 1st sess., S. Doc. 13.

———. 1936. "Notes on Inflexible Prices." *American Economic Review* 26 (supp.): 23–35.

————. 1957. In U.S. Congress (1957, pp. 74–125).

Meltzer, A. H. 1976. "Monetary and Other Explanations of the Great Depression." *Journal of Monetary Economics* 2: 455–71.

Mund, V. A. 1965. *Government and Business*. New York: Harper & Row.

Nelson, S., and Keim, W. S. 1940. *Price Behavior and Business Policy*. TNEC monograph no. 1. Washington, D.C.: Government Printing Office.

Nutter, G. W. 1951. *The Extent of Enterprise Monopoly in the United States, 1899–1939*. Chicago: University of Chicago Press.

Peltzman, S. 1976. "Toward a More General Theory of Regulation." *Journal of Law and Economics* 19: 211–40.

Posner, R. A. 1970. "A Statistical Study of Antitrust Enforcement." *Journal of Law and Economics* 13: 365–419.

————. 1976. *The Robinson-Patman Act*. Washington, D.C.: American Enterprise Institute.

Simons, H. C. 1934. *A Positive Program for Laissez Faire*. Chicago: University of Chicago Press.

Stigler, G. J. 1942. "The Extent and Bases of Monopoly." *American Economic Review* 32 (supp.): 1–22.

————. 1947. "The Kinky Oligopoly Demand Curve and Rigid Prices." *Journal of Political Economy* 55: 432–49.

————. 1949. "Competition in the U.S." In *Five Lectures on Economic Problems*. London: Longmans, Green.

————. 1962. "Administered Prices and Oligopolistic Inflation." *Journal of Business* 35: 1–13.

————. 1971. "The Theory of Economic Regulation." *Bell Journal of Economics and Management Science* 2: 3–21.

————. 1972. "The Process of Economic Regulation." *Antitrust Bulletin* 17: 207–35.

Stigler, G. J., and Kindahl, J. K. 1970. *The Behavior of Industrial Prices*. New York: Columbia University Press, for the National Bureau of Economic Research.

Temin, P. 1976. *Did Monetary Forces Cause the Great Depression?* New York: W. W. Norton.

Thorp, W. L., and Crowder, W. F. 1941. *The Structure of Industry*. TNEC monograph no. 27. Washington, D.C.: Government Printing Office.

Tugwell, R. G. 1935. "The Economics of the Recovery Program." In *The Battle for Democracy*. New York: Columbia University Press.

U.S. Congress. 1938. *Message from the President of the United States Transmitting Recommendations Relative to Strengthening and Enforcement of the Antitrust Laws*. Senate. 75th Cong., 3rd sess., S. Doc. 173.

————. 1939. *Hearings*, statement of W. J. Ballinger, Director of Studies and Economic Advisor to the Federal Trade Commission. Senate, Temporary National Economic Committee. 76th Cong., 1st sess., pt. 5.

————. 1941. *Final Report and Recommendations*. Senate, Temporary National Economic Committee. 77th Cong., 1st sess., S. Doc. 173.

————. 1957. *Administered Prices: Hearings.* Senate, Committee on the Judiciary, Subcommittee on Antitrust and Monopoly. 85th Cong., 1st sess., pt.1.

————. 1959. *Administered Prices: Hearings.* Senate, Committee on the Judiciary, Subcommittee on Antitrust and Monopoly. 86th Cong., 1st sess., pts. 9, 11.

U.S. Council of Economic Advisors. 1962. *Annual Report.* Washington, D.C.: Government Printing Office.

U.S. Federal Trade Commission. 1941. *Relative Efficiency of Large, Medium-Sized, and Small Business.* TNEC monograph no. 13. Washington, D.C.: Government Printing Office.

Wallace, D. H. 1936. "Monopolistic Competition and Public Policy." *American Economic Review* 26 (supp.): 77–87.

Weidenbaum, M. L. 1977. *Business, Government, and the Public.* Englewood Cliffs, N.J.: Prentice-Hall.

Weston, J. F., and Lustgarten, S. 1974. "Concentration and Wage-Price Change." In *Industrial Concentration: the New Learning,* ed. H. J. Goldschmid et al. Boston: Little, Brown.

Wilcox, C. 1960. *Public Policies toward Business.* Rev. ed. Homewood, Ill.: Richard D. Irwin.

Wilcox, C., and Shepherd, W. G. 1975. *Public Policies toward Business.* 5th ed. Homewood, Ill.: Richard D. Irwin.

9 COMMENTS ON "MONOPOLY EXPLANATIONS OF THE GREAT DEPRESSION AND PUBLIC POLICIES TOWARD BUSINESS"

William Poole

The Cox paper has two main themes. The first concerns the validity of monopoly explanations of the Great Depression. The second concerns the effects of monopoly explanations on public policy since the 1930s. I will discuss these two themes in turn.

VALIDITY OF MONOPOLY EXPLANATIONS

A central problem of macroeconomic theory has been why downward shifts of demand generate lower output rather than lower prices. As a matter of economic theory we all agree that *if* prices are rigid, *then* a downward shift in demand will generate lower quantity. The monopoly explanations of price rigidity may or may not be correct; nevertheless, these explanations have the characteristic that they will do the job if they are correct.

Cox argues that monopoly explanations of the depression were displaced by Keynesian explanations. This argument, it seems to me, is not quite right. The Keynesian model is built upon the assumption of wage and price rigidity. While it is true that as a formal matter wage and price rigidity is treated as an assumption, it is also true that in the Keynesian tradition this assumption tends

208

to be justified by appeals to institutional factors, including monopoly power. Thus, the Keynesian explanation is in good part consistent with the monopoly explanation.

What is involved here, it should be emphasized, is the use of the monopoly explanation to account for wage and price rigidity. This argument is clearly not, as Cox suggests, a "dead issue." There is still much controversy over the reasons for sluggish wage and price adjustment—sluggish as compared to the adjustments that would be necessary to maintain output. What is true—and this is probably what Cox has in mind—is that the monopoly explanation cannot be an explanation in the sense of itself explaining the business cycle. There is simply no evidence of a cyclical pattern to monopoly that would make an explanation in this sense plausible. However, the monopoly explanation for price rigidity, accompanied by explanations for fluctuations in aggregate demand, has a continuing following.

EFFECTS OF MONOPOLY EXPLANATIONS ON PUBLIC POLICIES

Cox seems to suggest that monopoly explanations primarily date from the 1930s. This view is surely wrong. Monopoly explanations long predate the '30s and were clearly of concern in the latter part of the nineteenth century. I would suppose that what really changed in the 1930s was public attitudes toward government intervention rather than theoretical accounts of the role of monopoly.

This view would seem to be supported by the federal regulatory statutes listed in table 1 of Cox's paper. Of the 76 statutes listed, 23 date from the 1930–39 decade. Clearly there was an outburst of regulatory legislation in the 1930s that was not seen before or since.

The legislation listed in table 1 seems inconsistent with the argument that monopoly explanations had a major effect on the course of legislation. The legislation in the 1930s and since has involved at best very minor extensions of antitrust law and some extensions of industry price regulation. More importantly, though, from the table 1 list, I count five statutes since 1930 explicitly designed to provide certain exemptions from antitrust and a number of other statutes explicitly designed to raise wages or prices. But most of the legislation since 1930, particularly in the 1960s and '70s, is designed as protective of health, safety, and environment. Cox himself emphasizes this aspect of the more recent legislation, and it is clear that it does not seem to fit an antimonopoly cast.

The discussion of the administered-price doctrine also gives the impression that this doctrine is a product of the 1930s. While the words date from the 1930s, the basic idea is far older. The notion that market power explains inflation dates from the nineteenth century at least. In addition, it does not seem correct to attribute the form of the Nixon wage-price controls to the administered-price doctrine. That doctrine, if it has any explicit public policy message at all, would have led to controls only on large firms and large unions. In fact, the 1970s' controls were levied against all firms and all workers regardless of the degree of market power that might be possessed. While it is true that the controls later on exempted smaller firms in some respects, this exemption is primarily explained by administrative considerations rather than the administered-price doctrine.

In his discussion Cox mentions but does not really examine the rational–self-interest theory of regulation. Surely there is much truth to this argument. But I would also mention in passing the importance of the intellectual climate of distrust of business and faith that government can set matters right. I suspect also that certain accidents of history have had much to do with the nature of the legislation listed in table 1. Certainly the timing, if not the very existence, of some legislation is explained by particular events in the form of scandals, bankruptcies, poisonings, and so forth, within the context of a climate conducive to regulatory extensions. It is not very satisfactory, to be sure, to attribute certain legislation to random events, but we should not try to explain more than we know how to explain.

10 COMMENTS ON "MONOPOLY EXPLANATIONS OF THE GREAT DEPRESSION AND PUBLIC POLICIES TOWARD BUSINESS"

Thomas Mayer

Cox starts his paper with a rejection of the prevailing monopoly explanation of the Great Depression. He argues that monopoly was not increasing, that industrial prices were not really inflexible, and that the administered-price theory, in addition to having its facts wrong, also lacks an acceptable theoretical foundation. But, ill-founded as the administered-price theory was, it had a major impact on policy. It led to increased efforts to limit concentration and many years afterward made peacetime price controls politically acceptable. But, although Cox connects the Nixon price controls to the prevalence of the administered-price explanation in the 1930s, he rejects the view that an increased receptiveness toward government regulations resulting from the Great Depression led to our current flood of regulations. These regulations are primarily oriented toward protecting consumers and employees and therefore seem unrelated to the monopoly argument of the 1930s. At the end of his paper he mentions the possibility that the monopoly explanation of the Great Depression has undermined the public's faith in capitalism and thus has led indirectly to our current willingness to accept more and more regulations. But he rejects this line of approach as too vague.

In these comments I will deal with two issues. One is Cox's evaluation of the administered-price explanation, and the other is the indirect way the depression prepared the way for our current wave of regulations by undermining public confidence in the market system.

FLEXIBILITY OF INDUSTRIAL PRICES

I certainly do not intend to defend all the elements of the monopoly explanation of the Great Depression; on many major points it is clearly wrong. For example, the inflexibility of industrial prices was not a new development in the 1930s. The bimodal distribution of frequency of price changes that Means found for this period already existed in earlier recessions (Humphrey 1937) and hence cannot readily explain the unique severity of the Great Depression.

But Cox is not arguing primarily that industrial prices have been inflexible all along. Instead, on two grounds he argues that industrial prices are *not* inflexible. First, the evidence for price inflexibility relates to list prices rather than to actual transactions prices; and second, the theory that attempts to rationalize sticky prices in concentrated industries, the kinky oligopoly demand curve, is invalid. But Cox's evidence is unconvincing. He attempts to document the difference in the behavior of list prices and transactions prices by citing the work of Stigler and Kindahl, who claim to have shown that administered prices are in large part merely a statistical illusion. But are they? If one looks at the figure in which Stigler and Kindahl compare BLS wholesale prices to their own transactions prices (Stigler and Kindahl 1970, fig. 6–6), the so-called illusion turns out not to be such a great illusion after all. Transactions prices also show little flexibility. In general, as Milton Moore (1972) and Leonard Weiss (1977) have shown, an analysis of actual transactions prices confirms what the wholesale price data show.

Cox rejects the administered-price approach, not only because he believes that the Stigler-Kindahl data disconfirm it, but also because he believes that it has no valid theoretical underpinning. With a one-sentence reference to Stigler's classic article, he claims that the underlying theory, the kinky oligopoly demand curve, has been disconfirmed. This is much too cavalier a dismissal. There exists by now a very large literature on the kinky oligopoly demand curve, much of it favorable.[1] To ignore completely this opposing point of view, as though it were not worthy of discussion, is hardly good procedure.

Besides, one does not have to accept the kinky oligopoly demand curve to believe that many industrial prices are inflexible. As good a neoclassicist as Phillip Cagan (1974, pp. 18–21), while rejecting the kinky oligopoly demand curve, believes that industrial prices are inflexible due to the difficulties that firms experience in coordinating price changes. And Arthur Okun (1975) has recently presented an alternative theory in which price inflexibility emerges as the consequence of an attempt to reduce search costs. This approach gives one a sharply different view of price inflexibility from the one presented by Means. The notion underlying Means's analysis is that price flexibility is the norm and that inflexibility has to be explained by a special factor, market power. To Okun, however, price inflexibility of custom goods is the normal state of affairs, and what has to be explained is not why certain prices change infrequently but why other prices change so frequently. And the answer is, of course, that these highly flexible prices are disproportionately the prices of raw materials.[2]

The idea that the limited extent to which prices responded to the Great Depression is somehow "normal" may seem bizarre. Given the unprecedented severity of the depression, shouldn't industrial prices have fallen much more? Part of the answer may be that in 1930 and 1931 the Great Depression was so unprecedented only by hindsight. To be sure, in 1930 unemployment stood at 14.2 percent of the nonfarm labor force, but it had been higher than this in 1908, 1914, 1915, and 1921. Given the previous experience that some depressions, despite being severe, were short-lived, it is not so surprising that industrial firms decided to cut their prices only moderately in 1930 and 1931.

In fact, a very crude test suggests that the response of wholesale prices in the period 1929–33 was not very different from that in some previous severe recessions. In the 1907–08 recession, wholesale prices fell by 5.2 percent (Warren and Pearson 1933, p.13), that is, at a monthly rate of 0.40 percent.[3] In the 1913–14 recession they fell by 4.4 percent (U.S. Bureau of Labor Statistics 1970), that is, at a monthly rate of 0.19 percent. By comparison, wholesale prices fell by 37.5 percent between August 1929 and March 1933, which amounts to 0.87 percent per month. Admittedly, the 1929–33 depression was much more severe. One can make a very rough adjustment for this difference in severity in the following way. Lebergott (1964, p. 512) gives yearly unemployment rates for nonfarm employees. They show an increase in the unemployment rate by 12.5 percentage points between 1906 and 1908, by 7.4 points between 1913 and 1915,[4] and by 32.3 points between 1924 and 1933. One can divide the change per month in the wholesale price index by these increases in the unemployment rates to obtain a very crude measure of the change in wholesale prices per one percent increase in unemployment. If so one gets ratios that are fairly similar for all three depressions. They are 0.032 for 1907–08, 0.026 for 1913–14, and 0.027 for 1929–33. While this comparison is exceedingly rough, it suggests that wholesale prices were not unusually inflexible in the 1929–33 period compared to some previous depressions.[5] When one adds to this the previously cited fact that in earlier recessions the frequency of price changes also had a bimodal distribution, this greatly weakens the administered-price theory of the Great Depression. The factor alleged to have made this depression so uniquely severe and persistent was also present in other depressions.

But if prices were not unusually inflexible in the early 1930s, why did this inflexibility attract so much attention? Perhaps this was due in part to the more recent experience during the 1920–21 recession, and perhaps the explanation lies in the length of the depression. Previous depressions were over soon enough that one could not discover how much time is required for many industrial prices to decline. By 1934, however, this had become apparent.

But Means and his supporters did more than just argue that industrial prices had become inflexible. They also claimed that this worsened the depression. But this is good neoclassical economics. If aggregate demand falls, one can restore full employment either by raising aggregate demand back again through fiscal and monetary policies or by reducing the price level. In a neoclassical model, price reductions, by raising the real stock of money, are an effective remedy. But this is not so in a crude, old-fashioned Keynesian model, for here aggregate demand depends, not on the real stock of money, but on nominal income. And since wage and price cuts reduce nominal income, they are not an effective remedy for a depression. Given the way Keynesian theory swept the field, it is not surprising that mainstream economists soon abandoned the idea that we could get out of the depression by a fervent antitrust policy that would lower prices.

Modern neo-Keynesian theory, however—as it is embodied in the MPS model, for example—tells us that the real quantity of money is important, so that price cuts could, in principle, be an effective weapon against unemployment. Thus, as Weinstein's paper in this volume shows, the NRA-induced price increases were a "bad thing." To this extent, the monopoly explanation of the Great Depression, for all its obvious weaknesses, is consistent with both our major macroeconomic approaches.

All in all, despite the fact that hardly any serious economist would argue nowadays that the Great Depression was caused by monopoly power, some of Cox's criticisms of the monopoly explanation are too severe.

EXPLAINING THE GROWTH OF REGULATION

Cox concludes his paper by saying that the monopoly explanation of the Great Depression may be responsible for an increase in regulation by creating a distrust of the free market. But he then rejects this approach, arguing rather cryptically that in this way "almost any regulation could be related to those explanations, but it would add nothing to our understanding of how policy develops." One of the purposes of this conference, however, is to elucidate how the experience of the 1930s shaped current events, and hence there is something to be said for discussing its indirect effects via changes in public opinion, even if such a discussion need be vague and tentative.

Many of the events of the 1930s could, in principle, have been responsible for shifting the public's view of the proper dividing line between government and business. First, the very occurrence of any serious and widely perceived economic problem is likely to shift public opinion, because it gives people an incentive to reexamine previously held beliefs. And since we started with a primarily free enterprise economy, any shift was more likely to increase, rather than reduce, the desired role of the government. Second, many people saw unemployment as the fault of the private sector. This must obviously have enhanced public support for government regulation—even on issues not directly related to unemployment—by reducing the perceived benefits of a private enterprise system. Third, public exposure in various congressional hearings of questionable practices in business and finance must surely have reduced the legitimacy of a free market system. Fourth, the rise of the monopoly theory of the depression must also have weakened the case for the status quo. Finally, the very fact that *some* regulations are imposed makes the imposition of still other regulations more likely by reducing the ideological barriers against them.

Although it is therefore very likely that the Great Depression fostered a willingness to accept government regulation of business, it does not necessarily follow that it bears a substantial responsibility for the current spate of regulations. Its role *might* be minor compared to the secular factors—so well described by Schumpeter (1942, chap. 12)—that are weakening capitalism. Two considerations make this superficially plausible. One is that the current environmental regulations bear little similarity to the regulations imposed in the 1930s. Second, much time elapsed between the New Deal regulations and current upsurge in regulatory activity.

But neither of these considerations is persuasive. American business has traditionally fended off unwelcome regulations by ideological slogans such as "government regulation is un-American" and "you cannot repeal the laws of supply and demand."[6] Once some regulations are imposed, other regulations—even if they deal with different problems—no longer look so un-American, and the "law of supply and demand" does *seem* to be repealable after all. Moreover, it would be naive to expect that, if the Great Depression made government regulation politically more acceptable, there would then be a continuous stream of new regulations. Government activity does not expand merely because the barrier against it is weakened; strong positive pressure for it is required, too. In the immediate postwar years this pressure did not exist. Both the unemployment rate and the inflation rate were low, and externalities were not yet perceived as a serious problem. But when externalities did burst upon the public's awareness, government regulation could expand rapidly, since the barrier against it had been weakened by the Great Depression.[7]

Can one test empirically the hypothesis that the Great Depression reduced the political barriers to regulations? Ideally, one should compare public opinion polls in the 1920s, in the late 1930s, and in the 1970s to see if the current attitude toward government regulations already prevailed in the late 1930s but not in the late 1920s. Unfortunately, such public opinion polls do not exist for the 1920s. But the view that the public was then hostile to government regulations is very plausible. Thus, in discussing public attitudes toward welfare payments, a public opinion expert wrote:

> The early-to-rise and early-to-bed thrift and work ethic may well have made an about face just before the pollsters appeared on the scene [1935]. It must have begun to dawn on people that hard work and dedication were not always insurance against unemployment and poverty at a time when there was actually not enough jobs to go around. [Erskine 1972, p. 256]

I will therefore assume that the public was hostile to government regulation prior to the Great Depression and will just compare the public opinion polls taken in the late 1930s and early 1940s with those taken in the 1960s and '70s. Unfortunately, I could locate only two issues on which comparable questions were asked in both periods.[8] On the question of whether the government should "provide for all people who have no other means of obtaining a living," 65 percent agreed in 1940 and 73 percent in 1948; while in 1964, 68 percent agreed that the "government must see that no one is without food, clothing or shelter." When asked whether the government should see to it that everyone who wants to work can find a job, 77 percent agreed in 1935 and 61 percent in 1939; while in 1960, 67 percent of the sample, when asked how much they would like to see that the government guarantee the availability of jobs, responded "a great deal or fair amount," and only 26 percent said "very little or nothing" (Erskine 1975, pp. 258–59, 263–64).

Public opinion polls in the late 1930s and early 1940s asked a number of other relevant questions on which, unfortunately, no comparable responses from current polls are available. On a number of issues the public showed substantial support for government intervention or a general antibusiness attitude.[9] In May 1937, 57 percent of a sample agreed that a company "doing business in more than one state should be required to get a license from the Federal Government" (*Public Opinion Quarterly* [*POQ*] Oct. 1939, p. 595). In January 1941, 71 percent of a sample agreed that the government should take over a factory "that refuses to make defense materials for the government at a price considered reasonable by the Defense Commission" (*POQ* June 1941, p. 330). In the same year, while 32 percent of a sample thought that the federal government had too much power, 59 percent thought that there was "too much power in the hands of a few rich men and large corporations" (*POQ* Fall 1941, p. 475). And in 1940, almost a quarter of a sample believed that there should be a law "limiting the amount of money an individual is allowed to earn in a year." Only 37 percent of a 1940 sample agreed that "if business pays top wages it is fully entitled to keep for its shareholders any amount of profit it could earn," while an equal percentage thought that shareholders should get a "certain fixed percent, and the remainder should somehow be divided between workers and stockholders" (*POQ* June 1940, pp. 354, 346–47). In a 1939 sample the food stamp plan [then in effect] was approved by 70 percent of those who expressed an opinion (*POQ* Mar. 1940, p. 92).

To be sure, responses to other questions showed a more probusiness attitude. In 1940, 51 percent of a sample agreed, and only 27 percent disagreed with the view that there should be less regulation of business by the federal government over the next four years (*POQ* Mar. 1941, p. 149). And in 1938, when asked about the causes of the depression, respondents ranked "Roosevelt and the New Deal policies" ahead of the other nine alternatives; in a 1939 poll, 55 percent of the sample agreed that to create new jobs and reduce unemployment "it would be better to follow the ideas of big businessmen" than those of the Roosevelt administration (*POQ* Oct. 1939, pp. 590–91, 587). Similarly, in 1940 the public thought balancing the budget to be the most important economic task for the next administration (*POQ* Sept. 1940, p. 541). Finally, in a 1940 sample, 56 percent of the respondents said that the interests of employers and employees were basically the same and only 25 percent saw them as opposed (*POQ* June 1940, p. 346).

Despite their rather mixed nature, these views show considerable hostility toward business—in all probability, much more hostility than would have been found in the 1920s. And they probably do not differ very much from the contemporary public opinion that supports, or at least acquiesces in, our current wave of regulations.

It is, of course, possible that the public became less favorable to government controls as the memory of the Great Depression faded and then became again more favorably disposed to government controls only recently. Unfortunately, only a few relevant polls appear to be available for the "middle period." One of them (University of Michigan 1951), taken in October 1950, shows that 76 percent of a sample believed that the good things about big business outweigh the bad things, while only 10 percent held the opposite view (p. 18). But while this suggests that the public had changed its opinion, another question tells a different story; 53 percent of the sample thought that government control over the activities of big business was a "good thing," and another 18 percent agreed to this statement with qualifications (p. 44). Only 18 percent opposed such control. And among those who indicated that they would not disapprove of all government controls, 32 percent wanted to see the government exercise control over prices (p. 47). Admittedly, by October 1950 when this survey was taken, prices had risen by 4.4 percent since January—an unusually high inflation rate for that period.[10]

All in all, the above data, spotty though they are, suggest that by 1940 a firm belief in the free market was no longer a barrier to government regulations. If one assumes, as seems plausible, that these attitudes were different before the Great Depression, then the Great Depression did bring about a major shift in public opinion. And the very limited evidence that is available does not provide much reason for thinking that opinions changed back again toward faith in the free market after the Great Depression. This suggests that a change in public attitudes during the Great Depression was a major factor that permitted the rapid growth of government regulations in recent years.

NOTES

1. See, for instance, Efroymson's (1955) brilliant criticism of Stigler's article. For a discussion of the growth of the literature on the kinky oligopoly demand curve, and its tenor, see Stigler (1978).

2. Among the prices classified as "most rigid," in the period 1890–1933, 93 percent were those of finished goods, and only 2 percent were prices of raw materials. By contrast, among the flexible prices, 39 percent were those of raw materials, and 46 percent were prices of finished goods (Humphrey 1937, p. 656).

3. The monthly rate cited is simply the average monthly price decline disregarding compounding.

4. Although the NBER chronology has the trough in 1914, I am using the 1915 unemployment rate since this is higher than the 1914 rate.

5. Of course, wholesale prices were much more flexible in the 1920–21 depression, but this probably was due to the fact that the war inflation had driven prices up to what was considered an unrealistic level.

6. The public responds to ideological argument for a reason akin to transaction costs. It is not worth most people's time to study the details of a political question. Hence, they select an intellectual supermarket on the basis of its advertising and then acquire most of their opinions there.

7. Concern about pollution spread amazingly fast. In a poll taken in 1965, only 28 percent of the population considered air pollution to be a very or somewhat serious problem; in 1970, 69 percent did. The corresponding figures for water pollution are 35 percent and 74 percent. Erskine called "the unprecedented speed and urgency with which ecological issues have burst upon the American consciousness" a miracle (Erskine 1972, pp. 121, 120).

8. A warning is in order; seemingly trivial variations in the wording of a question can elicit substantially different results.

9. It is surprising, however, that in 1939 the public was still fairly optimistic about employment. Only 13 percent had accepted the stagnation thesis, agreeing that "the great age of opportunity and

expansion in the U.S. is over," while 72 percent saw expansion ahead. And in 1940, 61 percent of the sample preferred a job "that pays a high wage, but with a fifty-fifty chance of getting promoted or fired" while only 33 percent preferred a "steady job earning just enough to get by on, but with no prospect for advancement" (*Public Opinion Quarterly,* March 1940, p. 93; June 1940, p. 355).

10. In addition, as discussed previously, support for government welfare payments was as strong in 1948 as in 1940, or stronger.

REFERENCES

Cagan, P. 1974. *The Hydra-Headed Monster.* Washington, D.C.: American Enterprise Institute.

Efroymson, C. 1955. "The Kinky Oligopoly Demand Curve Reconsidered." *Quarterly Journal of Economics* 69: 119–36.

Erskine, H. 1972. "Pollution and Its Costs." *Public Opinion Quarterly* 36: 120–35.

――――. 1975. "The Polls: Government Role in Welfare." *Public Opinion Quarterly* 39: 257–74.

Humphrey, D. 1937. "Rigid Prices, 1890–1933." *Journal of Political Economy* 46: 651–61.

Lebergott, S. 1964. *Manpower in Economic Growth.* New York: McGraw-Hill.

Moore, M. 1972. "Stigler on Inflexible Prices." *Canadian Journal of Economics* 4: 486–93.

Okun, A. 1975. "Inflation: Its Mechanics and Welfare Cost." *Brookings Papers on Economic Activity* 2: 351–90.

Public Opinion Quarterly, various issues.

Schumpeter, J. 1942. *Capitalism, Socialism and Democracy.* New York: Harper.

Stigler, G. 1978. "The Literature of Economics: The Case of the Kinked Oligopoly Demand Curve." *Economic Inquiry* 16: 185–204.

Stigler, G., and Kindahl, J. 1970. *The Behavior of Industrial Prices.* New York: Columbia University Press, for the National Bureau of Economic Research.

University of Michigan. 1951. *Big Business from the Viewpoint of the Public.* Survey Research Center. Ann Arbor.

U.S. Bureau of Labor Statistics. 1970. *All Commodities Wholesale Price Index.* Washington, D.C.: Government Printing Office.

Warren, G., and Pearson, F. 1933. *Prices.* New York: John Wiley.

Weiss, L. 1977. "Stigler, Kindahl and Means on Administered Prices." *American Economic Review* 67: 610–19.

11 THE IDEOLOGICAL ORIGINS OF THE REVOLUTION IN AMERICAN FINANCIAL POLICIES

George D. Green

The title for this paper deliberately paraphrases Bernard Bailyn's masterful work, *The Ideological Origins of the American Revolution*. Economic historians in recent years have devoted great energy and ingenuity to measuring the economic burdens on (or benefits for) the American colonists of British imperialism, on the presumption that their answer might reveal the economic basis for that political conflict. Bailyn's book makes this debate over the economic costs of imperialism largely irrelevant by reminding us that the conflict did not involve "rational" economic or political men maximizing their individual or national interest. He portrays the political rebels of the 1770s as unconscious victims of cultural lag, interpreting the actions of king and parliament through the distorted ideological lens of a fading political theory inherited from some angry English Whigs of the preceding century. To understand fully the action of our revolutionary ancestors, we must see it first through their eyes, from within their ideological perspective, and then recognize where that ideology sometimes diverged from the economic and political reality of their day.

As the depression of the 1930s becomes almost as historical as the American revolution, we can acquire a similar perspective on its "ideological lags." As our own economic and political theories move out from beneath the shadow of the New Deal paradigm, we can take a bifocal view of its economic policies. First we look for the "old" theories or ideologies through which the economists and political leaders of the 1930s interpreted their experience and formulated their policy responses. Then we step back and use the "new" theories of our own day to assess the impacts of those policies upon the 1930s' economy. First the political and intellectual history of the *origins* of economic policy, then the (sometimes) econometric history of the *impacts* of economic policy.

I have borrowed my title from Bernard Bailyn, so I will take my sermon text from a more familiar source, the final paragraph of Keynes's *General Theory*:

> The ideas of economists and political philosophers, both when they are right and when they are wrong, are more powerful than is commonly understood. Indeed, the world is ruled by little else. Practical men who believe themselves to be quite exempt from any intellectual influences, are usually the slaves of some defunct economist. Madmen in authority, who hear voices in the air, are distilling their frenzy from some academic scribbler of a few years back. I am sure that the power of vested interests is vastly exaggerated compared with the gradual encroachment of ideas. Not, indeed, immediately, but after a certain interval; for in the field of economic and political philosophy there are not many who are influenced by new theories after they are twenty-five or thirty years of age, so that the ideas which civil servants and politicians and even agitators apply to current events are not likely to be the newest. But, soon or late, it is ideas, not vested interests, which are dangerous for good or evil. [1936, pp. 383–84]

My short sermon on this Keynesian text has two parts, one on "temptation" and the other on "the path to salvation." I would first urge you to avoid the temptation of showing "what fools our ancestors were." There is a tendency in economics and other social (and natural) sciences to look upon the history of the discipline (economic thought) as demonstrating our progress out of past error into present enlightenment. The first danger of this approach lies in its lack of humility and charity: judge not, that ye be not judged! It denies us the opportunities to discover the limitations of our own theories in the wisdom and variety of theories of the past. The second danger is that we may misread the earlier theories by aligning them according to our own theoretical categories, when these categories were not so clearly or neatly drawn in the minds of earlier writers. We may distort past theories by reading back our modern factional concerns, dividing the previous generation of economists into sheep or scapegoats. Keynes himself and his followers did this to "Keynes vs. the Classical Economists." Others have done it to "monetarists" vs. "commercial loan" theorists. The New Dealers stereotyped their "laissez faire" opponents, and now a new generation of "neoclassical" economists attacks the New Dealers for naive planning and overregulation.

Another variation of this backward projection of current theoretical concerns is the search for "prophets crying in the wilderness," earlier theorists who anticipated our splendid modern insights. For Keynes the prophets were Mandeville and Malthus and even Major Douglas. For the American Keynesians they were Alexander Hamilton and Marriner Eccles, while for the monetarists we have the greenbackers or Lauchlin Currie, according to your taste. Rather than searching for such scapegoats or prophets, we might examine the past theories more in terms of the issues and conceptual problems of their own times, allowing for a greater variety of ideas, a range of sophistication and intellectual confusion, and the drift of theory and opinion even within the lifetime of one person.

The "path to salvation" that I draw from Keynes's text follows his emphasis on the priority of ideas over "vested interests." Notice that he does not deny vested interests; instead, he boldly asserts that even politicians, businessmen, and bankers have ideas! This insight frees us from the need to pursue a detailed, political narrative of the making of financial policy during the depression. We can take it for granted that bankers and farmers and labor leaders and other "vested interests" fought politically for their economic interests. Our task is to find out how they perceived and articulated those interests, what theory and ideology they used to persuade others as policies were debated and developed.

We will take one major shortcut in this intellectual history of 1930s' financial policy. Our interest is in the "prevailing interpretations of the major events," that is, the interpretations that "prevailed" politically and became embodied in legislation or administrative policy. The theories of the political losers will receive less attention than they deserve, except where they were powerful enough to limit or modify the policy outcome.

BUSINESS LEADERSHIP, THE MARKET ECONOMY, AND THE ROLE OF GOVERNMENT

The many specific changes in economic thought and financial policy during the depression years all took place against the backdrop of broader shifts in prevailing American attitudes toward the relative power and responsibility of business and government. The substantial increase in government power, and the shift of that power toward the federal government and away from state and local governments, required and reflected major shifts in prevailing ideology.

Obviously, many people hesitated or resisted this transformation of thought and policy, but by 1940 even major elements of the business community had moved a great distance from the intellectual assumptions of 1929. The traditional opposition to big government had been repeatedly weighed in the balance against the potential benefits of specific government actions and the desperate needs of the moment. One small episode will illustrate this general tension between the older business ideology and the acceptance of new government actions to meet the depression crisis. In August 1934, A. J. Byles, president of the American Petroleum Institute, delivered a memorial address on the site of the first American oil well in Pennsylvania. His historical observations carried an obvious political message:

> The pioneers of the oil industry were rugged individualists. . . . What else, if not rugged individualism, could have ignored ease, risked life and fortune, taken victory and defeat with stoic courage, wrested from an unwilling and hostile nature one of her most dangerous and priceless possessions, and subdued and harnessed it in the service of mankind? . . . They believed in the Jeffersonian maxim that people least governed are best governed. . . . Democracy and autocracy or bureaucracy cannot live side by side or long breathe the same air. . . .

Yet moments later in the same speech, Byles offered the following policy recommendation: "The public's interest, both in conservation and price, may be safeguarded through government control of the volume of crude oil allowed to be produced" (Byles 1934).

Many changes had been rationalized and accepted initially as temporary or "emergency" policies, only to become permanent institutional fixtures a few years later. Senator Carter Glass reluctantly accepted a temporary relaxation of his cherished "eligibility" rules for rediscounting commercial paper and agreed to sponsor the Glass-Steagall Act of 1932 only because President Hoover told a breakfast meeting of senators and administration leaders that the United States would be forced off the gold standard within two weeks unless the legislation was passed. Yet within two years the gold standard had been abandoned, and a year later (in the Bank Act of 1935) Glass accepted, still reluctantly, the permanent displacement of the narrow "eligibility" rules. Similarly, President Roosevelt justified his earliest budget deficits by segregating the regular (balanced) budget from the "emergency" budget for relief expenditures. By 1938 the president was defending deliberate deficit spending as a contribution to raising national income and thereby achieving the still-desired balanced budget out of a "balanced income."

One major impetus for the rising acceptance of government economic leadership was the declining faith in the business community and the market economy. In the late 1920s business leaders reached the pinnacle of self-confidence and popular support. The older business values of "rugged individualism" and "laissez faire" still ran strong. But they had been complemented by the emerging ideology of a new generation of corporate progressives who believed in scientific management, technological progress through institutional research, mass consumption funded by high productivity and high wages, and economic stability through cooperative forecasting and voluntary planning by business and government. Herbert Hoover was the high priest of this progressive business ideology, but it had other spokesmen in Ogden Mills, Gerard Swope, Owen D. Young, and Edward Filene, as well as a number of economists and business school professors (Horowitz 1971).[1]

The promised "new era" of permanent prosperity and mass consumption dissolved into years of depression. The image of a professional business elite guiding the economy for the general welfare was shattered even more dramatically by the business failures and the Pecora investigation's allegations of fraud, mismanagement, and selfish speculations with corporate funds. It is hardly surprising that the 1930s witnessed a greater suspicion of business motives and a particular desire to regulate the behavior of financiers and "speculators." The Securities Act of 1933, the Securities Exchange Act of 1934, the separation of commercial and investment banking, and the Public Utility Holding Company Act of 1935 all bear witness to this disillusionment and suspicion.

The competitive market economy also lost credibility in the depression. This attack on the market system was sometimes linked with the attack on businessmen and their behavior, but it also went in some quite different directions. Many critics of business behavior sought (through government intervention) to purify and restore the competitive market ideal by eliminating fraud and monopoly. But others, including some of Hoover's corporate progressives and even some small businessmen, renounced the competitive faith and searched for an alternative economic structure (Hawley 1966). The recurring talk about "destructive competition" found its strongest fulfillment in the National Recovery Administration, whose administrator, Gen. Hugh Johnson, contended somewhat melodramatically that "the very heart of the New Deal is the principle of concerted action, in industry and agriculture, under government supervision, looking to a balanced economy—as opposed to the murderous doctrine of savage and wolfish competition and rugged individualism, looking to dog-eat-dog and devil take the hindmost" (Johnson 1935, p. 169). This skepticism toward competition found expression in such financial policies as the ceilings on the interest rates paid on bank deposits and the limitations on chartering of new banks.

As the faith in business leadership and market competition declined, the role of government gradually expanded. The American value of equal opportunity had long been affirmed through government attacks on monopoly power. The more liberal New Dealers went beyond equal opportunity to economic egalitarianism. The depression undermined the traditional theory that wealth or poverty is determined by individual character, hard work, and thrift. The liberal economic theories also suggested that egalitarian redistribution would alleviate "underconsumption" and thus contribute to stabilization.

Accompanying this increased egalitarianism was a growing acceptance of government's obligation to assure personal economic security to its citizens. This first took the limited form of emergency relief and rescue from bankruptcy, then the provision of emergency public employment, and finally the responsibility for stabilizing (or even "planning," in the minds of some) the entire economy. Many of the financial reforms of the 1930s reflected this increased government commitment to personal economic security: the insurance of deposits, home mortgages and farm commodity prices, the regulation of stock exchange transactions, and even the partial maintenance of gold reserves behind Federal Reserve notes.

THE STOCK MARKET BOOM AND CRASH

In the popular mind of the 1930s (and even today) the opinion surely prevailed that the stock market boom and crash triggered or caused the depression. This was more an unquestioned belief than a reasoned explanation, and thus it was probably completely unaffected by the technical debates that economists conducted over the issue during the 1930s. The historical sequence was just too obvious, the timing too perfect, to be a mere coincidence. The "speculative mania" of the boom phase lifted security prices to unsupportable and irrational levels; the inevitable crash in security values wreaked widespread financial havoc that brought on the depression.[2]

A classic assertion of this widespread opinion, full of the typical moral indignation, appeared in the report of the Pecora investigation on stock exchange practices, published by the Senate Committee on Banking and Currency in 1934:

> In retrospect, the fact emerges with increasing clarity that the excessive and unrestrained speculation which dominated the securities markets in recent years has disrupted the flow of credit, dislocated industry and trade, impeded the flow of interstate commerce, and brought in its train social consequences inimical to the public welfare.... The economic cost of this downswing in security values [September 1929 to July 1, 1932] cannot be accurately gauged. The wholesale closing of banks and other financial institutions; the loss of deposits and savings; the drastic curtailment of credit; the inability of debtors to meet their obligations; the growth of unemployment; the diminution of the purchasing power of the people to the point where industry and commerce were prostrated; and the increase in bankruptcy, poverty, and distress—all these conditions must be considered in

some measure when the ultimate cost to the American public of speculating on the securities exchanges is computed. [U.S. Congress 1934, pp. 5, 7]

Closely related to this boom-crash-depression doctrine was the question of what had caused the stock market boom in the first place. Some people blamed the stockbrokers and bankers who had allegedly promoted "unsound" securities, manipulated the market through secret pools and other schemes, created investment trusts to keep the spiral going, and defrauded the investing public by depriving it of meaningful information about the true financial condition of the companies or governments whose securities were being sold. These same "insiders" were also suspected of having profited from the crash, by selling out early and then selling short on the way down. The Pecora investigation provided dramatic testimony and documentation to embarrass Wall Street before the bar of public opinion. President Hoover had initially encouraged such a congressional investigation (though he intended a more limited and less sensational one) because of his own belief that his recovery program was being blocked by a powerful group of Wall Street "bears" who were driving stock prices down through short selling (Carosso 1970, pp. 322, 325, 329–46).

The shocking accusations of the Pecora investigation added to the political momentum for legislative reforms of stock market practices. The first response, the Securities Act of 1933, concentrated on public disclosure of information about the issuing company, the securities, and the underwriters. This added information offered some limited protection to investors against fraudulent or wildly inflated new security issues, but it certainly did not outlaw speculation or even prevent most of the transactions that so scandalized Mr. Pecora (Carosso 1970, pp. 356–63).

The Securities Exchange Act of 1934 supplemented the 1933 law by imposing detailed regulations on stock exchange transactions (not just new issues), requiring annual financial reports from all listed corporations, and creating an agency, the Securities Exchange Commission (SEC), to exercise ongoing surveillance over the industry. It also set a minimum margin requirement (55 percent of market value) on brokers' loans and empowered the Federal Reserve Board to vary the percentage above that minimum level (Carosso 1970, pp. 375–79).[3]

The SEC seems to have accomplished most of the reform goals envisioned for it during the 1930s. Continuing regulatory efforts have minimized the incidence of fraud, exploitation of privileged information, and other abuses. Continuing sharp fluctuations in market values and the volume of transactions have not reproduced the "panicky" dynamics or liquidity crises of 1929, although brokerage firms themselves have failed or been forced into rescue mergers on several occasions. For reasons still sharply debated among economists today, the stock market fluctuations of recent years have apparently not generated the serious macroeconomic instability that popular opinion attributed to the crash of 1929.[4] In the 1970s the SEC, by inaugurating variable commission rates, has even broken somewhat free of the cartel-enforcing role of a "captured" regulator.

A truly significant structural change came with the Glass-Steagall Banking Act of June 1933, which required the separation of commercial and investment banking into separate firms. This action forced a drastic reorganization of the investment banking industry and temporarily reduced the amount of capital available to float new security issues. Of greater concern to Senator Glass and other believers in the "commercial loan" theory of sound banking, it also reduced the vulnerability of the commercial banks to illiquidity arising from the financial troubles of their security affiliates. The divorce of commercial and investment banking was opposed by most bankers when it was first proposed, though after the Pecora testimony about the abuses of the National City Company, a number of major bankers, led by Winthrop Aldrich of Chase National Bank, decided that the split was inevitable and supported the legislation (Carosso 1970, pp. 368–75; Kennedy 1973, pp. 212–13).

Economists seem to have supported the reform, and it has been unquestioned in the years since, as far as I can determine. This unanimity seems more remarkable in an era when bank portfolios and trust accounts have come to include a wide variety of noncommercial securities, and bank holding companies have been formed to permit diversification into a variety of financial services. Certainly the investment banking industry and stock exchanges have endured dramatic adjustments to shotgun mergers, negotiated commission rates, and the increasing role of institutional investors; yet none of these stresses has suggested a reunion with the great financial resources of the commercial banking industry. The division imposed in 1933 may not have been structurally efficient at the time, as many bankers complained, but after 45 years of political and economic adaptation it seems irreversible.

While a segment of popular opinion blamed the stock market boom (and "resulting" crash and depression) on the speculative manipulations of bankers and stockbrokers, most economists and other expert observers of the day attributed the boom to preceding conditions of "easy credit." There were a variety of (often vague and implicit) definitions of this "easy credit" condition and a similar variety of theories about how it affected the stock market and the rest of the economy. Each different diagnosis of the "easy credit" malady led to a different financial policy remedy. Debate among economists and policymakers over this issue was prolonged and vigorous, so that no single "prevailing interpretation" dominated financial policy.

Some writers related their conceptions of "easy credit" to the classical gold standard and attributed the "inflationary" expansion to gold imports from Europe or to Federal Reserve money creation (multiplied by a gold-reserve ratio well below 100 percent) upon this expanding gold stock. This "overexpansion" of money and credit began in 1921, and finally the excessive credit seeped into the security markets after 1927. The proper remedy according to this view would be a more conservative central-bank policy, which "may well act to curb undue expansion and to discourage contraction of credit but it should rarely, if ever, act to enforce expansion of credit" (Noyes 1930, pp. 188–91).[5]

A larger and more prominent group of observers relied upon the "commercial loan" theory and defined "easy credit" as bank loans to brokers or to others to finance purchases of securities. They believed that the Federal Reserve's low rediscount rate and especially its open-market purchases of securities in 1927 had encouraged bankers to expand the "speculative" types of loans and that these "speculative" loans absorbed credit that might otherwise have gone to finance "legitimate" commercial activities. Once this "easy credit" got a stock market boom under way and made "speculative" loans even more profitable, any attempt by the Federal Reserve to contract credit would only restrict commercial activity even further while the boom ran its inevitable disastrous course. The only possible remedy would be some regulatory action specifically designed to restrict bankers to commercial loans by outlawing their loans for "speculative" purposes (Chandler 1971, pp. 18, 47).

Key officials in the Federal Reserve System apparently followed approximately this "commercial loan" model in determining their discount and open-market policies during the last two years of the boom in 1928–29. They had pursued an expansionary policy in 1927 in order to combat recession at home and to help ease the pressure on European exchange rates (thus helping Britain maintain its commitment to the gold standard). But as signs of "speculative" price increases and a rapid rise in the volume of brokers' loans occurred early in 1928, policy shifted sharply toward restriction. Discount and bill rates were sharply increased and member-bank reserves put under pressure through gold losses and open-market sales (Chandler 1971, pp. 37–39).

By August 1928, Federal Reserve officials had begun to face what they perceived as a policy dilemma, one that lasted until the stock market crash late in 1929. They wanted to discourage stock market "speculation" by restricting the flow of credit into that channel, but they did not want a general restriction of credit that might bring on a recession. These goals were agreed upon, but sharp disagreements arose over the methods to achieve them (Chandler 1971, pp. 47–48, 55).

Agricultural representatives opposed all increases in the discount rate and preferred open-market sales of securities for restriction (plus preferentially low interest rates on acceptances, to help move the crops to market). Governors Strong and Harrison of the New York Federal Reserve Bank generally advocated more active use of open-market operations for general stabilization and minimal concern over the stock market. If it were to become necessary to act against speculation, they preferred a brief, sharp rise in discount rates, hoping (implausibly, perhaps) that this would quickly shock the stock market downward without seriously restricting the rest of the economy (Chandler 1971, pp. 42–53).

In February 1929, the Federal Reserve Board tried Adolph Miller's proposed solution for the dilemma, sending a letter to the Reserve banks urging them to deny rediscounts to a member bank "when it borrows either for the purpose of making speculative loans or for the purpose of maintaining speculative loans." The letter asserted that "the extraordinary absorption of funds in speculative security loans" had caused a "firming of money rates to the prejudice of the country's commercial interests." This "direct action" strategy against speculation generated immediate controversy and prolonged theoretical arguments among economists. How would "speculative loans" be defined, they asked, since the use of funds need not correspond to the form of a loan or the collateral behind it? Critics also denied, both theoretically and by examining credit data, that the stock exchange "absorbed credit." They also pointed out that much of the increased funding for brokers' loans in 1929 came not from banks but from corporations and other sources out of reach of Federal Reserve restrictions. In any case, the "direct action" program had little real impact, mainly because of the inability or unwillingness (especially in New York) of the Federal Reserve banks to implement it (Chandler 1971, pp. 55–70; Reed 1930, pp. 154–74; Hardy 1932, pp. 153–72; Snyder 1930; Currie 1934a).

These internal debates within the Federal Reserve, and the dialogue with critics outside, did not vanish after the stock market crashed. The interpretations and evaluations of the 1927–29 policy struggles lingered on to shape policy responses during the emerging depression. The prevailing retrospective view within the Federal Reserve System followed the outlines of the "commercial loan" theory and blamed "easy credit" in 1927 for launching the boom and "aggravating the speculative fever." Emmanuel Goldenweiser, director of research for the Federal Reserve Board, believed (in 1951) that the 1928 policy of restraint had been insufficiently restrictive and that it was particularly compromised by the low rate on acceptances. He agreed with many of the early critics' arguments against the 1929 "direct action" strategy, emphasized that most of the "speculative" credit came from nonbank sources, and considered the board's increase of the discount rate in August 1929 "tardy and too mild to have any effect on the frenzy of speculation." He basically argued that once it had accidentally let the "speculative frenzy" get started in 1927, the board was powerless to prevent the boom and crash without bringing on an earlier recession. "What monetary authorities could do in such circumstances was limited to making money more expensive. Since then the situation has changed; loans for account of non-banking correspondents are prohibited by law and the Board has a new weapon against excessive use of credit in the stock market through the determination of margin requirements on security loans." Goldenweiser also believed that immediately after the stock market crash the board had "embarked on a policy of easy money which it pursued through the depression," except for brief restraints to fight the 1931 gold drain and to raise reserve requirements in 1936–37 (Goldenweiser 1951, pp. 142–55).[6]

Policy discussions within the Federal Reserve System from 1930 to 1934 seem quite consistent with Goldenweiser's retrospective view of the 1927–29 period. Since the central bank was believed powerless to halt a "speculative fever" once it got under way (without imposing a recession on "legitimate business"), it became doubly important to "nip it in the bud." The Federal Reserve did lower discount, bill, and acceptance rates after the crash (which they considered proof of "easy credit"), but they were generally unwilling to carry on significant open-market purchases, because such "artificial stimulation" might reignite speculation (even in the midst of depression!). There was much of the "commercial loan" and "accommodation" theories behind these decisions, of course, but I think also a lingering anxiety about the dangers of reviving "speculation."

At first glance it would seem that the power over margin requirements granted to it by the Securities Exchange Act of 1934 should have enabled the Federal Reserve Board to stop worrying about the dangers of stock market speculation. Goldenweiser and his assistant Woodlief Thomas both claimed that this reform removed the policy dilemma of 1927–29. But notice how perfectly that "reform" still fits within a theory concerned about the "quality of credit," still assumes that bank loans to finance "speculation" are dangerous and undesirable, and assumes that they can be identified by form or collateral.

Even the enactment of margin requirements did not remove fear of stock market speculation. Marriner Eccles was no believer in the "commercial loan" theory of sound banking, as many of the Federal Reserve bankers of 1930–33 had been. Yet when the stock market experienced a modest speculative flurry in the spring of 1937, he reacted strongly. In a memo of March 11 he wrote to the president that, unless coordinated government policies prevented inflationary developments in particular industries, "there is grave danger that the recovery movement will get out of hand, excessive rises in prices encouraging inventory speculation will occur, excessive growth in profits and a boom in the stock market will arise, and the cost of living will mount rapidly. If such conditions are permitted to develop, another drastic slump will be inevitable (Eccles 1951, pp. 296–97). Eccles's remarkable fear of inflation in the presence of high unemployment was widely echoed at the time and clearly owed its persuasive power to the fear of repeating the uncontrollable boom-bust sequences of 1929. In fairness to Eccles, he worried more about inventory accumulations, declining construction (due to an inflationary cost-push squeeze on profits), and declining federal deficits than he did about the stock market. And he was not immobilized as the Federal Reserve had been in 1928–29; he proposed a combination of increased deficit spending, voluntary price restraints by labor unions and corporations, and increased reserve requirements (to gain the power to stop inflation quickly if it should develop). I do think that the premature anti-inflationary element of his program (the increase in reserve requirements) was prompted by a belief in the "danger" of another "1929." The theory of uncontrollable stock market boom and bust cast a long shadow indeed when it touched a liberal expansionist like Marriner Eccles.[7]

There was significant criticism and debate during the early 1930s over the prevailing theory of the stock market boom and crash. Specific elements of the theory—the absorption of credit, the identifiability of "speculative" loans— were rejected, and the "commercial loan" doctrine itself came under such heavy attack that many economists regarded it as discredited and pointedly announced their rejection of it. But, of course, this academic debate had little influence on the thinking of Senator Carter Glass, the heads of Federal Reserve banks, and countless other bankers and policymakers whose ideas, as Keynes said, had been shaped by "defunct economists" of an earlier day. Perhaps the prevailing idea also survived because most of the critics did not really offer a coherent alternative interpretation of the historical events and policy options of 1927–29. The prominent exception, the most coherent alternative interpretation, came from Lauchlin Currie in a book published in 1934, *The Supply and Control of Money in the United States.*

Currie joined the attack on the "commercial loan" doctrine but broadened it to criticize economists for using vague terms like "credit" or "bank credit" in place of a well-defined and carefully measured concept of money. He contended that the Federal Reserve should have focused its policymaking on controlling the supply of money rather than the quality or composition of "credit" or even the level of various interest rates. (His discussion of the exogenous influences on that money supply and of the variations in velocity, or demand for money, is sophisticated beyond the level of other "quantity theorists" of that era.) After a close statistical review of the impact of Federal Reserve actions (or inactions), Currie came to several novel conclusions. There had been no real inflation in 1928–29 in commodity prices nor any of the other signs of excess demand or "boom": excess profits share, commodity speculation, labor scarcity and inefficiency, or inventory hoarding. The Federal Reserve's 1927 expansion to alleviate recession was excellent, and its 1928 policy of slightly raising interest rates to prevent recovery from overheating was also appropriate, if slightly too restrictive. But by spring or summer 1929, the Federal Reserve had enough information to justify a shift toward monetary expansion to fight the recession. Instead, its policy was *highly effective* in *restricting* the money supply (although "ineffective" against "total credit" and only "slightly effective" against "bank credit"). Rather than being ineffective against credit inflation and runaway speculation, Currie said, the Federal Reserve had been much too effective in restricting the money supply and bringing on the recession it had hoped to avoid (Currie 1934a, pp. 160–61, 168–76; 1934b).

Despite its clarity of analysis and its coherent alternative interpretation, Currie's version did not displace the prevailing interpretation. (It may have helped Currie toward his influential career as a senior staff member in the Treasury and Federal Reserve, where this articulate young monetarist helped Marriner Eccles develop a statistical series on the government's "net contribution to community purchasing power," that is, its cash deficit, and became one of the early New Deal advocates of Keynesian deficit spending.) Nor did it prevent another liberal economist, Harold Barger, from accepting most of Currie's analysis while supporting the quite different conclusion that 1928–29 had been a period of "overinvestment and excessive profits" and of disguised inflation—because rigid prices had denied the fruits of rising productivity to consumers and had raised profit shares (Barger 1935). Barger's interpretation blended neatly into the New Deal's structuralist and "underconsumption" views of the depression and reaffirmed that the Federal Reserve had overexpanded "credit" in 1927–29. New Dealer Currie must have read liberal Barger with a sign of despair.

FINANCIAL POLICIES DURING THE HOOVER YEARS

Herbert Hoover brought to the presidency exceptional career experience, strong convictions about the relationship between government and the economy, and strong intellectual background in the problems of depression. After a successful worldwide business career in mining engineering and brief humanitarian service in Europe at the end of World War I, Hoover became the progressive star of the Harding and Coolidge cabinets as secretary of Commerce (and "undersecretary of everything else," as one rival complained). One of his first tasks as secretary of Commerce was to promote and organize the President's Conference on Unemployment. The results of that conference and of Wesley Mitchell's follow-up report on business cycles for the Department of Commerce in 1923 largely shaped Hoover's policy responses to depression in the 1930s. Edward E. Hunt, secretary to the 1921 conference, summarized their implications:

> The [Mitchell] study showed that the influences which cause business booms and slumps lie within business, and that the most productive results in controlling the so-called business cycle are likely to be obtained from a consideration of business methods rather than from efforts to explore remote considerations. It showed that business booms are an evil: they create a false "prosperity" which is like fever; they are always followed by slumps and indeed are the cause of slumps. Slumps in the main are due to wastes, extravagance, speculation, inflation, over-expansion and inefficiency in production developed during booms, so that these evils are most effectively attacked by preventing booms. This result may be accomplished in part by provision for such economic information as will show the danger signs, and by the use of this information by bankers, manufacturers and merchants. Conservative business policies then tend to flatten the top of the threatened boom and thus to fill up the trough of the depression. [Hunt 1927]

As secretary of Commerce, Hoover did work energetically with the business community on programs to eliminate waste and to improve business statistics to help businessmen identify trends and better match their production to forecasted demand. He relied on the Federal Reserve to control inflation by controlling the credit expansion of individual banks. He believed that, in addition to coordinating these programs and promoting voluntary cooperative action in the private sector, the federal government should coordinate the engineering and financial development of a standby program of construction projects (federal, state, local, and private), unemployment reserve funds, and employment bureaus ready for use in case of depression. Late in 1928 he proposed a $3 billion federal-state reserve fund "to be used for public construction work, so as to ward off unemployment in lean years" (Brandes 1962, pp. 3–34; Warren 1959, pp. 65–66). Unfortunately, the fund was not actually created before the depression.

Despite all this prior theorizing and "preventive" activity, Hoover obviously did not act very effectively once the depression was upon him. I think that some of his hesitation resulted from slow diagnosis of conditions; some of it was quite consistent with his 1920s' thinking and his basic values; and some of it reflected political deadlock and his growing concern with balancing the federal budget.

In the midst of the market crash in October 1929, Hoover issued a public statement reassuring the nation that "the fundamental business of the country, that is production and distribution of commodities, is on a sound and prosperous basis." (He offered no such assurance about the stock market.) In the months thereafter he offered similarly optimistic public statements, evidently intended to bolster public confidence and thus encourage sustained spending. During the same months he was telling leading businessmen in private that a severe depression had arrived and that he would need their cooperation to minimize its impact, especially by maintaining wage rates and accelerating or increasing construction projects. A series of conferences and contacts with construction-industry leaders, governors, and mayors indicated immediate construction projects for $5 billion, and in his December 3 message to Congress, Hoover proposed $700 million of federal construction and a reduction of $160 million in federal income taxes. In these early efforts there was little emphasis on financial policies beyond a brief recommendation in his December message for reform of the banking system. The combination of confidence-building publicity, presidential coordination and promotion of voluntary efforts from the private sector and local governments, and modest spending on federal public works exemplified Hoover's consistent policy response to the entire depression (Galbraith 1954, p. 111; Warren 1959, pp. 114–20).

It was not until the fall of 1931, in fact, that Hoover offered major proposals on domestic financial policies. By this time the international economy had suffered the Kredit Anstalt crisis and subsequent departures from the gold standard, and the American economy had suffered nearly a year of accelerated bank failures. Even in this atmosphere of international financial crisis Hoover's first approach was to seek the voluntary cooperative action of the banking community. Calling the leading New York bankers to a secret White House meeting on October 4, 1931, he proposed that they charter a National Credit Corporation that would assemble a capital of $500 million (from the stronger banks) to be lent to banks in financial difficulty who could not borrow from the Federal Reserve. Hoover was aware that individual bankers had been seeking their survival individually through efforts at liquidation that only dragged the economy downward; he hoped that this instrument for mutual support and cooperation would give them the "courage" and "confidence" to provide credit more liberally. Within a few weeks it was evident that the banking community was unable to assume these risks on a grand scale, that the National Credit Corporation was a failure (Nash 1959).

At this juncture Hoover finally abandoned voluntarism and private financing and accepted the proposals that Eugene Meyer (governor of the Federal Reserve Board) and Ogden Mills (undersecretary, soon to be secretary, of the Treasury) had been urging on him for months. In December he sent a message to Congress proposing the establishment of a Reconstruction Finance Corporation, modeled closely after the War Finance Corporation that Meyer had directed for most of its existence (1919–20 and 1921–29). As established by Congress in January 1932, the RFC was authorized to lend to virtually all types of financial intermediaries (including closed or liquidating banks) and to railroads; an amendment of July 1932 extended coverage (much to Hoover's dismay) to permit loans to finance local governments' relief expenditures. Capitalized at $500 million, it was allowed to issue debentures for an additional $1.5 billion (raised to $3.3 billion in July). In its first five months the RFC lent over $800 million, and by the end of Hoover's presidency it had disbursed about $2 billion, about half of it to banks and trust companies. RFC debentures were not eligible for purchase by the Federal Reserve, so none of this debt was directly monetized. But since nearly all the debentures were sold to the Treasury (whose debts the banks could purchase) and since RFC loans enabled banks and other financial intermediaries to "rediscount" a variety of frozen assets, the RFC did substantially enhance their solvency, liquidity, and probably even their willingness to lend (Nash 1959; Warren 1959, pp. 140–45; Friedman and Schwartz 1963, p. 320; Sprinkel 1952).

In his meetings with congressional leaders in the fall of 1931, Hoover had outlined several other supporting financial proposals, some of which followed close behind the RFC. Some limited relief for farmers threatened with foreclosure of their mortgages came through the addition of $125 million to the capital of the Federal Land Banks and the creation of Regional Agricultural Credit Corporations. After the banking industry lobbied to block a comprehensive system of mortgage discount banks, Hoover finally settled for the more limited system of Home Loan Banks, which began rediscounting mortgages for savings banks and savings and loan institutions. The Glass-Steagall Act allowed more flexible discounting powers by the Federal Reserve banks. Hoover had also advocated structural reforms of the banking system (requiring all banks to join the Federal Reserve System, separating commercial and investment banking, and allowing branching by national banks), but the bankers defeated these measures in the halls of Congress (Warren 1959, pp. 157, 163–67).

Each of these "reconstruction" programs (except the banking reforms) compromised Hoover's commitment to voluntarism and decentralized financing and reflected his response to pressures from Congress and the progressives within his administration. Ogden Mills explained the theory behind the "reconstruction" proposals in a series of speeches in 1932.

> The outstanding fact today is that deflation has proceeded too far. Every additional decline in credit and prices and securities brings with it further bank failures, and bank failures in their turn lead to further contraction in credit and

prices. The deflation has now reached a point where it feeds upon itself, and where forces working for economic recovery are nullified by the psychological momentum of the downward movement. . . .

Business as we know it cannot be conducted without credit, and credit cannot function without confidence. . . .

Our sole purpose in the development of the reconstruction program has been to set free the recuperative and constructive forces within business itself by removing the pressures which were stifling them—to clear away major obstacles so that the nation's business might have an opportunity to do for itself what the Government cannot hope to do for it, and so that the normal vigor of our economic life might again assert itself.

In February 1933, just a month before the inauguration of the new president, Mills added the following defensive footnote to his explanation:

Credit cannot be brought into active use by brute force. The increased employment of credit depends upon an expansion of business activity, that is, the buying and selling of commodities, employment of labor and the acceleration of all the manifold economic activities that form part of the modern economic mechanism. Potential credit is a favorable factor to business recovery, but until the credit actually goes to work it can affect neither business nor prices. It will go to work only when the lender feels secure enough to lend, and the borrower confident enough of the use he can make of the money to borrow. [Cited in Romasco 1965, pp. 195–97]

Mills (and Hoover) clearly believed by this time that "credit" contraction and bank failures might have contributed to the downward spiral of depression. But the explanation mixes such restraints on spending arising from limits on the *supply* of "credit" with psychological ("confidence") restraints on the *demand* for both credit and spending. (Politicians have problems with model "identification" too!) Hoover clearly did not intend for the RFC to provide a direct fiscal stimulus to aggregate demand (as he did envision for public works, for example). Even Congress, in adding the loans to finance relief, was apparently more agreed upon providing food and shelter for the desperate than upon providing stimulus to consumer spending for recovery. The prohibition against sale of RFC debentures to the Federal Reserve makes it equally clear that neither Hoover nor Congress intended for the reconstruction program to expand the money supply. The stimulus to spending would come indirectly, by "removing the pressures" of illiquidity in the financial intermediaries and "clearing the major obstacles" of heavy debt burden and imminent default for the railroads, farmers, and home owners.

The RFC and programs for refinancing of farm and home mortgages were greatly expanded under the New Deal, and similar programs of selective financial support to distressed industries have become a permanent and growing feature of our political economy in recent years. Certainly the RFC was not the first occasion of selective government loans to the private sector; recall the funding of transportation and banking during the nineteenth century, for example. But the RFC may have been the first occasion on which such federal aid was justified, not for promotion of development but for rescue from distress and support of macroeconomic stabilization (Sprinkel 1952, pp. 211–24). The RFC is in this sense the grandfather of the Lockheed loan, selective credits to Appalachia, and a host of other federal programs. In the 1930s' depression, few people questioned the allocative-efficiency aspects of such financial rescue missions. Today the macroeconomic justifications must meet the microeconomic criticisms of most such programs.

COLLAPSE AND REFORM OF THE BANKING INDUSTRY, 1933–38

As the number of bank failures grew and the surviving banks scrambled to liquidate and yet to protect their solvency, the bankers themselves became more open to considering changes in their industry and in its relationship to government. Even where they resisted change, the investigations of Wall Street "scandals" and "abuses" and the growing popular distrust of the "soundness" of banks strengthened the political voices for change. By 1933 a small army of monetary reformers badgered Congress and other government agencies with radical proposals for reorganizing the banks or replacing them with some alternative monetary mechanism (greenbacks, silver, or scrip, for example). In Congress, especially in the House of Representatives, the sentiment for inflationary monetary reform was vociferous. The nationwide bank holiday of March 1933 offered a unique potential for radical reorganization of the entire system (Reeve 1943, pp. 33–110). Given the divisions among the bankers, the depth of popular distrust and openness to monetary experimentation, and sentiment in Congress, it seems truly remarkable in retrospect that the banking reforms of 1933–35 were so conservative.

One aspect of the legislative reform of banking began in the Hoover years and represented a partial erosion of the "commercial loan" principles of sound banking. Under the Glass-Steagall Act of February 1932, the sacred priority of "eligible commercial paper" for rediscounting was compromised ever so slightly: a banker might borrow on ineligible assets at a penalty rate from his Federal Reserve bank with the consent of five members of the Federal Reserve Board. Little came of this initial provision, but the heresy was soon extended. An amendment of July 1932 permitted individuals and corporations (not just member banks) who were unable to obtain funds elsewhere to borrow directly from their Federal Reserve banks against eligible assets (only $1.4 million was loaned by March 1933.) The Emergency Banking Act of March 1933 allowed member banks to borrow, "in exceptional and exigent circumstances," on their own notes with collateral of any acceptable assets. This provision was continued by presidential proclamation until March 1935, then replaced permanently in the Banking Act of August 1935 by a broader provision allowing discounting on any satisfactory security at any time subject to the board's rules. In practical terms, the special rediscounting status of commercial paper had been far more significantly undermined by the RFC, which provided very large funds to banks by loans against their ineligible assets or purchases of their preferred stock (Friedman and Schwartz 1963, pp. 321, 422, 447–48).

Yet even as the "commercial loan" theory was written out of the Federal Reserve's discount mechanism and was sharply attacked by many professional economists, it was reincarnated in the legislative attacks against "speculative" bank loans and in the cautious lending practices of the bankers themselves. The Banking Act of June 1933 severely penalized banks (including threatening loss of discount privileges!) for providing credit "for the speculative carrying of or trading in securities, real estate, or commodities, or for any other purposes inconsistent with the maintenance of sound credit conditions," or for excessive "loans secured by stock or bond collateral." Of course, the forced divorce of commercial and investment banking activities and the Federal Reserve's new power to set margin requirements (both discussed above) formed part of this same attack on "speculation" and reaffirmation of "commercial" banking. In a careful 1934 study of bank-lending practices, Charles Hardy and Jacob Viner discovered that bankers (and bank examiners) had backed away from types of business loans common in the 1920s (renewable working-capital loans) toward more narrowly commercial loans. Lauchlin Currie and many other economists may have defeated the "commercial loan" theory in the academic world, but there were still powerful congressmen and cautious bankers who followed the "defunct economists" of the old school (Friedman and Schwartz 1963, p. 443; Chandler 1971, pp. 237–38).

A second major policy question relating to the banking industry was the appropriate number of bank charters and the degree and structure of competition. American banking had operated for 70 years under a "dual" system of state and federal charters and regulation. Until the mid-1920s, state banking authorities and the comptroller of the currency had engaged in vigorous chartering competition; since about 1924, both had slowed the chartering race sharply and given more attention to "the banking needs of the community" (not chartering new competitors where established banks already served the community adequately). Even during the prosperous 1920s, over 5,400 banks had failed, most of them small state-chartered banks and the great majority of them located in rural communities suffering depressed incomes and high debt burdens (left over from the rapid expansion of agriculture during World War I). From 1930 to 1933 another 8,800 banks had failed, as depression and the downward spiral of illiquidity spread its toll. By 1933 the conclusion had become nearly universal that the 1920s had been a decade of "overbanking" and that this practice had contributed to the depression's severity (Robertson 1968, pp. 125–31). Another version of the "boom-bust" theory blossomed here, often ignoring the other structural causes of bank failures or the obvious (to us) fact that after 1929 those failures were presumably as much the result as the cause of depression. The remark of Leo Crowley, chairman of the Federal Deposit Insurance Corporation (FDIC), to the Senate Committee on Banking and Currency is typical: "We cannot return to the overbanked condition of 1920 if we wish to have a sound banking structure. The growth of excessive banking facilities was one of the most destructive influences which existed prior to the banking holiday of 1933" (U.S. Congress 1935*b*, p. 31; Kent 1963).

The obvious policy response to this belief in "overbanking" was severe restriction of charters for new banks. The comptroller of the currency stated as his duty and purpose (in his 1934 *Annual Report*) "to prevent the organization of a new national bank unless it has adequate, sound capital, and unless there is a need for additional banking facilities in the location chosen, and a reasonable prospect that the bank will operate successfully." State chartering authorities had reached the same "overbanking" conclusion and had become equally restrictive. The Banking Act of 1935 merely wrote these prevailing practices into law and gave Mr. Crowley's FDIC indirect federal restraining power over new state charters through its capacity to deny deposit insurance protection. This whole rationale certainly illustrates the diminished faith in the benefits of a competitive economy that characterized the 1930s, as well as the greatly increased concern for stability, security, and the safety of the monetary system against default. The fear of "overbanking," or at least the satisfaction with the limited-entry cartel structure that it produced, lasted far beyond the end of the depression and was not really challenged until James Saxon became comptroller of the currency in 1961 (Robertson 1968, p. 128).

More controversial than chartering of new banks was the structural issue of branch banking, one of the truly classic conflicts in American banking theory and practice. Since the nineteenth century, some states had permitted branch banking on an intracity or even statewide basis, while other states (especially in the South and West) outlawed or severely restricted branching in favor of "community-service-oriented" unit banking. Where branching was limited, bankers of the 1920s sought to capture the emerging economies of scale (of better management and more efficient data-processing facilities) through "chain" or "group" banking that joined ostensible unit banks into larger systems. National banks were severely restricted in establishing branches until the McFadden Act of 1927 allowed limited intracity branching where states allowed this privilege to state-chartered banks (Robertson 1968, pp. 100–05, 131–32; Gayer 1935; Williams 1936; Currie 1934b, pp. 126–29, 182–83).[8]

The idea of branch banking, even perhaps nationwide branching, had gained in popularity. By the 1930s it was clear that the small unit banks were more prone to failure and that intercity branching might even provide a mechanism whereby stronger banks could rescue failing ones. By then a large number of academic economists had come to endorse an expanded system of branch banking. But the unit bankers and their intellectual and political allies replied vehemently (and classically) that branch banking represented monopolistic concentration of power, the threat of Wall Street, and the demise of institutions dedicated to meeting the credit needs of the farmers and small-business owners in their local communities.

This issue may represent the exception to Keynes's dictum: the outcome was determined more by old-fashioned pressure politics, since the opposing ideas were as frozen as bank assets of the day. The comptroller of the currency and Senator Glass both offered proposals for state-wide branching (and even a little beyond, where "trade areas" crossed state boundaries); the American Bankers Association softened its opposition; and it appeared for a moment that liberal branching provisions might pass. In its final form the Banking Act of June 1933 did allow statewide branch banking by national banks where state banks enjoyed the same power, but it set for such institutions a discriminating high capital requirement that largely killed its appeal. The unit bankers had won the political battle, partly by winning approval of a policy that could reassure worried Americans of the safety of their small banks: deposit insurance.

Closely related to the debate over chartering and branch banking was the appeal for unification of the banking system under one regulatory and supervisory agency. The usual form advocated was to require all state banks to become members of the Federal Reserve System. Most academic economists, then as now, saw this as a reform that would correct the confusion and inequity arising from the "dual" banking system. It would overcome the laxity of state regulation and strengthen the effectiveness of the monetary powers of the Federal Reserve Board. This strengthening of federal power was exactly what opponents of "unification" objected to. State bankers and their allies feared that the Federal Reserve System would impose undue restrictions on real estate or agricultural loans or otherwise limit their local autonomy and profitability. Even national bankers preferred decentralization and competition among regulators as a check on their potentially "dictatorial" powers. The other major source of opposition was the comptroller of the currency, and the FDIC once it began operations; neither agency wished to surrender its jurisdiction to the Federal Reserve. The Banking Act of 1933 required insured state banks to join the Federal Reserve System by 1936; but the act of 1935 postponed the deadline until 1941, and then in 1939 the state banking forces won legislation that dropped the membership requirement entirely. The three regulatory agencies resolved their quarrels over jurisdictions and procedures for bank examinations by 1938 and apparently concluded that the near-universality of FDIC membership did give the federal agencies reasonably effective control over the business performance of the state banks. But the issue of "unification," especially as it pertains to the Federal Reserve's macroeconomic effectiveness, obviously did not die out in 1938 and has surfaced again as the proportion of member banks has declined in recent years.[9]

Perhaps the most controversial feature of the Banking Act of June 1933 was the provision for insurance of demand deposits through creation of the FDIC. Deposit insurance had been tried in various forms on the state level since early in the nineteenth century and had long been advocated for two purposes: protecting the circulating medium, monetary liquidity, and protecting the savings of depositors. Monetary liquidity would be strengthened, first, because the insurance would discourage runs on banks that brought on monetary contractions and, second, because the fund would quickly replace any deposits in failed banks while it slowly liquidated the frozen assets. As noted previously, politicians from the South (notably, Vice-President Garner of Texas and Henry Steagall of Alabama, chairman of the House Committee on Banking and Currency) and the West saw deposit insurance as strengthening the independent small banks (and their customers) against the spread of branch banking and Wall Street power. Senator Glass initially opposed deposit insurance, preferring instead to increase Federal Reserve surveillance over the state banks. President Roosevelt was also strongly opposed, suspecting that any such scheme would fail financially (as the state schemes had) and perceiving such guarantees as special protection for bankers that was not being offered to other depressed businesses. The American Bankers Association and the comptroller of the currency also bitterly opposed the FDIC because it would delay branch banking and might compel the large and strong banks to rescue and subsidize the small and weak ones. The FDIC won out in the hard legislative bargaining in the last days of the congressional session, and its subsequent operations have justified nearly everyone's hopes or fears except Roosevelt's. It has prevented runs on banks, protected depositors, limited the extension of Federal Reserve powers (and, to some extent, branch banking) over independent state banks, and provided an implicit subsidy of small and weak banks (Golembe 1960; Friedman and Schwartz 1963, pp. 434–42; Freidel 1973, pp. 183–84, 441–44; Viner 1936, pp. 110–12; Emerson 1934).

Once the banks enjoyed deposit insurance, other similar institutions had to obtain it in order to remain competitive. Mutual savings banks were eligible under FDIC and joined slowly (they had remained relatively untarnished by depression and so had no fear of runs and delayed joining while campaigning for lower insurance rates.) Building and loan associations obtained their separate coverage under the Federal Savings and Loan Insurance Corporation, which was created by the National Housing Act of 1934. They had demanded the deposit insurance in return for the creation of the Federal Housing Administration, which they strongly opposed because its new low-interest insured mortgages would enable commercial banks to compete with them in mortgage lending (Eccles 1951, pp. 149–50; Friedman and Schwartz 1963, p. 437).

While much of the controversy focused on insurance of deposits, the Banking Act of June 1933 included another provision, for ceilings on deposit interest rates, that has assumed new and different significance since the 1950s. The act of 1933 prohibited payment of any interest on demand deposits (including interbank deposits) and permitted the Federal Reserve and the FDIC to set maximum rates on time deposits. Since no hearings were held on the act of 1933 and little public debate focused on interest rate ceilings, we can probably never be certain which ideas or motives counted most. Senators Glass and McAdoo recalled the purposes of these rate ceilings during hearings on the Bank Act of 1935:

> *Senator McAdoo:* You know that great abuses had risen out of that practice—the bidding by banks against each other for the deposits of customers who had large deposits and who were relatively highly favored while the small depositors got practically nothing. It led to unwholesome competition between the banks and an unwholesome condition, so far as demand deposits were concerned because the big depositors usually had some knowledge of what might happen and they pulled their deposits out when they got scared, which weakened the condition of the bank more than the withdrawal of a large number of small deposits. . . .

> *Senator Glass:* Country banks had what they call standard rates of discount. It is almost impossible ever to get them to depart from that standard rate of discount. They would rather bundle up their surplus funds and send them to the money centers at a nominal rate of 2 percent than to give the merchants of the town or the industries of the town or the locality the benefit of an abundance of money and an abundance of credit. . . . But it resulted in the withdrawal of all the interior funds of the country banks and the transferring of them to the money centers for speculative purposes. That was a major reason why we prohibited the payment of interest on demand deposits.

> *Senator McAdoo:* And also for another reason, that where we were requiring the bank to pay a premium to insure any part of their deposits, to relieve them of this payment of interest on demand deposits we gave them an additional means by

which they could pay premiums upon insurance. [U.S. Congress 1935*b*, pp. 491–92; see also Goldenweiser 1951, p. 94]

The primary considerations seem to have been the belief that bidding for mobile interbank deposits left city banks temporarily illiquid when deposits were withdrawn (either to other banks or for shifting the funds into other assets, such as brokers' loans) and deprived the country folk of access to bank credit. The comment that reduced payment of interest on deposits helped the city bankers afford the costs of deposit insurance seems to have been more a political argument for the FDIC than a reason for ceiling rates as such.

Subsequent research suggests that the beliefs that supported ceilings on deposit interest rates were inaccurate even during the 1930s. Payment of interest on deposits did not actually draw bankers into riskier investments or increase the likelihood of their failure. Since the imposition of interest ceilings, rural bankers have still maintained urban correspondent accounts (or transferred funds to city banks through the "Fed Funds" market), demonstrating that Senator Glass was wrong to assume that ceilings would stop the drain of funds from rural banks. At the time these ceilings were imposed, bankers had been reducing the rates paid on deposits (often to zero) anyway, because of the declining rates earned on their assets. The law merely accelerated this trend and perhaps gave bankers a small cartel profit on a government-fixed price. But after World War II, when market rates of interest on liquid financial assets rose to new heights, bankers found themselves paying "implicit" interest through nonprice competition for deposits (prizes, advertising, convenient branch offices, free checking services, etc.) and suffering large deposit shifts among institutions or "disintermediation" when ceiling rates were changed or fell below the market level. These inefficiencies and episodes of financial instability have raised new questions about deposit ceilings once imposed to protect bankers from their own "unwholesome competition" (Friedman and Schwartz 1963, pp. 443–45, 645–51; Axilrod 1977; Benston 1964).

CENTRALIZING THE CENTRAL BANK

The main concerns behind the financial legislation of 1933 and 1934 had been to correct a variety of perceived "abuses" and "speculative excesses" and to rescue financial intermediaries from illiquidity and insolvency. In the debates over the Bank Act of 1935, primary attention shifted from the health of the banks to the strength of the Federal Reserve and its stabilization powers. This debate occurred in a political atmosphere supercharged with tension by a variety of proposals for drastic reorganization of the monetary system. Father

Coughlin was arousing his radio audience with a variety of inflationary schemes for monetizing the entire debt with paper currency. Followers of Dr. Townsend wanted to issue currency through $200 monthly pension payments to the elderly, with stamping provisions to assure its high velocity. In the House hearings on the bill, Robert Hemphill, journalist and spokesman for the National Monetary Conference (a coalition of farm groups and other monetarists), urged Congress to commit itself to achieving stable prices (at some 1920s' level), to set the target of monetary circulation of $250 per capita to achieve this goal, and to create a new Federal Monetary Committee to carry it out. Economist and monetary lobbyist Irving Fisher testified in support of Hemphill's proposals and also endorsed the idea of ''100 percent reserves,'' which a number of different economists had proposed, as a means to give the government, rather than the bankers, control over money. Meanwhile, Walter Spahr and other conservatives in the Economists' National Committee on Monetary Policy attacked all the proposed ''reforms'' and demanded a return to the natural discipline of the gold standard. In this political atmosphere, technical details of the composition of the Federal Reserve Board and its sharing of powers with the Federal Reserve banks took on larger symbolic significance (Reeve 1943, pp. 80–94; U.S. Congress 1935*a*, pp. 483–585; U.S. Congress 1935*b*, pp. 989–1004).

The administration's banking-reform proposals, reflecting primarily the views of Marriner Eccles, were received sympathetically in the House Committee on Banking and Currency (whose leaders, Henry Steagall and Alan Goldsborough, were both advocates of more radical proposals) and were passed nearly intact by the House of Representatives. Senator Glass had his own distinctive views, and it was through his Senate committee hearings that bankers and conservative economists expressed their opposition to Eccles's proposals.

Eccles favored a variety of measures designed to remove monetary policy powers from the Federal Reserve banks, which he believed too much under banker influence (through their local boards of directors and general professional backgrounds), and transfer them to the presidentially appointed (with Senate confirmation) Federal Reserve Board in Washington. Eccles won most of the issue, including the board's power of approval over the appointments of the bank presidents and vice-presidents. Glass sought to assure the board's freedom from undue political pressure by removing the secretary of the Treasury and comptroller of the currency as nonvoting members. Despite Eccles's efforts to establish new professional criteria for board members (expertise in national economic and monetary policy), Glass retained the old system of selecting by region with representations for industry, commerce, and agriculture (Eccles 1951, pp. 222–24).

The hottest issue, and the target of the most hostile banker lobbying, was Eccles's proposal to remake the Federal Open Market Committee (FOMC). The Banking Act of June 1933 had just given it official legal sanction and specified that it consist of one representative of each of the twelve Federal Reserve banks. Eccles wanted to dramatize that open-market operations were not businesslike investment decisions of the individual banks (as they had first been conceived in the 1920s) but crucial instruments of national money management. He therefore proposed that the FOMC membership be transformed from the twelve "bankers" to the board itself, with five of the bank presidents sitting in as nonvoting advisers! The final compromise gave those five bank presidents full voting rights along with the seven board members. Within a year it became clear that the center of power in the FOMC had shifted from the New York bank to the board in Washington (Eccles 1951, pp. 224–26).

While Eccles eagerly cut down the internal influence of the Federal Reserve banks and their banker allies, he also discreetly tried to preserve the Federal Reserve's "independence" against intrusions by his more radical congressional allies and against the growing monetary leverage of the Treasury. The opportunity for congressional domination arose in rewriting the "mandate" for the Federal Reserve Board, the legislative statement of its policy goal. Eccles wanted to remove obsolete language of the original Federal Reserve Act— "accommodating commerce and business"—because it sounded too passive and too reminiscent of the "commercial loan" doctrine. But what should replace it? There were many monetary enthusiasts abroad (and in Congress) who wanted to mandate "price stabilization" (preceded by "reflation" to 1926 or 1929 or other suitable base price levels) and perhaps even to specify a "commodity dollar" or other specific form or mechanism for achieving permanent price stability. Eccles managed to avoid these hazards and also to suggest that monetary solutions alone might not always control the economy. With Steagall's cooperation he drafted a mandate for the board "to promote conditions conducive to business stability and to mitigate by its influence unstabilizing fluctuations in the general level of production, trade, prices, and employment so far as may be possible within the scope of monetary action and credit administration." This version also left the board ample "discretion" for selecting the policy means by which to achieve the goal. In the end, Senator Glass held out, and the 1914 language remained elegantly, irrelevantly intact (Eccles 1951, p. 228; Reeve 1943, pp. 24–26, 44–46, 87–90). But the struggles over Federal Reserve "independence" (from Congress, Treasury, president, or whomever), over "discretion" versus monetary "rules," and over the "mandate" of monetary policy (what is to be "stabilized") could not be silenced and have reverberated through the halls of Washington and academe ever since. I personally think that more of the issues and alternatives were articulated in the lively debates of 1935 than in the more devious and decorous discussions of the postwar years.

The Treasury acquired new monetary powers as a result of the departure from the gold standard, devaluation, and the creation of an Exchange Stabilization Fund in 1934 and a similar "sterilized gold" account beginning in December 1936. Problems of financing the growing federal debt had long since given the Treasury a strong concern for keeping interest rates low and stable. Throughout the New Deal years, Eccles and Secretary Morgenthau worked to maintain cooperative relationships and consistency between the policies of their two agencies. There was some personal distrust because Morgenthau resented Eccles's vocal advocacy of "compensatory" fiscal policies, and there were occasional episodes of conflict and policy crisis (over reserve requirements and gold sterilization in 1936–37, for instance), but there do not seem to have been fundamental differences over financial (as contrasted to fiscal) policy. Obviously, the uneasy alliance between Eccles and Morgenthau foreshadowed the many "border incidents" between Federal Reserve and Treasury in the years ahead (Chandler 1971, pp. 307–10; Eccles 1951, pp. 290–93; Blum 1959, pp. 338–79).

The Banking Act of 1935 concentrated more on changing the political structure of the Federal Reserve System than on modifying its basic instruments of monetary policymaking. Open-market operations were unaffected, and member-bank borrowing of reserves was liberalized somewhat. But the most notable change was the granting of power to the Federal Reserve Board to modify reserve requirements. A very limited version of this power had been included as an option in the "inflation tools" of the Thomas Amendment to the Agricultural Adjustment Act of 1933. Eccles sought now to remove from it the "emergency" stigma and to make it a permanent policy option, without limitation as to the range of change. Senator Glass succeeded in limiting the permissible range of acceptable change in the final bill; the board could not lower reserve requirements below the level then prevailing nor raise them beyond twice that level (Friedman and Schwartz 1963, p. 446; Eccles 1951, p. 226).

Because the board was engaged in raising reserve requirements within a year after the passage of the 1935 law, and because that decision became quite controversial, our attention has been diverted from some aspects of the 1935 intellectual context in which the change occurred. There may have been early signs of worry about the potential dangers of "excess reserves" at that time, especially in the New York Federal Reserve Bank. But there were no systemwide memoranda or discussions yet. On the other hand, during 1935 and the preceding year there was intense discussion of a quite different reason for changing reserve requirements, the "100 percent reserve" ideas. Such plans had been proposed by Congressman Wright Patman and a group of University of Chicago economists, among others, and Irving Fisher had recently joined the throng. Moreover, Lauchlin Currie had endorsed a version of 100 percent reserves in his own writings and in a 1934 proposal for monetary reforms submitted to Treasury Secretary Morgenthau. Eccles's proposals certainly included the possibility of 100 percent reserves, though he gave the board ample "discretion." The Glass amendment ruled out the option of radical reform (Friedman and Schwartz 1963, p. 446; Eccles 1951, p. 226; Currie 1934*b*, pp. 151–56; Currie 1968, p. 198; Reeve 1943, pp. 87–90).

EXCESS RESERVES AND THE RECESSION OF 1937–38

By mid-1935 the Federal Reserve policymakers became concerned about the large volume of excess reserves held by member banks (over $2 billion). They studied and discussed the problem for months, then decided in July 1936 to raise the reserve ratios by 50 percent. When excess reserves again exceeded $2 billion in January 1937, the board scheduled the remaining 50 percent increases (effective in March and May 1937) authorized by the Banking Act of 1935. In making and announcing both decisions, the board repeatedly affirmed that these actions were not intended to modify its "easy credit" policy. They believed that the member banks would still have ample excess reserves (at least $500 million) to satisfy their liquidity needs and finance further recovery. But they were increasingly concerned about the recovery turning eventually into an unhealthy, inflationary boom and wanted to take up the slack in excess reserves in order to be prepared to exert money and credit restraint promptly if the need should arise. When the government bond market tightened in March 1937, Secretary Morgenthau angrily blamed the increased reserve requirements, urged cancellation of the scheduled May increases (refused), and demanded Federal Reserve open-market purchases to support the bond market. When the board recognized that the economy was in a recession, in September 1937, it initiated modest ($38 million) open-market purchases and encouraged the Treasury to expand reserves by desterilizing $300 million of gold. In April 1938 the board also lowered reserve requirements, adding $750 million to excess reserves (Chandler 1971, pp. 31–39, 326–29; Friedman and Schwartz 1963, pp. 461, 517–34).

Neither at that time nor in later years did Federal Reserve leaders accept the view that their 1936–37 increases had been a mistake. Both Eccles and Goldenweiser continued to insist in the 1950s that excess reserves had been sufficient for banker liquidity and that credit had not tightened significantly. They asserted that the recession had been caused by "serious maladjustments" in relative prices, inventory speculation, and reduction in the federal cash deficit (Chandler 1971, pp. 31–39, 326–29; Friedman and Schwartz 1963, pp. 461, 517–34; U.S. Congress 1938, pp. 54–80; Eccles 1951, pp. 289–99, 308–10; Goldenweiser 1951, pp. 175–82).

Many economists have reviewed the evidence on monetary aspects of the 1937–38 recession. Some early supporters of the Federal Reserve and believers in the Keynesian liquidity trap accepted Eccles's view that the Federal Reserve was not at fault. Monetarists such as Brunner and Friedman and Schwartz gathered evidence to show the damage from monetary restraint, and recent Keynesian interpretations have accepted this view while still pointing to contributing nonmonetary causes of recession and emphasizing the contribution of Roosevelt's deficit spending to recovery (Gordon 1952, pp. 398–99; Horwich 1963; Brunner 1958; Morrison 1966, pp. 2–62).

These previous studies have answered most of our questions about the beliefs and theories motivating Federal Reserve policy on reserve requirements. I only have several points of emphasis to add. First, it appears that one reason for the board's desire to mop up excess reserves (beyond assumed "normal" liquidity needs) *early* was its continuing fear that speculative enthusiasm would produce another "1929" uncontrollable boom-bust sequence. Goldenweiser told the board in January 1937 that "the most effective time for action to prevent the development of unsound and speculative conditions is in the early stages of such a movement when the situation is still susceptible of control." This fear of a speculative boom led them to risk some premature and restrictive impact. Second, the board apparently held the view that in the midst of a well-advanced recession their actions to ease "credit" would be relatively weak and ineffective. Thus they welcomed Treasury financial and fiscal initiatives. This view in 1938 was remarkably similar to the sense of powerlessness that dominated the board in 1931–33, though the theory behind it was more sophisticated (Friedman and Schwartz 1963, p. 525; Morrison 1966, pp. 4–5).

The fear of "another 1929" and the belief that monetary expansion is relatively ineffective in advanced recessions carried over into the postwar years not only in the minds of Eccles and Goldenweiser but in the implicit theories of Chairman William McChesney Martin and a number of Keynesian economists. They are part of the historical legacy from the 1930s that still flows into the intellectual currents today.

NOTES

1. See also the writings of Ellis Hawley on Herbert Hoover, especially Hawley (1973).
2. For one statement among many, see Noyes (1930).
3. For a more detailed political history, see Parrish (1970, chap. 5).

4. Not all economic historians subscribe to the popular 1930s' opinion of the role of the stock market crash in causing the depression. See Green (1972) and Cagan (1972). Compare Galbraith (1954, pp. 173–93) and Temin (1976, pp. 42–43, 69–83). For a sampling of the continuing discussion of the links between the stock market and the macroeconomy, see Bosworth (1975, pp. 257–300) and Mishkin (1977, pp. 123–74).

5. For a similar gold-standard theory of credit inflation by a historian, see Rothbard (1963).

6. For an earlier statement of the same historical interpretation by Goldenweiser's assistant director, see Thomas (1935).

7. The memory of 1929 and the fear of losing control of a speculative boom lingered to influence Federal Reserve thinking even in the 1960s. Chairman William McChesney Martin addressed the Alumni Federation of Columbia University in 1965 on the historical lessons of 1929:

> Most observers agree that to a large extent the disaster of 1929–33 was a consequence of maladjustments born of the boom of the twenties. Hence, we must continuously be on the alert to prevent a recurrence of maladjustments—even at the risk of being falsely accused of failing to realize the benefits of unbounded expansion. Actually, those of us who warn against speculative and inflationary dangers should return the charge: our common goals of maximum production, employment, and purchasing power can be realized only if we are willing and able to prevent orderly expansion from turning into disorderly boom. [Martin 1966, p. 220; the entire address is reprinted, pp. 213–26.]

8. For the background on the McFadden Act and changing attitudes toward branch banking in the 1930s, see Fischer and Golembe (1976) and White (1976). I am grateful to Roger White for pointing out these studies.

9. One major dispute between the agencies came over Eccles's proposals for countercyclical examining policies, liberalizing allowable bank loan portfolios, and valuing the assets at their long-term rather than depression values. Eccles won some points, but his basic scheme never went far (Gayer 1935, p. 103; Williams 1936, p. 105; Viner 1936, pp. 107–10; Robertson 1968, pp. 105–16, 126–27, 134–38; Eccles 1951, pp. 266–86; Schlesinger 1958, p. 443; Blum 1959, pp. 344–46, 428–31; Goldenweiser 1951, p. 97).

REFERENCES

Axilrod, S. H. 1977. "The Impact of the Payment of Interest on Demand Deposits." Unpublished. Washington, D.C.: Federal Reserve Board of Governors.

Barger, H. 1935. "The Banks and the Stock Market." *Journal of Political Economy* 43: 763–77.

Benston, G. J. 1964. "Interest Payments on Demand Deposits and Bank Investment Behavior." *Journal of Political Economy* 72: 431–49.

Blum, J. M. 1959. *From the Morgenthau Diaries: Years of Crisis, 1928–1938.* Boston: Houghton Mifflin.

Bosworth, B. 1975. "The Stock Market and the Economy." *Brookings Papers on Economic Activity.*

Brandes, J. 1962. *Herbert Hoover and Economic Diplomacy.* Pittsburgh: University of Pittsburgh Press.

Brunner, K. 1958. "A Case Study of U.S. Monetary Policy: Reserve Requirements and Inflationary Gold Flows in the Middle 30's." *Schweizerische Zeitschrift fur Volkwirtschaft und Statistik* 94: 160–201.

Byles, A. J. 1934. "Memorial Address." *Oil and Gas Journal,* August 30.

Cagan, P. 1972. "Comments on 'The Economic Impact of the Stock Market Boom and Crash of 1929.' " In *Consumer Spending and Monetary Policy: The Linkages.* Boston: Federal Reserve Bank of Boston.

Carosso, V. P. 1970. *Investment Banking in America: A History.* Cambridge, Mass.: Harvard University Press.

Chandler, L. V. 1971. *American Monetary Policy, 1928–1941.* New York: Harper & Row.

Currie, L. 1934a. "The Failure of Monetary Policy to Prevent the Depression of 1929–32." *Journal of Political Economy* 44: 149–54.

―――. 1934b. *The Supply and Control of Money in the United States.* Cambridge, Mass.: Harvard University Press.

―――. 1968. "A Proposed Revision of the Monetary System of the United States." In *The Supply and Control of Money in the United States,* ed. K. Brunner. Rev. ed. New York: Russell & Russell.

Eccles, M. 1951. *Beckoning Frontiers.* New York: Alfred A. Knopf.

Emerson, G. 1934. "Guaranty of Deposits under the Banking Act of 1933." *Quarterly Journal of Economics* 48: 229–44.

Fischer, G. C., and Golembe, C. H. 1976. "The Branch Banking Provisions of the McFadden Act as Amended: Their Rationale and Rationality." In *Compendium of Issues Relating to Branching by Financial Institutions.* U.S. Congress, Senate, Committee on Banking, Housing and Urban Affairs, Subcommittee on Financial Institutions. 94th Cong., 2d sess.

Freidel, F. 1973. *Franklin D. Roosevelt: Launching the New Deal.* Boston: Little, Brown.

Friedman, M., and Schwartz, A. J. 1963. *A Monetary History of the United States, 1867–1960.* Princeton, N.J.: Princeton University Press, for the National Bureau of Economic Research.

Galbraith, J. K. 1954. *The Great Crash, 1929.* Boston: Houghton Mifflin.

Gayer, A. D. 1935. "The Banking Act of 1935." *Quarterly Journal of Economics* 50: 103–04.

Goldenweiser, E. A. 1951. *American Monetary Policy.* New York: McGraw-Hill.

Golembe, C. 1960. "The Deposit Insurance Legislation of 1933." *Political Science Quarterly* 75: 181–200.

Gordon, R. A. 1952. *Business Fluctuations.* 2nd ed. New York: Harper & Row.

Green, G. D. 1972. "The Economic Impact of the Stock Market Boom and Crash of 1929." In *Consumer Spending and Monetary Policy: The Linkages.* Boston: Federal Reserve Bank of Boston.

Hardy, C. O. 1932. *Credit Policies of the Federal Reserve System.* Washington, D.C.: Brookings Institution.

Hawley, E. 1966. *The New Deal and the Problem of Monopoly*. Princeton, N.J.: Princeton University Press.

———. 1973. In *Herbert Hoover and the Crisis of American Capitalism*. ed. J. Huthmacher and W. Susman. Cambridge, Mass.: Schenkman.

Horowitz, D. A. 1971. "Visions of Harmonious Abundance: Corporate Ideology in the 1920's." Ph.D. diss., University of Minnesota.

Horwich, G. 1963. "Effective Reserves, Credit, and Causality in the Banking System of the Thirties." In *Banking and Monetary Studies*, ed. D. Carson. Homewood, Ill.: Richard D. Irwin.

Hunt, E. E. 1927. "Business Cycles and Unemployment." Hunt Papers, Box 28. Hoover Institution Archives, Stanford, Calif.

Johnson, H. 1935. *The Blue Eagle from Egg to Earth*. Garden City, N.Y.: Doubleday.

Kennedy, S. E. 1973. *The Banking Crisis of 1933*. Lexington: University Press of Kentucky.

Kent, R. P. 1963. "Dual Banking between the Two World Wars." In *Banking and Monetary Studies*, ed. D. Carson. Homewood, Ill.: Richard D. Irwin.

Keynes, J. M. 1936. *The General Theory of Employment, Interest, and Money*. New York: Harcourt, Brace.

Martin, W. M. 1966. Address to the Alumni Federation of Columbia University. In *Money and Finance*, ed. D. Carson. New York: John Wiley.

Mishkin, F. S. 1977. "What Depressed the Consumer? The Household Balance Sheet and the 1973–75 Recession." *Brookings Papers on Economic Activity*, no. 1: 123–64.

Morrison, G. R. 1966. *Liquidity Preferences of Commercial Banks*. Chicago: University of Chicago Press.

Nash, G. D. 1959. "Herbert Hoover and the Origins of the Reconstruction Finance Corporation." *Mississippi Valley Historical Review* 46: 455–68.

Noyes, C. R. 1930. "The Gold Inflation in the United States, 1921–1929." *American Economic Review* 20: 181–98.

Parrish, M. E. 1970. *Securities Regulation and the New Deal*. New Haven, Conn.: Yale University Press.

Reed, H. L. 1930. *Federal Reserve Policy, 1921–1930*. New York: McGraw-Hill.

Reeve, J. E. 1943. *Monetary Reform Movements*. Washington, D. C.: American Council on Public Affairs.

Robertson, R. M. 1968. *The Comptroller and Bank Supervision: A Historical Appraisal*. Washington, D.C.: Office of the Comptroller of the Currency.

Romasco, A. U. 1965. *The Poverty of Abundance: Hoover, the Nation, the Depression*. New York: Oxford University Press.

Rothbard, M. 1963. *America's Greatest Depression*. Princeton, N.J.: Princeton University Press.

Schlesinger, A. M., Jr. 1958. *The Coming of the New Deal*. Boston: Houghton Mifflin.

Snyder, C. 1930. "Brokers' Loans and the Pyramiding of Credit." *Journal of the American Statistical Association* 25 (supp.): 88–92.

Sprinkel, B. W. 1952. "Economic Consequences of the Operations of the Reconstruction Finance Corporation." *Journal of Business* 25: 211–24.

Temin, P. 1976. *Did Monetary Forces Cause the Great Depression?* New York: W. W. Norton.

Thomas, W. 1935. "Use of Credit in Security Speculation." *American Economic Review* 25: 21–30.

U.S. Congress. 1934. *Stock Exchange Practices*. Senate, Committee on Banking and Currency. 73rd Cong., 2nd sess.

————. 1935a. *Hearings on the Banking Act of 1935*. House, Committee on Banking and Currency. 74th Cong., 1st sess.

————. 1935b. *Hearings on the Banking Act of 1935*. Senate, Committee on Banking and Currency. 74th Cong., 1st sess.

————. 1938. *Hearings*. Senate, Special Committee to Investigate Unemployment and Relief. 75th Cong., 3rd sess.

Viner, J. 1936. "Recent Legislation and the Banking Situation." *American Economic Review* 26 (supp.): 106–19.

Warren, H. G. 1959. *Herbert Hoover and the Great Depression*. New York: W. W. Norton.

White, R. S. 1976. "The Evolution of State Policies on Multioffice Banking, from the 1930's to the Present." In *Compendium of Issues Relating to Branching by Financial Institutions*. U.S. Congress, Senate, Committee on Banking, Housing and Urban Affairs, Subcommittee on Financial Institutions. 94th Cong., 2nd. sess.

Williams, J. H. 1936. "The Banking Act of 1935." *American Economic Review* 26 (supp.): 106–8.

12 COMMENTS ON "THE IDEOLOGICAL ORIGINS OF THE REVOLUTION IN AMERICAN FINANCIAL POLICIES"

George J. Benston

Professor Green sets forth a very interesting framework for his paper. His title and purpose are taken from Bernard Bailyn's *The Ideological Origins of the American Revolution*. Green states that his approach is based on that author's following assumption: "To understand fully the action of our revolutionary ancestors we must see it first through their eyes, from within their ideological perspective, and then recognize where that ideology sometimes diverged from the economic and political reality of their day"(p. 220). Green then takes his "sermon text" (as he puts it—I would prefer "hypothesis") from Keynes's *General Theory,* to the effect that the ideas of past and often forgotten so-called academic scribblers are much more important than those of vested interests in determining the actions of authorities. I believe that a historian who uses this framework and hypothesis to examine changes in American financial policies is likely to provide economists with valuable insights. Before considering the extent to which Professor Green's paper fulfills this expectation, I want to place the paper into a larger context of the alternative contributions of historical analysis for economic understanding.

One major contribution of historical analysis is the narrative recounting of financial history. It is useful to learn what presumably important people said and to whom they spoke and wrote. We rely on historians to determine

253

whether or in what ways and to what extent presumably important people really were important. Many years after these people are dead, we find it difficult to determine whether they are known to us because they had an effective following, had a skillful biographer, were interesting chroniclers of their times who exaggerated their own importance, or were colorful characters whose remarks were quoted and exploits cited because they were entertaining rather than because they affected people or events. (For example, was Eccles really as important as his book indicates, or was he perhaps overly modest in describing his accomplishments?) We also want to learn about the shadowy forces "behind the throne," the people whose names are not known to us but whose ideas and other interests were influential. (Who were the advisors to key legislators?)

Once the important people are identified, it would be useful to distinguish the sources of their importance. Did they act directly, did they get others to act, were their ideas the causal factors of actions even though they never were in contact with those in power? In short, what were the channels through which they influenced events?

A historian's task (I suggest), though, is more than a recounting of what others say people said and did. We would like to know whether they really did say and do what onlookers, journalists, and other writers of the time and afterwards report. It is not unusual to find that such reports were consciously or subconsciously falsified. We rely on historians to uncover such situations. We hope to learn from them who really maneuvered legislation through the administration and Congress, whether specific arguments really were taken seriously or were understood at the time to be mere "puffery." (For example, was the argument that bank failures were caused by competition in the form of interest payments on demand deposits an important factor in the passage of the legislation?)

Next, we would like to learn whether events occurred as they were reported. Contemporaneous views are interesting. For example, at the time of the 1929 stock market crash, did the newspapers, trade journals, stock market reports, letters, etc., say that the crash was a disaster? Then we would like to know whether the events were really as important as they were claimed to be. Did the Pecora hearings actually change public opinion, or did they reflect it? Did the public really believe that paying interest on demand deposits caused banks to fail? Did people realize that the doubling of reserve requirements in 1937 would cause a recession, or did they support the move as desirably anti-inflationary?

Perhaps it is more the task of the empirical economist—or the cliometrician—to determine what so-called events actually occurred. Thus, one wants to know whether the 1929 crash actually caused the Great Depression, or, at least, whether brokers and distraught investors really did defenestrate themselves in record numbers. What was the extent of corporate financial disclosure before passage of the securities acts? Did the Pecora hearings actually show a widespread pattern of fraudulent and inept behavior by brokers and bankers? Did interest payments on demand deposits actually cause banks to fail? Did overbanking result in bank failures?

Of course, history need not be limited to a description or determination of people and events as they occurred. Historians also can propose and test hypotheses about, say, why legislation was or was not enacted. As Professor Green indicates, one group of hypotheses might rely on the assumption that legislation is enacted to further the self-interests of individuals and groups. Those who accept this basic assumption could structure research designed to test hypotheses about who benefited from specific legislation. For example, were the large underwriters the beneficiaries of the Glass-Steagall Act provisions that separated investment from commercial banking? Or the role of groups—such as labor unions, consumer advocates, and trade associations—in the enactment and administration of legislation could be analyzed.

A second set of hypotheses is related to the effect of exogenous events on ideas and legislation. For example, the immigration to the United States in the late 1800s of large numbers of relatively unskilled people may have influenced concepts of the role of government in the economy. Of specific relevance to this conference, the Great Depression may have affected people's beliefs about the efficacy of the Protestant work ethic, the desirability of government actions to increase security, and the effectiveness with which the private marketplace allocates and employs resources. (For these hypotheses, it is necessary to consider the effect of events on beliefs rather than the truth of those beliefs.)

Finally, a third group of hypotheses is the announced concern of Professor Green's paper—the effect of ideas on the formation, enactment, and administration of legislation. This set of hypotheses is distinguished from the second in that ideas derived from "academic scribblers" or others—rather than exogenous events, such as the Great Depression—are assumed to be the direct causal factors. Thus, the historian might delineate and document the ideas that were generally accepted during the period when the legislators and administrators in power in the 1930s were growing up. He might specifically trace the personal history of such influential legislators as Senator Glass, bankers such as Marriner Eccles, and academics such as H. Parket Willis. The prevalent and presumably influential ideas of the 1920s also might be documented and their hypothesized effect on the interpretation of the events of the 1930s tested.

Perhaps of greatest interest, I suggest, would be a joint testing of these three groups of hypotheses in the hope of determining which of them is the most relevant. Each could be brought to bear on specific legislation. The degree to which the alternative hypotheses were consistent with the legislation enacted would provide us with considerable insights into the factors that tend to shape our legislative process.

Turning now to Professor Green's paper, I am disappointed that he has not fulfilled my expectations about what a historical analysis should provide. The paper essentially is in the genre of historical narrative. For the most part, we are presented with an uncritical recounting of what legislation was passed and what some well-known persons said and did about it. In this regard, Professor Green's paper is not very different (or any worse) than many (perhaps most) history books. Indeed, it is very much like the section of money and banking textbooks that walk the student through recent monetary and fiscal policy events. Thus we are told, in the second postintroduction section, that the 1929 stock market crash and the Pecora hearings preceded passage of the Securities Acts and the Glass-Steagall Act, though the causal relationship (if any) is not analyzed or examined carefully. The effect of the crash on banking theories also is considered and, were it developed more fully, could have been very useful. As it is, the relationships are briefly sketched and insufficient evidence is brought to bear on the question. Consequently, not much more is established than that legislation was enacted and a few presumably important people may have influenced its passage. Though Professor Green does provide some discussions on the effect of some Federal Reserve officials' beliefs about speculation and the "real bills doctrine" on Fed policy, the narrative form he uses does not permit a clear statement and testing of hypotheses. Hence, one cannot determine the extent to which these past ideas of academic (or applied) scribblers influenced events.

The next (short) section of the paper, which discusses the supply and control of money, is concerned largely with Currie's work. Considering Currie's thesis, that the money supply was the causal factor of the depression, etc., I would have appreciated some explanation of why he "became one of the early New Deal advocates of Keynesian deficit spending" (p. 232). I also wonder that Green did not attempt to analyze why, "despite its clarity of analysis and its coherent alternative interpretation, Currie's version did not displace the prevailing interpretation" (p. 232).

The section "Financial Policies during the Hoover Years" does contain some description of Hoover's belief in voluntarism and the effect of the events and personages during his presidency that got him to change his ideas about the role of government. However, a more thorough analysis or at least a recounting of the interaction of forces, particularly with references to the specific "academic scribblers" or ideas that influenced Hoover's thinking and actions, would have been more in keeping with Professor Green's announced plan for the paper.

The next section of the paper, "Collapse and Reform of the Banking Industry, 1933–38," includes an interesting discussion of the banking concepts that affected (and apparently failed to effect) the Banking Act of 1933 and subsequent legislation. The final two sections, "Centralizing the Central Bank" and "Excess Reserves and the Recession of 1937–38," essentially summarize what happened and what presumably important people (particularly Eccles) argued and did.

Considering Professor Green's paper in its totality, I must conclude that he either was unable to test what I take to be his basic hypothesis (that past ideas are more important determinants of present actions than are vested interests) or forgot about it in the course of recounting the events of the period. Perhaps because I found the hypothesis intriguing, I was disappointed.

I also was disappointed to see so few references to the empirical research on events with which the paper was concerned. Many researchers have analyzed diligently the folklore about the alleged market failures and events that justified much of the New Deal legislation. The paper would have benefited considerably had the opinions of the contemporary observers quoted and the secondary sources cited been contrasted with or supported by this research.

13 COMMENTS ON "THE IDEOLOGICAL ORIGINS OF THE REVOLUTION IN AMERICAN FINANCIAL POLICIES"

James L. Pierce

Green's paper is a valuable contribution to the literature on the 1930s. He provides a succinct discussion of many of the proposals for financial reform as well as of the reforms actually accomplished during that traumatic decade. For Green, the reforms should be viewed as the result of the shift in American attitudes "toward the relative power and responsibilities of business and government" as well as an acceptance of greater power for the federal government relative to the states. Green views the 1930s as characterized by government concern for the economic security of its citizens. He also points to the erosion of such cherished concepts as the commercial loan theory as evidence of the triumph of economic analysis over conventional wisdom. In this regard, he quotes from Keynes, who argues, in effect, that the ideas of "practical men" are the products of the work of "some defunct economist."

While I agree, in part, with Green's approach, I think he overstates the case. Available evidence suggests that vested interests played a far larger role in the financial reform activities of the 1930s than Green indicates. These interests changed their approach with the times by using the federal government to achieve their objectives, but they did not lose their effectiveness. Furthermore, if Keynes's assertion is correct concerning the power of economic ideas, one can only conclude that the lags are truly long and variable. Most of the financial reforms suggested in the 1930s have yet to occur! It was fascinating to read the arguments used in the 1930s to thwart financial reform; they are almost exactly the same ones still used successfully today. The "path to salvation" may follow "the priority of ideas over vested interests," as Keynes argued, but the financial system has not moved very far down the path. I am afraid that Keynes's statement is more an academic ego trip than a useful analytic approach.

Many changes in the nation's financial structure were legislated in the 1930s. Some were good, some were bad, and most were a mixed blessing. All reforms were exceedingly mild; there certainly was no revolution in the nation's financial environment. For example, the securities acts and the establishment of the SEC were useful reforms, but the legislation provided mild medicine for a major disease. The requirement of increased disclosure can be applauded, but one wonders if the reform really represented a concern for the protection of the general public. Large investors have a vested interest in obtaining information on the operations of the firms in which they invest. Large, well-managed firms often have an interest in supplying information. It is not surprising that they could get together and use the federal government as the vehicle for disclosure. Gains to the general public were probably incidental to the pressures from vested interests. It would be interesting to learn who were the moving elements behind passage of the securities acts. The establishment of limits to the use of margin credit can only be viewed as a triumph for the commercial loan theory. Despite Green's claims that the theory was under attack, it weathered the storm intact.

The establishment of deposit insurance was probably the greatest financial reform of the 1930s. But it too can be viewed as a triumph for vested interest that only incidentally helped the general public. Small banks had a strong vested interest in deposit insurance because the government would guarantee that their deposits were just as safe as those of large, well-known banks. Furthermore, the FDIC would help assure these small banks that their correspondent balances held at large banks would be safe. The nation's large banks apparently were willing to accept deposit insurance in return for the prohibition of interest on demand deposits. One could argue plausibly that deposit insurance was achieved because of the power of the thousands of small banks in the nation coupled with an absence of strong opposition from the large banks. It is unlikely that concern over the safety of the checking accounts of the general public would have been sufficient to achieve the reform. There was a fortunate coincidence of vested interests and the public interest.

Confirmation of this assertion can be found in the manner in which the FDIC has operated since its inception. The FDIC has always been in the business of protecting banks, not deposits. By emphasizing protection of banks, the FDIC has guaranteed the safety of deposits but at the cost of encouraging anticompetitive practices by banks. The FDIC has worried about "overbanking" and has restricted new entry, branching, and certain merger activities. Deposit insurance was an important reform, but it came at the price of restricted competition and protection for small banks.

The Glass-Steagall Act is another interesting case. The separation of commercial from investment banking has been viewed by some observers as an important reform. Perhaps it was, but it was also a triumph for the commercial loan theory. The Glass-Steagall Act is a strange piece of reform legislation. It prevents commercial banks from underwriting securities issued by private firms but allows the trust departments of these banks to purchase the securities once underwritten. It is far from clear that removing banks from underwriting while retaining activities of their trust departments is an important reform. One wonders what combination of vested interests produced this strange result. It certainly was not the power of the proponents of public protection and the critics of conflicts of interest. The act also has not prevented banks from making private placements, and it explicitly allows them to underwrite state and municipal securities. One would like to have seen a discussion of the forces that produced this weak and strange law.

The McFadden Act started with a series of good proposals and ended up as a victory for small unit banks. The McFadden Act prevented branching across state lines and subjected national banks to whatever restrictions were imposed by the states within their boundaries. Federal legislation on branching is anticompetitive and represents another triumph for vested interests. By a like token, Green described the impressive proposals that were made to consolidate the federal regulation of banks and to reform the Federal Reserve System. Nothing came of the consolidation proposals, and little came of the proposals to reform the Fed. The FOMC was established, and power over Federal Reserve affairs was concentrated in Washington, but other important reforms were swept aside. Among the excluded reforms were universal membership (or at least reserve requirements), qualifications for governors, elimination of bank ownership of Reserve Banks, a clear mandate of Fed responsibilities, and the question of independence of the Fed.

I conclude that financial reform occurred in the 1930s when the wishes of vested interest coincided with the efforts of reformers. Vested interests saw that they could use the rising power of the federal government as a vehicle to further their ends. When the reformers were opposed by the vested interests, the reformers failed. I think that a careful study of the role of vested interest in the 1930s could teach us something about that decade and also provide clues for the future of financial reform. The efforts of well-intended reformers is not sufficient, and neither are the ideas of "defunct economists" (or even "funct" ones). In most cases, financial reform must await the day when market and technological forces have produced vested interests that conform to the interest of reformers.

14 SOME MACROECONOMIC IMPACTS OF THE NATIONAL INDUSTRIAL RECOVERY ACT, 1933–1935

Michael M. Weinstein

History will probably record the NIRA as the most important and far-reaching legislation ever enacted by the American Congress.

— Schlesinger (1959, p. 102)

With these words, President Roosevelt signed the National Industrial Recovery Act on June 16, 1933, and so began an unprecedented two-year experiment in regulating the entire U.S. economy. Between June 1933 and May 1935, staggering reforms were promulgated in the quest for economic recovery and reform. Of course, other New Deal legislation, also signed during the famous "100 days," had similar objectives.[1] The NIRA promised to extract the United States from the continuing depression through cooperative action: pro-

Some of the content of this paper is taken from Michael M. Weinstein, "Some Redistributive and Macroeconomic Impacts of the National Industrial Recovery Act, 1933–1935," Ph.D. dissertation, Department of Economics, Massachusetts Institute of Technology, 1978. Robert Hall and Peter Temin have provided invaluable advice to me during this project. E. Cary Brown has also provided helpful comments. Of course, none of these individuals is responsible for the remaining contents.

moting cartels to aid industry and promoting unions to aid employees. Within one year, codes of "fair competition" for 450 individual industries, covering 23 million workers, were passed. By the time the law was declared unconstitutional on May 27, 1935, over 550 codes had been passed covering almost the entire private, nonagricultural economy.[2]

The codes were designed to fulfill five primary objectives (U.S. National Recovery Administration 1937, pp. 1–16):

1. The purchasing power of labor was to be increased, primarily by the institution of economy-wide minimum-wage regulations.
2. Employment was to be spread over more individuals as the result of limitations on the number of hours any employee could work.
3. "Predator" or "destructive" competition was to be curtailed by minimum-price regulations (and other restrictions on employers).
4. "Inhumane" working conditions—such as child labor—were to be eliminated.
5. The relatively disadvantaged were to be aided; the codes were to progressively redistribute income.

Obviously, the NIRA was ambitious. The legislation promised recovery, reform, and redistribution.

Great controversy has surrounded the passage and implementation of the NIRA: the debate has only slightly diminished with time. Is the NIRA to be dismissed as a quickly aborted, two-year experiment of little lasting significance? Or was it the harbinger of increased national planning and government regulation that would characterize the United States in the second half of the twentieth century? Was the NIRA the "Magna Charta" for labor, as William Green predicted, or was it biased against labor, as William Leuchtenberg and Bernard Bellush now claim? Should the NIRA be condemned either as "fascistic" (according to Norman Thomas) or as "a socialistic dictatorship" (according to William Randolph Hearst)? Or should the legislation be credited, as Arthur M. Schlesinger, Jr., claims, with accomplishing "fantastic" and "staggering" reforms (such as the elimination of child labor and sweatshops, establishment of collective-bargaining protections, promotion of consumer protection, and defeat of "economic fatalism" [Schlesinger 1959, pp. 174–75]).

In addition to the political and social debates indicated above, there has also been controversy concerning specific economic issues, including (1) to what extent the NIRA was responsible for the aberrant (inflationary) behavior of wages and prices in the aftermath of the Great Depression, when approximately one-quarter of the labor force remained unemployed; (2) whether the NIRA successfully redistributed income to labor, in general, and to the relatively disadvantaged, in particular; and (3) whether the NIRA promoted economic recovery. This paper will analyze only the last of these economic issues—the extent to which the NIRA affected the course of economic recovery from the 1929–32 depression years.

Although economists and historians have tended to dismiss the importance of the macroeconomic impact of the industrial codes, this study will argue that the NIRA's macroeconomic impact was considerable and deleterious to recovery from the Great Depression. By reducing the real money supply, diminishing real wealth, and increasing the relative wage rate, the codes induced considerably more unemployment than would have occurred in their absence.

Arthur M. Schlesinger, Jr., summarizes his findings by claiming that the "NRA's strictly economic contributions to recovery were limited. . . . The enduring achievements of NRA lay not in the economic but in the social field" (1959, pp. 174–75). It is the determination of the present study that, whatever the achievements in the social field, the NRA's "strictly economic contributions" were not negligible. The legislation hindered, rather than promoted, recovery. It should also be noted that there is evidence that the legislation did, nonetheless, accomplish many of its redistributive goals—including a redistribution of income to labor and a spreading of employment to an increased number of individuals.

The remainder of this paper is divided into five sections. The first briefly describes the NIRA. The second section summarizes estimates of the impact of the industrial codes on nominal wages and prices. The third section estimates the impact of the codes on real money balances and, thereby, macroeconomic equilibrium. The fourth section summarizes the impact of the codes on macroeconomic equilibrium due to the NIRA-induced reduction in real wealth, redistribution of income toward labor, and rise in the real wage rate. The last section summarizes the findings.

PROVISIONS OF THE NIRA

Title I of the National Industrial Recovery Act (the only part of the legislation discussed in this paper) suspended the antitrust laws and authorized industry members to draft "codes of fair competition" that, when approved by the president, would apply to the entire industry and be enforceable by law. Title I (Section 7a) also established labor's right to bargain collectively and to organize without management interference. Under the auspices of Title I, over 500 codes of industrial self-government were promulgated, covering virtually all of the nonagricultural, private (and profit-making) economy.

Individual industry codes were the product of time-consuming negotiation between representatives of management (who themselves were often divided in their suggestions), labor, consumers, and the National Recovery Administration (NRA). Delays were unavoidable. In order to expedite implementation of wage and hour regulations, the President's Reemployment Agreement (PRA) was distributed in July 1933. Employers voluntarily agreed to (among other provisions) a limit of 35 hours per week per employee for industrial workers and a minimum wage of 40 cents per hour (as well as section 7a protections).

Most of the industry codes were proposed and approved between the spring of 1933 and the winter of 1934. By January 1934, 80 percent of industry was codified; and by December 1934, only a fraction of the eligible industries were not codified.

The wages and hours provisions of the NIRA codes varied from industry to industry, but all established minimum wages (frequently, 40 cents per hour, with many demographic differentials), restrictions on the number of hours that any individual could work per week (generally a maximum 36 to 40 hours per week, with a complicated set of exceptions and qualifications), and section 7a protections. Individual codes were far more vague in specifying the adjustment of wages for individuals earning more than the minimum. Many codes called for "equitable readjustment," though *equitable* was never defined; frequently, the codes prohibited reductions in employees' weekly wages (Lyon et al. 1935, p. 344).

As implied by the title "codes of fair competition," the trade provisions of the codes were designed to restrict competitive forces (which were the cause of continuing economic stagnation, both labor and management agreed). Trade-practice restrictions were even more varied than were the labor provisions; more than 1,000 different types of regulations appeared in the industrial codes. Most codes included provisions for minimum prices (below which no firm could charge), accompanied by complicated provisions to prevent secret price reductions or other competitive practices. The trade-practice provisions have often been accused of fostering monopolistic control of markets and favoring large, well-organized firms (U.S. National Recovery Administration n.d.).

EFFECT OF CODES ON NOMINAL WAGES AND PRICES

Before the macroeconomic effect of the NIRA can be determined, the impact of the codes on nominal wages and prices must be determined. This section will provide a summary of estimates that are provided elsewhere (Weinstein 1978, chap. 2) of the extent to which the NIRA codes caused wages and prices to rise above the levels that would have otherwise occurred.

The economic events following the precipitous economic downturn of 1929–33 in the United States have never been adequately explained by existing economic theory. Though unemployment exceeded one-quarter of the labor force in 1933, and never fell below 14 percent during the entire decade of the 1930s, nominal wages and prices steadily increased once the trough of the Great Contraction (March 1933) had been passed. Between May 1933 and December 1934, wholesale prices increased by more than 20 percent despite an unprecedented unemployment rate exceeding 20 percent. It will be argued in this section that the institution of economy-wide wage and price controls under the NIRA explains at least a part of the "anomalous" price behavior after June 1933.

To estimate the impact of the economy-wide wage and price controls instituted by the NIRA, a familiar two-equation Phillips curve system was estimated from monthly data on individual industries. The first of the two equations specified the determination of wages; the second, the determination of prices. Estimates of the two equations support the following conclusions:

(1) The unemployed continued—even after 1932 and initiation of the codes—to have a significant deflationary impact, but the NIRA codes had a more than offsetting inflationary impact. The coefficient of the wage-inflation equation associated with the unemployment variable was not significantly altered after passage of the NIRA. A 1 percent increase in the unemployment rate produced an approximately 0.33 percent change in the rate of wage inflation (for unemployment rates in the range of those experienced during the early 1930s) for *both* the pre- and postcode periods. There is, therefore, no statistical evidence, despite the anomalous price movements, that the labor markets became any less capable of exerting deflationary pressure in the mid-1930s than previously.

(2) The codes did add considerably to both wage and price inflation (i.e., the code provisions shifted the constant term of the Phillips curve equations): passage (elimination) of the codes increased (decreased) the inflation rate for any given level of unemployment.

The NIRA codes contributed to *continuing* wage inflation primarily through two mechanisms. First, as individual industry codes were successively approved, the wages of employees earning below the minimum rate were raised. Second, normal competitive mechanisms, as well as explicit pressure on employers by the NRA, increased the wages of employees who were already earning above the minimum wage rate; these forces worked to restore, at least in part, the wage differentials that prevailed prior to the NIRA. Hence, the institution of the NIRA codes led to a *progression* of wage increases—a shift in the *rate* of inflation—following initial code approval and not just a once-and-for-all increase in the wage rate.

Similarly, the NIRA codes furthered continuing price inflation by (*a*) contributing, as described above, to wage inflation and (*b*) increasing through newly approved codes the monopoly power of industry members, which, over time, allowed prices to be increased relative to costs. Subsequently, these price increases would spread, over time, throughout the economy.

(3) Initiation of the codes increased wages by approximately 26 percent per year for the two-year NIRA period. Nullification of the codes decreased the wage level by 14 percent per year. Initiation of the codes increased prices by 14 percent per year; nullification decreased prices by approximately 7 percent per year.

In the absence of the NIRA, average hourly earnings in manufacturing would have been less than 35 cents per hour by May 1935 instead of the actual level of almost 60 cents (assuming unemployment to have been unaltered). Similarly, the wholesale price index would have been less than 62 (for 1926 = 100) instead of the actual value of 80.2.

EFFECT OF NIRA ON ECONOMIC RECOVERY

Few New Deal historians have attributed to Title I of the NIRA much importance in the recovery from the Great Depression. While the ideological and political ramifications of the codes have been thoroughly explored by a plethora of historians, economists have generally confined their analysis to Title II (Public Works and Construction Projects) in order to ascertain the impact on employment and output.

Some economists—particularly Armen Alchian (1970), Milton Friedman and Anna Schwartz (1963), and Kenneth Roose (1954)—have recognized the possible recessionary consequences of the many New Deal regulations (including the NIRA) that autonomously raised wages and prices. These studies have not, however, analyzed the particular provisions of the NIRA. Consequently, the precise mechanisms by which codes affected the economy and, most importantly, the quantitative importance of the codes have been left undetermined.

Most of those who have considered the macroeconomic impacts of the codes have either dismissed their importance or considered them to have been weakly salutary. In a study completed in 1935, George Filipetti and Roland Vaile, for example, found that "there was practically no expansion in purchasing power, that is, in the quantity of goods that could be bought either by the individual factory employee or by all of the factory employees taken together" (p. 16). In a more recent study, Ellis Hawley concluded:

The gains were certainly limited ones, and it was doubtful that even those could be credited to the NRA. More than likely they were due much less to the NRA codes than to the spending and relief programs, and the working of natural recuperative forces.

What the NRA might be credited with was a sort of holding action, a program that for a season did provide a psychological stimulant. [1966, pp. 131–32]

Historians have often concurred in these conclusions. Arthur M. Schlesinger, Jr., is not atypical when he argues:

Indeed it is hard to resist the conclusion that the question of price policy per se consumed far more time in NRA (and far more space in subsequent analyses of NRA) than its importance warranted. . . .

The ending of the NRA price-fixing would certainly not, for example, have induced much expansion. The problem here was not the level of price, but the gross failure of demand, *and this was something that NRA by itself could not reverse.* [1959, p. 172, emphasis added]

It is the purpose of this section to disprove the contention that the NIRA did not significantly affect the course of economic recovery from the Great Depression. The NRA's importance cannot be relegated only to the "social field."

Most previous analyses have been preoccupied with discerning a break in the trend of output and employment after code initiation. Without an explicit model of what output and employment would have been in the absence of the codes, however, no definitive statement can be made about the macroeconomic impacts of the industrial codes. The analysis provided in the next two sections will show that the NIRA-induced inflation in nominal wages and prices, as discussed in the second section, had a sizable contractionary impact on the economy. By reducing the real money supply and diminishing real wealth, for example, the industrial codes caused a reduction in output and employment. Furthermore, the code-induced rise in the real wage rate encouraged firms to reduce employment even further. These contractionary consequences of the codes were only minimally offset by the increase in consumption due to the redistribution of income toward labor that was attributable to the NIRA (Weinstein 1978, chap. 4).

Of course, many factors other than the industrial codes influenced macroeconomic equilibrium during the NIRA period. This paper considers the extent to which the industrial codes—even if all other economic variables were unchanged from their 1933–35 levels—independently affected the levels of real output and employment during the NIRA period.

Modern macroeconomic models identify the importance of private spending, the government budget, and real money balances to the determination of real output and employment (for unchanged autonomous private spending and given price and income elasticities of the relevant spending functions and money-demand function). Thus, to initiate an investigation of the impact of the codes, the effect of the codes on private spending, the government budget, and the real money supply must be investigated. Since the NIRA codes did not independently alter government expenditures or taxes, the next two sections will analyze the impact of the wage and price provisions on private spending, real money balances, and, thereby, on macroeconomic equilibrium. By significantly raising wages and prices, the codes did diminish the real value of money balances (and other net financial assets of fixed nominal value). By redistributing income (e.g., by raising, on average, wages more than prices), diminishing real wealth (due to the wage and price inflation), altering expectations, and raising the real wage rate, the codes affected private autonomous spending and employment.

The economic stagnation, to which the above quotations refer, is evident in the data for industrial production. The monthly industrial production index includes many of the same sectors that were covered by the NIRA codes (especially the manufacturing sectors) and generally excludes sectors that were not covered by the codes. Most importantly, the use of yearly data (e.g., GNP data) can be exceedingly misleading in studying the NIRA period and the impact of the industrial codes.

For example, in the months of 1935 preceding code nullification (May 1935), industrial production declined by 0.7 percent (1.6 percent annual rate of decline); during the months following the *Schechter* decision, industrial production rose by more than 15 percent (27 percent annual rate of increase). Thus a yearly average for 1935 production would confound the distinct experiences before and after the NIRA codes were nullified. In fact, GNP did rise between 1934 and 1935, despite the stagnation during the NIRA period as indicated by the industrial production index.

In the year following passage of the NIRA in June 1933, industrial production was almost stagnant—increasing by less than 1 percent despite the fact that the economy had passed the trough of the Great Depression. By May 1935, industrial production had increased by less than 6 percent during the two years of the National Industrial Recovery Act. In fact, after June 1933 industrial production reached a plateau that was not finally surpassed until more than a year and a half later. Though industrial production spurted in the early months of 1933 (just prior to the legislation), it fell in the second half of the year, recovered somewhat in the first half of 1934 (though only to the level achieved in the previous year), and then fell once more during the second half of 1934. There was a brisk, if abbreviated, recovery between the very end of 1934 and the beginning of 1935, but production remained virtually unchanged throughout the early months of 1935. Only in the second half of 1935 (after NIRA nullification) was there a sustained and brisk recovery.

The relative stagnation of industrial production during the NIRA period—or, more precisely, the pause in the recovery of industrial production from the middle of 1933 through the latter part of 1934—seems, at first consideration, baffling. After all, this was a period of unprecedented governmental (New Deal) spending programs and monetary expansion. Furthermore, such fiscal and monetary stimuli should be most effective during such a period of massive underutilization of economic resources. On the contrary, while industrial production was relatively unchanged during the year following June 1933, prices, on the other hand, increased by 15 percent during the same interval.

Nor was the aberrant behavior of prices and output after June 1933 typical of the prewar economy. In 1932 prices plummeted in the face of increasing unemployment and economic stagnation, as most economic models would predict. Similarly, during the 1920–21 recession (May 1920 through June 1921) both wholesale prices and industrial production tumbled (by 44 percent and 28 percent, respectively, accompanied by a 9 percent drop in the money supply). More interesting, during the 1921–23 recovery, prices rose (as they did after 1933), but the 1920s' upturn was characterized by an unprecedented swift and extensive recovery (rather than the massive continuing underutilization of production resources and economic lethargy of the 1930–35 experience). Between July 1921 and May 1923, real output increased by a spectacular 63 percent (accompanied by a 14 percent rise in the money supply). Thus, the combination of stagnation, inflation, and massive unemployment in the mid-1930s appears to be not only theoretically anomalous but also atypical of the prewar U.S. economy.

Though E. Cary Brown's seminal paper (1956) addressed the potential importance of the fiscal programs that were initiated under the New Deal, the impotence of the monetary expansion remains unresolved. After all, between June 1933 and June 1934 the nominal money supply increased by approximately 10 percent—regardless of whether one considers M_1 (currency held by the public plus demand deposits at commercial banks) or M_2 (M_1 plus time deposits at commercial banks). Between June 1933 and June 1935, the nominal money supply (M_1) increased by more than 31 percent (between the same two dates, M_2 increased by 26.5 percent). Table 1 provides the growth of the money supply during the period 1933–35.

The dramatic increases in the money supply after June 1933 must be contrasted with the previous precipitous decreases in the nominal money supply that had characterized the economy during its downward spiral prior to the

Table 1. Nominal Money Supply, 1933–35 (millions of current dollars)

	1933		1934		1935	
	M_1	M_2	M_1	M_2	M_1	M_2
Jan.	20,627	34,154	19,720	30,954	23,648	36,035
Feb.	19,982	32,607	20,298	31,614	24,353	36,765
Mar.	19,052	29,970	20,748	32,240	24,259	36,817
Apr.	19,039	29,747	20,880	32,571	24,586	37,377
May	19,449	30,100	20,997	32,798	24,774	37,581
June	19,232	30,087	21,068	33,073	25,199	38,049
July	19,087	30,160	21,539	33,566	25,434	38,229
Aug.	19,115	30,192	22,127	34,234	26,804	39,658
Sept.	19,171	30,261	22,024	34,097	26,381	39,352
Oct.	19,313	30,387	22,557	34,745	26,714	39,749
Nov.	19,558	30,563	23,017	35,178	27,268	40,351
Dec.	19,759	30,807	22,774	35,061	27,032	40,338
Yearly Average	19,449	30,753	21,479	33,344	25,538	38,364

Source: Friedman and Schwartz 1963, table A–1.
Note: M_1 = Currency held by public plus commercial-bank demand deposits.
M_2 = Currency held by public plus commercial-bank demand and time deposits.

spring of 1933. In just the six months between January and June 1933, M_1 decreased by almost 7 percent (approximately a 14 percent annual rate of increase) and M_2 decreased by approximately 12 percent (or slightly less than a 24 percent annual rate of decrease). These figures reinforce the accounts of many researchers who attribute the radical reversal of the trend in money to (1) New Deal changes in the banking structure (federal deposit insurance, e.g.) and (2) explicit reversal of the monetary policy by the Federal Reserve Board.

Common to all factors that have been cited as responsible for the reversal of the money-supply trend is their independence of the NIRA industrial codes. Milton Friedman and Anna Schwartz have argued that, in contrast to the 1920s, the Federal Reserve System abandoned its attempts to sterilize gold movements or to smooth fluctuations in high-powered money. Because no systematic attempt to alter the quantity of high-powered money was made, the dominant influence on the money supply during the NIRA period became fortuitous inflows of gold. Friedman and Schwartz argue convincingly that the "accidental" gold inflow "occurred despite rather than because of the actions of unions, business organizations, and government in pushing up prices" (1963, p. 499; see also pp. 499–534).

The question remains: What effect did the NIRA codes have on the economic recovery from the depression? To answer this question, recall one of the primary characteristics of modern macroeconomic models: the long-term features of the model do not depend on the nominal quantity of money; only the real money supply is critical (e.g., Hickman and Coen 1976). It is this consideration that helps to identify the impact of the NIRA codes and perhaps explains, in part, the otherwise anomalous sluggishness of the unemployment rate during the NIRA months, despite vigorous monetary expansion. First recall that the monetary expansion after June 1933 was mainly due to gold inflows; for reasons previously discussed, the (approximately) 14 percent average annual rate of increase in the money supply during the two-year NIRA period can be considered an exogenous shock—independent of the NIRA legislation itself. Second, the discussion in the second section indicated that the industrial codes contributed to prices approximately 14 percent per year during the NIRA period. The codes exactly nullified the monetary expansion! Despite nominal expansion of the money supply, there was literally no expansion of the *real* money supply. Thus there was no stimulus to any real variables in the economic system. In the absence of the codes, the monetary stimulus would have been expansionary; in the presence of the codes, the monetary stimulus was impotent.

Because the codes generated a 14 percent annual rate of inflation during the NIRA, they imposed a 14 percent reduction per year in the real money supply (relative to what it would have been in the absence of the codes). For the specific historical episode under investigation, the reduction of 14 percent in real balances is equivalent to the nullification—in real terms—of the 14 percent rate of increase in the nominal money supply after June 1933. Note that in the absence of the codes the monetary stimulus would have contributed to real output and employment; however, the combination of the monetary stimulus and the NIRA-induced inflation left real output virtually unchanged. Thus the contractionary impact of the codes can be measured, at least in part, by what contributions to real output and employment the monetary stimulus would have made in the absence of the codes.

In order to determine the effect on real GNP of a 14 percent annual increase in the nominal money supply, it would be convenient to use money multipliers for real GNP (the change in real GNP per dollar change in the nominal money stock) from a suitable large-scale macroeconomic model of the 1930s' U.S. economy. Although there is one such macroeconomic model—the Hickman-

Coen annual growth model of the U.S.—money multipliers for the 1930s have yet to be determined for this model. Nevertheless, reasonable conjectures can be made about the potential impact of the codes.

The maximum stimulus that a 14 percent annual increase in the money supply could provide is, of course, 14 percent annually. There are two necessary conditions for this maximum stimulus to be achieved, as can be seen by examining the following definition of V, the income velocity of money:

$$V \equiv \frac{P \cdot Y}{M},$$

where $P \cdot Y$ is nominal income and M is nominal money stock; or

$$M \cdot V \equiv P \cdot Y.$$

The maximum real impact would have resulted from the monetary stimulus only if (1) the income velocity of money remained constant and (2) the entire change in nominal income was comprised of changes in real output—that is, prices did not rise after the monetary stimulus.

Of course, neither of these two conditions would have strictly prevailed—perhaps not even approximately—during the 1930s. Thus, 14 percent is certainly an overestimate of the real impact of the monetary expansion. To appreciate the possible extent of the overestimation, consider the postwar experience of the U.S. economy. If money multipliers for real GNP were approximately the same during the 1930s as they have been in the postwar economy (an assumption that will be discussed below), the potential stimulus from a 14 percent annual increase in the nominal money stock can be readily estimated. Data reported in a comparative study of postwar macroeconometric models indicate that the average value of the money multipliers for real GNP from the major postwar macroeconomic models are 2.6, 5.4, and 6.4, respectively, for the first three years following the monetary stimulus (Fromm and Klein 1976, table 9).

From these estimates, a continuing 3.1 billion dollar (approximately 14 percent) increase in the money supply, continuing for two years, would be expected to produce a 4.1 billion (1929) dollar increase in real output in the year following June 1933.[3] In the year following June 1934, real output could be expected to have increased by 8.5 billion (1929) dollars due to the continuing money-supply increase. For the entire NIRA period, monetary expansion itself would have contributed, in the absence of the codes, more than 12 billion 1929 dollars. Thus, monetary expansion alone would have increased real output by, on average, 8 percent annually during the NIRA period. Though the estimate that real GNP would have increased 8 percent (on average) because of the

Table 2. Comparison of Lebergott and Hickman-Coen Yearly Averages for Unemployment, 1933–35 (percentage of civilian labor force)

	Lebergott Estimate	Hickman- Coen Estimate
1922	6.7	7.3
1923	2.4	4.5
1931	16.3	13.0
1932	24.1	18.8
1933	25.2	19.8
1934	22.0	21.3
1935	20.3	19.5

Sources: Lebergott 1964, table A–3; Hickman and Coen 1976, p. 239.

monetary expansion after June 1933 is sizable, it is well below the theoretically maximal impact.

The consequence of forgone expansion under the codes would have been continued misery for the unemployed. The unemployment rate was particularly persistent throughout the NIRA period. Hickman and Coen (the series to be used in the following discussion) estimate that unemployment, on an annual basis, was only 0.3 percent lower in 1935 than it was in 1933 (and actually increased by more than 1 percent in 1934). This complete stagnation occurred despite the brisk recovery after June 1935—after nullification of the industrial codes (the yearly averages confound the NIRA and non-NIRA periods in 1933 and 1935). Table 2 compares the yearly averages for two different series on unemployment: Hickman-Coen and Lebergott.

The Hickman-Coen model indicates that an 8 percent increase in real GNP during the NIRA period would be associated with at least a 3 percent (on average) fall in the unemployment rate. In the absence of the codes, approximately 1.5 million individuals each year could have been spared the misery of unemployment (if the postwar money multipliers do not seriously overestimate the prewar response to monetary stimuli). In other words, evidence based on postwar money multipliers indicates that the codes were responsible for vitiating a potential 15 percent reduction in the number of individuals who were unemployed.[4]

These postwar money multipliers, of course, do not account for structural differences in the pre- and postwar economy. Current evidence cannot yet definitively answer whether the monetary expansion during the 1930s would have been more or less powerful than the postwar experience.

It is quite possible, however, that a monetary stimulus would not have raised prices as much between 1933 and 1935 as it has in the postwar period (the source of the money multiplier used above). After all, the NIRA codes were imposed, in part, to halt what was perceived as a persistent *downward* spiral of prices. Thus, for given increases in nominal income, real output might be expected to have risen more, on average, in the aftermath of the Great Depression than in the postwar period.

It is to be expected that fiscal and monetary stimuli should be most effective—in real terms—during this period of massive underutilization of economic resources. When the economy is suffering excessive underutilization of productive capacity, as was true during the 1930–35 period, the response of real output to, for example, a spending stimulus should be strong.

This theoretical presumption is confirmed by the simulations of the Hickman-Coen macroeconomic model for the U.S. economy. The Hickman-Coen estimates indicate that, for the years immediately following a fiscal stimulus, the government-spending multipliers for real GNP (that is, the change, relative to a control solution, of real GNP per dollar change in nominal spending) during the NIRA period were considerably larger than the respective multipliers for other prewar years.

In fact, Hickman and Coen find that the spending multipliers are higher, on average, during the prewar period (not just the depression years) than during the postwar years. Hickman and Coen attribute the differences, in part, to well-recognized structural changes in the economy. They emphasize the development of built-in stabilizers in the U.S. economy since the prewar period, such as the larger federal tax base, the unemployment insurance system, changes in import and export propensities, and the smaller response of business fixed investment and state and local government expenditures to changes in GNP (Hickman and Coen 1976, p. 193).

For the above reasons, it would seem that, compared to the postwar period, given increases in nominal income during the NIRA period would be characterized by relatively larger real output changes. Even if this statement were true, however, it would not necessarily follow that real output would rise relatively more during the prewar period in response to a monetary stimulus. For example, changes in velocity during the NIRA period might have vitiated changes in the money stock, leaving nominal income relatively immune to monetary stimuli. The bulk of previous research, however, does not indicate that velocity behaved significantly differently in the pre- and postwar periods. In a study conducted for specific years during the 1930s, Gandolfi (1974) concluded that the elasticity of the demand for money did not increase substantially during the depression years. In fact, he found that it actually declined in 1933. Nor did the studies of Teigen (1964), Brunner and Meltzer (1963), or

Laidler (1966) find any tendency for the interest elasticity of the demand for money to be significantly altered during the 1930s. And, after reviewing all of the major studies of the demand for money, Laidler concluded that "there appears to be little evidence" that the liquidity trap hypothesis is true (1977, p. 130).

If, for the reasons cited above, (1) velocity did not negate monetary stimuli more in the pre- than in the postwar period, and (2) increases in nominal income were likely to produce larger changes in real output in the pre- than in the postwar economy, then the money multipliers from the postwar macroeconomic models should serve as a reasonable, albeit conservative, estimate of the prewar money multipliers. Thus, the post-war-based estimate that the codes nullified a potential 8 percent average annual increase in real GNP would be credible.

Despite the above arguments, it has *not* been proved that the money multipliers during the 1930s were at least as large as those for the postwar period. Hence, the 8 percent estimate, derived above for the real output loss due to the codes, cannot be definitely interpreted as an underestimate. For example, evidence has not been presented that proves that spending would have responded to whatever fall in interest rates would have accompanied monetary expansion (even assuming Gandolfi et al. are correct that the money-demand function was unchanged in the prewar period). Existing macroeconomic models of the 1930s' U.S. economy are either too primitive (e.g., Klein-Goldberger) or insufficiently tested (e.g., Hickman-Coen) to reveal the true response of the prewar economy to monetary expansion. Klein and Goldberger, in an early macroeconomic model of the 1929–52 economy, conclude that "in using our highly aggregative measure of investment, we find no reasonable empirical results for the effect of interest" (1955, p. 67). In the Hickman-Coen model, interest rates do enter the equations for investment in automobiles and in housing starts, but market rates "have no direct influence on business fixed investment in our model" (1976, p. 106). Personal-consumption expenditures are similarly unaffected by market interest rates. Examination of these individual functions of the Hickman-Coen model does not reveal any obvious mechanism by which monetary expansion could have had a powerful impact during the 1930s. Nevertheless, the interest elasticities of most of the major spending functions (as well as the interest elasticity of the demand for money) in the Hickman-Coen model are not significantly different in the pre- and postwar periods; there is, therefore, no specific indication that money multipliers would be lower in the prewar period (and recall, the Hickman-Coen spending multipliers are higher in the 1930s, which would produce, all else the same, a larger response to monetary expansion).

Nor could these macroeconomic models of the 1930s be expected to capture the entire impact of monetary changes. For example, the models fail to incorporate in the spending functions any wealth effects by which monetary policy could be expected to influence macroeconomic variables.

In the absence of definitive empirical evidence, the potential response of the 1930s' economy to the monetary expansion after June 1933 remains uncertain. Evidence based on postwar experience suggests, however, that the codes, by nullifying the real impact of the monetary expansion, precluded an (approximately) 8 percent average annual increase in real output during the NIRA period. The imposition of the industrial codes precluded the kind of dramatic recovery that a depressed economy might have realized when subjected to a massive monetary infusion (and as occurred, for example, after the 1920–21 recession).

The analysts quoted at the beginning of this section confused the continuing stagnation of the economy with what they argued was a neutral impact of the industrial codes. Because the economy displayed neither renewed growth nor renewed recession, the initiation of the codes was interpreted to have been relatively insignificant. It is the implication of the above discussion, however, that the NIRA codes were deleterious to economic growth; and economic production, once sacrificed, can never, of course, be recaptured.

EFFECT OF NIRA ON REAL WEALTH

Even though existing macroeconomic models cannot pinpoint the overall impact of monetary expansion during the 1930s, some of the partial mechanisms by which money affected real output and unemployment can be identified and quantified. This section will summarize the impacts of the NIRA-induced diminution in real wealth, redistribution of income, and rise in relative wages (Weinstein 1978, chap. 4). Though no estimate of the entire effect of the codes is possible from the separate examination of these partial mechanisms, the analysis does provide an indication of the possible magnitudes involved.

The contractionary effects of the NIRA, discussed in the third section, were derived from the postwar macroeconomic models. These models, in general, explicitly capture the extent to which lower real money balances (due to the NIRA-induced inflation) cause interest rates to rise and thereby cause (especially) investment and consumer durable spending to fall. However, many of these models (e.g., the Hickman-Coen specification) exclude any direct role for net financial assets of fixed nominal value in determining consumer expenditures. Thus, some of the models do not *systematically* estimate the extent to which the diminution in real wealth, due to the NIRA-induced inflation, reduced consumer spending. Nor did the estimates in section 3 explicitly determine either (1) the extent to which the NIRA-induced rise in real wages promoted direct substitution away from the employment of labor or (2) the extent to which the NIRA-induced redistribution of income toward labor (primarily through work spreading and the rise in real wages) stimulated total spending.

Estimates derived from a variety of economic models suggest that the independent effect on spending (and income) due to the NIRA-induced diminution in the real value of net financial assets (from inflation) was responsible for a 6–11 percent reduction in annual GNP during the NIRA years. Also, the NIRA-induced relative wage increase, in the absence of any other effects, would have added another 2 percent to the unemployment rate. As a partial offset, the redistribution of income did stimulate spending, and therefore output and employment. At the very most, however, this impact would have been of a magnitude similar to merely the real wealth effect alone (but probably would have been less). Unfortunately, the total contractionary effect of the NIRA codes cannot be derived from the above information: one cannot simply add the separately estimated effects of the NIRA-induced impact on real money balances (and thus interest rates), real wealth, and the distribution of income. Just because the macroeconomic models may not *explicitly* incorporate wealth effects, for example, does not necessarily imply that the multiplier estimates of the model do not capture at least part of the wealth effects that do characterize the economic system. The omission of wealth from the consumption function represents a specification error, which in general biases the estimates of the other parameters of the model. Part of the impact of real wealth on spending might already be included in these biased estimates. Thus, adding the effects of the reduction in real wealth to the macroeconomic impacts estimated from the Hickman-Coen model might involve some double counting of the total impact of the NIRA codes on the economy.

The extent of the possible double counting cannot be determined, since the extent to which the postwar multipliers happen (implicitly) to capture wealth and redistributive effects cannot be accurately quantified (without simulation experiments). The multipliers of a nonlinear, multiequation system depend not only on the parameters of the individual equations but also on the complicated interactions between the variables and the dynamic properties of the model.

CONCLUSION

The NIRA industrial codes contributed to prolonged stagnation of the economy after the trough of the Great Depression. The NIRA-induced price inflation was more than enough to vitiate whatever expansion would have resulted from the vigorous (though fortuitous) monetary expansion that began in June 1933.

It cannot be definitively argued, on the basis of the present evidence, that the monetary expansion, fiscal expansion, or other recovery forces that were operating in the mid-1930s would have provided an economic boom (similar to the recovery from the 1920–21 recession) in the absence of the NIRA. No evidence has been presented to prove that there were not other economic depressants besides the industrial codes. What has been established, however, is the fact that the NIRA codes were a significant and independent contractionary influence; the economy could not have recovered in historically expected ways as long as the NIRA wage and price regulations were effective.

Though the evidence is conjectural, the NIRA-induced inflation vitiated a potential 8 percent rate of growth (and the accompanying 15 percent reduction in the number of individuals who were unemployed) that might have resulted from the monetary expansion during the NIRA period. Other evidence suggests that the diminution of real wealth alone was responsible for a 6–11 percent reduction in annual GNP during the NIRA years. Also, the NIRA-induced relative wage increase added another 2 percent to the unemployment rolls.

As a partial offset, the redistribution of income toward labor would have increased consumer spending and, through the multiplier effect, output and employment; this impact was probably less stimulatory than the real wealth effect was depressing.

What has *not* been provided is a single estimate of the total NIRA impact on employment and output. It cannot be assumed that the total effect is the simple sum of the previously mentioned partial mechanisms, all of which are imbedded in a mutually determined and determining general-equilibrium system. Nor have all the links between the codes and the economy been analyzed in this paper (e.g., the impact of the codes on investment spending or business expectations has not been considered). To determine the NIRA's total effect would require the simulation of a macroeconomic model that incorporated all of these partial mechanisms (which no existing macroeconomic model of the period can provide). It is nevertheless the implication of the partial mechanisms analyzed in this paper that the NIRA codes were a nontrivial—more likely, significant—retardant to economic progress and a cause of the prolonged recovery from the depths of the depression. Of course, this is not to suggest that the other forces did not contribute to the economic lethargy that characterized the mid-1930s.

NOTES

1. For example, the Emergency Banking Act (March 9), Civilian Conservation Corps Act (March 31), Federal Emergency Relief Act (May 12), Agricultural Adjustment Act (May 12), Tennessee Valley Authority Act (May 18), Truth in Securities Act (May 27), Home Owners Loan Act (June 13).
2. By January 1, 1934, 90 percent of all industrial workers were covered by NIRA regulations.

3. For the multiplier experiments summarized here, the money supply during the NIRA period is considered to have increased at a constant annual rate (the average of the actual changes) during the two years. A constant rate, rather than the actual trend in the money supply, is used because the Hickman-Coen simulations were conducted only for the hypothetical situation in which the exogenous variables changed by a constant amount each year. Estimates using the actual money-supply figures did not change qualitative results.

4. See Hickman and Coen (1976). From their table 9.3 (p. 188), it can be determined that for the years 1933–35, a one-dollar increase (in 1958 terms) in real GNP was associated with, on average, a 0.28 percent reduction in the unemployment rate.

REFERENCES

Alchian, A. A. 1970. "Information Costs, Pricing, and Resource Unemployment." In *Microeconomic Foundations of Employment and Inflation Theory,* ed. E. S. Phelps. New York: W. W. Norton.

Brown, E. C. 1956. "Fiscal Policies in the Thirties: A Reappraisal." *American Economic Review* 46: 857–78.

Brunner, K., and Meltzer, A. 1963. "Predicting Velocity: Implications for Theory and Policy." *Journal of Finance* 18: 319–54.

Filipetti, G., and Vaile, R. 1935. *The Economic Effects of the NRA: A Regional Analysis.* Minneapolis: University of Minnesota Press.

Friedman, M., and Schwartz, A. J. 1963. *A Monetary History of the United States, 1867–1960.* Princeton, N.J.: Princeton University Press, for the National Bureau of Economic Research.

Fromm, G., and Klein, L. R. 1976. "The NBER/NSF Model Comparison Seminar: An Analysis of Results." In *Econometric Model Performance,* ed. L. R. Klein and E. Burmeister. Philadelphia: University of Pennsylvania Press.

Gandolfi, A. E. 1974. "Stability of the Demand for Money during the Great Contraction—1929–1933." *Journal of Political Economy* 82: 969–83.

Hawley, E. W. 1966. *The New Deal and the Problem of Monopoly.* Princeton, N.J.: Princeton University Press.

Hickman, B. G., and Coen, R. M. 1976. *An Annual Growth Model of the U.S. Economy.* Amsterdam: North-Holland.

Klein, L. R., and Goldberger, A. S. 1955. *An Econometric Model of the United States, 1929–1952.* Amsterdam: North-Holland.

Laidler, D. 1966. "The Rate of Interest and the Demand for Money: Some Empirical Evidence." *Journal of Political Economy* 74: 545–55.

———. 1977. *The Demand for Money: Theories and Evidence.* New York: Dun-Donnelley.

Lebergott, S. 1964. *Manpower in Economic Growth: The American Record since 1800.* New York: McGraw-Hill.

Lyon, L. S., et al. 1935. *The National Recovery Administration: An Analysis and Appraisal.* Washington, D.C.: Brookings Institution.

Roose, K. D. 1954. *The Economics of Recession and Revival*. New Haven, Conn.: Yale University Press.

Schlesinger, A. M., Jr. 1969. *The Coming of the New Deal*. Boston: Houghton Mifflin.

Teigen, R. 1964. "Demand and Supply Functions for Money in the United States." *Econometrica* 32: 477–509.

U.S. National Recovery Administration. N.d. *Minimum Price Regulation under Codes of Fair Competition*. Trade Practice Study No. 56. Washington, D.C.: NRA.

――――. 1937. *Report of the President's Committee of Industrial Analysis*. Washington, D.C.: Government Printing Office.

Weinstein, M. M. 1978. "Some Redistributive and Macroeconomic Impacts of the National Industrial Recovery Act, 1933–1935." Ph.D. diss., Massachusetts Institute of Technology.

15 COMMENTS ON "SOME MACROECONOMIC IMPACTS OF THE NATIONAL INDUSTRIAL RECOVERY ACT, 1933–1935"

Phillip Cagan

Here we are again returning to the 1930s, an obsession monetary economists share with the proverbial criminal who supposedly cannot resist returning to the scene of his crime. In our case we return to the scene of our major failure to explain events. It is not, I hasten to add, that monetary developments fail to explain the severity of the Great Contraction and ensuing recovery. The monetary explanation fits very well. The other question raised at this conference—whether monetary developments were exogenous and so provide a self-contained explanation of the 1930s—cannot be resolved by inferences drawn from this one observation. When we put together all the relevant episodes, however, as I argued in an earlier study (1965, pp. 263–68), the combined evidence strongly supports the proposition that business contractions became severe when monetary growth declined substantially for any of a variety of reasons and not otherwise, and that most of the monetary declines could not be attributed to the severity of the accompanying business contractions.

Our failure to explain the 1930s pertains to the behavior of prices and wages in the face of continuing massive unemployment. After declining sharply from 1929 to 1933, prices and wages rose thereafter. It seems strange that they did not continue to fall in an adjustment to remove the excess supply of resources and seems stranger still by the new theory of rational expectations. There has been some nibbling away at the edges of this anomaly. Darby (1976) swept several million of the alleged unemployed under the rug of government employment. Others have argued that the public expected the long-run price level to be higher because of the 1933 devaluation of the dollar, and these expectations counteracted the short-run market pressures on prices and wages to fall. Friedman and Schwartz (1963, p. 498) list the NIRA codes as one among several important reasons for the perverse behavior of prices and wages in the 1930s. A suspicion has nevertheless lingered that all these explanations fall short.

Michael Weinstein now proposes to allay this suspicion by making the NIRA codes the major culprit. The codes, he claims, raised prices and wages that otherwise would have continued to decline after 1933, consistently with previous historical experience. This is a satisfying step to those in the monetarist tradition; for them, only governmental interference seems capable of explaining such a major deviation from the market's normal tendency to bring demand and supply into equilibrium. I think Weinstein is correct to assign major importance to the codes, though I am still puzzled over the strength they supposedly had and hesitate to surrender all doubts.

I am puzzled how the codes could be enforced with such power as to raise wages sharply against the market forces of excess supply. I am puzzled why some prices and wages rose even before the codes became effective. Was the mere anticipation of the codes catalytic for an economy so prone to collusion that prices rose before legal enforcement was necessary? And why, when the codes were no longer enforceable after 1935, did no reassertion of market forces to reduce prices and wages become evident? The data series show nary a ripple (Creamer 1950, chart 1, p. 12). Weinstein does not present major evidence on the detailed operation of the codes to overturn these doubts.

In his statistical analysis Weinstein assumes that the codes fully account for the deviation of wages from a Phillips equation. To fit the equation to periods when the codes were not in effect, he relies on the 1921 business contraction, 1931–33, and a short period after May 1935. (Wages underwent very little variation in the intervening years of the 1920s, and little would be gained by including them.) Given the lack of earlier data, there is nothing else that can be done, but we should note that one and a half business contractions is not an overwhelming amount of evidence to work with. His fit of the Phillips equation also covers 1933–35 with a dummy for the codes period (there is another dummy for the subsequent period of their removal). The dummies shift the constant term; hence the slope of the equation is assumed to be the same in all years. The equation,[1] disregarding the dummies, is:

monthly rate of change of wages = $-0.015 - 0.090$ (reciprocal of unemployment in percent).

When wages are constant, the implied rate of unemployment works out to be 6 percent. (According to my analysis [1977] of the post–World War II period, the noninflationary full-employment rate in 1977 was again 6 percent. By the preceding equation, therefore, 1 percent excess unemployment in 1977 would *reduce* wages at a rate of 2.4 percent per year. The labor market has clearly changed since the 1930s!) In the period of the codes, June 1933 to May 1935, unemployment averaged about 22.5 percent (without Darby's correction). By the preceding equation, this would have produced a monthly decline in wages of 1.095 percent, or a total decline of 22.4 percent over the 23 months the codes were in effect. Actually, average hourly earnings rose 33.1 percent in that period.

The codes were estimated to raise wages by 2.2 percent a month, or in total from June 1933 to May 1935, by 65 percent. (Were the beneficiaries of these cartels actually so greedy?) The equation predicts a total rise in wages of only $(1 + 0.022 - 0.01095)^{23}$, or 27.2 percent. Since the equation underpredicts the actual rise in wages over this period, its estimate of the effect of the codes could even be too low.

Weinstein's estimate of the effect on prices (1978, p. 299) is 14 percent per year—sufficient to wipe out the stimulative effect of the entire increase in the money stock during the NIRA period. He then discusses the implications for real GNP and employment, concluding that employment was held as much as 15 percent lower during the NIRA period.

There are reasons to believe, however, that this effect of the codes is overstated. First, there is the absence of Darby's correction, which would reduce the estimated effect. Second, the cyclical direction of economic changes could intensify the decline in wages and enhance their recovery, in which case part of the cyclical variation in wage changes should not be related to the level of the unemployment rate. (This possibility calls for adding the change in the unemployment rate to the equation.) Third, it is not clear how to handle expected price changes during this period, but Weinstein's method of adding the current price change to a second fit of the equation (which had little effect on the other coefficients of the regression) may not be adequate. Conceivably, price expectations accounted for some of the rise in wages.

In the final analysis, however, we face in the 1930s' experience the need to explain a perplexing combination of large-scale unemployment and substantial increases in wages. Although I would not dismiss as unimportant the widespread belief at the time that low prices were the cause and not simply the symptom of depression and the acceptance this created for collusive arrangements, the legal enactment of the NIRA codes was clearly very important. Weinstein has examined the workings of the codes in material not presented at the conference. We need to learn more of how they worked in practice. I commend him for alerting historians to an effect whose economic significance appears to have been previously understated.

NOTE

1. Shown in the extended manuscript of Weinstein (1978, table II–5, p. 100), circulated at the conference but not reproduced in this volume.

REFERENCES

Cagan, P. 1965. *Determinants and Effects of Changes in the Stock of Money, 1875–1960*. New York: Columbia University Press, for the National Bureau of Economic Research.

———. 1977. "The Reduction of Inflation and the Magnitude of Unemployment." In *Contemporary Economic Problems, 1977*, ed. W. Fellner. Washington, D.C.: American Enterprise Institute.

Creamer, D. 1950. *Behavior of Wage Rates during Business Cycles*. Occasional Paper 34. New York: National Bureau of Economic Research.

Darby, M. 1976. "Three-and-a-Half Million U.S. Employees Have Been Mislaid: Or, an Explanation of Unemployment, 1934–41." *Journal of Political Economy* 84: 1–16.

Friedman, M., and Schwartz, A. J. 1963. *A Monetary History of the United States, 1867–1960*. Princeton, N.J.: Princeton University Press, for the National Bureau of Economic Research.

Weinstein, M. 1978. "Some Redistributive and Macroeconomic Impacts of the National Industrial Recovery Act, 1933–1935." Ph.D. diss., Massachusetts Institute of Technology.

16 THE DEPRESSION IN SWEDEN AND THE UNITED STATES:

A Comparison of Causes and Policies
Lars Jonung

The depression of the 1930s was a worldwide phenomenon. The economic activity of practically every country was strongly influenced by the depression. This was the case for a small open economy like the Swedish one as well as for a large and fairly closed economy like the American. The character of the depression, however—particularly its duration and its severity—differed significantly from one country to another. Generally, countries that had left the gold standard at an early stage of the depression experienced a less pronounced decline in prices and output than those that remained on gold.

There has been considerable discussion among American economists about the causal interpretation of the American depression. Two general classes of alternative explanations have been proposed. The first one, the money hypothesis, stems in its modern version from the work of Friedman and Schwartz (1963) and suggests that monetary developments played a key role during the depression. The second one, the spending hypothesis, which has recently been

I have benefited from the comments of Lennart Jörberg and Eskil Wadensjö of the University of Lund, of Bertil Ohlin, of members of the money workshop at the University of Western Ontario, London, and of participants of the conference. I am especially grateful to Bertil Ohlin, who has given me valuable suggestions concerning Swedish economic policies in the 1930s.

advocated by Peter Temin (1976), states that changes in autonomous spending caused the contraction. The present discussion about the causes of the depression is to a large extent based on the work of these economists, although both classes of explanations have been advanced earlier within as well as outside of the United States.[1]

The purpose of this paper is to compare the depression of the 1930s in Sweden and in the United States by focusing on (1) the causes of the start and development of the depression and (2) the impact of macroeconomic policies in the two countries. The aim of this comparative analysis is to discriminate between the money hypothesis and the spending hypothesis on the basis of the evidence from Sweden. When examining the 1930s, American economists have generally regarded the American record as the benchmark case. Instead, the Swedish record will be adopted here as the basis for comparison. For the following reasons Sweden provides an interesting comparison with the United States, one that is highly suitable for examining the American depression:

1. Monetary and fiscal policies were applied in Sweden in a countercyclical manner. Two unique experiments in economic policy were carried out. First, a monetary program of price stabilization based on Knut Wicksell's recommendations was adopted after Sweden had left the gold standard in 1931. Second, and better known but of less actual impact, a deliberate countercyclical fiscal policy—inspired by the work of Gunnar Myrdal, Bertil Ohlin, and others—was initiated in 1933. In the United States neither fiscal nor monetary policy was applied on any significant scale to counteract the contractionary forces. Rather, the behavior of the Federal Reserve System has been assigned a crucial role in the explanation of the development of the American depression.

2. In Sweden, a small open economy, the depression was primarily "imported" through the foreign sector, while the depression in the United States generally is regarded as having been generated domestically.

3. In Sweden the economic profession exerted a significant influence on the framing of economic policy. Economists often had direct contact with the Swedish central bank, the Riksbank, and the Department of Finance throughout the 1930s.

4. Reliable data on monetary and real developments are available from both countries. The minutes from the board meetings of the Riksbank in the 1930s have also been made available recently, allowing for an inside examination of its policy.

This article is organized in the following way. First, the statistical picture is presented, displaying the behavior of several economic variables such as income, output, prices, and various monetary aggregates. Second, the Swedish experience of the 1930s is considered. Here the policy of the Riksbank is assigned great importance, for two reasons: (1) there are significant differences in the behavior of monetary aggregates and in the policy of the Riksbank and the Federal Reserve System; and (2) fiscal policy had a relatively minor impact in both countries. Third, the American record is discussed from the viewpoint of the money hypothesis and the spending hypothesis. A number of comparisons are made with the Swedish experience in order to examine the explanatory power of these two hypotheses. Fourth, the role of the economic profession is examined. Finally, the discussion is summarized.[2]

THE STATISTICAL PICTURE

This section traces and compares the behavior of several key economic aggregates in Sweden and the United States. The year 1929 has been adopted as the basis for comparison as this was a year of fairly high economic activity and a low rate of unemployment in both countries.

Income and Production

The depression started earlier, became deeper, and lasted longer in the United States than in Sweden. This is seen from the behavior of real income shown in figure 1 and table 1. Between 1929 and 1933, U.S. real income declined for four consecutive years by roughly one-third. In the same period Swedish real income was reduced by 10 percent. (It actually increased by 3 percent in 1929–30.) Generally, 1929 is regarded as the beginning of the American depression. In Sweden, 1930, or more precisely the second half of 1930, is commonly designated as the start of the downturn. The recovery began at roughly the same time in the two countries, that is, in 1932–33, but it proceeded at a faster rate in the United States. Nonetheless, the index of Swedish real income in 1937 was one-fifth larger than the American. Real income in the United States had not reached the level of 1929 by 1937. In Sweden the level of 1929 had already been surpassed by 1934.

Data on industrial production reveal roughly the same pattern as those on real income. Figure 1 and table 1 show the reduction in industrial production to be of a larger magnitude in the United States, where it declined by 46 percent between 1929 and 1932, than in Sweden, where it fell by 21

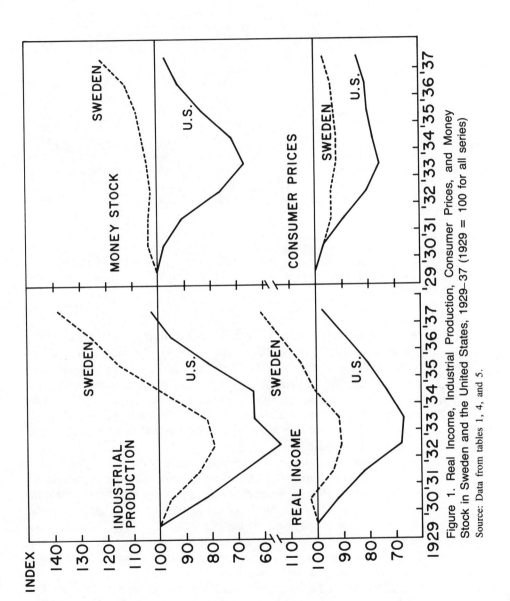

Figure 1. Real Income, Industrial Production, Consumer Prices, and Money Stock in Sweden and the United States, 1929–37 (1929 = 100 for all series)

Source: Data from tables 1, 4, and 5.

Table 1. Real Income, Industrial Production, and Employment in Sweden and the United States, 1929–37 (1929 = 100)

	Real Income		Industrial Production		Employment	
	Sweden (1)	U.S. (2)	Sweden (3)	U.S. (4)	Sweden (5)	U.S. (6)
1929	100	100	100	100	100	100
1930	103	92	96	83	102	96
1931	94	82	85	69	99	89
1932	91	68	79	54	97	82
1933	92	67	82	64	95	81
1934	101	73	99	64	99	86
1935	106	80	115	80	102	89
1936	114	89	125	95	105	93
1937	122	98	138	103	106	97

Sources: Col. (1): Johansson 1968, p. 153. Col. (2): U.S. Department of Commerce 1966; gross national product according to Kuznets's estimates, p. 166. Col. (3): The industrial production index of the Swedish Federation of Industries, 1929–32, linked with the revised index, starting in 1932 and in 1934; Sweden, Kommerskollegium. Col. (4): U.S. Department of Commerce 1966, p. 168. Col. (5): Johansson 1968, p. 157. Col. (6): U.S. Department of Commerce 1960, p. 70.

percent in the same time span. Total employment dropped in both countries, albeit more markedly in the United States (table 1). The rate of unemployment reached considerable levels. There are, however, no suitable data available for comparison. The American rate of unemployment reached a high of 25 percent in 1933; in Sweden unemployment peaked in 1933, when 23 percent of the members of the labor unions were out of work. In both countries, unemployment was widespread throughout the 1930s until World War II changed this picture.

The depression had different effects on the output of various sectors of the American and Swedish economies. American domestic investments had practically disappeared by 1932, commanding only 2 percent of the gross domestic product in that year, while it held 18 percent in 1929 (table 2). In Sweden the corresponding share of the gross domestic product displayed a considerably smaller reduction, nowhere near the size of the American decline. In the United States the share of consumption increased markedly as a consequence of the decline of investments.

Table 2 reveals an important difference between the two economies. Exports and imports commanded about one-fifth of the Swedish domestic product

Table 2. Percentage of Gross Domestic Product Held by Exports, Imports, Domestic Investments, and Private Consumption in Sweden and the United States, 1929–37

| | Exports | | Imports | | Domestic Investments | | Private Consumption | |
	Sweden (1)	U.S. (2)	Sweden (3)	U.S. (4)	Sweden (5)	U.S. (6)	Sweden (7)	U.S. (8)
1929	20	5	18	4	14	16	76	76
1930	18	4	17	4	16	11	76	77
1931	15	3	16	3	15	7	78	80
1932	13	3	14	3	13	2	78	84
1933	15	3	13	2	12	3	77	82
1934	16	3	14	3	14	5	75	79
1935	15	3	15	3	17	9	75	78
1936	16	3	16	3	17	10	74	76
1937	19	4	18	3	18	13	74	74

Sources: Sweden: computed from Johansson 1968. United States: U.S. Department of Commerce 1960.
Note: The volume of investments for Sweden includes both private and public investments. The data for the United States cover only private domestic investments. The volume of public investments in Sweden was, however, of a relatively small size in the 1930s.

prior to the depression, while the corresponding shares were much smaller for the United States—about 4 to 5 percent. The depression had an extremely strong impact on Swedish exports and imports. Exports declined in current prices from 2.7 billion kronor in 1929 to 1.2 billion in 1932 (Johansson 1968, pp. 151–52). The share of exports in gross domestic product fell from 20 percent in 1929 to 13 percent in 1932 (table 2). In less than three years the demand for exports was practically halved—in some branches the decline was much stronger. The fall in exports was accompanied by a reduction in imports of roughly the same size.

The depression reduced the relative size of the Swedish export-import sector. Industries producing for the domestic market remained less affected than the export industries by the decline in the world economy (table 3). The production of the export industries fell by one-third from 1929 to 1932. Industries selling products for domestic use experienced a 13 percent drop in these three years. Furthermore, the consumption goods industries fared better than industries producing investment goods.

Table 3.   Industrial Production Indices for Sweden, 1929–34 (1929 = 100)

	Industries Producing for the Domestic Market (1)	Industries Producing for Export Markets (2)	Industries Producing Investment Goods (3)	Industries Producing Consumption Goods (4)	Total Index (5)
1929	100	100	100	100	100
1930	97	96	94	100	96
1931	89	78	78	95	85
1932	87	66	69	96	79
1933	88	72	73	95	82
1934	108	85	91	113	100

Source: Sweden, Kommerskollegium.
Note: The indices were constructed and collected by the Swedish Federation of Industries. Industries were grouped into four categories depending on the (a) the main market of their output (domestic or foreign) and (b) the main type of goods produced (consumption goods or investment goods). Thus, every industry included in the statistics is represented in two of col. (1)–(4).

Prices

The world price level had fallen secularly since the first half of the 1920s. This decline was accentuated during the depression. Those countries that left the gold standard early in the 1930s, however, were as a rule able to reduce the rate of deflation compared to the experience of those countries that remained on gold. Sweden went off gold almost at the same time as Great Britain in September 1931. After this step the Swedish consumer price index remained practically constant until the rise in world prices around 1937 (figure 2). This is one of the longest periods of price stability in Swedish history according to available statistics. The development of consumer prices from 1931 to 1936 should be regarded primarily as the result of the monetary program of 1931, which aimed at stabilizing the domestic purchasing power of the Swedish krona. American consumer prices, however, continued to fall until the dollar went off gold in 1933. By then, U.S. consumer prices were 25 percent below the level of 1929, while the corresponding figure for Sweden is only 8 percent (table 4).

Wholesale prices fell more than consumer prices, particularly in Sweden (table 4). The decline was of almost the same size and had nearly the same timing in the two countries. This pattern was due to the world deflation, which affected prices of internationally traded raw materials more strongly than those

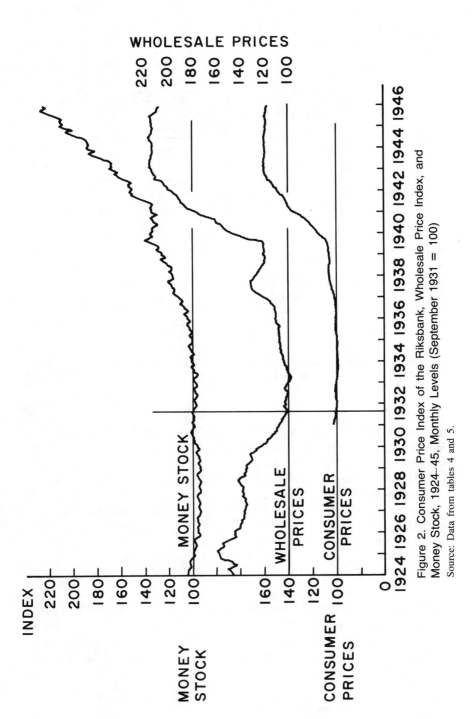

Figure 2. Consumer Price Index of the Riksbank, Wholesale Price Index, and Money Stock, 1924–45, Monthly Levels (September 1931 = 100)

Source: Data from tables 4 and 5.

Table 4. The Behavior of Prices in Sweden and the United States, 1929–37
(1929 = 100)

	Wholesale Price Index		Consumer Price Index		Deflator	
	Sweden (1)	U.S. (2)	Sweden (3)	U.S. (4)	Sweden (5)	U.S. (6)
1929	100	100	100	100	100	100
1930	86	91	97	97	96	96
1931	78	77	94	89	90	85
1932	75	68	94	80	87	77
1933	75	69	92	75	84	75
1934	80	79	92	78	87	80
1935	83	84	93	80	88	79
1936	87	85	94	81	90	82
1937	104	91	97	84	97	83

Sources: Col. (1): Wholesale price index of the Svensk Finanstidning. Col. (2) U.S. Department of Commerce 1960, p. 116. Col. (3): Consumption price index of the Riksbank, 1931–37, linked with the cost-of-living index of the Socialstyrelse for 1929–30. Col. (4): U.S. Department of Commerce 1960, p. 125. Col. (5): Deflator of the Swedish domestic product according to Krantz and Nilsson 1975, pp. 130–40; this is a weighted price index where agriculture, manufacturing, and personal private services represent 75 percent of the weights. Col. (6): Implicit price index of the U.S. gross national product, U.S. Department of Commerce 1960, p. 139.

of domestically produced and consumed goods. (The wholesale price indices included a larger fraction of the first-mentioned type of goods than did the consumer price indices.) The sharper fall of U.S. prices is also seen in the behavior of the implicit deflator of the American gross domestic product. It declined by one-fourth from 1929 to 1933 (table 4). The deflator of the Swedish domestic product exhibited a reduction of 16 percent within the same time period.

Monetary Aggregates

There are significant differences between the Swedish and American monetary experiences. The contrast between the sharp reduction in the American money stock and the constancy of the Swedish volume of money in the period 1929–33 is a striking feature of table 5 (see also figure 1). The American

Table 5. Money Stock, Currency-Money Ratio, and Reserve-Deposit Ratio in Sweden and the United States, 1929–37 (Money stock: 1929 = 100)

	Money Stock		Currency Ratio		Reserve Ratio	
	Sweden (1)	U.S. (2)	Sweden (3)	U.S. (4)	Sweden (5)	U.S. (6)
1929	100	100	11.8%	8.4%	1.8%	7.7%
1930	104	98	11.9	8.2	1.8	7.8
1931	104	91	11.9	9.6	1.8	8.5
1932	103	76	11.8	14.0	3.6	9.7
1933	104	67	12.0	16.3	6.7	12.2
1934	106	72	12.8	13.8	9.4	15.7
1935	108	83	14.2	12.5	8.4	5.6
1936	112	92	15.7	12.1	8.4	17.8
1937	122	97	16.0%	12.3%	16.3%	18.9%

Sources: Cols. (1), (3), and (5): Jonung 1975, tables A–1, B–1. Cols. (2), (4), and (6): Friedman and Schwartz 1963, tables A–1, B–3.

money stock (M_2) declined by about one-third while the Swedish (M_2) actually increased by a few percentage points in these years. The absolute level of the American money stock fell successively between February 1929 and April 1933, shown in table 6. The growth rate of the Swedish money stock was negative between July 1930 and January 1932—a much shorter period than in the United States. The contraction phase prior to the trough of 1931 in the specific growth cycle of the money stock was considerably longer in the United States than in Sweden (col. [1] in table 6). The expansion phases of the two countries, however, were of roughly the same length.

A breakdown of the growth rate of the money stock with the purpose of discerning the contributions of its proximate determinants—the monetary base, the currency-money ratio and the reserve-deposit ratio—reveals the following pattern. The U.S. currency ratio accounted for a larger average absolute contribution to the growth of the money stock than its Swedish counterpart. This may be seen from column (4) in table 6. The rise in the American currency ratio from a level of 8.2 percent in 1930 to 16.3 percent in 1933 contributed negatively to the growth rate of the money stock. This rise was closely associated with a number of banking panics, when the American public tried on a massive scale to convert deposits into cash. These runs on the American banking system are clearly represented in the cycle stages covering June 1930 to April 1933 in table 6. After this turbulent period the U.S. currency ratio declined in size.

Table 6. Contributions of the Proximate Determinants of the Money Stock to Specific Cycles in the Growth Rate of the Money Stock in Sweden and the United States during the Contraction Phase prior to the Trough of 1931 and during the Following Expansion Phase

	Cycle Stage	Dates	Length (months) (1)	Change in Money Stock (2)	Contributed by:		
					Monetary Base (3)	Currency Ratio (4)	Reserve Ratio (5)
Sweden							
Contraction	V	Oct. 1929–Jan. 1930	3	+ 5.1	+ 5.8	+ 0.3	− 0.8
	VI	Dec. 1929–July 1930	7	+ 4.6	+ 4.1	+ 0.3	+ 0.2
	VII	July 1930–Apr. 1931	9	− 0.1	− 0.4	+ 0.0	+ 0.4
	VIII	Apr. 1931–Nov. 1931	7	− 1.8	+ 4.8	− 0.5	− 5.7
	IX	Oct. 1931–Jan. 1932	3	− 2.1	+12.2	− 2.8	−13.0
Expansion	I	Dec. 1931–July 1933	19	+ 0.4	+16.0	+ 0.1	−15.8
	II	July 1933–Apr. 1935	21	+ 1.8	+10.5	− 5.1	− 3.7
	III	Apr. 1935–Nov. 1936	19	+ 5.0	+17.0	− 4.8	− 7.0
	IV	Oct. 1936–Jan. 1937	3	+ 9.3	+42.5	+ 0.1	−33.7
United States							
Contraction	V	Sept. 1927–Dec. 1927	3	+ 2.8	− 0.8	+ 5.7	− 1.9
	VI	Nov. 1927–Feb. 1929	15	+ 1.3	− 0.1	+ 0.6	+ 0.7
	VII	Feb. 1929–June 1930	16	− 1.6	− 2.6	+ 1.0	+ 0.0
	VIII	June 1930–Sept. 1931	15	− 8.2	+ 6.8	−10.6	− 4.4
	IX	Aug. 1931–Nov. 1931	3	−31.4	+ 4.7	−33.1	− 2.6
Expansion	I	Oct. 1931–Apr. 1933	18	−18.7	+ 4.5	−15.9	− 7.5
	II	Apr. 1933–Sept. 1934	15	+10.3	+13.3	+ 7.0	−10.2
	III	Sept. 1934–Mar. 1936	6	+12.3	+12.7	+ 2.7	− 3.2
	IV	Feb. 1936–May 1936	3	+16.5	+ 1.6	+ 4.4	+10.5

Sources: United States: Cagan 1965, table F–1. Sweden: numbers computed in the same way as Cagan's.

The constancy and thus the small contribution of the Swedish currency ratio to the growth in the Swedish money stock are primarily explained by a strong public confidence in the solvency of the Swedish commercial banking system, effectively preventing any runs on banks similar to the events in the United States. No banks defaulted or suspended payments in Sweden in the 1930s. This picture provides a stark contrast to the American record.[3] The Swedish currency ratio started to rise in 1933, but this development, which continued until the 1950s, is explained by factors other than those directly associated with the monetary chaos of the early 1930s.

Tables 5 and 6 show that the Swedish reserve-deposit ratio exhibited larger fluctuations than the American ratio. The rise in 1931–32 was due to the uncertainty created by the depression concerning, in part, the outflow of capital from Sweden and the international economic situation and to the fear of domestic bank runs in connection with the Kreuger crash in the spring of 1932. Commercial banks responded then by borrowing substantially from the Riksbank. The 1933–37 increase in the reserve ratio was caused by (1) a large inflow of capital following the boom for the export industries and (2) the disappearance of the international capital market in the 1930s, inducing a shift from foreign into domestic assets.[4] The U.S. reserve ratio also increased in the 1930s. Runs and bank failures, forcing banks still in existence to increase their holdings of reserves, were a major factor behind this change. The continuous rise of this ratio after 1933 has been regarded as the result of a buildup of desired reserves in response to the bank runs and the inadequate support provided by the Federal Reserve System during the panics.

In both countries the monetary base expanded during the years 1930–36—that is, even during the trough of 1931. This pattern is explained to a large extent by a sharp rise in the demand for cash in the form of notes. The liquidity crises occurring in several countries took the form of massive conversions of bank deposits to notes. In both Sweden and the United States the expansion of the total amount of base money after 1933 was closely linked to the rise in the volume of base-money reserves held by the commercial banking systems.

The annual percentage fluctuations of the income velocity of money (M_2) in Sweden and the United States during the depression were as a rule of the same sign as the changes in the money stock—that is, movements in velocity were not offsetting fluctuations in the money stock. Velocity declined markedly during the first years of the 1930s—in Sweden, between 1930 and 1933, and in the United States, between 1930 and 1932. The annual percentage changes in velocity were considerably larger than the movements in the money stock for several of the depression years.

Summary

The depression of the 1930s had an immense impact on the Swedish and American economies. In both countries real income, industrial production, employment, and prices declined sharply. There are considerable differences in the patterns of economic change. The depression was deeper and longer-lasting in the United States. The American monetary sector was the subject of greater disturbances, judging from the decline in the American money stock, the sharp increases in the currency ratio, and the spread of banking panics and bank failures. In Sweden the foreign sector was affected more strongly than other sectors of the economy.

Americans have termed the early years of the 1930s in their history the Great Depression—no previous downturn in American economic activity has been as extensive. In Sweden, however, these years have not acquired a name of similar connotations. Actually, the postwar depression in the early 1920s was more severe than the recession of the 1930s as measured by the decline in real income, employment, prices, and the money stock.[5] The depression of 1920–23 was primarily caused by the policy of restoring the prewar gold parity of the Swedish currency after the monetary expansion and inflation of World War I. A strong deflation, produced by a contractionary monetary policy, accomplished a return to gold at the old parity of the krona. Thus, the Swedish depression at that time was basically the outcome of political decisions and generated by domestic policy measures—as opposed to the downturn of 1931–33, which was strongly influenced by foreign developments.

THE CASE OF SWEDEN

The Causes of the Depression

The Swedish recession was caused by foreign developments, that is, by the worldwide depression of the international economy, transmitted to Sweden through the foreign sector—specifically, by the large reduction in the demand for Swedish exports. The world depression did not influence the Swedish economy to any noticeable extent until the summer and fall of 1931. Domestic economic activity remained at a fairly stable level during 1930 compared to the experience of the United States (figure 1). The world recession and world deflation eventually had an impact, however. Swedish exports fell rapidly between 1931 and 1933, reducing aggregate demand and causing rising unemployment and falling industrial production. As a consequence of the international recovery, exports started to rise in 1933–34 and kept on expanding until the international recession of 1937–38.

According to this account, the Swedish depression and recovery were caused, *not* by domestic developments, but by international changes. Some domestic events, however, aggravated the recession. In March 1932 Ivar Kreuger, a well-known industrialist, committed suicide in Paris. The news of his death and the disclosures concerning his business dealings were a severe shock to the Swedish public. The bankruptcy of his enterprises caused heavy financial burdens and spread public distrust about the future of the Swedish economy. Labor strikes, especially the long strike of the construction workers from April 1933 to February 1934, were also a source of domestic disturbances, hampering implementation of the new fiscal policy. These two events had a minor impact, however, compared to the effects of international developments.[6]

The Conduct of Monetary Policy

The Swedish economy was fairly unaffected by the depression prior to the summer of 1930. The Riksbank lowered the discount rate in 1930 in four steps, in order to follow the changes of the Bank of England. In spite of a rapidly growing trade deficit, the Riksbank's foreign reserves remained high in the first half of 1931, due partly to a large inflow of capital from abroad. Sweden was at this time considered a financially and politically stable country. As a result of the financial crisis in continental Europe, however, the foreign reserves of the Riksbank started to decline in June 1931. When the Bank of England left the gold standard in September, Swedish authorities were initially optimistic, believing that the krona would be able to remain on gold. One week later, however, on September 27, the government and the Riksbank were forced to let the krona leave the gold standard and to adopt a paper standard, as practically all foreign reserves with the exception of the holdings of gold were depleted.[7]

At the same time as Sweden left the gold standard, the authorities declared that the aim of the policy of the Riksbank should be to "preserve the domestic purchasing power of the krona using all available means." The new paper standard was thus to be based on a norm of price stabilization. This is the first time that price stability was made the official goal of a central bank. The monetary program of 1931 remained the official basis for Swedish monetary policy in the 1930s.

The management of the bank lacked knowledge about the conduct of monetary policy aimed at price stability. It turned in October to Sweden's most renowned monetary economists at that time—Gustav Cassel, David Davidson, and Eli Heckscher—with a questionnaire dealing with a large number of the monetary issues of the day. Among other things, the bank inquired about the choice of price index to adopt as the guide for its policy—should consumer prices, wholesale prices, or some other index of prices be used? It also wanted to know at which level prices should be stabilized—a level prior to the depression or the level of September 1931—and which norm to adopt—Wicksell's norm of constant prices or Davidson's norm of a price level falling in proportion to the rise in productivity.

In reply to the questionnaire, the three economists gave the bank a considerable number of recommendations. They advised the bank to construct a consumer price index and to stabilize this index at the level of September 1931, that is, to adopt Wicksell's norm, and not to attempt to inflate or deflate the Swedish economy to reach any other level of prices before the stabilization program was started.[8] The bank constructed a consumer price index under the auspices of Erik Lindahl. This index was made available on a weekly basis, and it became an important part of the framing of monetary policy in the ensuing years.

When Sweden left the gold standard in September 1931, the krona was effectively depreciated in terms of the currencies remaining on gold. The exchange rate between the dollar and the krona rose from the gold standard parity of 3:74 to above 5 kronor in December 1931. This depreciation had favorable effects on the Swedish economy by isolating it from the world deflation. The fall in wholesale prices and consumer prices was arrested (figure 2 and table 4).

The Riksbank actually expected and feared rising prices after Sweden left gold, and raised the rate of discount from 6 to 8 percent in September 1931. At the end of 1931 and at the beginning of 1932, the authorities started to view falling prices as the major problem, and the rate of discount was lowered. The policy of the bank, though, remained fairly passive prior to the Kreuger crash in March 1932, except for allowing a large volume of rediscounting.[9] The Swedish commercial banks had been indebted to the Riksbank during the 1920s. As the depression began to affect the Swedish economy, borrowing from the Riksbank by the commercial banks increased rapidly. The management of the Riksbank generally provided the banks with funds with no apparent hesitation. Actually, the Riksbank became heavily involved in the lending to the Skandinaviska Kreditaktiebolag, at that time Sweden's second-largest commercial bank and the bank most closely associated with the Kreuger enterprises.

The death of Kreuger caused a sharp decline in the foreign value of the Swedish currency. The pound rate rose from around the gold parity of 18:15 to close to 20 kronor. The financial position of the Skandinaviska Kreditaktiebolag became precarious. The government and the parliament took quick action and arranged for a large loan to the bank. This loan, combined with other forms of lending to the banking system, contributed to financial stability and to a reduction of the impact of the Kreuger crash on the Swedish economy. Actually, the depreciation of the krona following Kreuger's death counteracted the deflationary forces. Once the demand for foreign reserves by the Kreuger enterprises disappeared, the Riksbank was free to carry out a more expansionary policy than it had previously.

In the spring of 1932, as the depression became more severe in Sweden, the parliament requested a more expansionary monetary policy. The Riksbank was asked to induce a rise in the level of wholesale prices—without significantly raising consumer prices. In the summer of 1932 the Riksbank made large purchases of foreign assets, holding the pound and dollar rates well above parity. Consumer prices as well as wholesale prices were kept constant, checking the deflationary tendency. In the fall and winter of 1932, however, the bank depressed the exchange rate of the pound and also of the dollar by selling foreign assets. This policy—which was clearly not in the spirit of the monetary program—contributed to a decline in wholesale prices by about 4 percent and in consumer prices by 1 percent between October 1932 and March 1933. After this event the Riksbank again started to make large purchases of foreign assets in 1933 and 1934. This policy expanded the monetary base and raised the reserve ratio of the commercial banking system.

In the summer of 1933 the Riksbank decided on its own initiative to peg the krona to the pound at the rate of 19:40, representing a depreciation relative to the gold parity of 18:15. The bank maintained this rate for the rest of the 1930s. The recovery from the depression was well under way when the pound rate was pegged. The volume of Swedish exports rose steadily, and the surpluses in the balance of payments gave rise to a huge inflow of reserves. The minutes of the board of the Riksbank of the mid-1930s reveal that the major problem for the bank was to find suitable investments for its foreign reserves.

The Effects of the Policy of the Riksbank

The policy of the Riksbank after the introduction of the paper standard in the fall of 1931 kept the Swedish money stock on practically the same level for five years until the boom of 1937 (figure 2). The monetary program of price stabilization was followed in the sense that the consumer price index of the bank was kept stable in these years. The monetary program was an effective restriction on the actions of the bank, preventing the bank from carrying out a deflationary policy aimed at tying the krona to the pound or to gold at the parity rate. Attempts in this direction were actually made (Jonung 1979*b*). The policy of the bank held the money stock constant through various measures—first of all, by leaving the gold standard and depreciating the krona in 1931; second, by liberal lending and support to the commercial banking system; third, by large purchases of foreign assets from the Swedish public, representing a form of expansionary open-market operations. The monetary program of 1931 and the subsequent declarations of the government and the parliament about the aim of monetary policy maintained public trust and confidence in the banking system. The determined actions to support the Skandinaviska Kreditaktiebolag prevented speculations and expectations concerning impending financial turmoil. To sum up, the conduct of monetary policy counteracted the contractionary impulses and created public confidence in the Swedish financial system.

The Role of Fiscal Policy

Stabilization policy was synonymous with monetary policy in Sweden prior to the depression of the 1930s. In the early 1930s, however, Swedish economists like Gunnar Myrdal, Erik Lindahl, and Bertil Ohlin developed a theory for a countercyclical fiscal policy based on the Wicksellian heritage. The nonsocialist government that ruled Sweden in the early 1930s founded its economic policy on monetary measures and was critical of fiscal actions that could cause budget deficits. Still, government expenditures were held at a roughly unchanged level during these years in spite of a decline in government revenues. Considerable deficits in the budget were the result. The Social Democrats came to power in 1933, after the election of 1932, by forming a coalition government with the Farmers' party. The new government initiated a fiscal policy that was openly based on budget deficits to be financed through government borrowing. The fiscal authorities publicly declared that the budget should be underbalanced. The new fiscal policy—called the "crisis policy" in Sweden—met with strong opposition from the old generation of economists, while the young generation supported the policy. Some of them, like Bertil Ohlin, had worked in favor of an "active employment policy."

The effects of the fiscal program launched in 1933 were only minor. There are two major arguments for this conclusion. First, the "crisis policy" was carried out for a fairly short time, that is, between 1933 and 1935. Second, the fiscal measures actually implemented were of a comparatively small magnitude. They had hardly any noticeable effects on the trend of government expenditures in the 1930s. The long strike of the construction workers in

1933–34 was also detrimental to the fiscal program. It is thus safe to conclude that the new economic policy had an insignificant impact on the business cycle. In political discussion within Sweden, however, the experience of the 1930s has frequently been used as an argument for the use of fiscal policy, although there is little empirical support for such an argument. Specifically, a comparison of the behavior of exports and imports with the pattern of government expenditures clearly indicates that changes in the foreign sector were the major source of economic fluctuations in the 1930s. On the other hand, the steady level of the expenditures of the government sector was a source of stability in the 1930s.[10]

Summary of the Swedish Record

The depression in Sweden was caused by foreign developments. Swedish exports declined sharply in size between 1929 and 1933. This represented a substantial fall in autonomous spending. Swedish authorities adopted a host of monetary measures to counteract this reduction in aggregate demand. The devaluation of 1931, when Sweden left the gold standard, isolated Sweden from the world deflation. The authorities managed to stabilize domestic prices by maintaining a stable money stock. The countercyclical fiscal policy launched in 1933 did not have any prominent effects, although it had a far-reaching impact on the theoretical discussion among Swedish economists and on the framing of Swedish stabilization policy in the postwar period.

THE CASE OF THE UNITED STATES

Explanations of the American Depression

Most observers agree that the Great Depression was generated primarily within the United States, although there is no agreement over which domestic developments actually caused the depression to become as deep and as long lasting as it turned out to be. It is difficult to argue that the U.S. recession was caused by foreign factors—as was the case for Sweden—for a number of reasons. First, the American foreign sector commanded a fairly small share of U.S. national income in these years (table 2). Changes in exports could not, per se, produce a major recession. Second, American monetary authorities had considerable autonomy in the framing of monetary policy. The gold-standard system of the 1920s did not restrict the actions of the Federal Reserve System as much as it did for the central bank of a small open economy such as Sweden's.[11]

Third, the downturn in economic activity was considerably stronger in the United States than in most European countries in 1930–31, suggesting that the depression started in the American economy and spread to the rest of the world. Foreign developments exerted a contractionary influence on the American economy, in particular when the depression outside of the United States grew in strength. This influence, however, cannot be regarded as the main cause of the American contraction in the same way as the Swedish depression is explained by the decline in the demand for Swedish exports.

Several explanations of the American depression have been proposed. The differences between them generally concern the weights assigned to monetary and nonmonetary factors in the causal interpretation. The recent American discussion has focused on two competing hypotheses, "the money hypothesis" and "the spending hypothesis," following the terminology proposed by Peter Temin (1976, p. 7). The money hypothesis ascribes a central role to monetary policy and monetary events. The spending hypothesis attaches great weight to an exogenous shift in autonomous expenditures. Both of these explanations suggest that the Great Depression was generated by forces essentially working within the U.S. economy, implying that the depression spread from America to the rest of the world.

The basic elements of the two hypotheses can be expressed in the following way. The money hypothesis states, asserting the relative stability of the money-demand function, that a reduction in the supply of money caused the decline in real income and prices; that is, changes in the growth rate of the supply of money were a driving force behind the depression. An expansionary monetary policy, increasing the money supply, could thus have prevented the depression from becoming as deep as it did. The spending hypothesis in its various versions postulates that a decline in some component of national income, such as investment or consumption, through a multiplier process caused a reduction in national income; that is, changes in autonomous expenditures were the main force behind the depression. A fall in the demand for money, due to the reduction in autonomous spending and income, occurred along a stable money-supply function. An expansionary monetary policy would not have counteracted the depression effectively, according to this hypothesis, because any increases in the money supply would have been offset by changes in the demand for money.

Thus, the spending hypothesis suggests basically the opposite causal relations of those implied by the money hypothesis. The essential discrepancy concerns the analysis of the behavior of the monetary sector and monetary policy. An attempt will be made here to discriminate between these rather simplified versions of the two opposing hypotheses by comparing the Swedish and American records. Such a comparison will bring out the basic issues involved in the present American debate about the character of the contraction of the American economy in the 1930s.

The Money Hypothesis

The money hypothesis is intimately connected with the work of Friedman and Schwartz, specifically, with *A Monetary History of the United States* (1963). There are two main arguments in their analysis of the American 1930s. First, the basic reason why the recession of 1929–30 turned into the Great Depression was that the policy of the Federal Reserve System contributed significantly to a reduction of the American money supply by more than one-third in the period 1929–33. They do not rule out influences from nonmonetary developments (pp. 300–01). These, however, could not have accounted for the severity and duration of the depression, in their opinion. Second, an alternative expansionary monetary policy could have reduced the contraction in economic activity and made the depression milder and shorter.

Chapter 7 in *A Monetary History* describes in detail a number of developments that caused the reduction in the U.S. money stock from the onset of the stock market crash in October 1929 to the final banking panic of 1933 that paralyzed the financial system and left the United States without a working central banking system. According to Friedman and Schwartz, two factors interacted to bring about the decline in the money stock: first, four waves of banking panics, the first one starting in the fall of 1930, the second in March 1931, the third in September 1931, and the fourth in January 1933, which led to the collapse of the Federal Reserve System in March 1933; and second, the inability of the Federal Reserve System to prevent the panics from spreading by applying a more expansionary monetary policy. The banking panics reduced the money stock by raising the currency ratio and the reserve ratio and by forcing a large number of banks to close for business (table 5).

The Federal Reserve System did not effectively check the fall in the money stock; rather, the actions of the system contributed to the decline in the money stock. According to Friedman and Schwartz there are several reasons for this passive and contractionary policy. The attitude of the Federal Reserve System was one of inactivity and lack of understanding of the problems facing the American commercial banking system. The Federal Reserve System also had an aversion to lending to commercial banks. Many members of the board regarded the defaults ''as regrettable consequences of bad management'' and had ''no feelings of responsibility for non-member banks'' (pp. 357–59). The Federal Reserve System had simply not developed the proper analysis necessary for a successful conduct of central bank policy. The views of many of the officials were more aptly those of commercial bankers than those of central bankers. The inactivity is also attributed by Friedman and Schwartz to the size of the Federal Reserve Board. The large number of governors made it difficult to reach decisions on specific actions, thus creating a bias toward a policy of inaction. Furthermore, Friedman and Schwartz point to the lack of an informed public opinion that could exert influence on the framing of monetary policy (pp. 407–11).

Friedman and Schwartz argue strongly that the Great Depression was not an inevitable consequence of the workings of economic forces. A more expansionary monetary policy could have eliminated the decline in the money stock, checking the fall in nominal income and making the depression shorter. An alternative monetary policy could thus have prevented the recession of 1929–30 from turning into the Great Depression. In their own words:

> Prevention or moderation of the decline in the stock of money, let alone the substitution of monetary expansion, would have reduced the contraction's severity and almost as certainly its duration. The contraction might still have been relatively severe. But it is hardly conceivable that money income could have declined by over one-half and prices by over one-third in the course of four years if there had been no decline in the stock of money. [P. 301]

They have no direct evidence for this view. To support their contention, Friedman and Schwartz point to the effects of open-market operations in 1932. The Swedish record, however, provides a case of a country that actually carried out a policy that has much in common with the alternative proposed by them. Thus, a comparison with the Swedish experience may shed light upon their argument that a different monetary policy would have reduced the effects of the depression in the United States.

The Swedish money stock was held at roughly a constant level after Sweden had left the gold standard and depreciated its currency. The monetary program of domestic price stability forced the central bank to maintain a policy of a stable money stock. This policy undoubtedly was the major factor explaining why the depression in Sweden was shorter and milder then in the United States. During the 1920s, when the decline in the Swedish money stock was stronger than in the 1930s, domestic prices and economic activity fell more than in the 1930s. Consequently, the Swedish case supports the view that an alternative monetary policy would have reduced the decline in U.S. nominal income.

Swedish monetary policy was more expansionary than its American counterpart in the early 1930s, judging from the growth pattern of the Swedish money stock (figure 1). Still, Swedish monetary policy could have been more expansionary in these years—as some economists also requested—allowing for a more rapid monetary growth. Conceivably, such a policy would have been more effective in checking the Swedish contraction. Furthermore, Swedish monetary policy affected primarily the domestic price level and the output of domestic goods and services. Industries producing for domestic markets fared better than the export industries (table 3). As the American economy was more closed than the Swedish economy, an expansionary monetary policy would have influenced a larger share of the economy in the United States than in Sweden. The Swedish monetary authorities were faced with the task of offsetting the disappearance of the foreign demand for the export industries. This was less of a problem in the United States.

There is a major difference between the behavior of the Swedish and American central banks in the 1930s. Swedish central bank policy aimed at creating, and did create, monetary stability and public confidence, while the actions of the Federal Reserve produced the opposite result. The Swedish central bank had no aversion to lending to the commercial banks. The Riksbank had fully accepted the role of being the lender of last resort supporting the commercial banks. The Federal Reserve System, however, did not operate as the lender of last resort and denied assistance to the U.S. commercial banking system. The public declaration of the goal of monetary policy and the construction of the price index by the Riksbank in 1931 reduced uncertainty about the future, increasing the predictability and stability of the future. As time passed and the public gradually discovered that the consumer price level had been stabilized, public trust in the conduct of monetary policy was also strengthened. In the United States, however, the successive banking panics eventually eroded public confidence in the solvency and stability of the banking system. These differences in the conduct and effects of monetary policy strengthen the criticism by Friedman and Schwartz and others of the behavior of the Federal Reserve System in the early 1930s.

The Spending Hypothesis

There are several versions of the spending hypothesis, depending on which type of autonomous expenditure is postulated to have initiated the decline in aggregate demand. In the present discussion, Peter Temin's argument (1976) that a large and unexplained fall in U.S. consumption in 1930 caused the depression has attracted much debate.[12] According to him, the reduction in consumption set off a multiplier process, reducing aggregated demand and national income. Essentially, the contraction of the succeeding years appears to be the result of the behavior of autonomous spending in 1930. In the analysis of the monetary sector, Temin suggests that the decline in income produced a downward shift in the demand-for-money schedule and thus an excess supply of money. The banking panics during the early stages of the depression are assigned a minor role:

> There is no evidence that the banking panic of 1930 had a deflationary effect on the economy. Instead, the data are consistent with the hypothesis that the demand for money was falling more rapidly than the supply during 1930 and the first three-quarters of 1931. They are consistent with the spending hypothesis, not the money hypothesis about the causes of the Depression. [P. 137]

Temin is consequently arguing that the American supply of money adjusted to a falling demand for money. With respect to the effects of monetary policy, this reasoning implies that an expansionary monetary policy would not have been able to counteract the contraction of the American economy.

The Swedish experience can be used to examine this line of argument. The world depression was transmitted to Sweden by a sharp decline in autonomous expenditures, that is, by a fall in Swedish exports. The spending hypothesis applied to the Swedish record postulates that the Swedish demand for money would shift downward in the succeeding years along a stable supply-of-money schedule. Monetary policy would not have been able to maintain a constant money stock under these circumstances and thus not been able to check the contractionary multiplier effects stemming from the reduction in exports. The Swedish record, however, does not lend support to this interpretation of the spending hypothesis. The sharp decline in autonomous spending in Sweden did not cause a downward shift in the demand for money that reduced the Swedish money stock. The policy of the Riksbank maintained roughly a constant money stock during the depression years. Consequently, this chain of events is inconsistent with the spending hypothesis as interpreted here.

It should be noted in this context that the reduction in expenditures at the early stages of the Swedish depression was of the same relative magnitude as that of the United States. The years 1930–31 roughly represent the beginning of the recession in Sweden in the same way as the period 1929–30 marks the beginning of the American depression. From 1930 to 1931 the Swedish gross domestic product declined by 13 percent in current prices and by 8 percent in constant prices. The corresponding numbers for the United States between 1929 and 1930 are 13 percent and 9 percent. Swedish exports fell by 27 percent and consumption by 10 percent. The corresponding figures for the American economy are 26 and 10 percent, respectively. Thus, the initial declines in aggregate spending in the two countries were of approximately the same size. The initial recessionary impact, however, was transformed into a much deeper contraction in the United States than in Sweden, primarily because of differences in the framing of monetary policy.

When Temin studies the impact of macroeconomic policy in the 1930s, he draws the following conclusion:

> What can we say about the role of macroeconomic policy in this story? It is clear from the fact that the Depression occurred that effective countermeasures were not used. Those countermeasures that were tried clearly were ineffective; the Depression took place. To show that a macroeconomic policy can be effective, a historian is forced into the uncomfortable position of attempting to prove that it was not used. If it was used, it did not work. Only if it was not used can it emerge from the debacle of the 1930s unscathed. [P. 173]

This represents a rather skeptical view of the possibilities of evaluating the effects of monetary and fiscal measures during the depression. This paper, however, builds upon a cross-country comparison of two different records of stabilization policy. This method of evaluation, not explicitly considered by Temin, suggests in the case of Sweden and the United States that monetary policy deserves to emerge from "the debacle," if not unscathed, then at least regarded as an effective policy alternative.

THE INFLUENCE OF THE SWEDISH ECONOMISTS

A major difference between the Swedish and the American depression is to be found in the conduct of monetary policy. Why, then, was the policy of the Riksbank more expansionary than the policy of the Federal Reserve System? Differences in the level of knowledge of economic matters as well as in the influence of the economic profession on the framing of monetary policy is part of the answer to this question. Friedman and Schwartz argue that one reason for U.S. monetary policy being "so inept" was the lack of a proper economic analysis to account for what was happening in the American economy. Consequently, good policy advice was not forthcoming.

> Contemporary economic comment was hardly distinguished by the correctness or profundity of understanding of the economic forces at work in the contraction, though of course there were notable exceptions. Many professional economists as well as others viewed the depression as a desirable and necessary economic development required to eliminate inefficiency and weakness, took for granted that the appropriate cure was belt tightening by both private individuals and the government, and interpreted monetary changes as an incidental result rather than a contributing cause. [Pp. 408–09]

It is tempting to conclude that exactly the opposite situation prevailed in Sweden. The Swedish economists presented policymakers and public opinion with a thorough and, ex post, surprisingly correct analysis as well as reasonable policy recommendations. The political parties, the government, and the Riksbank were also ready to listen to the advice of the economists.

In order to understand the strong influence exercised by the economists as a professional group in the 1930s, one has to go back to the economic events in Sweden during and after World War I. In these years monetary matters were the subject of an extremely lively discussion in Sweden. Almost all the economists active at that time, such as Cassel, Davidson, Heckscher, Ohlin, and Wicksell, participated. The debate is documented in a large number of articles in *Ekonomisk Tidskrift*, in newspapers and various journals, in books, in reports of government committees, and in the proceedings of the Swedish Economic Society. Representatives from industry, commercial banking, the Riksbank, and the political parties also took part in the exchange of ideas.[13]

The opinions of the economists and their recommendations became well known to the general public. Wicksell's norm of price stabilization was in these years proposed as a serious policy alternative. After the war most economists, however, advocated a return to the prewar gold parity of the krona. This return required a strong deflation. The economists at that time generally did not expect the social consequences of the deflationary policy, measured in terms of unemployment and social unrest, to be as large as they turned out. The deflation of the 1920s made the profession critical toward any monetary policy involving a falling price level.

When Sweden left the gold standard in 1931, Gustav Cassel apparently drafted the monetary program of price stabilization. Economists were as a rule favorable toward this program in 1931. The Riksbank turned to Cassel, Heckscher, and Davidson for advice about the conduct of Swedish monetary policy. The three economists presented the bank with a document rich in policy recommendations, particularly urging the bank to stabilize the domestic price level, to avoid deflation, to lend liberally to commercial banks, and to establish public confidence in the policy of the Riksbank. These recommendations represent a level of knowledge in monetary questions considerably above that reflected by the opinions of American economists in the early 1930s.

In the 1930s economists were active in the public discussion in the same manner as during World War I and in the 1920s—writing in newspapers and magazines, preparing committee reports on macroeconomic policies, and advising the policymakers. Cassel, Heckscher, and Ohlin were associated with various newspapers and contributed columns regularly. Ohlin was the most prolific writer of them all. In 1932, for example, he published about 60 articles in the *Stockholms Tidning*, dealing with various domestic and foreign economic issues. After Sweden had left the gold standard in 1931, Cassel and Heckscher remained strong proponents of the program of price stabilization. They advocated, in part, an appreciation of the Swedish krona in 1937 in order to stabilize Swedish prices when the world price level was rising. They acted as "watchdogs" over the policy of the Riksbank through their articles in the newspapers. The younger generation of economists, however, came gradually to focus their interest on fiscal measures and to propose employment stabilization—instead of price stabilization—much to the dismay of Cassel and Heckscher. This new generation came to inspire the framing of fiscal policy. This policy, however, had only a minor impact on the Swedish business cycle in the 1930s compared to the monetary measures. To sum up, the Swedish economic profession exerted a considerable influence directly as well as indirectly on the conduct of Swedish stabilization policies in the 1930s. This influence is an important part of the explanation of why Swedish monetary policy was based on Wicksell's norm of price stabilization and was more expansionary than the policy of the Federal Reserve System during the depression.

CONCLUSION

This paper has compared the economic record of the depression of the 1930s for Sweden and the United States. The depression in Sweden was shorter and less severe than in the United States. This difference is explained primarily by the conduct of monetary policy in the two countries. Swedish policy aimed at stabilizing the domestic price level and thus the money stock, while American policy contributed to a sharply reduced money stock. The difference in the framing of monetary policy is to a considerable extent due to the influence of Swedish economists on the policy of the Riksbank.

In economic research it is generally impossible to study experiments similar to controlled testing in a laboratory, but the experience of Sweden and of the United States in the 1930s may be regarded as two interesting test cases. One was the case of an economy where the money stock was kept constant, the other the case of an economy with a falling money stock. When the money stock was held at stable level, domestic prices remained constant and the downturn in industrial production was smaller and of shorter duration than in the economy with a sharply falling supply of money.

The comparative analysis provides conclusions concerning the money hypothesis and the spending hypothesis considered in American debate. The comparison of Sweden and the United States makes a strong case for assigning great importance to monetary developments in the depression of the 1930s in Sweden as well as in the United States.

APPENDIX: GUSTAV CASSEL ON THE AMERICAN DEPRESSION

Gustav Cassel was the most prominent Swedish economist after the death of Wicksell. He was probably also the most renowned economist in the world from the early 1920s until the publication of Keynes's *General Theory*. He played a leading role in various committees of the League of Nations; he traveled extensively and published a large number of articles on world monetary issues. Cassel was a strong proponent of a monetary interpretation of macroeconomic events, specifically, of the world depression. He presented a good summary of his views in an article published in October 1932, that is, in the middle of the crisis, called "A Contribution to Characterization of the Crisis." This article is interesting to look at more closely because Cassel discusses from a Swedish viewpoint various hypotheses concerning the causes of the U.S. depression.

Cassel states initially that the crisis was a crisis of the world's monetary system. He summarizes the "chain of causes" behind it in the following way:

> The principal links in this chain are the unnatural demands for the payment of reparations and war debts; the reluctance of the recipient countries to take payment of reparations and war debts in the form of goods and services; the lopsided distribution of gold in the world, greatly aggravating the effects of the existing shortage in the supply of gold; the sharp fall of prices; the general insolvency and loss of confidence; the paralysis of enterprise; the increasing trade barriers and the collapse of the world economy.

In this chain of events the policy of the United States played the central role, according to Cassel.

Then Cassel examines various explanations of the U.S. depression, like (1) underconsumption, (2) excessive consumption, (3) overproduction, and (4) stock speculation. He dismisses all these hypotheses, arguing that it is

> perfectly clear that the course of economic events in the United States is essentially a pure process of deflation, quite distinct from ordinary economic movements, a process which began on a small scale as far back as 1929, and which has afterwards developed with such momentum that it is grinding to pieces the entire national economy.

This process of deflation was started by the Federal Reserve System in the spring of 1928, when, fearing stock-exchange speculation, it introduced restrictions on credits. The restrictive policy caused a pronounced fall in commodity prices in the United States. They had fallen from 95 by June 1929 to 64 by June 1932. "This very marked and continuous fall of prices cannot possibly be interpreted as a result of preceding economic, nonmonetary disturbances.'' The fall in prices triggered a chain of events that aggravated the crisis. Various institutional developments contributed to this. The "prevalent views that the member banks ought not to be indebted to the Federal Reserve banks" prevented the Federal Reserve System from a policy of liberal lending that would have counteracted the deflationary process. Due to the absence of big banks with many branch offices, small banks were left on their own to face bank runs with no resort to central support from large banks. Big banks, on the other hand, tried to improve their reserve positions. They cut down their loans and contributed further to deflation.

The process of deflation "could have been checked only by a determined policy of antideflation on the part of the Federal Reserve banks" and by an active intervention extending the "effective supply of means of payment." Such a policy was not implemented because of the system's "almost superstitious dread of anything that could be stamped as inflation." Furthermore, the Federal Reserve banks were hampered in their actions by the legal framework, specifically, by the restrictions eliminated by the Glass-Steagall Bill of February 1932 and by the amendment of the Federal Reserve Act of July 1932.

To sum up, Cassel is advocating a strong monetary interpretation, stating that (1) the U.S. depression was caused by monetary factors, and (2) an expansionary monetary policy could have effectively checked the depression. It is worth noting that Cassel was writing this in the midst of the crises and that he was observing American economic events from Sweden. In his later writings he remained a staunch proponent of a monetary view of the depression. He became extremely critical of the fiscal activism of the Stockholm School and of the work of Keynes and his followers.

NOTES

1. Temin's study has been the subject of several critical comments; see Gandolfi and Lothian (1977), Mayer (1978), and Meltzer (1976).

2. This paper deals primarily with the contraction phase of the depression, that is, with the years 1929–33. The recovery phase has not attracted as much interest as the downturn in economic activity.

3. The number of commercial bank offices was reduced in Sweden in the 1930s, but this was part of a trend that started in the early 1920s.

4. The Swedish krona was depreciated when Sweden left the gold standard in 1931. The prices of foreign assets were then regarded as attractive, since a return to the parity rates of the gold standard was expected by many in the first half of the 1930s.

5. The Swedish money stock was reduced by 29 percent and the implicit deflator of the gross domestic product by 35 percent between 1920 and 1925.

6. What follows builds upon and summarizes the analysis of Swedish monetary and fiscal policy in the 1930s in Jonung (1979b).

7. The Riksbank tried to obtain loans from New York and Paris in order to stay on the gold standard but was denied financial support. Thus, Sweden was forced off gold fairly rapidly and in this way avoided a prolonged period of deflation compared with those countries that remained on gold.

8. Jonung (1979a) gives a detailed presentation of the reports of Cassel, Davidson, and Heckscher. Their reports until recently have remained classified documents kept in the archives of the Riksbank.

9. In his report to the Riksbank in 1931, Gustav Cassel urged the bank to rediscount and lend to the commercial banking system on liberal terms. He also advised the bank to supply as many notes as demanded by the public and to announce that any increase in the demand for notes would be satisfied. See Jonung (1979a).

10. Swedish economists commonly agree that the "crisis policy" had minor effects on the recovery of the Swedish economy (Jonung 1979b).

11. Davidson argued in his report to the Riksbank that the American monetary system was based on a paper standard in the 1920s and that the Riksbank could learn from the behavior of the Federal Reserve System how to manage a paper standard (Jonung 1979a).

12. Temin's conclusion is based on a number of econometric tests of consumption functions for the United States in the interwar period. Mayer (1978) reports econometric results that are critical of Temin's arguments.

13. See Jonung (1979b) for a presentation of this debate.

REFERENCES

Cagan, P. 1965. *Determinants and Effects of Changes in the Stock of Money, 1875 –1960*. New York: Columbia University Press, for the National Bureau of Economic Research.

Cassel, G. 1932. "A Contribution to Characterization of the Crisis." Skandianaviska Kreditaktiebolaget *Quarterly Review*, October.

Friedman, M., and Schwartz, A. J. 1963. *A Monetary History of the United States, 1867 –1960*. Princeton, N.J.: Princeton University Press, for the National Bureau of Economic Research.

Gandolfi, A. E., and Lothian, J. R. 1977. "Did Monetary Forces Cause the Great Depression?" *Journal of Money, Credit and Banking* 9: 679 –91.

Johansson, Ö. 1968. *The Gross Domestic Product of Sweden and Its Composition, 1861 –1955*. Uppsala: Almquist & Wiksell.

Jonung, L. 1975. "Studies in the Monetary History of Sweden." Ph.D diss., University of California at Los Angeles.

———. 1979a. "Cassel, Davidson and Heckscher on Swedish Monetary Policy—A Confidential Report to the Riksbank in 1931." *Economy and History:* 85 –101.

———. 1979b. "Knut Wicksell's Norm of Price Stabilization and Swedish Monetary Policy in the 1930's." *Journal of Monetary Economics* 5: 459 –96.

Krantz, O., and Nilsson, C-A. 1975. *Swedish National Product, 1861 –1970*. Kristianstad: Gleerup.

Mayer, T. 1978. "Consumption in the Great Depression." *Journal of Political Economy* 86: 123 –39.

Meltzer, A. 1976. "Monetary and Other Explanations of the Start of the Great Depression." *Journal of Monetary Economics* 2: 455–71.

Sweden. Kommerskollegium. Various issues. *Economisk oversikt*. Stockholm: Kommerskollegium.

Temin, P. 1976. *Did Monetary Forces Cause the Great Depression?* New York: W. W. Norton.

U.S. Department of Commerce. 1960. *Historical Statistics of the United States, Colonial Times to 1957*. Washington, D.C.: Government Printing Office.

———. 1966. *Long Term Economic Growth, 1860–1965*. Washington, D.C.: Government Printing Office.

17 EPILOGUE:
Understanding the Great Depression
Karl Brunner

THE RANGE OF ISSUES

The interpretation of the Great Depression still offers a major intellectual challenge. The conflict of ideas, conjectures, and hypotheses bearing on this important historical event permeates the papers and comments contributed to this volume. One of the participants concluded that "[Anna] Schwartz and I do not seem to have any common ground on which to discuss our historical stories. How can we talk about the historical facts when we perceive them so differently? How can we test hypotheses unless we agree on the mechanism by which monetary forces affect aggregate demand? . . . Can the issue of the causes of the Great Depression be debated fruitfully at all?" (Temin 1981, p. 122).

A first and somewhat impressionistic reading of the various papers may easily foster such a despairing view. But a closer inspection hardly supports

An earlier draft of this chapter received detailed comments from Robert J. Gordon, James Lothian, Anna Schwartz, and James Wilcox. These comments influenced the final draft and are gratefully acknowledged. As always, the close collaboration with Allan H. Meltzer affected the basic view presented. This applies most particularly to the argument bearing on the supply side of the problem.

316

such moods. Scholarly work and the associated disputes rarely proceed with an immediate and explicit summary of issues settled or of the partial and always provisional consensus achieved. We would hardly accept today some of the legends purveyed over many decades by the Federal Reserve authorities and even enshrined in textbooks. The story of the powerless Central Bank acting valiantly but in vain in order to contain the economic storm has been effectively exposed as a fallacy. This story influenced the perception of the Great Depression that many textbooks conveyed to early postwar generations of students and teachers.[1]

The product of scholarly endeavor, however, is not confined to the elimination of untenable views expressed by their gradual disappearance from serious consideration. The exchange of arguments published in this volume also reveals the emergence of a partial consensus on some important aspects of the story.[2] Lastly, the nature of the unsettled issues reflected by disagreements and contentious arguments offers a guide to future research with the aim to understand the phenomenon more completely and reliably. Any cognitive progress in this range depends on clear recognition concerning the nature of alternative hypotheses more or less implicitly used to buttress conflicting views. Differences in perception of the same "historical facts" reveal corresponding differences in conjectures about the social processes at work—that is, they reveal different hypotheses or theories used to interpret reality. The question raised in the second sentence of this passage quoted above thus finds a simple answer: Anna Schwartz and Peter Temin advocate substantially different theories. The crucial question confronting us under the circumstances bears on the procedures actually used and potentially applicable to assess the competing contentions. The noise and confusion produced by our discussions seems frequently to suggest that "social nature," in contrast to "physical nature," obstructs our intellectual groping with inherent difficulties. This may be the case, and any debate about the Great Depression or other socioeconomic problems may be fruitless beyond the use of language for strategic purposes in contexts of political conflicts. We should hesitate, however, to drift into an essentially nihilistic intellectual position. The noise and confusion do not just reflect an obnoxious social reality or the hostile game of the gods controlling (and obscuring) the nature of social processes. We may create our own difficulties and obstruct our vision through inadequate formulation or erroneous conception bearing on our assessment of alternative conjectures (Brunner 1967).

The passage quoted above exemplifies this surmise with a peculiar misdirection of attention. It suggests that no assessment is feasible unless participants agree on a common view of the basic monetary mechanisms. But the interpretations developed and evaluation procedures used by various participants are logically tied to very *different* views pertaining precisely to these basic mechanisms. The suggestion quoted thus requests that different hypotheses be tested by disregarding their crucial differences. But these very differences determine the variations in the interpretations observed and form the centerpiece of any critical comparison. The common ground required for relevant mutual critique and assessment of conflicting conjectures is in our context and at this stage not a common view of "basic monetary mechanisms." The common ground necessary for our purposes consists of generally accepted standards of analysis involving the formulation and also the assessment of hypotheses.

The first round for any further investigation of the Great Depression involves a clarification of the range of unsettled issues. This examination should probe more or less implicit aspects of divergent hypotheses. It should also consider the quality and relevance of evaluations addressed to various propositions. The current chapter suggests a modest beginning of this task.

The range of issues requiring our attention is well defined by the contributions included in the volume. The papers contributed by Schwartz, Gordon and Wilcox, and the comments offered by Meltzer, Temin, Lothian, and others demonstrate that the nature and working of dominant causal or contributing factors plunging the American economy into the deepest recorded recession still require systematic attention. The discussion bears at this point on the comparative role of monetary and nonmonetary forces and conditions in the socio-economic process producing the events of the 1930s. But a general emphasis on the causal significance of nonmonetary events and conditions is hardly informative. The dispute extends to different types of nonmonetary conditions. They may involve a shifting variety of spending categories organized in accordance with standard national income accounts. Alternatively, the nonmonetary conditions invoked may dominantly address sociopolitical and institutional aspects of society.

The dispute about the role of monetary and nonmonetary events and conditions also includes the interpretation of the observed monetary evolution. The significance of "reverse causation" and the potential role of Central Bank policy belong to this subject. Some progress toward a consensus with respect to the latter subject appears among the discussants. But a closer scrutiny also reveals at this point some remaining implicit differences pertaining to the views about the nature of the transmission mechanism. The analysis of the observed behavior of monetary aggregates is closely associated with still pending issues bearing on a useful interpretation of monetary policy and of specific events (the stock market crash and banking failures).

A last set of unresolved questions remains directed at the long duration of the Great Depression—over more than ten years. The diversity of answers centers on contrasting views about the nature of price-wage processes expressing different explanations of price-wage behavior. Alternative answers are also controlled by different views concerning relevant nonmonetary factors (for example, Gordon and Wilcox and Meltzer about the low recovery rate in the late 1930s). Lastly, the alternative views of price-wage processes also express substantial differences about the interpretation of price-wage mechanisms as a basically self-correcting social process.

My discussion of these issues proceeds in three sections. The first part surveys the major alternative views offered by Schwartz, Gordon and Wilcox, and Temin. The second part examines the alternative conjectures concerning the causal and conditioning forces operating on the Great Depression. The third part addresses price-wage processes, the role of supply behavior, and the interpretation of price-wage "inflexibility." The last section summarizes some aspects for an agenda of research and refers in this context particularly to the potential use of systematic comparisons of very different patterns exhibited by a variety of countries.

THE COMPARATIVE ROLE OF MONETARY AND NON-MONETARY CONDITIONS: A SURVEY OF THREE VIEWS

A Framework for the Discussion

Our examination of the issues proceeds in the context of a schema describing the interaction between aggregate demand and aggregate supply. Aggregate demand is defined by the quantity equation relating changes in the price level with changes in the excess of output over normal output. We write thus

$$\Delta m + \Delta v - \Delta ny = \Delta p + \Delta x, \qquad (1)$$

where variables refer to logarithma of the money stock (m), velocity (v), normal output (ny), the price level (p), and to the deviation x of the output from normal outputs. The measure of velocity represents a variety of influences on aggregate nominal demand ($\Delta m + \Delta v$) beyond the immediate measure of monetary evolution.[3] It includes all influences operating on domestic private sector velocity. It also reflects, however, any effects of fiscal policy and foreign influences. Changes in foreign money stock, foreign monetary velocity, foreign prices, or the exchange rate affect the standard easure of velocity used in equation (1).

Equation (1) defines the demand relation d occurring in figure 1. The slope is necessarily minus unity. The position of the demand line, expressed by the

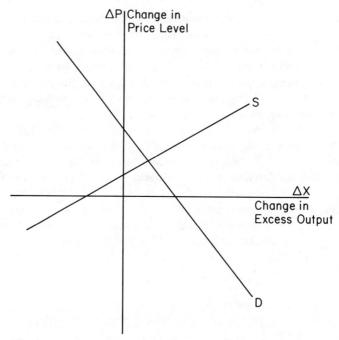

Figure 1. An Aggregate Demand and Supply Framework

vertical intercept, is determined by the adjusted nominal aggregate demand
($\Delta m + \Delta v - \Delta ny$). An excess of nominal demand ($\Delta m + \Delta v$) over normal
real growth thus produces a positive intercept.

The supply line is specified in terms of its slope and position. This involves
a decomposition of the change in the price level Δp into two components,
according to equation (2).

$$\Delta p_t = \Delta p_{1t} + \Delta p_{2t} \qquad (2a)$$

$$\Delta p_{1t} = E_{t-1}[\Delta m_t + \Delta v_t - \Delta ny_t / I_{t-1}] \qquad (2b)$$

$$\Delta p_{2t} = \Theta \Delta x_t + u_t \qquad (2c)$$

The slope represents the response of a more or less transitory component of
price changes to excess changes in output. Changes in the price level due to
the second component exhibit, under the circumstances, movements along a
given supply line. The position of this line reflects, on the other hand, the
prevailing expectations bearing an adjusted aggregate nominal demand. These
expectations are determined by the information available at the time. Vertical
shifts of the supply line result, therefore, from revisions in expectation patterns
induced by a changing information set.

The schema is quite neutral thus far with respect to the conflicting views about our phenomenon. It offers an organizational device for the accommodation of all conjectures. Unavoidably, the formulation possesses no empirical content. Infusion of content occurs with the characterization of the alternative hypotheses about the evolution of events from 1929 onward. The problem to be explained by the diverse conjectures may be summarized as a cluster of points in the diagram concentrated in quadrants I and III. Each one of the alternative hypotheses offers a different story about the relative movement in demand and supply required to produce a pattern of intersection points covering the observed cluster of pairs (Δx, Δp). Two major issues emerge immediately from this organization. The first addresses the dominant processes "behind" the fall in the demand line. The second involves a search for an explanation of the pronounced asymmetry in the shifts of demand and supply revealed by the cluster of available observations.

A Monetary Explanation

Anna Schwartz assigns to monetary forces and conditions a central role in the explanation of the shifts in the aggregate demand line. A series of negative shocks beginning with an initial deceleration of the U.S. money stock, reinforced by the stock market crash and four banking panics, persistently lowered the money stock over four years by magnitudes never before experienced. Two transitory positive shocks, which halted for a short duration the economy's decline, reflect the continued potency of monetary influences at this time.

The monetary explanation fully recognizes the large decline in velocity reflected by persistent large negative values of Δv. But at least some part of this decline in velocity is interpreted to occur as a consequence of the monetary deceleration. A monetary explanation emphasizes most particularly that substantial and persistent declines in velocity are unlikely in the absence of a prior monetary deceleration. Similarly, a substantial and persistent increase of velocity will hardly emerge without a corresponding monetary acceleration. The evidence from inflation and hyperinflation forms in the context of the monetary explanation of the business cycle an essential strand of the story bearing on the endogenous responses of velocity to monetary evolutions. It should be noted that the monetary explanation does not claim to offer a complete account of velocity behavior. Such a claim would not be substantiated by the available observations.

Two aspects in the movement of velocity need be recognized in this context. First, the economy does not respond with an invariant pattern to monetary impulses. The monetary explanation acknowledges, at least implicitly, the pervasive stochastic nature of the socioeconomic process. It follows under the circumstances that the systematic responses of velocity to changing monetary evolutions will most likely vary between different occasions and experiences. It is also admitted that various nonmonetary events, conditions, and forces affect the behavior of velocity. Advocates of a monetary explanation would, in general, emphasize nonmonetary conditions controlling the relative yields and attractiveness of real and financial assets. They tend to discount, on the other hand, the relevance (with respect to aggregate demand) of autonomous variation in spending components. Such variations are limited in the monetary explanation to the ineradicable randomness built into social processes and are impounded into the shorter-run drift of velocity but otherwise domina ntly absorbed by allocative adjustments. An interpretation of such random characteristics in terms of autonomous spending changes falsely attributes to essentially stochastic events a systematic meaning. This interpretation of velocity patterns implies that expansionary monetary policy directed to accelerate the money stock successfully raises aggregate nominal demand. "Offsetting velocity" behavior typically occurs in response to monetary accelerations or decelerations but hardly extends much beyond a quarter. A persistent positive response by the Federal Reserve authorities to the stock market crash, in the spirit of the Federal Reserve Bank of New York, well maintained beyond 1930 would have at least moderated the decline in velocity by a very substantial margin.

The central proposition of the monetary explanation about the nature of the interrelations between velocity and monetary changes determined an important strand of the research strategy followed by proponents of this explanation. They explored with great detail the properties of the money-supply process. These studies were largely motivated by an attempt to clarify the causal significance of monetary changes and to interpret the pervasive correlation between income and money so uniformly observed over many periods and in different countries. The large variations in the properties of money-supply processes in the face of a persistent money-income correlation pattern are difficult to reconcile with a dominant operation of reverse causation. We also should note two pieces of additional evidence, advanced in the present paper, that bear on the main thrust of the argument. A Granger causality test applied to two distinct sample periods, both covering the Great Depression, yields some support for the monetary explanation. The data reveal uniformly larger probabilities for the *absence* of "reverse causation" from income to money, than for the absence of "causation" from money to income. The strength of the support derived from the statistical procedures is not high, but the pattern is remarkably uniform and clear. The other piece of evidence relates the monetary evolution with the movement of the reciprocal of a price index. The pattern observed seems certainly consistent with the monetary explanation.

An "Eclectic" Explanation

The monetary explanation cannot be subsumed under the traditional $IS-LM$ framework with its usual interpretations. Some comments addressed by Anna Schwartz at Peter Temin's argument are clearly incompatible with the constraints imposed by the $IS-LM$ framework on the nature of the monetary transmission mechanism. Some issues associated with this aspect will be examined in more detail in a subsequent section. But the implicit difference in analytical vision should be recognized even if a more explicit clarification is suspended for the moment.

The eclectic position so articulately advanced by Gordon and Wilcox appears clearly grounded within the traditional $IS-LM$ framework supplemented with an aggregate supply function. This apparatus clearly influenced the organization of the authors' arguments. The eclectic view is motivated by the observation of a comparatively small decline in the money stock within the first year of the depression compared with the large decline of velocity measuring around 10 percent. This comparatively large decline of velocity from 1929 to 1930 suggests to the authors the operation of nonmonetary events autonomously compressing some components of aggregate demand. The autonomously caused decline in spending would be expressed by a leftward shift in the IS curve. Gordon and Wilcox argue, moreover, that the long duration of the depression lasting over the whole decade cannot be explained without an essential recourse to the operation of autonomous nonmonetary forces. They also find the hesitant economic expansion observed beyond 1937 into 1940–41 difficult to reconcile with the magnitude of the monetary impulse prevailing at the time.

The nature of the eclectic conjecture presented by Gordon and Wilcox requires a two-stage approach in the empirical investigations pursued. In a first round the authors proceed in the same manner as Anna Schwartz. They present two sets of Granger tests assessing the dominant causal relation between income and money. One set uses quarterly, and the other, monthly data. The data used include both the narrow and the wider measure of the money stock, both original data and first differences, and they also cover subperiods of the total period 1920 to 1941. The broad results summarized in tables 1 and 2 of the Gordon-Wilcox study essentially confirm the patterns found by Schwartz.

There is clearly more support for the "money causes income" view than for the opposite conjecture that "income causes money." The authors also find that the patterns deteriorate for both formulations in the second subperiod covering the "dismal 1930s." It is noteworthy, however, that for the only completely reported case using quarterly data the deterioration of the results for the "reverse causation hypothesis" is a multiple of the deterioration observed for the "causation hypothesis."

The authors carefully note the large coefficient in both formulations attached to concurrent variables. The regressions thus leave us with some uncertainty about the interpretation of concurrent relations between money and income. The issue is not further examined with the required study of characteristic properties controlling the money-supply process. But Gordon and Wilcox explicitly place their investigation into a broader context of monetary research developed over the past decades. This research, which covers very different periods and countries and is executed with a variety of methods, uniformly supports the conjecture that "money does matter" in specific ways with respect to the movements of economic activity and the price level. All these results taken in conjunction lead the authors to reject a nonmonetary explanation of the Great Depression. They reject, in particular, a purely nonmonetary explanation for the first two years of the downswing.

The denial of a purely nonmonetary account does not involve the acceptance of a monetary view of the events. The large role of velocity adjustments in arithmetical decompositions of the fall in nominal income is accepted as prima facie evidence of a shift in the *IS* curve occurring independently of monetary shocks. In order to buttress the case for an eclectic position, Gordon and Wilcox also investigate the simulation patterns extracted from the regressions subjected to a Granger test. Tables 3 and 4 in their paper and the corresponding figures supply the relevant information. The simulated income level falls at the trough to about $71 billion, whereas the actual income dropped to $52 billion. The simulation thus accounts for slightly less than 50 percent of the collapse in nominal income observed over the whole downswing. Gordon and Wilcox conclude from this pattern that nonmonetary events must have contributed substantially to the deflationary thrust imposed on the U.S. economy. A purely monetary explanation fails in their judgment to explain adequately the contours of the depression.

An examination of the first two years reinforces their judgment. Only about 25 percent of the total decline in nominal income can be attributed to the receding monetary impulse according to the information extracted from the regressions. Nonmonetary influences thus appeared to dominate the initial phase of the downswing, with monetary forces emerging more strongly in the second and final decline of the U.S. economy. The upswing from early 1933 to early

1937 and the subsequent depression are, on the other hand, well approximated by the simulation results. We find here no clues for any relevant contribution emanating from nonmonetary events. The recovery phase beyond 1937 reveals, however, the operation of negative nonmonetary influences. The monetary stimulus determines a momentum of the simulated income not shared by actual observations.

The assignment of significant nonmonetary influences affecting the U.S. scenario between 1929 and 1933 and again between 1938 and 1941 naturally poses a question about the nature of these nonmonetary conditions. Gordon and Wilcox conclude their search for appropriate nonmonetary influences with assigning causal significance to the evolution of housing and construction expenditures, the evolution of the stock market, and the Hawley-Smoot tariff legislated by Congress in 1930. Housing expenditure moved, according to the authors, since 1926 on a declining trend conditioned by retardations in population growth and by overbuilding. Demographic evolution lowered, according to Gordon, the desired stock of housing, while overbuilding produced an excessive stock. The resulting excess supply induced a longer-range stock adjustment, which contributed to lower aggregate demand. The effect of the stock market boom on private consumption expenditures more than offset, for some time, the deflationary macroconsequences of this particular allocative maladjustment. The crash of October 1929 removed the compensating effect of consumption and even lowered this demand component. The deflationary impact of nonmonetary influences was finally unleashed with the crash. The Hawley-Smoot tariff retarded the price decline and channeled a larger portion of the receding aggregate demand into adjustments of output. The tariff legislation also destabilized at the time an international monetary system already weakened by the U.S. downswing, the reparations imposed on Germany, and an overvalued pound sterling. The retaliations and repercussions amplified the deflationary impulse distributed over the world. This impulse fed back into the U.S. economy in the form of rapidly shrinking exports.

A Nonmonetary Explanation of the First Phase of the Depression

A third position expressing our attempts to understand the Great Depression was introduced several years ago in a volume published by Peter Temin (1976). The author responded to the extensive critique addressed to his book by Gordon and Wilcox and Schwartz with some detailed comments included in this volume. The succinct presentation offers the reader an excellent opportunity to appreciate Temin's views on the subject under consideration.

Temin is clearly impressed by the same set of observations as Gordon and Wilcox: the massive decline in velocity over the first year of the downswing accompanied throughout by falling interest rates even through the first banking panic, a fall in the price level and even more in output, and lastly, an increase in real balances. These observations are neatly subsumed under a traditional *IS –LM* framework augmented at this stage with an aggregate supply relation. Temin then examines whether the monetary explanation could possibly offer a coherent account of the set of observations noted. The framework used implies that a pronounced monetary shock would raise nominal interest rates, most particularly short-term rates emphasized by the author in this context, as a result of the leftward shift in the *LM* curve. Adjustments in anticipated price changes shifting the *IS* curve to the left could have moderated or even offset these interest-raising effects of a monetary shock. The role of expectational effects is, however, substantially discounted by the author. Perfect foresight would have produced full adjustment of prices to the new situation without any output effects. Under the circumstances inherited from the 1920s, Temin finds no reason to assign any significance to the operation of adaptive expectations.

The persistent fall of short-term nominal interest rates, combined with the rise in real balances pushing the *LM* curve to the right, determines Temin's conclusion that no monetary forces or events contributed in any way to the deflationary evolution observed over the first two years of the Great Depression. He acknowledges, however, the emergence of negative monetary shocks by the fall of 1931 after the devaluation of the pound sterling. The fall in velocity, that is, the substantially negative Δv, forms the centerpiece in Temin's argument. The author judges this fall to form an autonomous event independent of any prior monetary evolutions. In spite of the emphatic role attributed to a falling price level expressed by rising real balances, no feedbacks into adjustments of anticipated price movements are admitted. The decline in velocity was not even partly influenced by decreasing real rates of interest.

The rejection of any monetary influences on the events from 1929 to 1931 imposes the whole burden on the *IS* curve. Appropriate nonmonetary causes must be found that can be made responsible for autonomous leftward shifts in the *IS* curve. Such influences are explored, according to the direction predetermined by the analytic framework, among the spending components constituting aggregate demand. Temin discards autonomous declines in private investment expenditures and concentrates on consumption expenditures. A regression of consumer expenditures on disposal income and wealth estimated for the interwar period determines, apparently, a substantial negative residual for 1930. This residual contrasts with a positive residual estimated for 1921 and 1938. The negative residual obtained for 1930 is interpreted as the negative nonmonetary shock initiating the Great Depression. The resulting shift in the *IS* curve yields in Temin's account, in contrast to the monetary shock, precisely the pattern actually observed. Temin concludes that the set of observations can be coherently explained by a nonmonetary hypothesis but contradicts the monetary conjecture of the depression.

The story offered by Temin essentially reverses the account developed by Schwartz. The autonomous forces operate in this case only on velocity and cause the large decline ($\Delta v < 0$) observed in 1930. The very magnitude of Δv relative to Δm seems to suggest an autonomous nonmonetary force compressing velocity. The monetary changes, on the other hand, are purely endogenous and are simply the consequences of the nonmonetary shocks and the decline of velocity. The deceleration of the money stock obtains no independent meaning. The residual character of monetary changes in Temin's account implies that no monetary forces contributed or aggravated the downswing over the first phase of the Great Depression. This argument involves a variety of details and important aspects that will be considered in the following section.

THE ROLE OF MONETARY AND NONMONETARY INFLUENCES: A TENTATIVE EVALUATION

The general summary of the various conjectures omitted some revealing detail and neglected important strands of the arguments presented and counterarguments made. This section probes deeper into the issues associated with the comparative role of monetary and nonmonetary events and conditions.

The Search for Nonmonetary Influences

The title of this paragraph, taken from the Gordon-Wilcox article, is singularly descriptive and most informatively summarizes the state of affairs. The rejection of a monetary explanation necessarily directs the advocates of nonmonetary influences on a search for autonomous changes in spending components that explain the exogenous drop in velocity. It is this very decision that rationally suggests that the formulation presented with equation (1) be replaced or at least supplemented with an income-expenditure formulation involving appropriate subdivisions of total expenditures. The basic idea guiding the search is the conjecture that some allocative shifts are converted into global changes of nominal demand expressed by corresponding changes in velocity occurring autonomously relative to monetary evolutions or conditions. Understanding the stochastic processes governing velocity thus requires a sufficiently detailed attention to the stochastic processes controlling *specific* expenditure categories. The stochastic processes shaping velocity operate, at least to this extent, independently of the money-supply process and its properties. This conception naturally fosters an analytic-empirical research program formulated in terms of expenditure categories. An emphasis on nonmonetary forces thus encourages a procedure confined to the Keynesian framework. It will be argued in a subsequent paragraph that this commitment, conditioned by the vision of the major driving forces, involves for our purposes implicit problems not examined by the participants. The monetary approach argues, on the other hand, that the stochastic process controlling velocity is at least partly conditioned by the money-supply process. It also contends more or less implicitly that the process guiding velocity produces even in the context of systematic dependence on monetary evolution a substantial "stochastic looseness" in the behavior of velocity. And lastly, attempts to a systematic explanation of the "unexplained variability" in terms of specific combinations of nonmonetary forces are unlikely to succeed.

The discussion among the participants and various comments addressed to specific investigations offer sufficient material to ponder the basic problem inherent in "the search for nonmonetary forces." The most immediate aspect confronting us is the *diversity of conjectures* submitted to our examination. This diversity reveals also the central problem of *the* nonmonetary explanation of the Great Depression. The issue is, of course, an old one. Our literature developed "real" and "monetary" theories of the business cycles decades before the "Keynesian revolution." And the variety of "real factors, conditions, events or forces" selected for our attention today seems not much smaller than in pre-Keynesian days of business-cycle theories.

Problems Inherent in the Search
for Nonmonetary Influences

The various nonmonetary explanations are hardly consistent. If we accept the thesis advanced by Gordon and Wilcox, then Temin and Kindleberger are just as wrong as the monetary explanations. Corresponding statements hold in the other directions. We need to consider the nature of the supporting arguments. The procedure of Gordon and Wilcox clearly reflects the basic pattern of the search for a nonmonetary force. Having decided that a monetary explanation fails to account sufficiently for the phenomenon under consideration, the authors look for an expenditure category moving in the right direction. So they settle on housing but find it necessary for the reason stated above to supplement this event with the autonomous component of boom and crash on the

U.S. stock market. Temin uses, on the other hand, a regression to find a substantial negative residual for the proper time period. And Kindleberger (1973) emphasized some economic "maladjustments" to be perceived ex post facto.

The procedure used in all these cases does not produce, as it stands, any assessable propositions. Gordon and Wilcox present informative discursive elaborations about the selected aspects of the U.S. economy and refer for evidential support to the Hickman model about the housing sector and Mishkin's study of wealth effect on consumer expenditures. But the latter observation is consistent with a purely monetary explanation denying a systematic autonomous component in the stock market crash. The search relies essentially on arithmetical considerations pertaining to the structure of the national income accounts. Temin's procedure begs the question of the consumption function used for the computation. There is little reason to assign more weight to Temin's explanation than to any other "real hypothesis" offered for our scrutiny in the absence of any evidence yielding good grounds for the selection of this hypothesis over alternative consumption hypotheses with different residual patterns. In addition, we note that the various nonmonetary explanations encounter a timing problem not covered by their arguments. The real factors addressed by Gordon and Wilcox cannot explain the occurrence of the turning point months before the stock market crash with a substantial decline in economic activity until November 1929. Temin, on the other hand, must rely on the emergence of a negative residual around mid-1929, certainly before the stock market crash. His comments offer neither argument nor evidence in support of the relevant timing. The monetary explanation emphasizes in this context the deceleration of the money stock emerging in 1928 and persisting until early 1933.

The behavior of construction from 1925–29 and of the stock market during the late fall and winter of 1929–30 deserves in this context some closer attention. Construction expenditures in current dollars fell from $547 million in July 1925 to $518 million in July 1926. They *rose* subsequently every year until they reached $652 million in July 1929. The volume of expenditures thus exhibits no persistent weakening prior to the great turning point. These expenditures fell during the third post–World War I recession but recovered and expanded over the subsequent three years with a remarkable force. The square footage of total construction did reach a record level of 85.5 million in July 1925 and fell in the subsequent recession to 68.1 million. It recovered by 1928 almost two-thirds of the prior loss and reached 74.9 million in July 1929 (Lipsey and Preston 1966).

Both data thus exhibit little supportive evidence for a persistent deflationary thrust produced by the construction industry. The square footage produced was lower in July 1929 than in July 1925 but higher than in July 1926 and July

1927. Expenditures, on the other hand, were much higher in July 1929 than in any previous July over the preceding four years. We note that the contraction in the building industry observed in 1926 unleashed no major economic depression even without the offsetting effect of rapid increases in stock values.

The stock market data pose a similar problem. The Standard and Poor common stock price index measured 237.8 in September 1929 and dropped to 159.6 in November 1929. It recovered over the subsequent months until it reached 191.1 in April 1930. It fell over the subsequent two years without interruption to a bottom level of 35.9 in June 1932. Which portion of these movements should count as the autonomous impulse? Surely, the decline beyond April 1930 must be recognized as a consequence—that is, an event induced by the progressive decline in economic activity. But what portion of the movements observed between September 1929 and April 1930 could be reasonably considered as "autonomous?" No answer has been provided thus far. The issue is actually important for any assessment of the relative role of alternative causal forces. Meltzer and Schwartz argue that the stock market essentially responded to the preceding boom in the economy occurring during 1928 (until mid-1929) and reflected subsequently with a lag a tightening monetary policy. A similar question needs also be directed to the construction expenditures. We can hardly assign an autonomous character to the continued decline during the Great Depression. The persistent decline of economic activity must have lowered the desired stock of buildings.

One more difficulty remains for any thesis assigning major autonomous significance to the stock market. Stock values fell in real terms over seven months (September 1929–April 1930) beginning September 1929 by somewhat less than 20 percent. We experienced episodes in the mid-1970s during which the real value of stocks fell by a multiple of the decline in 1929–30 and construction expenditures also receded rapidly. But there ensued no Great Depression. Normal output was permanently lowered by 5 percent, and the cyclic decline in actual output was probably at most 3.5 percent, similar in magnitude to the first three post–World War II recessions. It seems hardly possible to recognize in the nonmonetary account provided by Gordon and Wilcox much more than a suggestive idea. It emerges at best as a potential explanation of the observed decline in velocity.

Advocates of a real theory are confronted with the problem of linking the selected nonmonetary impulses with the evolution of aggregate demand. The Wicksellian process solved this problem by relating monetary growth via divergences between market rates and the expected real rate of return on real assets with the autonomous drift in the real return. Keynes used, of course, for his purpose the investment-multiplier assuring "autonomous" variations in velocity. But should we really continue this process and invent a specific multiplier arbitrarily linking aggregate demand with any real event or relatively maladjusted branch of the economy? The procedure implicitly assigns systematic global significance to specific allocative patterns selected from a range of possible choices in accordance with the direction of aggregate demand established ex post facto. But this assignment remains essentially ad hoc and has so far not been integrated into an assessable hypothesis of cyclic movements. The combination of real events or conditions selected to "explain" economic evolution always seems to occur *after* the event when the movement of expenditure categories has already been observed. The arbitrariness of the procedure is, of course, fully reflected by the fact that every author can easily find "his own real event." So long as the "real conditions" are not integrated into a systematic movement persistently operating as repetitive patterns in contexts of cyclic evolution, or of economic declines or major economic declines, we can only conclude that the minimal requirements of an empirical hypothesis are not satisfied. The ex post facto search for nonmonetary conditions confirms with its futility so far the conjecture that the allocative real events emphasized remain essentially random with respect to the evolution of aggregate nominal demand. This conclusion remains also quite provisional and tentative. It is not impossible that some venturesome and skilled researchers may find some real conditions contributing systematically to the movements of aggregate nominal demand.

The role of the Hawley-Smoot tariff also deserves some attention among the candidates for nonmonetary influences shaping the Great Depression. This massive tariff legislation produced three distinct consequences: It redistributed wealth among different domestic groups; it lowered the marginal product of real capital; and it unleashed deflationary feedback impulses on the U.S. economy via the international repercussions on U.S. exports. The first effect could affect stock market values only to the extent that negatively affected firms are dominantly incorporated, whereas positively affected firms (by the pure distribution effect) are dominantly unincorporated. This is hardly the case in a state with agriculture operating as the major export industry. The second effect would lower real stock values but only by a fraction of the 20 percent observed over the September-April period. Under no circumstances could it explain the decline from 237 to 35 in the Standard and Poor index over the full period. The decline in the marginal product of capital could hardly exceed a few percentage points. Neither of the first two effects can thus explain the decline in velocity observed over the first year of the depression. The decline in the expected rate of real return on real capital in Italy during the 1970s may have substantially exceeded this effect of the Hawley-Smoot tariff without triggering a Great Depression. The last effect, on the other hand, did lower domestic velocity. The definition of velocity used in equation (1) implies that the induced decline of the foreign money stock, the vast adjustments of exchange rates, and increasing protectionism contributed to depress velocity. But this effect did not initiate the Great Depression. It did not operate as an initiating causal impulse but worked as a reinforcing deflationary condition on the ongoing process.

Motivation of the Search and Some Interpretation of Results

This state of search for nonmonetary events responsible for at least some major phases of the Great Depression should be pondered in the context of the motivation for this search. The Gordon-Wilcox study elaborates the motivation with particular explicitness. The large decline in velocity is judged to offer prima facie evidence of nonmonetary forces at work. This judgment was buttressed by the simulation results which determined that only 25 percent of the decline in nominal income observed over the first two years could be attributed to negative monetary shocks. There remained for these two years, according to this count, a 75 percent margin still to be explained. Gordon and Wilcox cite in this context Gottfried Haberler's strictures against "single cause" explanations. Obviously, multiple causes seem more "realistic." There is, however, no justification for this a priori belief arbitrarily qualifying possible research strategies.

A strategy expressing our cognitive groping to understand reality begins usefully with broad and simple hypotheses. Complications need be justified in terms of the "cognitive leverage" achieved with their aid or in terms of their "cognitive marginal productivity." The current state of more or less nonmonetary explanations establishes in my judgment that the "unexplained residual" remains in fact at the moment unexplained, at least with respect to the particular monetary explanation formulated by Gordon and Wilcox. There emerges at this point, beyond the partial explanation achieved by the monetary impulse hypothesis, no relevant, systematic, and even provisionally assessed contribution from nonmonetary conjectures. The occurrence of substantial residuals poses a challenge but offers no evidence concerning the systematic operation of other events.

The monetary approach fully appreciates, as indicated before, that the stochastic process governing velocity, conditioned on monetary growth patterns, exhibits some broad "looseness" revealed by a conditional variance. It follows that a monetary explanation successfully accounts for direction and some orders of magnitude of the phenomenom. But the degree of approximation to the observed magnitude may also be quite rough on many occasions. It appears most natural to explore systematic explanations for the unexplained rest. One will surmise that the observed "stochastic looseness" reveals the operation of other and neglected factors at work. It may also reflect an inadequate formulation of the monetary mechanism, or result from shifting policy regimes, or simply describe the ineradicable stochastic nature of basic economic relations. We will never know the answer with any certainty. We may attempt, however, at any moment to assess our views. It appears to me at this stage that nothing has been gained so far beyond the available monetary explanation. The "unexplained rest" has not been effectively addressed by references to a moving array of autonomous changes in more or less conveniently selected expenditure categories. These explorations pose at the moment a challenge and define a potential research program.

The state of our research efforts was clearly recognized in my judgment by Friedman and Schwartz (1963) and Schwartz (1981). When Schwartz concluded that a monetary account seems preferable to a nonmonetary account, she made a purely *comparative* statement. It is a position that remains essentially agnostic with respect to the nonmonetary factors stressed by others. Such factors may be hidden in the variance of the monetary relation. The same position seems to be stated, as I understand it, in a statement advanced by Friedman and Schwartz and quoted by Gordon and Wilcox that the events observed could possibly involve the operation of autonomous nonmonetary factors affecting velocity.

Some previous remarks already anticipated the range of interpretations consistent with the regressions presented by Gordon and Wilcox. A more explicit attention is required, however. Zellner and Palm (1974) have shown that any multiple linear-time-series process can be decomposed or transformed into a set of ARIMA processes, one for each variable in the multiple process. When this result is applied to the special case of structural models, we obtain solutions for each endogenous variable in the form of an ARIMA process with transfer functions containing the exogenous vector of the system. The solution appears thus in the form

$$a(L)y_t = b(L)x_t + c(L)e_t,$$

where y is an endogenous state variable, x is a vector of exogenous variables, and e is a vector of random disturbances operating on the system. $a(L)$ is a polynomial in the lag operator defining the autoregressive part. It is identical for all endogenous variables of any given system and is specified by the system's determinant. $b(L)$ and $c(L)$ are row vectors in polynomials determined by the system's structure.

The formulation of Gordon and Wilcox appears as a special case of the above formula with the x-vector curtailed to money and all coefficients attached to lag operators in $c(L)$ equated to zero. Some reflections related to previous arguments indicate that the interpretation of the regression results are not unambiguous. Four possible cases can be distinguished:

1. The true variance of the stochastic term is sufficiently large.
2. The sampling error associated with a short sample creates substantial simulation residuals.
3. Changes in policy regime from the sample period to the simulation period modify the structure expressed by the lag polynomials $a(L)$, $b(L)$, and $c(L)$.
4. Some relevantly operating exogenous variables were omitted.

Gordon and Wilcox settled on interpretation (4) and proceeded with their search for the neglected exogenous nonmonetary factors. It would have been useful in this context to include actually some measure of consumers' expenditures determined by autonomous stock market changes with some measure for autonomous construction expenditure in the regressions used. Meltzer emphasizes in his comment, most particularly for the halting recovery 1938–40, the operation of aspect (3) mentioned above. A vast array of institutional changes and the emergence of a wide range of new policies created pervasive information problems and corresponding uncertainties. They particularly affected, according to this conjecture, the expected real rate of return on real assets. Such developments lowered velocity and thus compressed the net magnitude of the monetary stimulus. The operation of this process would be revealed by increasing errors produced by the simulation analysis. But these errors, by themselves, do not discriminate between interpretation (4) offered by Gordon and Wilcox and Meltzer's interpretation (3). Additional evidence needs to be examined for this purpose, and this would require a detailed study of this period and the impact of institutional and policymaking innovations in the public sector on the behavior of the private sector.

Initiating Causes and Accompanying Conditions

It appears on occasion that discussions about the role of monetary and nonmonetary influences on the business cycle are hampered by some shifting meaning of the terms used. Consider for purposes of clarification an autonomous decline in velocity produced by a negative real shock of one kind or another. This induces under given monetary arrangements an endogenous decline of the money stock. Such a situation appears to justify a "nonmonetary explanation" of the depression and in a sense it does. But we should also consider the question whether a change in monetary regime could prevent the endogenous response $\Delta m < 0$ to the fall in velocity.

Two situations need to be distinguished here. We partition at the moment $\Delta m = \Delta\mu + \Delta\beta$ where μ designates the log of the monetary multiplier and β the log of the monetary base. In one case a change in regime produces a positive $\Delta\beta$ in response to $\Delta v < 0$ so that $\Delta m + \Delta v > \Delta v < 0$. In the other case, any positive $\Delta\beta$ only produces offsetting (further) declines of μ and v, so that aggregate demand ($\Delta\beta + \Delta\mu + \Delta v$) is unaffected by any changes in the policy regime. Monetary conditions clearly operate in the first case with a significant role even in the context of an autonomous nonmonetary shock. The same shock produces very different results under alternative monetary processes shaping Δm. The second case describes, on the other hand, a world where monetary arrangements cannot possibly modify the business-cycle process determined by nonmonetary conditions and driven by nonmonetary shocks. This "real" theory of business cycles implies that monetary events and arrangements are but epiphenomena of real processes that can be safely neglected in any examination of cyclic episodes.

A discussion of the comparative role of monetary and nonmonetary conditions need thus distinguish between initiating shocks and accompanying conditions. This recognition seems implicit in the argument advanced by Gordon and Wilcox pertaining to the potency of monetary policy. The relevance of accompanying monetary conditions is equivalent to their *potential* operation as initiating shocks. Any explanation of selected cyclic episodes needs to attend beyond the discussion of nonmonetary shocks to an examination of monetary arrangements reinforcing or attenuating the process unleashed by the negative shock. The exemplary study by Friedman and Schwartz of the banking failures and associated institutional or policy issues seems essentially guided by such a view. Even in the context of an open issue concerning the nature of the initiating shock there still remains room for a careful appraisal of the role of monetary conditions affecting the subsequent process.

Our argument applies, of course, to the reverse situation and naturally qualifies the meaning of a "monetary explanation." Meltzer's interpretation of the stock market events and the recovery period of 1938–40 reveals the relevant point. Suppose one accepts on good grounds the operation of an initiating monetary shock. The impact of this stimulus on putput and prices will be affected by nonmonetary conditions. These conditions link in Meltzer's example the monetary evolution with the break in the stock market and influenced the magnitude of the decline. They probably contributed to the emergence of runs on banks and the ensuing banking failures. We find some evidence for such influences in the chapter on the Great Depression published by Friedman and Schwartz (1963).

Meltzer's argument pertaining to the comparatively poor recovery beyond 1937 noted by Gordon and Wilcox should alert us, however, to a subtle but important difference. Proponents of a monetary explanation tend to emphasize a different range of relevant nonmonetary conditions, both as shocks and modifying circumstances, than do advocates of (more or less) nonmonetary explanations. The latter search for autonomous shocks in expenditure categories, and the former invoke more frequently real shocks (including institutional changes and sociopolitical factors) that modify incentives on labor markets, affect output suppliers, or change the expected real yields on real assets. It would appear that this range of issues still deserves some attention in future business-cycle research.

On Reverse Causation

Occurrence and interpretation of "reverse causation" from income to the money stock involves arguments closely tied to the previous paragraphs. Both Gordon and Wilcox and Temin touch on these issues but in a somewhat different context.

The occurrence of "reverse causation" cannot discriminate per se between the two worlds experiencing nonmonetary shocks considered in the previous section. The comments advanced by Gordon and Wilcox are quite explicit in this context. Two aspects need be considered here: There is first the question of occurrence and magnitude of reverse causation; and second, there is also the issue pertaining to the appropriate interpretation of the phenomenon. The accumulated evidence about the position of money in the economic nexus rather thoroughly rejects at this stage the *pure* nonmonetary thesis of the business cycle. Gordon and Wilcox and Meltzer concur in this assessment. The pure nonmonetary thesis implies that Δm is endogenously determined by autonomous influences operating via Δv. It denies, furthermore, that Δm could potentially emerge as a major autonomous force shaping the business cycle. The rejection of this thesis means that any occurrence of reverse causation thus addresses our attention to the monetary conditions that produce this pattern. This examination should also reveal the nature of arrangements that minimize reverse causation.

An examination of various European countries (France, Belgium, Germany, Spain) suggests that reverse causation dominantly results from the prevailing arrangements governing the supply of base money and seems less influenced by processes shaping the movement of the monetary multiplier. But such arrangements can be changed, and a survey of different countries and different periods indicates that the supply of base money can be regulated by radically different regimes. Such changes modify the role of reverse causation and most particularly modify or even remove amplifying responses of Δm to autonomous variations in velocity. Monetary policy understood in a broader sense subsuming attention to institutional arrangements can thus affect the business cycle. But the circumstances also allow expansionary actions in the narrower sense and actively raise the monetary base and offset any autonomous (or induced) decline in velocity. The opportunity for effective action of this kind persists into the depression once one dismisses the *pure* nonmonetary explanation on the ground of its incompatibility with accumulated evidence.

But the actual occurrence of relevant reverse causation still requires our attention. Temin explains the monetary deceleration in the early phase as a pure case of reverse causation. This thesis is a necessary block in his denial of any role assignable to initiating monetary shocks. Temin simply dismisses at this point evidence in the form of Granger tests presented by Gordon and Wilcox and Schwartz. The only justification offered is the proxy character of bank debits used by Schwartz and the poor relation of bank debits with cyclic turning points. But both Gordon and Wilcox and Schwartz use other measures of economic activity. Temin's case, however, is not supported by a detailed analysis of the money supply process, which would locate the crucial mechanisms producing the reverse causation. Proponents of a nonmonetary thesis seem often inclined to invoke reverse causations with little attention to the properties of the money-supply process. Some regressions produced by Gordon and Wilcox offer an ambiguous case in this context. Most of the weight of the coefficients is concentrated at current values of income and money. This pattern seems consistent with a large operation of reverse causation. But major events affecting the money stock over the period sampled can hardly be interpreted as examples of reverse causation. We note in this context the accelerations of the base due to politically induced gold inflows, or the gold inflow triggered by the devaluation, the turnaround in the movement of the currency ratio after the "Bank Holidays" in 1933, and lastly, the open-market purchases raising the base in response to a congressional ultimatum in the spring of 1932. A detailed study of money-supply processes in the United States appears to raise substantial doubts about the dominant operation of reverse causation over an intermediate run. Moreover, whatever magnitudes of reverse causation occur result from specific and modifiable institutional arrangements or policy procedures governing the supply of base money.

The Perspective of the *IS–LM* Framework

Temin's insistence on reverse causation and his dismissal of initiating or autonomous monetary shocks are ultimately grounded in his analytic perception formulated in terms of the traditional *IS–LM* apparatus. This framework conditioned Temin's vision and interpretation. It contains, however, structural problems disregarded in the discussion that seriously condition the interpretation of the data.

The interpretation of the *IS–LM* approach has traditionally been ambiguous. A "Hicksian" interpretation opposes a "Metzlerian" interpretation. According to the former view, money substitutes only with financial assets but not with real assets. The alternative view recognizes that money substitutes over the full range of assets. Real assets and money are substitutes and so are money and nonmoney financial assets or nonmoney financial assets and real assets. The Metzlerian interpretation combines the unconstrained range of substitutions for money with the assumption of "perfect substitutability" between real and nonmoney financial assets. This assumption is hardly to be understood in any literal sense. This would be too obviously false. It should be understood as an artifice to squeeze a three-asset world into a framework fitted for two assets (money and nonmoney). "Perfect substitutability" really refers to a composite good. It confines, therefore, useful application of the framework to periods with comparatively negligible changes in relative yields between nonmoney financial and real assets. The alternative interpretations implicitly involve, furthermore, very different specification of the "rate of interest" occurring in the *IS* or the *LM* relation (Brunner 1971).

These aspects embedded in the *IS–LM* framework are not sufficiently recognized in the literature. They undermine, under either interpretion, the relevance of Temin's framework as an analytic guide to understand the Great Depression or, more generally, the broad contours of business-cycle phenomena. The "Hicksian" interpretation cannot be reconciled with the facts suggesting a range of substitution for money reaching beyond financial assets to include goods. The evidence drawn from inflation (or deflation) experiences of countries with (at best) rudimentary "money" or capital markets (Turkey, Israel, Belgium, the Netherlands, Korea, South America, and others) is hard to reconcile with a "Hicksian" substitution pattern. It appears that the "Hicksian" interpretation expresses a somewhat parochial "City of London syndrome." The Metzlerian interpretation is confined, on the other hand, to episodes of moderate relative yield changes. But these conditions hardly fit the Great Depression, during which large changes in relative risks and gross yields between groups of assets occurred. The neglect of these yield changes blurs the vision of the ongoing process and falsifies the story in essential respects.

Temin's argument shifts on occasion between the two interpretations. He concludes a passage devoted to the nature of the transmission mechanism outlined by Friedman and Schwartz with the statement that "deficient money balances are made up by sales of a variety of assets, among which financial assets are included." This interpretation is not compatible with a "Hicksian" notion of the transmission of monetary shocks. Just before the quoted sentence Temin propounds that the range of substitution involving money poses no relevant issue in our context. It forms, on the contrary, a crucial issue in order to evaluate Temin's evidential procedure. Most of the time Temin adheres, however, to a Hicksian interpretation. This occurs, for instance, in the context of his argument criticizing Schwartz's explanation why short-term rates of interest in 1930–31 failed to rise in response to a negative monetary shock. Schwartz emphasized in this context the institutional link between bank reserves, or the supply of base money, and some categories of short-term instruments. An increasing uncertainty about reserve flows was translated under the institutional circumstances prevailing into a rising demand for short-term assets. The institutional link between the supply of base money and short-term financial assets thus prevented the rise in short-term interest rates. Temin argues at this point that the "perverse behavior" of interest rates, produced under Schwartz's "institutional" explanation, suspended the connection between the real and the monetary sector. Temin concludes that "the failure of interest rates to rise . . . shows that the banking panics did not have the macroeconomic effect" claimed by the monetary explanation. Whatever negative monetary shock may have occurred could not be communicated to the real sector. It was effectively blocked by the failure of short rates to rise. This argument is, of course, only acceptable for the Hicksian world denying any transmission channels beyond the short-term rates and the term structure relation.[4]

This interpretation of Temin's argument is confirmed by the fact that the only transmission channels considered by the author reaching beyond interest rates on financial assets center on real balances and the expected rate of deflation. Both channels operate as shifts of the *IS* curve induced by monetary events. But this expectational channel is discounted by Temin (and also by Gordon and Wilcox). The Pigovian real balance effect vanishes to negligible proportions when properly placed in the context of a complete asset position. The choice of a short-term interest rate in the central argument denying the occurrence of any monetary shock over the period 1929–31 only makes sense in the context of a Hicksian view. This choice of interest rate as an independent variable of money demand requires, however, the addition of a term structure relation. The *IS* relation involves by general consensus a long-term real rate. Temin's analysis thus remains incomplete in the absence of the term structure relation. This relation introduces an additional element beyond "the expected rate of deflation" shifting the *IS* curve. If the turning point is accompanied by an (algebraic) increase in the spread between long and short rates, an additional channel operates to lower the *IS* curve. We note also in passing that Temin's reservation bearing on the efficacy of an expansionary monetary policy during a depression results from the Hicksian perception of the transmission mechanism. Once "the interest rate" is pushed to the minimal level where marginal yields are fully absorbed by transaction costs, monetary policy becomes impotent under this view. But this impotency is conditioned by the exclusion of other transmission channels beyond substitution with short-term liquid assets or even the range of financial assets.

The observation set motivating Temin's proposition that the first half of the Great Depression was the result of nonmonetary shocks centers on declining interest rates and rising real balances. These observations by themselves offer, however, no useful evidence. We note first an interesting counterpart to Temin's observation set: rising prices, rising interest rates, and falling real balances. This combination, characterizing pronounced inflationary accelerations, was frequently adduced by officials as "evidence" of a restrictive monetary policy. The comparison should not be pressed too much in the present context. The inflationary case depends crucially on the operation of expected price movements. These expectations were probably less pronounced in the early phases of the Great Depression than during highly inflationary episodes. Still, Meltzer argues that prices moved already before the turning point along a declining trend. The emergence of a sharp reversal in economic affairs around the middle of 1929 may have raised the anticipated rate of deflation and contributed to shift the *IS* curve leftward.

The repercussions unleashed by banking panics need not be confined to price expectations. The first banking panic expressed by a jump in the currency ratio lowered the money stock. The same uncertainties and expectations producing $\Delta m < 0$ probably also affected velocity. The monetary deceleration produced by the banking panic was reinforced, under the circumstances, by a decline of velocity. The resulting fall in aggregate nominal demand substantially affected the movement of prices at this stage. Rising real balances can thus be reconciled with the occurrence of a negative monetary shock.

The clarification of the analytic conditioning behind Temin's argument, however, requires a more explicit examination. The extension of analysis beyond the confines of *IS–LM* to a three-asset world involving substitutions of money in all directions shows that a falling interest rate can be consistently reconciled with the operation of a negative monetary shock. My argument uses the Brunner-Meltzer model of asset-market interaction supplemented with the output equation. Asset markets determine interest rate and the price on real assets in response to the prevailing stock values (monetary base, government debt) and expectations (of the rate of deflation, net real returns on real assets). The demand for output depends on nonhuman and human wealth, price level of output, price of real assets, and interest rate. A solution of the asset markets for the price of real assets in terms of the (relative to the asset markets) predetermined variables can be used to replace the asset price in the output market and the money market equation. The three-asset system is thus reduced to the standard form of *IS–LM*. The substitution over the full range of assets creates, however, interdependencies between the *IS* and *LM* curves neglected by the standard formulation. We note that a reduction in the monetary base shifts simultaneously both curves to the left.

An analytic examination summarized in the appendix establishes that the negative monetary shock *simultaneously* produces a fall in output and interest rate *provided* that the response of the price level for real assets to the monetary shock produced by the interaction on asset markets is sufficiently large and the negative monetary shocks are perceived by agents as a dominantly transitory event. These conditions are sufficient to produce a leftward shift of *IS* substantially exceeding the leftward shift of *LM*. The intersection point drifts toward the southwest. Temin's observation set is, under the circumstances, stated consistent with the occurrence of an autonomous monetary shock.

THE AGGREGATE-SUPPLY BEHAVIOR

The movement of the demand line in the price-output plane is not sufficient to explain the major contours of the Great Depression. Form and behavior of aggregate supply crucially affect the resulting patterns. The movement of the demand line determines the evolution of the nominal expenditures and income but cannot by itself explain the behavior of output or employment. Aggregate supply converts the nominal changes into price adjustments and output movements. Cagan emphasizes in his comments that we still need an adequate explanation of the price movements observed during the Great Depression. Many observers felt that the partial response of prices (and wages) to the persistent decline in nominal expenditures, expressed by a persistent negative vertical intercept of the demand line, reflected a major institutional problem. This interpretation contributed to the emergence of views that prices are "noncompetitively administered" with tenuous and uncertain adjustment to the state of the markets. The noteworthy increase in prices and wages after 1933 at a time of massive unemployment and excess capacity deepened the puzzle or reinforced the notion that prices and wages fail to behave in the manner presumed by economic theory. The experiences observed suggested a comparatively flat supply line in the diagram with slow and at best small adjustments of the vertical intercept Δp_1. Fluctuations in the demand line are naturally translated into variations of output with relatively small changes in the price level.

Keynes (1936) confronted the problem in the initial chapters of his *General Theory*. He interpreted the phenomenon on the labor market as a clear expression of "market failure." The market failed to produce an efficient solution to society's employment problem. The suppliers' marginal disutility of work "was clearly" much lower than the marginal product of labor. Pervasive opportunities existed for socially beneficial transactions that apparently were not exploited under voluntary arrangements. This interpretation essentially eroded the concept of a labor supply expressing a supplier's optimal allocation of his personal resources. At least for the shorter-run analysis, covering in this sense the business cycle, labor market phenomena seem demand determined and hardly involve any substantial interaction between demand and supply. Variations in employment over the shorter run reflect only to a minor extent movements along a supply curve representing underlying optimizing behavior. They reflect variations in demand along an institutionally fixed price-wage combination. The state points produced by the system in this manner typically occur "off" the "optimizing" supply curve. The latter may retain its relevance for very long-run aspects of an economy.

This scheme determines an obvious classification of unemployment. Changes along the supply curve involve variations in voluntary unemployment, whereas the distance between the state point and the supply curve expresses occurrence and magnitude of involuntary unemployment. The extension of the *IS–LM* framework to include a Phillips relation in order to explain price-wage movements did not modify the basic interpretation of the labor markets incorporated into the Keynesian tradition. This view reinforced, moreover, the denial of any self-correcting properties of the price-wage mechanism associated with the original analysis developed by Keynes. Such denials occur within the Keynesian tradition in two forms. In one form it follows from the proposition that the private sector is inherently unstable and without any self-correcting properties. The other strand admits the operation of self-correcting mechanisms. This recognition is qualified, however, with the view that its operation extends beyond any politically relevant or acceptable time horizon. We note in passing that Gordon and Wilcox interpret the behavior of prices during the downswing and the upswing as evidence supporting the denial of a price-wage mechanism with self-correcting properties.

The combination of a comparatively flat supply line and a volatile demand line certainly traces the broad contours of the business cycle in terms of output, price level, and nominal expenditures. But this explanation is bought at some costs. The Phillips relation has never been satisfactorily established, and the accumulated evidence remains remarkably tenuous (Santomero and Seater 1978). The underlying interpretation in terms of state points "off the labor suppliers" optimal-market combinations is inconsistent with a central building block of economic analysis. This state is clearly reflected in recent years by the attempts to explain the drift in Δp_1 over time or the large variations in

Δp_1 between different episodes or between countries by invoking shifting assortments of social entities or categories not subsumable under a systematic economic analysis. This analysis is anchored in a central building block, formulated by the model of a "resourceful, evaluating, maximizing man" (Meckling 1976). The building block still forms the most promising perceptions of man as a means to understand our social reality (Brunner and Meckling 1977). Thus emerged a new impetus to reconcile the observations of the labor market with a systematic economic analysis incorporating an explicit supply behavior. The work of Lucas and Rapping (1969) should be noted in this context as a much criticized pioneering piece. Subsequent work by Lucas, Sargent, and others contributed to the development of an equilibrium approach. This approach was constructed in order to interpret the observations as the result of an interaction between demand and supply reflecting optimizing behavior. This means in our context that the vertical intercept Δp_1 of the supply line is not left hanging outside the nexus of economic analysis but is integrated into a context of optimizing behavior.

These issues are most explicitly examined in the paper prepared by Gordon and Wilcox. The authors emphasize that our understanding of the Great Depression requires an adequate explanation of price-wage behavior. They explore in particular two specific alternative conjectures. One formulation expresses an "equilibrium aggregate supply" in a form suggested by Lucas and Sargent and previously investigated by Darby. The other formulation incorporates a traditional Phillips relation. The equilibrium aggregate supply explains unemployment or output relative to "normal output" as a function of actual relative to an expected price level. The latter magnitude is formed according to a standard adaptive scheme anchored in 1924. Gordon and Wilcox conclude, on good grounds apparently, that neither formulation offers an acceptable explanation of price behavior. The reestimation of Darby's "Lucas supply function" yields a high sensitivity of real variables to current prices. It is noteworthy that the estimates determine a slope of around unity for the supply line in our previous diagram. They also imply, however, that the vertical intercept, Δp_1, hardly moved over the Great Depression. This follows from the astonishing length of the mean expectation lag (infinite for one set of unemployment data, and nine years for another set). The estimates imply in particular that the anticipated price level remained close to the 1924 level. The supply line in the diagram would thus stay throughout the decade near the intersection of the two axes. Price-output changes result from the gyrations of the demand line along a comparatively stable supply line.

Gordon and Wilcox are properly skeptical about this result. They note in particular that arguments assigning significance to the difference between nominal and real interest rates during the period under consideration are difficult to reconcile without arbitrary artifices with the immense expectations of lag. Furthermore, this expectation of lag appears hardly compatible with any sensible behavior of "resourcefully evaluating" agents observing over four years successive waves of declining nominal demand and price levels.

The reservation about the Phillips relation is more immediately anchored in the poor statistical results. There emerges no significant relation between price *changes* and the *level* of unemployment or the level of relative output whenever *changes* in unemployment or *changes* in relative output are included. Gordon and Wilcox thus find no support for the traditional Phillips relation but do note a strong support for relations connecting changes in price level with changes in output, or between price level and level of output. This result confirms a prior result developed by Meltzer (1977).

Useful exploration of aggregate supply behavior may well begin with the observation pattern noted by Gordon and Wilcox and Meltzer. The relation imposes some constraints on the slope of supply and the joint shifts of demand and supply lines. The interpretation of "sticky" or "inflexible" prices and wages usually emerging from Keynesian contexts presents the phenomenon as a reflection of a market failure. This inflexibility in the price system prohibits market clearing and produces excess supplies of labor and output. The analytic foundation for the statement that prices and wages are inflexible remained, however, singularly vague. The context of the discussion suggests that "inflexibility" was revealed by insufficient adjustments of prices to changes in market conditions. A flexible adjustment would have, according to the apparent lessons of classical price theory, absorbed all ongoing shocks into price changes and consequently avoided any excess supplies on labor and output markets. The occurrence of such excess supplies offered prima facie evidence of inflexibility in the price system with associated inefficiencies in the private coordination of productive activities. Comparative inflexibility, therefore, seems properly expressed by a sloping line imposing movements of the state point away from the vertical axis in response to shifting nominal demand. Such inflexibility thus appears as a sufficient condition for the conversion of nominal impulses into fluctuations of real variables.

Henry Thornton recognized this pattern in the most explicit terms. Recent analytic work inspired by Lucas demonstrated, however, that "inflexible" or "sticky" prices are not a necessary condition for the transmission of nominal shocks into movements of output and employment. This equilibrium or market-clearing approach also establishes that nonmarket clearing is not necessary to explain variations in real variables. In particular, this market-clearing analysis yields implications consistent with the general pattern of the Gordon-Wilcox-Meltzer results. It is noteworthy in this context that real phenomena usually associated with "inflexible prices" are explainable, to some extent, in terms of market clearing and flexible prices. This flexibility means that market prices are continuously and completely adjusted to any underlying shocks operating on the economy. This approach establishes that incomplete information about the ongoing shocks, if not the shock structure itself, is a necessary condition for a link between nominal and real movements.

The classical dichotomy between nominal and real patterns was typically produced by an implicit assumption of full information. Nominal shocks were fully absorbed by the price level. The information problem of the Lucas schema centers on differences in the accrual of information bearing on local and aggregate market conditions. Agents know the contemporaneous local price but obtain aggregate information with a lag. It follows that agents encounter difficulties in the interpretation of observed price movements. The nature of the incomplete information makes it impossible to discriminate correctly between allocative and aggregative components of price changes or between real and nominal shocks. Global shocks affecting the aggregative price level are misinterpreted as relative price changes. This information pattern implies that the nature of the shock structure determines the division of nominal impulses between prices and output. The crucial aspects in this approach producing the Gordon-Wilcox-Meltzer relation between Δp and Δy (or Δx) depends on the variance of aggregate relative to the variance of allocative shocks (Barro 1976, 1979a).

The explanation of the prevailing persistence patterns exhibited by real variables requires special attention in the equilibrium approach. They can be accommodated with the aid of particular specifications of preferences and technology (Sargent 1979). There is also the problem of relating measured unemployment to categories contained in the analysis. The Keynesian differentiation between voluntary and involuntary unemployment loses content and meaning in this context (Lucas and Rapping 1969; Lucas 1978). The information structure centered on the inference concerning real and nominal shocks yields no rationale for the pervasive occurrence of more or less explicit contractual arrangements involving prices and wages. We seem to observe that price-wage changes do involve revisions in some dimensions of such arrangements. Lastly, the whole structure rests on empirically rather weak foundations. In the absence of any differential between local and global, or allocative and aggregate information, any connection between nominal shocks and the real sector is suspended. We obtain, therefore, the classic full information result with the partition between nominal and real aspects of an economy. The public supply of data about the aggregate state of a modern economy within a comparatively short time horizon undermines, it would appear, the relevance of the information structure shaping this particular form of the equilibrium approach.

The contract theory may appear to open opportunities for an alternative equilibrium approach (Azariadis 1975; Sargent 1979). This theory explains the rational emergence of fixed wages in the context of a specific kind of uncertainty confronting risk-averse employees and risk-neutral employers. The structure of the problem implies that every contract with variable wages adjusted to the prevailing state is dominated by a fixed-wage contract. The contract theory thus appears to explain comparatively inflexible wages based on a resourcefully optimizing behavior. Barro pointed out, however, that the Azariadis-Baily contract theory yields essentially the same employment patterns as the flexible wage equilibrium approach. He concludes that ''rather than rationalizing the non-market clearing model as a useful 'as if' approach contracting analysis suggests that—despite the possible existence of 'sticky' wages and prices—the continuous market clearing model may provide a satisfactory framework for the analysis of employment and output'' (Barro 1976b).

A further inspection of the Azariadis-Baily contract model reveals the location of the crucial problem. We note first the difficulties encountered for any explanation of ''inflexibility'' by this approach. Firms exhibiting a systematic risk-neutral behavior on the labor market would have to proceed in a randomly risk-averse sense on the output market. Alternatively, price inflexibility emerges from a mechanical mark-up link with inflexible wages. More important, however, is the fact that the analysis yields no statement about inflexibility of *nominal* wages. It derives a statement about the inflexibility of an *allocative* or *relative* real wage in particular branches of the economy. The uncertainty confronting agents (firms and labor suppliers) concerns purely allocative aspects expressed by variations of the firm's nominal output price over an array of unpredictable states *relative* to a perceived *given* aggregate price level. The nominal wage varies between the possible states relative to an ''externally determined'' aggregate nominal wage. The information structure built into the contract model differs substantially from the Lucas-Phelps information pattern. Agents are uncertain about the allocative state and possess full information about the aggregate state. But this aggregate remains outside the analysis and, consequently, also the problem of global price-output adjustments in response to nominal shocks. The insights offered by the ''contract theory'' (e.g., ex post deviations between marginal product of labor, marginal value of leisure, and real wage under efficient solutions) are not negligible, but they do not help us to understand aggregate supply behavior. The specific ''contract theory'' considered here is consistent with a structure producing the classical dichotomy of nominal and real aspects of an economy. This dichotomy holds whenever the aggregate price-wage level fully reflects the prevailing nominal shocks imparted on the economy.

This conclusion and the seminal contribution made by Lucas determine the crucial role of incomplete information. Full information about the economic structure and the realizations produced by a stochastic process necessarily disconnect the real sector from any monetary shocks. These shocks are fully absorbed under the circumstances of full information by the price level (and the aggregate wage level). We need to explore the model of incomplete information best suited, in our judgment and at this state, for the development of a better understanding of supply behavior in the context of an aggregative analysis addressed to the business cycle. The allocative-aggregative information differential, frequently identified with a rational expectations analysis or a Lucas-Sargent supply function, has already been noted. An alternative specification of the information problem may usefully exploit Milton Friedman's central idea, thus anchoring his theory of the consumption function. Agents are confronted with pervasive changes in conditions exhibiting different duration or persistence. The crucial differences in persistence patterns exhibited by underlying shocks affecting people's behavior are roughly approximated by the binary distinction between "permanent" and "transitory" conditions. Friedman emphasized that agents' real consumption plans are dominated by their perception of more durable, permanent conditions, whereas transitory shocks are essentially absorbed by asset accumulations (or decumulations). The notion was extended by Lucas and Rapping (1969) to the labor market. They argued that the labor supplier will respond very differently to a perceived permanent change in the real wage than to a presumed transitory change in the current real wage.

A generalization of Friedman's original idea seems to offer a useful approach to the explanation of aggregate supply behavior. It refers to a much more pervasive and fundamental information problem than the confusion between local and global information. Agents face continuously shifting conditions shaping the economic process. Variations in monetary growth, productivity, foreign impulses, and institutions modifying expected net yields of various assets affect the course of events. Agents will consider different actions in accordance with their perception of the nature of the shocks. Resourceful agents thus cope continuously with a basic inference problem posed by nature and the social process. They cannot observe or measure in any direct fashion the "permanent" or "transitory" components of emerging shocks. But optimizing behavior requires that they assess in the best manner possible broad temporal patterns of prevailing shocks. They must infer the more permanent component embedded in the actually observed shocks from all the information available to them.

The rationale of this ongoing inference problem appears to follow from the costs associated with the spectrum of potential transaction. All transactions may be linked with or represented by some contractual arrangements. These arrangements cover a wide range reaching from a complicated cluster called a business firm to casual and passing understandings. They usually involve more or less implicit and frequently explicit agreements on aspects pertaining to shifting dimensions of the object transacted. The crucial aspect for our purpose is the link between the inference problem and the types of contractual arrangements. It has been argued that the firm emerges in response to the peculiar benefits of input combinations characterizing team production (Alchian and Demsetz 1972). But the substantial gain in output achieved by team production determined by essentially nonseparable production functions cannot be achieved without a substantial cost associated with the setting up of the required organization. The larger the transaction costs associated with the contractual cluster defining the firm, the longer becomes the relevant time horizon for the motivating output gain. Potential initiators of such arrangements respond, therefore, only to underlying changes that promise some degree of permanence. No actions are spurred in this matter by more or less transitory evolutions. Shortest-run transitory events modify, on the other hand, some current market behavior as they open opportunities for alert market participants not burdened with heavy transaction costs. An extensive array of contractual arrangements between the extremes thus influences crucial conditions governing ongoing transactions. These conditions frequently include prices and subsume probably most of the wages. Costs of transaction and information encountered by market participants induce a diversity of price-wage-setting behavior. Such behavior characterizes the price-searcher (nonauction) markets in contrast to the price-taker (auction) markets. The costs rationally inducing the patterns observed on nonauction markets also imply that price-wage setting is generally linked with the agents' perception of comparatively more permanent market conditions. The diversity of relevant cost considerations determines that the horizon underlying price-wage settings exhibits a corresponding variation. But whatever the horizon may be, the more or less explicit contractual arrangements associated with price-wage settings are conditioned by the agents' assessment of the ongoing shocks driving the economic process. These arrangements and the associated price (or wage) setting inherited at any moment thus reflect the inferences made at their initial formulation. They express the necessarily incomplete state of information available to the agents at the time when the contracts were determined. Market conditions subsequently deviate in general from the expectations originally guiding price-wage-setting behavior. Inferences derived from incomplete information about the realizations of transitory and permanent shocks yield a wedge between the expected permanent condition and its actual realization. This wedge emerges even in the context of full information concerning the underlying stochastic structure. It consists of the sum of a transitory component and the difference between the actual and expected permanent condition. The central inference problem is magnified in case the range of incomplete information extends beyond realizations and subsumes aspects of the stochastic shock structure. Expectations of permanent conditions appear as sample approximations to the true shock structure. Variations in this structure produced by shifting behavior of policy institutions further extend the uncertainty defining the agents' inference problem. As markets evolve, agents need substantial sampling via new information to interpret the actual evolution. Larger transitory changes built into the economic process rationally induce agents to assemble a larger volume of information before they revise inherited price-wage settings. Substantial sampling will be desired before contracts are revised with the sense that the nature of ongoing shocks has been radically altered.

The general idea may be stylized for our purpose with a very simple and rough approximation. A more detailed analysis of price-wage setting associated with the inference problem pertaining to the discernment between "permanent" and "transitory" shocks has been developed at some other occasions (Brunner, Cukierman, and Meltzer 1979). This analysis reconciles market clearing with the appearance of inflexible prices or wages and unemployment. It also reconciles rational expectations in the sense of systematic exploitation of available information with the occurrence of gradually adjusting prices. It explains the "shorter-run" nonneutrality of money within a context of "longer-run" neutrality. And lastly, it characterizes the "shorter run" in terms of the underlying shock structure and the associated resolution of the basic inference problem.

The present stylization is linked with the partition of price changes into the components Δp_1 and Δp_2. The second component contains all price movements associated with the agents' perception of more or less transitory events. These price movements summarize events on auction markets and shorter-run adjustments granted on nonauction markets in contexts of maintained contractual arrangements (discounts and premia on basic prices). The first component expresses, in the average, the agents' inference pertaining to the more permanent conditions controlling their activities. This is expressed by the formulation

$$\Delta p_{1t} = E_{t-1}[\Delta m_t + \Delta v_t - \Delta n y_t | I_{t-1}],$$

that is, the "permanent" component expresses agents' expectations of the trend in adjusted nominal demand on the basis of the relevant information I_{t-1} about the underlying processes available at the time. These "longer-run" expectations thus anchor a comparatively flat aggregate supply line.

The story unfolds at this stage as outlined by Anna Schwartz. A unique series of events never experienced with this persistence or magnitude radically altered the ongoing shocks governing Δm and possible Δv. This pattern imposed serious information problems on all agents. The information set and the corresponding inferences expressed by Δp_1 lagged substantially behind the events. The supply curve thus shifted down along the vertical but more slowly and by lesser amounts than the demand line. The unfamiliar persistence and magnitude of the negative shocks may have imposed something akin to an overload on the information-processing system operated by the market mechanism. The informational disarray possibly explains the comparatively slow shift in the supply line noted with a different formulation by Gordon and Wilcox (1981).[5] It may also have contributed to the shift in demand among different types of financial assets noted by Lindert. This analytic approach to the role of supply and the resulting price behavior thus emphasizes the operation of an essentially self-correcting price-wage mechanism subjected to a long series of shocks and increasing uncertainties produced by political institutions.

The rapid motion of the state point into the first quadrant after the final turning point in 1933 indicates a remarkably swift move of Δp into the positive range. Weinstein attributes this change and the consequent retardation of the real economic expansion (i.e., Δx) to the price-wage policies formulated by the National Recovery Act (NRA) imposed by the Roosevelt Administration from May 1933 until June 1935. Cagan cautiously agrees with some interesting reservations worth pondering. The regressions listed by Gordon and Wilcox also provide some support for this contention. The abolition of the NRA in the middle of 1935 once again changed the relevant information set and substantially moderated Δp as shown by the regression results supplied by Gordon and Wilcox. The NRA clearly obstructed the recovery. The upward shift of the demand line produced by monetary acceleration resulting from the devaluation and the rapid decline of the currency ratio was matched by a large upward shift of the supply line produced by the activities proceeding under the NRA.

A similar situation prevailed, according to Meltzer, in the recovery beyond 1938. The role of the NRA with respect to the aggregate supply line was, however, replaced over this period by rapidly expanding unionization. The increase in uncertainty associated with this new event may have lowered Δv and simultaneously accelerated for a while Δp_1. This nonmonetary shock thus offset partly the monetary expansion Δm. The upward shift in supply and the moderated increase in demand due to lower Δv raised Δp and lowered Δx.

REMAINING ISSUES AND FURTHER WORK

Gordon and Wilcox recognized the potential usefulness of international comparisons for a systematic assessment of alternative conjectures. Their figure 6 and table 9 are particularly instructive for our purposes. Figure 6 compares the movement of the price level and real income in the United States with an average over a group of European countries. Output fell from 1929 to the trough approximately three times more in the United States than in Europe. The price decline was also larger in the United States, but the margin was much smaller than in the case of output. According to the authors' graph, the decline in U.S. prices was about 83 percent of the decline in output, whereas the average decline of European prices (from 1929 to the trough) measured about 180 percent of the decline in output. The price decline per unit decline of output proceeded in Europe at approximately double the rate of the U.S. decline in prices.

These data pose an interesting problem, and they appear to suggest more competitive price responses to market conditions in Europe. The data and the questions induced by their patterns certainly deserve some careful attention in further work. An analysis of interrelated open countries actually yields the pattern observed by Gordon and Wilcox even in the absence of differential responsiveness of prices to output changes (or output to price changes). A large monetary decline in a central economy lowers the price level in all countries. The decline of the central country exceeds the magnitude of the decline in the rest of the world. The decline of the domestic price level, composed of "nontraded" and "traded goods" prices, relative to the output decline, is, under the circumstances, however, larger in the rest of the world than in the central economy. The results reported by Gordon and Wilcox do not necessarily reflect, therefore, a failure of the U.S. price mechanism. They may more nearly express the international interdependence of price movements associated with divergent domestic monetary shocks modifying the relative output movements in various countries.

The investigations required in this context need to examine in some detail a variety of countries with radically different monetary and exchange rate policies. The observations made in the context of such variations should eventually supply some new information bearing on the major conjectures under consideration. Lars Jonung's examination of the Swedish experience offers a useful contribution to the research still required for our purposes. Swedish real income fell from 1929 to 1933 by 8 percent, whereas it declined by 33 percent in the United States. Sweden clearly experienced an economic downswing over the period. It is noteworthy, however, that it began much later and was much milder than in the United States. Within one year of the trough, Swedish real income moved beyond the level of 1929. The economic decline in Sweden obviously never evolved into a Great Depression.

How did this happen? The data show that the depression in Sweden was essentially "imported." It was not initiated in Sweden by autonomous shocks either affecting monetary growth or domestic (private spending) velocity. The transmission of the depression into Sweden via the decline in Swedish exports appeared in the form of a substantial fall in the standard measure of velocity.

But this decline initiated no reverse causation on the money stock. An active policy maintained the money stock and actually held it from 1930–33 at 4 percent above the level observed in 1929. Swedish monetary policy thus prevented the collapse of the money stock experienced in the United States. This determined course of monetary policy dampened the impact of the Great Depression conveyed via Swedish exports. Industrial production for the domestic market fell by only 12 percent over the four-year period 1929–33, and industries producing consumer goods suffered only a 5 percent decline over the same period in contrast to a much larger decline in the United States and Germany.

The relative movement of wholesale and consumer prices is also informative for our purposes. The index of wholesale prices fell in Sweden over the period under consideration by 25 percent (United States: 31 percent). The wholesale price index contains a comparatively large share of "traded goods" or goods closely associated with "traded goods." The consumer price index, in contrast, contains a more substantial share of "nontraded goods." The discrepancy between the two price movements thus reflects the Swedish situation characterized by an export-induced depression imported from abroad and dampened by a deliberate domestic monetary policy. The combination produced a comparatively large decline in a broadly based price level when measured against the U.S. experience. This pattern reflected the combination of events occurring in Sweden and should not, by itself, be interpreted as a failure of the price mechanism in the United States.

The Swedish experience clearly contributes some evidence bearing on the issues discussed in previous sections. It directs our attention to a specific and important location of autonomous shocks modifying velocity of comparatively small and open economies. This shock operates via the demand for a country's exports. Whatever the origin of these shocks, they are autonomous relative to the small open economies affected. But we also learn from the Swedish experience that suitable monetary policy *can* disconnect any reverse causation, as Gordon and Wilcox explicitly noted. And lastly, we learn that the deliberate exploitation of the technical opportunities available to monetary policy did make the difference between a depression, imported from the center of the Great Depression, and a Great Depression.

Jonung's study about the Swedish experience demonstrates the potential contribution we can reasonably expect from further detailed studies of selected countries. Our information would particularly benefit in case our examination concentrates on countries with substantial differences in economic policies. Switzerland, Germany, France, and the United Kingdom offer in this respect some unexploited opportunities. Switzerland differs both from Sweden and the United States. Until 1932 it resembled more the Swedish development. An increase of the money stock produced by large gold inflows delayed the onset of the depression. But beyond 1932 the Swiss economy slid, in contrast to both Sweden and the United States, deeper into depression as a result of a monetary policy fixed with rigid determination on the maintenance of a traditional gold parity. The Swiss data thus confirm the lesson conveyed by the Swedish experience. The significant operation of monetary conditions and monetary policy modified the effect of the Great Depression emanating from the United States.

The program of comparative studies of selected countries with diverse experiences could usefully explore the open issues revealed in our recent discussions. The following list may not be complete but should contain some of the major contentions examined by interested parties:

1. *The nature of "autonomous" nonmonetary shocks.* The discussion revealed a major difference pertaining to the nature of "nonmonetary" events and conditions between advocates of a monetary and those of a "nonmonetary" explanation of the Great Depression. One group addresses the role of sociopolitical or institutional development affecting either monetary growth or velocity via their effects on relative yields over a spectrum of assets. The other group is more concerned with the determination of exogenous expenditure components. The discussion of the halting recovery beyond 1937 exemplifies the issue. Neither group seems to have presented its case sufficiently at this stage.

2. *Initiating shocks and conditions of the propagation mechanism.* The examination of monetary policy presented by Gordon and Wilcox, supplemented by Jonung's discussion of Swedish experience, contributed to clarify the role of monetary conditions occurring as initiating shocks or properties of the transmission mechanism. A consensus appears to have emerged in this context that recognizes the relevant operation of monetary conditions in both senses. Some analytic-empirical effort may still contribute to a better understanding of the propagation conditions affecting occurrence and magnitude of "reverse causation."

   The discrimination between initiating shocks and properties of the transmission mechanism, combined with the distinction made under the first point, bears on the adequacy of alternative explanation. Any "monetary explanation" requires specification of the nonmonetary conditions or events shaping the transmission mechanism or occurring as autonomous shocks. Similarly, "nonmonetary explanations" need to clarify the role of autonomous monetary shocks and the role of monetary conditions influencing the operation of the transmission mechanism. The thrust of the discussion suggests that more attention be invested into these aspects in the future. These efforts may on occasion involve not so much a basic revision of our substantive views as a more careful formulation or a more adequate analytic expression.

3. *An evaluation of the four interpretations.* Four alternative interpretations of the statistical regressions obtained by Gordon and Wilcox were mentioned earlier. These interpretations involve most particularly a search for reliable and systematic operations of "nonmonetary initiating shocks" as arguments in an explanation of the sharp decline in velocity. This search contrasts with the effort to interpret a portion of velocity changes as movements induced by monetary accelerations (decelerations) or unanticipated monetary changes. The suggestions advanced by Gordon and Wilcox deserve some closer examination with proper integration of their autonomous expenditure components into the transfer function approach elaborated by Zellner and Palm. A persistent failure to offer good grounds for the systematic operation of such "nonmonetary initiating shocks" strengthens ultimately the case for the first two interpretations.

4. *Analysis of supply and price behavior.* This field confronts us most probably with the most serious intellectual challenge. Gordon and Wilcox interpret the data to reveal the absence of any self-correcting behavior in the price mechanism. An alternative view emphasizes a persistent overload with autonomous monetary shocks imposed on the U.S. economy over the whole downswing, supplemented during the recovery phase by a series of negative nonmonetary shocks in the form of sociopolitical or institutional events. This issue is closely associated with the nature of the aggregate supply function and the relevant information structure shaping price and output responses.

An approach to this range of problems would extend our understanding beyond the singular historical event experienced under the name of the Great Depression. This research program addresses essentially our understanding of the "business cycle" and would promise a better assessment of the monetary and nonmonetary conditions and events controlling our future evolution.

APPENDIX: THE SHIFTS OF *IS* AND *LM* IN A THREE-ASSET WORLD

The analysis is based on the following three equations:

$$y_t = d[i_t - (Ep_{t+1} - p_t), p_t, Ep_{t+1}, P_t, y_t] + g_t \qquad (1a)$$

$$p_t = p(y_t, Ep_{t+1}, \ldots) \qquad (1b)$$

$$a(i,\ldots) + B_t = \sigma[i_t - (Ep_{t+1} - p_t), p_t, Ep_{t+1}, P_t, y_t, S_t] \qquad (2)$$

$$m(i,\ldots) + B_t = \lambda[i_t, p_t, Ep_{t+1}, P_t, y_t] \qquad (3)$$

Equation (1a) describes the market for output y. Real demand d depends on the nominal rate of interest i, the expected rate of inflation $(Ep_{t+1} - p_t)$ the current price level p_t and the expected price level Ep_{t+1}, the asset price level P_t and real income. The latter operates on aggregate real demand via human wealth and the expected real return on real assets. Fiscal policy is represented by real government absorption and taxes impounded for simplicity into the demand function. Equation (1b) refers to supply behavior. A shortened expression is presented omitting some arguments. The crucial aspect in the present context is the dependence of price-setting behavior on prevailing expectations.

Equations (2) and (3) summarize asset-market behavior. The first describes the credit market with banks absorbing assets and the public supplying assets. Bank absorption is proportional to the monetary base B with a proportionality factor determined by the asset multiplier a. The public's stock supply σ of assets depends in addition to the variables occurring in the d-function also on the outstanding stock of government securities. The last equation describes the money market. The money stock is proportional to the monetary base B with a proportionality factor given by the monetary multiplier m. Both multipliers a and m depend on the nominal rate of interest and other, at this stage omitted, variables. Money demand depends on the nominal rate, current and expected price level, asset price level, and real income. The latter works its effect again via human wealth and the expected real return on real capital. This description is somewhat stripped down, as the stock of real capital has been omitted. We note lastly that all variables occur in form of log values.

The procedure is now as follows. The two asset-market equations are used to obtain a solution for the asset price level in terms of B, S, p, y and E. The latter term refers generically to expectation variables (i.e., Ep_{t+1}). After replacing the P variable in (1a) and (3) with its solution and similarly every occurrence of p with (1b), the following vertical shift elasticities of IS and LM with respect to the monetary base can be derived:

$$\epsilon(i,B|IS) = -\frac{\epsilon(d,P)}{\epsilon(d,i)}\,\epsilon(P,B|AM) - \frac{\epsilon(\bar{d},E)}{\epsilon(d,i)}\,\epsilon(E,B)$$

$$\epsilon(i,B|LM) = -\frac{1-\epsilon(\lambda,P)\cdot\epsilon(P,B|AM)}{\epsilon(m,i)-\epsilon(\lambda,i)} - \frac{\epsilon(\bar{\lambda},E)}{\epsilon(m,i)-\epsilon(\lambda,i)}\,\epsilon(E,B),$$

where $\epsilon(y,x)$ denotes the elasticity of y with respect to x. Insertion of AM in $\epsilon(P,B|AM)$ indicates an elasticity derived from the two asset markets. The reader should note that the elasticities, as expressions of vertical shifts, are derived under the constraint of a fixed output. We have, moreover, the following patterns:

$$\epsilon(P,B|AM) = \frac{\epsilon(MM,I) - \epsilon(CM,i)}{\epsilon(CM,i)\cdot\epsilon(MM,P) - \epsilon(CM,P)\cdot\epsilon(MM,i)} > 0,$$

with $\epsilon(CM,i) = \epsilon(a,i) - \epsilon(\sigma,i)$; $\epsilon(MM,i) = \epsilon(m,i) - \epsilon(\lambda,i)$.

$$\epsilon(CM,P) = \epsilon(a,P) - \epsilon(\sigma,P); \; \epsilon(MM,i) = \epsilon(m,i) - \epsilon(\lambda,i).$$

The total elasticities of the d and λ-function with respect to E are

$$\epsilon(\bar{d},E) = + \epsilon(d,P)\cdot\epsilon(P,E|AM) + \epsilon(d,P)\cdot\epsilon(P,p|AM)\cdot\epsilon(p,E)$$
$$+ \epsilon(d,p)\cdot\epsilon(p,E) + \epsilon(d,E)$$

$$\epsilon(\bar{\lambda},E) = + \epsilon(\lambda,P)\cdot\epsilon(P,E) + \epsilon(\lambda P)\cdot\epsilon(P,p|AM)\cdot\epsilon(p,E)$$
$$+ \epsilon(\lambda,p)\cdot\epsilon(p,E) + \epsilon(\lambda,E).$$

The elasticity $\epsilon(E,B)$ describes the responsiveness of expectations ultimately bearing on the policy regime with respect to the base. This elasticity depends on the public's perception of the composition of changes in the base in terms of transitory and permanent components. The larger the variance of transitory component and the less familiar the sequence of permanent shocks, the smaller this elasticity. The discussion in the section of the paper addressed to aggregate supply behavior argues essentially that $\epsilon(E,B)$ was quite small, at least over the first year of the depression. A sufficiently small $\epsilon(E,B)$ admits approximation by the first term in the definition of the shift elasticities. The first terms depend crucially on the responsiveness of P on B produced by the interaction on asset markets [i.e., $\epsilon(P,B|AM)$]. We thus obtain the following result:

A sufficiently large responsiveness of the asset price to changes in the monetary base and a sufficiently slow perception of a fundamental change in policy regime (exemplified by four years of monetary deceleration) form a sufficient condition for a comparatively large leftward shift of IS and a comparatively small shift in LM in response to a fall in the base. Under these conditions a negative monetary shock produces simultaneously a fall in output and interest rates.

NOTES

1. The fallacious nature of the Federal Reserve's official story was demonstrated at an early stage by Lauchlin Currie (1934) in *The Supply and Control of Money in the United States*.
2. The reader should consult Meltzer's comments in this context.
3. The standard measure of velocity V used in the text derived from a modified quantity equation incorporating international trade, government expenditures, and inventory accumulation. The equation reads

$$\phi M\bar{V} + (1 - \phi^*) M^*\bar{V}^*X + PG = P(Y - \Delta Inv),$$

where M refers to the money stock, V to velocity based on private sector expenditures, G to real government absorptions of output Y produced by the private sector, ΔInv designate inventory changes, and P denotes the domestic price level. The first term (i.e., $\phi M\overline{V}$) describes domestic private nominal demand for domestic output. This demand component is proportional to domestic private expenditures $M\overline{V}$ with proportionality factor ϕ. This proportionality factor describes the allocation of total private expenditures between domestic and foreign output. It depends on the exchange rate and relative domestic and foreign prices. The variables with an asterisk refer to the corresponding foreign magnitudes. The standard definition of velocity V, determined by $MV = PY$, is immediately obtained as follows:

$$V = \frac{\phi}{1-g-inv}\,\overline{V} + \frac{(1-\phi^*)}{1-g-inv}\,\frac{M^*X}{M}\,\overline{V}^*$$

where $g = G,Y^{-1}$, $inv = Inv \cdot Y^{-1}$.

4. Meltzer indicated that Temin's argument implies an excess demand for nonmoney assets. Under a Hicksian interpretation, this excess demand would be concentrated on assets fixed in terms of nominal yields. An alternative interpretation would experience difficulties in accounting for the massive fall in equity values in the context of an excess supply of money.

5. "Informational overload" can be observed on occasion on the Federal Funds Market or other financial markets (e.g., the bond market in the spring and summer of 1958). Rapid and uncertain changes in underlying conditions induce substantial search activities even on the classic auction markets. These activities are revealed by large dispersion of quoted prices, erratic movements of these quotes, and many quotes with little or no transactions. The duration of an "informational overload" problem depends on the relative role of transaction costs and the duration of the underlying information problem. The comparatively large transaction and information costs governing output markets would suggest that any "informational overload" would be much more serious for these markets than for financial markets.

REFERENCES

Alchian, A., and Demsetz, H. 1972. "Production, Information Costs and Economic Organization." *American Economic Review* 62: 777–95.

Azariadis, C. 1975. "Implicit Contracts and Unemployment Equilibria." *Journal of Political Economy* 83: 1183–1202.

Barro, R. J. 1976. "Rational Expectations and the Role of Monetary Policy." *Journal of Monetary Economics* 2: 1–32.

———. 1979a. "The Equilibrium Approach to the Business Cycle." Forthcoming in *Money Expectations and Business Cycles: Essays in Macroeconomics*. New York: Academic Press.

———. 1979b. "Second Thoughts on Keynesian Economics." *Proceedings of the American Economic Association* 69: 54–59.

Brunner, K. 1967. "A Case Study on the Importance of Appropriate Rules for the Competitive Market in Ideas and Beliefs." *Schweizerische Zeitschrift fur Volkswirtschaft und Statistik* 102: 173–90.

———. 1971. "A Survey of Selected Issues in Monetary Theory." Monograph. Konstanz: University of Konstanz.

Brunner, K.; Cukierman, A.; and Meltzer, A. H. 1979. "Stagflation, Persistent Unemployment and the Permanence of Economic Shocks." University of Rochester, Graduate School of Management Working Paper Series No. GPB 79–11.

Brunner, K., and Meckling, W. H. 1977. "The Perception of Man and the Conception of Government." *Journal of Money, Credit and Banking* 9: 70–85.

Currie, L. 1934. *The Supply and Control of Money in the United States.* Cambridge, Mass.: Harvard University Press.

Friedman, M., and Schwartz, A. J. 1963. *A Monetary History of the United States, 1867–1960.* Princeton, N.J.: Princeton University Press, for the National Bureau of Economic Research.

Gordon, R. J., and Wilcox, J. 1981. "Monetarist Interpretations of the Great Depression: A Rejoinder." In this volume.

Keynes, J. M. 1936. *The General Theory of Employment, Interest and Money.* London: Macmillan; New York: Harcourt, Brace.

Kindleberger, C. P. 1973. *The World in Depression, 1929–1939.* Berkeley: University of California Press.

Lipsey, R., and Preston, D. 1966. *Source Book on Statistics Relating to Construction.* New York: Columbia University Press.

Lucas, R. E., Jr. 1978. "Unemployment Policy." *Papers and Proceedings of the American Economic Association* 68: 353–57.

Lucas, R. E., Jr., and Rapping, L. A. 1969, "Real Wages, Employment and Inflation." *Journal of Political Economy* 77: 721–54.

Meckling, W. H. 1976. "Values and the Choice of the Model of the Individual in the Social Sciences." *Schweizerische Zeitschrift fur Volkswirtschaft und Statistik* 112: 545–60.

Meltzer, A. H. 1977. "Anticipated Inflation and the Unanticipated Price Change: A Test of the Price-Specie Flow Theory and the Phillips Curve." *Journal of Money, Credit and Banking* 9: 182–95.

Santomero, A. M., and Seater, J. J. 1978. "The Inflation-Unemployment Trade-Off: A Critique of the Literature." *Journal of Economic Literature* 16: 499–544.

Sargent, T. J. 1979. *Macro-Economic Theory.* New York: Academic Press.

Temin, P. 1976. *Did Monetary Forces Cause the Great Depression?* New York: W. W. Norton.

———. 1981. "Notes on the Causes of the Great Depression." In this volume.

Zellner, A., and Palm, F. 1974. "Time Series Analysis and Simultaneous Equation Econometric Models." *Journal of Econometrics* 2: 17–54.

LIST OF CONTRIBUTORS

George J. Benston: Graduate School of Management, University of Rochester

Karl Brunner: Center for Research in Government Policy and Business, Graduate School of Management, University of Rochester, and Universität Bern

Phillip Cagan: Department of Economics, Columbia University, and National Bureau of Economic Research

Charles C. Cox: Department of Economics, Ohio State University

Robert J. Gordon: Department of Economics, Northwestern University, and National Bureau of Economic Research

George D. Green: Department of History, University of Minnesota

Lars Jonung: Nationalekonomiska Institutionen, Lunds Universitet

Peter H. Lindert: Department of Economics, University of California, Davis

359

James R. Lothian: Citibank, N.A., and National Bureau of Economic Research

Thomas Mayer: Department of Economics, University of California, Davis

Allan H. Meltzer: Center for the Study of Public Policy, Graduate School of Industrial Administration, Carnegie-Mellon University

James L. Pierce: Department of Economics, University of California, Berkeley

William Poole: Department of Economics, Brown University

Anna J. Schwartz: National Bureau of Economic Research

Peter Temin: Department of Economics, Massachusetts Institute of Technology

Michael M. Weinstein: Department of Economics, Haverford College

James A. Wilcox: Department of Economics, University of California, Berkeley